DATABASES IN HISTORICAL RESEARCH

Databases in Historical Research

Theory, Methods and Applications

Charles Harvey and Jon Press

St. Martin's Press
New York

DATABASES IN HISTORICAL RESEARCH
Copyright © 1996 by Charles Harvey and Jon Press
All rights reserved. No part of this book may be used or reproduced
in any manner whatsoever without written permission except in the
case of brief quotations embodied in critical articles or reviews.
For information, address:

St. Martin's Press, Scholarly and Reference Division,
175 Fifth Avenue, New York, N.Y. 10010

First published in the United States of America in 1996

Printed in Great Britain

ISBN 0–312–15888–2

Library of Congress Cataloging-in-Publication Data
Harvey, Charles.
Databases in historical research : theory, methods, and
applications / Charles Harvey and Jon Press.
p.   cm.
Includes bibliographical references and index.
ISBN 0–312–15888–2 (cloth)
1. History—Data processing.   2. History—Research.   I. Press,
Jon, 1953–   .   II. Title.
D16.12.H37   1996
902.85—dc20   95–44035
                                                            CIP

Contents

List of Figures

Preface

This book is intended as a contribution to historical methodology: to the body of literature explicitly concerned with the ways and means of creating and representing historical knowledge. Its starting point is the observation that the construction of historical databases has become in recent years a widespread activity consuming resources on a large scale. A recent guide published by the Association for History and Computing, though 'far from being an exhaustive or definitive inventory', gives details of 376 projects carried out in the United Kingdom that have involved the creation of machine-readable data files.[1] These projects have been carried out on a wide variety of subjects covering all historical periods and many different types of source material. It is true that there has been a concentration on the nineteenth century, and that census, poll book and parish register data have predominated, but the fact remains that database-centred research is generally perceived to be applicable to all fields of historical enquiry.

The particular appeal of database-centred research is not difficult to understand. Data gathering, organisation, sorting and searching, are tasks routinely carried out by historians. Each is made less burdensome through the use of powerful computers and database management software, and the time and effort saved in this way have served to inspire ambition: historians at the leading edge nowadays conceive of very large databases, often incorporating diverse forms of data from many sources. The recurrent idea is that rich collections of data of this kind should form a collective resource, serving the needs of many scholars and many projects over many generations. This conception of databases as an enduring historical resource is expressed repeatedly in the landmark *History and Computing* set of three volumes published by Manchester University Press between 1987 and 1990. These contain versions of 113 of the papers delivered at the first three major conferences of the Association for History and Computing held in the United Kingdom. Databases and database technology are the main subjects of 53 papers and a minor subject of a further 16.[2]

The use of databases in historical research is set to increase to the point where a basic knowledge of database systems will be regarded as an essential skill for all professionally trained historians. The value of database systems is already widely understood, and as knowledge and experience increase so too will the number of database projects. An important factor encouraging the launch of fresh projects is the essentially non-threatening nature of database technology. Historians must create and interrogate sets of data whether or not these take the form of a computer database. Thus, in using a database system, the historian is not adopting a fresh research paradigm, but merely a technology which, on the face of it at least, supports traditional methods of research and analysis.

The rising popularity of database-centred research, none the less, poses very real challenges for the historical community. New skills, methods, standards and thinking are required if maximum advantage is to be gained from the technology. Historians must have a sufficiently deep technical understanding of database systems to select the right hardware and software for a project, to design databases that effectively satisfy the requirements of a project, and to construct, manage and exploit to the full the potentialities of project databases. They must also understand how databases fit within the bigger picture of computer-assisted historical research. Database design, construction and interrogation form just one of a number of sets of related processes that constitute *historical computing.* It is essential that historians working with databases should keep in mind the project as a whole and the interaction between processes. This indicates a need to think seriously about project management, and about standards of quality and transportability. There is little point in creating a database that, through a failure to conform to agreed standards, cannot satisfy the requirements of potential users.

In this book, we provide an introduction to database systems that will be of interest and immediate value to anyone undertaking a database-centred historical research project. We believe that a sound knowledge of database systems can assist the work of all sorts of historian: professional academics, postgraduate and undergraduate students, and amateurs working on regional and local projects. Our approach is to explore the subject within the broad framework of historical computing. We consider in depth the topics and issues which have most bearing upon the processes of historical research. Some of these are purely technical. Others are methodological. Our intention is to offer an account of database systems in historical research that will enable the reader to avoid costly mistakes and realise the full potential of available resources.

In Chapter 1, we consider the nature and processes of historical research, and the ways in which computers may be used to assist the historian obtain better results. The centrality of database systems to historical computing is explained. The main technical differences between database projects and types of database are established. On completing this chapter, the reader should have in mind the reasons for the importance of databases and database systems to computer-assisted historical research.

The next two chapters are fundamental. Chapter 2 is an introductory survey of database concepts, terminology and methods. This provides the conceptual underpinning which is needed before we can look in any depth at historical research projects. Though the discussion is necessarily technical, important terms and concepts are simply explained and illustrated diagrammatically. In Chapter 3, attention is given to the differing types of software available, from relatively simple file managers to powerful and complex relational database management systems, textual information managers, and multimedia systems. We note the dominance of relational systems in the marketplace, but stress that in recent years the development of database technology has progressed in new directions as users have demanded greater choice and flexibility. This is a theme to which we return in Chapter 7, where we consider some of the strategies and approaches which have been pursued by the critics of relational systems.

Chapters 4–6 are concerned with the design, construction and querying of databases. The planning, specification and management of database research projects is examined in Chapter 4. It is argued that effective planning and review procedures are critical to the success of large projects. A number of mundane but important issues relating to the development of a database are also discussed, including data preparation, entry and validation. In Chapter 5, we provide a step-by-step guide to two important approaches to database design – entity-relationship modelling and relational data analysis – and work through the actual creation of a database. Historians must be skilled in retrieving information from databases, and in Chapter 6 the main methods of forming queries and accessing databases are examined. Database reports and the presentation of information are also considered.

The example databases used in these chapters are implemented using two leading database management systems, ORACLE and Microsoft Access. ORACLE provides a very powerful set of programs which is available on a wide range of platforms from mainframes to personal computers. It is widely available on university networks. It uses SQL (Structured Query Language), the industry standard for creating, managing and querying databases, and has added extensions for managing large quantities of unstructured text, and displaying graphically the results of queries. Access is a much later arrival on the scene, but has rapidly established a dominant position amongst PC-based database management systems. Access is an up-to-date Windows product which is both powerful and easy to use. It provides a user-friendly form of information retrieval called query-by-example, and also offers SQL facilities for the benefit of more experienced users.

Chapter 7 reviews the concept of source-oriented data processing and the ambitious κλειω (kleio) project, and the advance of multimedia and hypermedia, object orientation, knowledge bases and expert systems. In Chapter 8, attention is given to two key issues in historical computing. The first concerns the need for historians to introduce codes into databases for reasons of order, classification and analysis. The second concerns the use of database systems as tools for record linkage: for drawing together disparate pieces of information relating to a single entity, most often a person.

The final chapter sets out the key points which must be borne in mind if the tremendous potential of database-centred research is to be realised. A select bibliography and a glossary of concepts and technical terms is also provided.

A distinctive feature of this book is the presentation of case studies at the close of each chapter. These are the work of project leaders and others closely acquainted with major database-centred research or software development projects: they are Peter Wakelin (CADW) and David Hussey (University of Wolverhampton); Catherine Harbor (Royal Holloway, University of London); Frank Colson (University of Southampton); Matthew Woollard (University of the West of England, Bristol); David Gilbert (Royal Holloway, University of London) and Humphrey Southall (Queen Mary & Westfield College, University of London); Edmund Green (Royal Holloway, University of London); Jean Colson (University of Southampton); and Kevin Schürer (ESRC Data Archive, University of Essex). The cases bring the book to life in a way that would otherwise be impossible. They are referenced throughout the main body of the text to illustrate key points. As stand-alone essays, they are records of achievement which we hope will inspire readers, suggest research possibilities, and highlight the main advantages of database systems and the methods of historical computing. We are most grateful to their authors for the time and trouble taken in preparing them.

We are also indebted to many other friends, colleagues and associates for their assistance in preparing this book for publication. They have given generously of their time, explaining their database projects in detail and helping us to clarify our thoughts on various matters. In particular, we would wish to record our thanks to Peter Denley (Queen Mary & Westfield College, University of London) and Deian Hopkin (London Guildhall University), the founders of the Association for History and Computing; Steve Baskerville (University of Hull); Leen Breure (Rijksuniversiteit Utrecht); Virginia Davis (Queen Mary & Westfield College, University of London); David Devlin (Bath College of Higher

Education); David Doulton (University of Southampton); Mike Goodland (University of Kingston); Philip Hartland (Roehampton Institute); Dave Hassall (Bath College of Higher Education); Noel Heather (Royal Holloway, University of London); Eddie Higgs (Welcome Unit for the History of Medicine, Oxford); Jack Hoare (Genealogical Society of Utah); Rosamund McGuinness (Royal Holloway, University of London); Roger Middleton (University of Bristol); Bob Morris (University of Edinburgh); Burkhard Pöttler (University of Graz); Manfred Thaller (University of Göttingen); Richard Trainor (University of Glasgow); John Turner (Royal Holloway, University of London); and Peter Wardley (University of the West of England, Bristol). Gwyn Price and Alec Gray (University of Wales College of Cardiff) kindly let us see a pre-publication copy of their paper on object-oriented databases and their application to historical research. Catherine Harbor and Matthew Woollard undertook a critical reading of the entire typescript. As a result of their collective efforts, we have been able to make substantial improvements in technical accuracy and clarity of explanation. As always, however, any errors or deficiencies which remain are ours alone.

We should also like to record our gratitude to the Scouloudi Foundation (formerly the Twenty-Seven Foundation) and the Research Committee of Bath College of Higher Education, which kindly supported our research through the provision of funds for travel and other expenses. Parts of Chapters 5 and 7 previously appeared in the pages of *History and Computing*, and we are grateful to the editor and publishers for permission to reprint them here. Finally, we would like to thank the staff of Macmillan Press, and especially Vanessa Graham, Simon Winder, Margaret Bartley, Pauline Underwood and Keith Povey, for their consideration, patience and warm support throughout.

CHARLES HARVEY
JON PRESS

■ Note on Terminology and Text Styling

Throughout the book, the term 'table' is used rather than 'relation' to describe the two-dimensional files that comprise a relational database. Although purists might object that, strictly speaking, the latter term is more correct, its use can lead to confusion between 'relation' and 'relationship'. 'Record' is generally preferred to 'row', and 'field' to 'column', though both terms are used. To distinguish them from the text, computer commands and printouts are in a Courier (monospaced) font. Additionally, for ease of identification, the names of tables and entities are in a bold type, and fieldnames in italics (though this would not be required in practice). All trade marks and registered names are acknowledged.

Chapter 1

Databases in Historical Research

The potential for the application of computers and computer-based methods in historical research is now generally understood: the Association for History and Computing is a flourishing international organisation with a growing membership and an attractive journal published thrice yearly by Edinburgh University Press; the academic establishment – embodied in the UK by the Royal Historical Society, the Historical Association, the British Academy and the Economic and Social Research Council – is lending active support to the advance of historical computing; journals such as the *Economic History Review* now feature articles on computers in history; academic conferences regularly have sessions devoted to computer applications and methods.

Yet, for all the vigour and enthusiasm of those at the leading edge of historical computing, and the general recognition amongst professional historians of the fundamental importance of computer methods to historical research, there remains a low level of computing expertise within the historical community as a whole. That historians should experience difficulty in coming to terms with the new technologies should come as no surprise, for the current situation is not very different in many other disciplines and walks of life. However, if costly mistakes are to be avoided, and full advantage taken of the opportunities now available, historians must have ready access to directly relevant knowledge and inspiration in the form of introductory, general and specialist books on computer applications in history.

Of all the subjects that deserves systematic treatment in book form, none is more important than that of database systems. The design and development of databases is central to the transformation of research methods in history which is now underway: to the development of superior systems for the location of primary and secondary sources; to the creation of transportable research resources of value to scholars in many fields and many nations; to the vital process of record linkage; to the organisation, searching and sorting of research materials; to the analysis and presentation of historical information. It is not claiming

1

too much to say that all research historians could benefit from a working knowledge of database concepts and methods.

■ 1.1 The Processes of Historical Research

History may be thought of as either product or process. As a product, a piece of history consists of a *representation of a past reality* based upon the interpretation of a body of known facts. Such representations of past realities are always bounded: they treat a subject chosen by the historian which might be static (the situation at point *x*) or dynamic (how the situation changed between points *x* and *y*). Collingwood argues in the same vein that:

> The historian's picture of a subject, whether the subject be a sequence of events or a past state of things, thus appears as a web of imaginative construction stretched between certain fixed points provided by the statements of his authorities; and if these points are frequent enough and if the threads spun from each to the next are constructed with due care, always by the *a priori* imagination and never merely by arbitrary fancy, the whole picture is constantly verified by appeal to these data, and runs little risk of losing touch with the reality which it represents.[1]

A sound piece of history, according to this view, is a logically consistent picture of a subject supported by all available data.

As a process, history may be conceived of as the *dynamic* and *directed* interplay of ideas and evidence. The word dynamic emphasises the fact that the process is circular rather than linear, and the word directed emphasises that there is an end to the process: a representation of a past reality as sharp and authentic as the historian is capable of producing. A more fully developed model of historical research is presented in Figure 1.1. In this model, historical research is represented as a circular, continuous and incremental set of processes which generate four related products. The products are shown in boxes and the processes are represented by the arrows linking the boxes. The four straight arrows describe the types of expertise the historian brings to bear on each process.

Consider by way of illustration the work of Charles Harvey and Peter Taylor on the contribution of mineral and metal exports to the economic development of Spain between 1851 and 1913. In this period, Spain emerged as one of the world's leading mining nations, with a booming export trade in lead, copper, iron and sulphur. A large part of the capital and enterprise promoting the boom came from overseas, mainly from Britain, and this, allied to fact that national economic growth

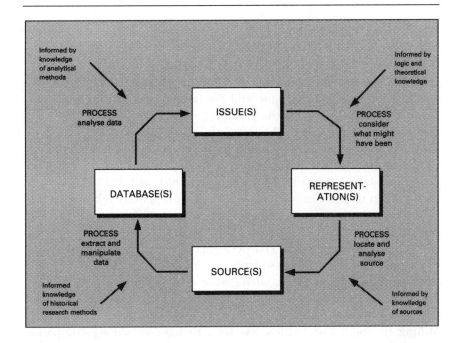

Figure 1.1   *The processes of historical research*

was very limited, has since led to the charge that the Spanish economy was 'dominated' by foreigners and exploited in 'true colonial fashion.' As a result, Spain has been seen by many scholars to have missed a glorious opportunity for generalised economic development, and the Spanish case has often been cited as a prime example of the damaging effects of foreign control of natural resource development.

The significant *issue* identified by Harvey and Taylor through their reading of the relevant historical literature was whether or not the exploitation of Spain's mineral resources by capitalists based in more economically advanced countries was detrimental to the country's economic growth. Nearly all those who had considered the issue previously had decided that it was. Spain was represented as a politically corrupt and economically backward nation ripe for exploitation by more knowledgeable foreigners. It was seen as a land of rich and easy pickings wherein the majority of foreign mining companies could employ cheap labour and earn fabulous profits. The researchers felt this *representation* of the past to be excessively generalised, simplistic and possibly wrong. Their main reason for taking this view was that logic, economic theory and the findings of other research projects suggested that a different historical reality might have existed. They reasoned that for every company which earned super-normal profits there would have been others which earned sub-normal profits or losses, and that the industry rate of return on capital employed would tend towards normal when due allowance was made for the risks involved in operating in Spain.[2]

Within the terms of Figure 1.1, the research of Harvey and Taylor was inspired by one main issue and the judgement, informed by logic, theory and experience, that the prevailing representation of an important element of modern Spanish economic history was inadequate. Thus the main aim of their project was to produce a fuller and more authentic representation of the relationship between mineral wealth and the economic development of Spain between 1851 and 1913. To do this they gathered together various *sources* of information relating to 174 British-owned mining companies formed to operate concessions in Spain during the period under review. Various data relating to the capital stocks, cash flows and financial performance of these companies were extracted from the original sources and logically organised to create a *database*. The data in the database were analysed in a variety of ways. The most important involved the aggregation of the individual company data series to form composite series for a hypothetical company, British Mining in Spain Ltd., which was seen to have subsidiary companies for each industry within the mining sector (copper, lead, iron etc.). In this way, and through the application of various techniques of investment appraisal, it was possible to develop a sophisticated and dynamic view of the foreign-dominated sector of the Spanish mineral industries. The results obtained showed that mining in Spain was in fact a high risk business in which most companies failed. When account was taken of the failed companies as well as the successful ones, and allowance made for the risks involved, profits were not of an exceptionally high order. Together with analyses of the data stored in secondary project databases, these findings led to a representation of foreign direct investment in Spain quite different from the existing orthodoxy.

The processes which supported the research effort of Harvey and Taylor were not carried out in simple stages. As more and more sources were located and data extracted from them, the project database grew larger and more complete. It was interrogated throughout and with every fresh round of analysis new issues were raised and thoughts stimulated. Visions of the past, of general and local situations, were constantly under revision. Awareness of lacunae in the total picture drove the search for additional primary materials – the survivals from the past on which the historian crucially depends to test propositions and validate ideas. As the project as a whole moved towards completion, the possibility of unearthing new sources sharply receded and it became apparent to the researchers that their understanding of the subject was as sharp and sound as was ever likely to be the case. At this point, they felt confident enough to publish their findings and their revisionist interpretation of mineral wealth and the economic development of Spain, while making clear to readers the limitations of their evidence and methodology.

Four additional points are worth stressing with regard to the view of historical research embraced in Figure 1.1. First, historians may begin projects for very different sorts of reason. Some, like Harvey and Taylor, may be gripped by a particular issue or set of issues. Others may simply feel that a subject is worth investigating because we know little about it and consequently our representation of the past is inadequate. Equally, many projects are begun because a body of source material has been discovered which is thought to have the potential to reveal something new about the past. Likewise it might be thought that a database created for one purpose might profitably be employed in researching another subject. Yet whatever the starting point for a project it is likely to involve, in varying degrees, imaginative and logical thought, the location and analysis of sources, the extraction and ordering of data, and systematic analysis of data of various types. A second point worth making is that the main processes of historical research are generic: they are not confined to any particular branch of history, nor are they dependent on any particular technology. A database, for instance, is simply a logically ordered collection of data which in the past may have been held on cards and ruled paper but nowadays is more typically held on computer files. Thirdly, it is plain that historical research, while differing in kind from research in the natural sciences, is characterised by a similar interplay between ideas and evidence. Logic, theory, analytical methods and imagination are as vital to knowledge creation in history as in any other subject. It follows, fourth and finally, that historical research is intellectually and technically demanding. Many things are required if a project is to yield good results. One of them, in the modern world, is a knowledge of how database systems may be used to facilitate each of the main processes of historical research.

■ 1.2 Databases in Historical Research

Historical computing is the term used by computer-literate historians to describe the various ways in which they use computers in their research. The subject-matter of historical computing is summarised in Figure 1.2 which illustrates how the main processes of historical research (introduced in Figure 1.1) may be supported and generally made more efficient through the use of computers and computer-based research methods. Consider again the research undertaken by Harvey and Taylor into mineral wealth and the economic development of Spain. In this case bibliographic and archival databases were searched over computer networks (local, national and international) to locate and access several hundred sources of quantitative and qualitative data. The quantitative data needed to determine the scale, scope and nature of foreign direct investment in Spain and to test various hypotheses were abstracted from the sources and entered into computer files. This process was made simpler and more certain through the use of the data entry and validation procedures of the computer software selected for the project. The database created by the researchers was sufficiently flexible to enable records relating to individual firms to be linked together and for subsets of the database to be selected as required for analysis. Numerous analytical procedures were developed and implemented using the statistical software package SPSS. The results gave the researchers a much clearer picture of the mineral industries in terms of output, foreign trade, income and expenditure, ownership, employment, profitability and productivity. The most interesting part of the project involved the development and testing of various statistical models which in turn enabled Harvey and Taylor to develop their revisionist interpretation of the relationship between foreign direct investment and the economic development of Spain.

The work undertaken by Harvey and Taylor would not have been possible without the use of computers. Many sources would not have been located. Insufficient data would have been available. Numerous analyses could not have been undertaken because of the number and complexity of the computations involved. The more advanced modelling parts of the project would have had to be abandoned for the same reason. What is true for Harvey and Taylor applies with yet more force to the large scale, resource-intensive projects which have shaped our understanding of two important historical subjects in recent years. To produce their remarkable book *The Population History of England, 1541–1871*, Wrigley and Schofield gathered data on baptisms, burials and marriages from a non-random sample of 404 Anglican parish registers. The original data 'consisting of about three and a half million monthly totals of events listed in the registers required much manipulation before they could plausibly be represented as national totals of vital events.'[3] Once these corrective procedures had been applied, a technique known as 'back projection' was used to derive from the series estimates of the size and structure of the population for a period of more than three hundred years. The authors acknowledge that 'back projection was a complex system, an example of a technique whose operation was made feasible only by the advent of high speed comput-

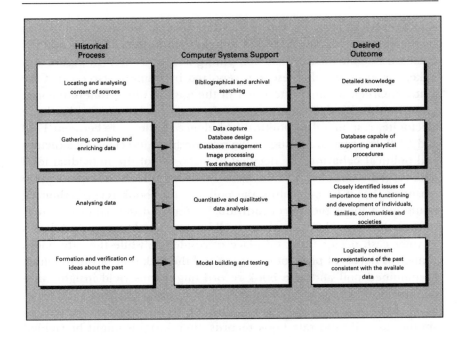

Figure 1.2 *Computing and the processes of historical research*

ing.'[4] Similarly complex estimation techniques were vital to the research
which led to Floud, Wachter and Gregory's pathbreaking book *Height,
Health and History: Nutritional Status in the United Kingdom, 1750–1980.*
On the basis of a sample of 170,000 individual recruits to the army,
the Royal Marines, the Royal Military Academy at Sandhurst and to
the Marine Society of London, Floud and his team were able to generate 'the longest single national series of height estimates yet published.'
Moreover, they were able 'to estimate not only the average height of
the whole population but also the average heights of various geographical
and occupational subgroups.'[5] Since height is a good indicator of health
and nutritional status, the estimates provide valuable evidence concerning the relationship between economic growth and the standard
of living. Prominent amongst the researchers' conclusions is the observation that 'the concept of a secular trend in height must be discarded. Height grew in the period of the Industrial Revolution, fell
back in the middle of the nineteenth century, gradually climbed back
to its previous peak by the time of the First World War, grew slowly
between the World Wars and then accelerated after World War Two.'[6]
Numerous other examples might be given of projects which have
been made feasible through the application of historical computing
methods. A small selection of interesting cases are reported in this
book in order both to indicate the potentialities and complexities of

computer-based research and to illustrate specific technical points. The case studies are further intended to help demonstrate the centrality of database systems to historical computing as represented in Figure 1.3. Take, for example, the research reported by Edmund Green in Case Study F. Green became interested in the ways in which different social groups within Westminster, an atypically open constituency with a large electorate, responded to political turbulence in the years between 1749 and 1820. In order to investigate the relationship between social structure and political behaviour he decided to make use of the individual level data records contained in numerous surviving poll and rate books. He reasoned that if he could link the poll and rate book records then he would get a fuller picture of individual voters and the pattern of their voting behaviour. The Westminster poll books invariably contained details of votes cast, occupation and place of residence, while the rate books contained details of place of residence and the rack rent of the dwelling. A combined poll and rate book record might thus yield insights into political preference, occupation and income (inferred from rack rent). If, in addition, records in one poll book were linked to records in another as well as to rate book records, then insights might be yielded into changes in political preference over time and the ways in which these related to social structure (as indicated by place of residence, occupation and rack rent).

The Westminster Historical Database constructed by Dr. Green to support his research contains in excess of 150,000 poll and rate book records. As an organised collection of data, it was established as the core resource of his research project. Its value was enhanced and systematic analysis made possible by the coding (categorisation) of occupations, places of residence, rack rents and voting patterns. Efficient management of the data made it possible easily to link poll and rate book records, to sort and search simple and linked records, to answer specific queries, and to retrieve valuable information. These might be thought of as the primary functions of a database system. For example, the researcher might wish to focus upon the voting behaviour of tailors at two consecutive elections, say 1818 and 1820. To do this, records derived from the 1818 poll book might be linked to those derived from the poll and rate books for 1820. This would require the implementation of a set of record linkage procedures. The end result would be a computer file containing linked records for tailors identified as voting in both elections and listed in the rate book for 1820. The linked records could then be sorted and searched to investigate the voting behaviour of individuals and groups of individuals with the aim of establishing underlying patterns and trends. In certain cases, conspicuous patterns and trends can be established simply by inspecting a carefully

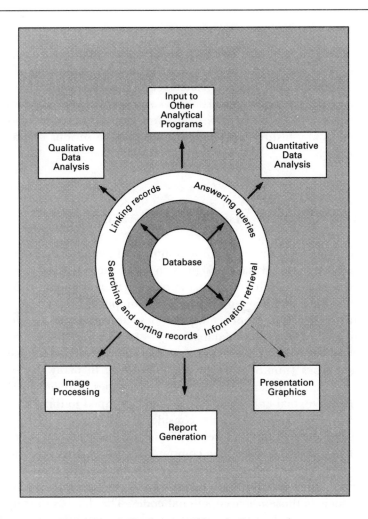

Figure 1.3 *Centrality of databases to historical computing*

ordered set of records. More often than not, however, a higher level of analysis is required to yield convincing results. In this case, the file of linked records might be exported to a subsidiary computer program incorporating appropriate routines for data analysis and presentation. Green made frequent use in his research of statistical, spreadsheet and graphics software in analysing data and presenting results.

As Figure 1.3 makes plain, flexibility is one of the most important advantages of database systems for historical research. Database systems provide an efficient means for gathering, organising and enriching historical data. They enable the researcher to create databases which are capable of supporting a variety of analytical procedures. In many cases, such as those reported above, the database consists of highly structured records which may be analysed using statistical software like SAS and SPSS. Increasingly, however, historians are also using databases to store unstructured text, sound and images (still and moving). These forms of data have their own associated set of analytical tools. However, the fundamental point remains: database systems are central to historical computing. A knowledge of how to use and get the best out of them is essential to any historian who seeks to undertake serious computer-based research.

■ 1.3 Types of Historical Databases

A database may be thought of, most simply and generally, as a collection of logically related data designed to meet the needs of multiple users. However, it is worth noting that in practice there are many different types of historical database and that among computing historians there is a continuing debate concerning the best approach to the design and construction of project databases.

We have already mentioned that the data held in a database may be of different types (numbers, text, sound, images). In many databases, the data are highly structured and consist of a series of relatively short numerical and textual entries (known as *fields*) grouped to form records. By way of illustration, for example, consider the Westminster Historical Database created by Edmund Green. Within this, each poll book record relates to an individual voter. The computer record mirrors the original source and has fields for voter name, voter occupation, voter residence, voter parish and vote. Additional fields have been added for analytical purposes such as those for occupational codes. The database is regular and highly structured with uniformly short alphanumeric fields. This stands in marked contrast to the Register of Music in London Newspapers (1660–1800) described in Case Study B of this volume by Catherine Harbor. The Register has a number of database fields for structured data, but the main entries consist of free text items of widely varying length. These are transcripts of articles, advertisements, editorials and the like containing references to musical events and activities of various kinds. In other databases, such as those required by art historians, images are stored together with textual and other data in ways which enable links to be established between database entries.

A second way of classifying historical databases is on the basis of the treatment of the sources used in their construction. At one extreme there are databases which may be thought of as *electronic editions*. An electronic edition seeks to capture an original source virtually whole.

The resulting database may be highly structured if the source is regular in form (as with census enumerators' books) or loosely structured (as with the computerisation of literary and other texts). Editorial comment may be embedded in the electronic version but without causing amendments or distortions to the original. A prime example of a large scale electronic edition is the machine-readable version of the 1881 census of England and Wales whose creation is reported by Matthew Woollard as Case Study D in this volume. At the other extreme to the electronic edition, there are databases which bear little resemblance to an original source. Typically, database entries in these composite databases are gleaned from many sources. The aim of such databases is to gather and systematically organise the data needed to support a well-defined research project. The work of David Gilbert and Humphrey Southall reported as Case Study E below falls into this category. The essential distinction is that databases of the electronic edition type are intended to serve a wide research community with varied and unspecified interests while multiple-source databases are designed to serve a smaller community with particular research questions in mind. Naturally, it is possible for databases to be developed with both ends in mind, and indeed many project databases are ultimately deposited in data archives and made available to other scholars.

Another way of classifying historical databases, which incorporates certain of the distinctions made above, has been highlighted by Peter Denley in a recent article in *History and Computing*.[7] Denley contrasts the *model-oriented* approach to database design with the *source-oriented* approach. There are two key features of the model-oriented approach. First, the researcher must decide in advance what data are to be stored in the database. Secondly, a series of design procedures should be followed which ensure that the data are organised logically to facilitate information retrieval. One advantage of this approach is that the researcher is obliged to think hard at an early stage of the project about the content and potential of the available sources and about project goals and desired outcomes. A second big advantage is that if the techniques of data modelling are applied correctly then a technically sound database capable of supporting many different research projects should result. Against these advantages must be set a number of disadvantages. The most obvious of these is that a large initial investment may be required of the researcher in the form of source analysis and data modelling. This means that subsequently there may be limited scope for organic development of the database design. A further limitation is that the established techniques of data modelling are best suited to structured data which are simple, complete and regular in form. Many historical sources do have appropriately simple structures, but equally many others have complex structures and contain data which are in some sense 'fuzzy'. Historical data can also be very incomplete and inconsistently recorded.

The perceived restrictions and limitations of the model-oriented approach to database design have led many computing historians to favour source over structure. The most essential feature of the source-oriented approach to database design is that priority should be given to capturing as completely as possible in electronic form the original source from which data are to be derived. It is up to the users of the electronic edition of the source to create a database by defining a structure for the document and inserting mark-up codes in the text. In the words of Manfred Thaller, the leading advocate of the source-oriented approach: 'source-oriented data processing attempts to model the complete amount of information contained in an historical source on a computer: it tries to administer such sources for the widest variety of purposes feasible. While providing tools for different types of analysis, it does not force the historian at the time he or she creates a database, to decide already which methods shall be applied later.'[8] One of the main advantages of prioritising source over structure is that it guards against the inadvertent loss of data and contextual information relating to the original source. Equally, database structures are not created in advance which might subsequently limit the freedom of enquiry of researchers in the future. In capturing sources whole, moreover, the historian does not have to cope all at once and in the early stages of a project with problems of irregular, incomplete, inconsistent, complex and ambiguous 'fuzzy' data.

In this book we consider both approaches to database design. The model-oriented approach was developed to meet the high technical requirements of the commercial world (where security, speed, retrieval and reliability are paramount). It is particularly well suited to the operating principles and environment of the most common type of database software: relational database management systems (RDBMSs). Relational databases (which are described further in the following chapters) typically consist of a number of tables (files) of structured data which can be linked together on the basis of common fields. If the historian is dealing with data which are regular and relatively straightforward in form, then use of a RDBMS and the model-driven approach will invariably yield good results. The best RDBMSs combine ease of use with advanced facilities for data analysis, presentation, security, import and export. Moreover, in recent years the relational model and RDBMSs have been extended to cope effectively with less structured data in the form of free text, sound and images, thus greatly increasing their utility as tools for historical research. It is now feasible to use commercial software *and* pursue the source-oriented approach to database design. This said, long-standing proponents of the source-oriented approach might well argue that feasibility is not the same thing as desirability. They would point out that RDBMSs capable of handling a variety of data types (unstructured as well as structured) still impose constraints on the historian wishing to retain the integrity of an original source. Commercial software, furthermore, is not designed to cope with history-specific technical problems such as the use of archaic and variable schemes of dating and measurement. It follows that it is preferable in many cases, especially when the researcher places a high priority on source replication, to use database software designed specifically to support historical research and the creation of electronic editions of complex historical sources. The κλειω system, designed and implemented by Manfred Thaller, is the most ambitious attempt to date to provide research historians with a comprehensive set of source-oriented database management tools. It is examined in some detail in Chapter 7 below.

The debate between the purist Dr. Thaller and those who believe in a more pragmatic approach to historical computing is set to continue. Both schools of thought have had an impact on the writing of this book. On the one hand, we certainly favour taking full advantage of technological and methodological advances made in the wider computing world. At the technological level, it is already apparent that new generations of database software are progressively more flexible and functionally capable than their predecessors. At the methodological level, techniques developed by computer scientists to deal with the complexities of database design and project management can be shown to be of great value to research historians engaged in a wide variety of projects. Some computing problems and solutions plainly are generic and apply as much to history as to business or any other subject which depends heavily on information processing. On the other hand, Thaller and his colleagues have drawn attention to what is special about historical research and historical computing. As we have demonstrated in this chapter, history has a distinctive research methodology which depends crucially upon the location, management and analysis of original sources. Equally, we believe that mastery of appropriate techniques and methods is essential if computing historians are to get the most out of highly functional commercial software such as database management systems. Our aim in the chapters which follow is to provide readers with a clear and practical introduction to the application of database systems in historical research. We believe that all research historians, irrespective of specialism, would benefit from a sound understanding of the ways in which historical databases are designed, managed and exploited.

Case Study A
Investigating Regional Economies: The Gloucester Portbooks Database

Peter Wakelin and David Hussey
CADW
University of Wolverhampton

The coastal Port Books of the sixteenth to eighteenth centuries are un-equalled as a quarry of data about internal trade before the Industrial Revolution. Records were kept for 122 official ports and harbours between 1565 and 1799 as part of the national system of Customs administration, and are now held as class E190 at the Public Record Office. The Portbooks Programme is a research initiative at the University of Wolverhampton which aims to release the huge potential of such records to advance understanding of trade, economic change and regional development. Work began in 1982 on the creation of a comprehensive database of the coastal Port Books for Gloucester. Since 1988 this has expanded with awards from the Economic and Social Research Council and the Leverhulme Trust to study Port Books and trade throughout England and Wales.[1]

The principal objective of the Gloucester Portbooks Database has been to analyse the coastal trade of Gloucester and the River Severn by com-puterising the port's 170 surviving coastal Port Books. They run from 1575 to 1765, and include records of over 35,000 voyages. Unlike the allied overseas Port Books, which controlled the collection of duties on foreign trade, the purpose of the coastal Port Books was to prevent evasion by recording mariners who claimed to be travelling solely between domestic ports. To this end, they noted coastal vessels and cargoes passing in and out of every port. Each entry described a single voyage, giving the date, the name of the boat and its 'home' port, the master and merchant as–sociated, the ports between which it was moving, and the quantities and types of goods transported. Typical entries are reproduced in Figure A.1. Because such documents were regulatory rather than fiscal in purpose, they were little affected by the smuggling and fraud which have been seen by historians to blight the overseas records.[2]

Port Books have long been recognised as providing an important in-sight into domestic trade, and evidence from them has been utilised by several scholars.[3] They have been widely used to illustrate the economic development of ports and regions and the production of particular goods and commodities. However, their use has been severely constrained by doubts about their interpretation and by the immense logistical problems of analysing them systematically. The Portbooks Programme has aimed to establish the full potential of the coastal Port Books by investigating their interpretation, demonstrating their applications, and proposing nationally

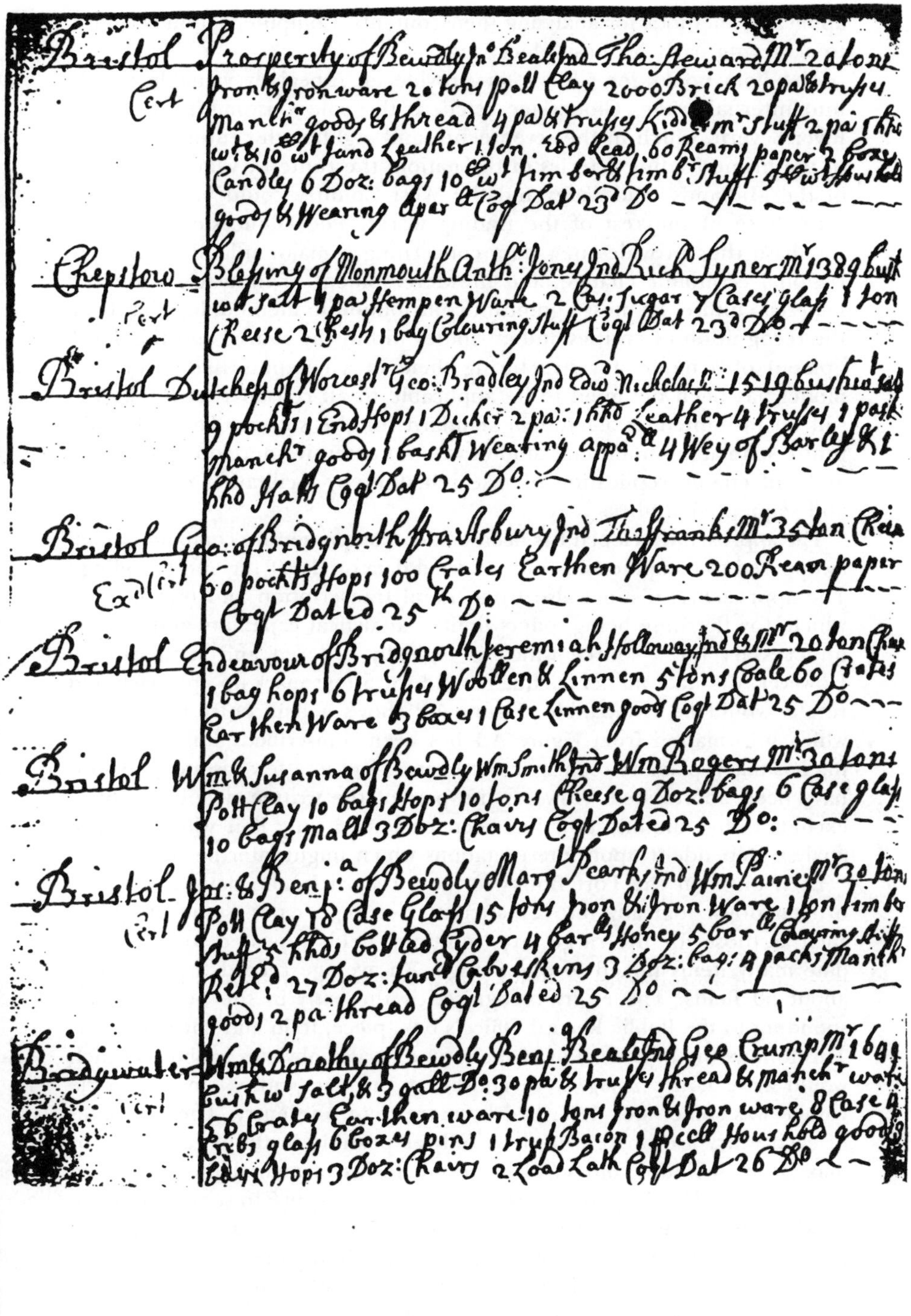

Bristol Prosperity of Bewdley Jno Beale fnd Tho: Steward Mr 20 tons
Cert Iron & Ironware 20 tons Pott Clay 2000 Brick 20 pa & trusses 4
Manchr goods & thread 4 pa & trusses Kiddermr stuff 2 pa ...
wt & 10 wt Sand Leather 1 ton ... Lead 60 Reams paper ... boxes
Candles 6 Doz: bags 10 wt ... Stuff ...
goods & Wearing Apparel Cogt Dat 23d Do

Chepstow Blessing of Monmouth Anth: Jones fnd Rich Syner Mr 1389 bush
Cert wt Salt 4 pa Hempen Ware 2 ... Sugar 7 Cases glass 1 ton
Cheese 2 ... 1 bag Colouring stuff Cogt Dat 23d Do

Bristol Dutchess of Worcestr Geo: Bradley fnd Edw Nicholas Mr 1519 bushels salt
9 pockts 1 End Hops 1 Dicker 2 pa: 1 hhd Leather 4 trusses 1 pack
manchr goods 1 baskt Wearing appa 4 Wey of Barley & 1
hhd Malt Cogt Dat 25 Do

Bristol Geo: of Bridgnorth Fra: Asbury fnd Tho: Franks Mr 35 ton Cheese
Exd Cert 60 pockts Hops 100 Crates Earthen Ware 200 Ream paper
Cogt Dated 25th Do

Bristol Endeavour of Bridgnorth Jeremiah Holloway fnd Ditto Mr 20 ton Cheese
1 bag hops 6 trusses Woollen & Linnen 5 tons Coale 60 Crates
Earthen Ware 3 boxes 1 Case Linnen goods Cogt Dat 25 Do

Bristol Wm & Susanna of Bewdly Wm Smith fnd Wm Rogers Mr 30 tons
Pott Clay 10 bags Hops 10 tons Cheese 9 Doz: bags 6 Case glass
10 bags Malt 3 Doz: Chairs Cogt Dated 25 Do:

Bristol Jno: & Benja: of Bewdly Mary Pearks fnd Wm Paine Mr 30 tons
Cert Pott Clay 18 Case Glass 15 tons Iron & Iron Ware 1 ton Timber
Stuff 3 hhds bottled Cyder 4 Barll Honey 5 barll Colouring stuff
Kettles 27 Doz: Sand Calveskins 3 Doz: bags 4 packs Manchr
goods 2 pa thread Cogt Dated 25 Do

Bridgwater Wm & Dorothy of Bewdly Benj: Beale fnd Geo Crump Mr 1699
Cert bush wt Salt & 3 gall Do 30 pa & trusses thread & manchr ware
56 Crates Earthen ware 10 tons Iron & Iron ware 8 Case ...
Cribs glass 6 boxes pins 1 truss Bacon 1 ... Houshold goods
... Hops 3 Doz: Chairs 2 Load Lath Cogt Dat 26 Do

Figure A.1 *A typical page from the Port Books*

applicable methods for analysing their contents. Computerisation is central to achieving each of these objectives.

The Port Books for Gloucester provide an especially valuable insight into internal trade. Gloucester acted as the sole Customs port on the River Severn, which in the seventeenth and eighteenth centuries was one of the prime trading arteries of the nation: the route by which the goods of the Midlands, mid-Wales and the West Country could be exchanged with those of the rest of the trading world. The Gloucester Portbooks Database thus provides new data concerning a major inland navigation, regional economic change, and the development of industry, trade and material culture. Its most significant contribution to methodology has been the recognition of entities and attributes within the source and the development of a model for structuring them in a computerised form. The model has been designed to be applicable to all coastal Port Books and will be promoted as a national standard for the source. This will assist future scholars to undertake studies without extensive developmental work and will enable replication of research, thereby facilitating comparative and sequential studies.

The approach developed has been one of 'comprehensive computerisation' as opposed to computerising only selected data or classifying and encoding.[4] The approach is distinct also from literal transcription and text markup which, for the time being, offers limited analytical capability and may be unnecessary for a source which is logically ordered and standardised. However, the data model is equally valid for a text mark-up approach and results would be compatible. Figure A.2 shows a data entry form on to which information from Figure A.1 has been transcribed. Some re-ordering has taken place to regularise the format, and in a few cases expressions have been abbreviated. However, no part of the written details has been excluded, and modification has been permitted only if it will not make analysis dependent upon interpretations which might later be revised.

Each entry in the Port Books forms a record in the database, and is broken down logically into 21 attributes or field types, some of which, such as those for the cargo, are 'multiple' fields repeated to accommodate many items linked to one voyage. An average record thus contains about 50 fields. The entity recognised is the *entry* in the books, corresponding to the Public Record Office's box, piece, folio and entry number. This follows the organisation of the source. It also obviates problems which would arise if the *voyage* were chosen as the data entity, since a single voyage was sometimes described by more than one entry. The attributes of each entry are broken down as fully as possible in the data model for maximum flexibility and so as to permit forms of analysis not predicted at the outset. This is quite different from the procedure in some databases, in which data are summarised or conflated because enquiries have been precisely pre-defined. The attributes of the Gloucester Portbooks Database are summarised in Figure A.3. Minor revisions are being made in the light of examinations of other Port Books.

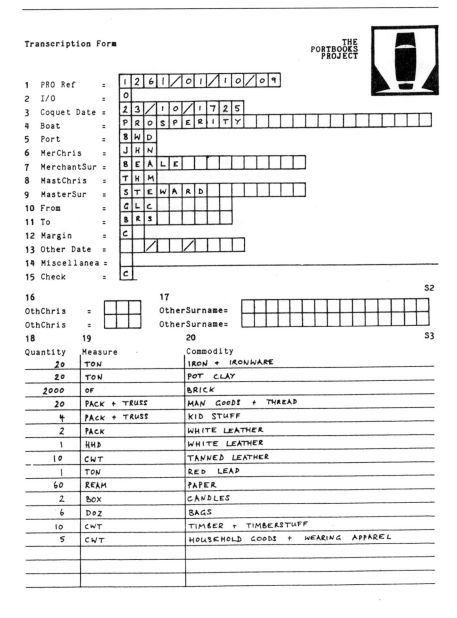

Transcription Form

THE
PORTBOOKS
PROJECT

1	PRO Ref	=	1	2	6	1	/	0	1	/	1	0	/	0	9
2	I/O	=	0
3	Coquet Date	=	2	3	/	1	0	/	1	7	2	5
4	Boat	=	P	R	O	S	P	E	R	I	T	Y
5	Port	=	8	W	D
6	MerChris	=	J	H	N
7	MerchantSur	=	B	E	A	L	E
8	MastChris	=	T	H	M
9	MasterSur	=	S	T	E	W	A	R	D
10	From	=	G	L	C
11	To	=	B	R	S
12	Margin	=	C
13	Other Date	=		/			/
14	Miscellanea	=
15	Check	=	C

S2

16		17		S3
OthChris	=	OtherSurname=
OthChris	=	OtherSurname=

18	19	20
Quantity	Measure	Commodity
20	TON	IRON + IRONWARE
20	TON	POT CLAY
2000	OF	BRICK
20	PACK + TRUSS	MAN GOODS + THREAD
4	PACK + TRUSS	KID STUFF
2	PACK	WHITE LEATHER
1	HHD	WHITE LEATHER
10	CWT	TANNED LEATHER
1	TON	RED LEAD
60	REAM	PAPER
2	BOX	CANDLES
6	DOZ	BAGS
10	CWT	TIMBER + TIMBERSTUFF
5	CWT	HOUSEHOLD GOODS + WEARING APPAREL

Figure A.2 *Sample data entry form*

Attribute name	Definition and explanation
PRO Ref	Entity key and unique number identifying Public Record Office box, piece, folio and entry number.
I/O	Direction of entry, inward or outward.
Coquet Date	Date of coquet or other Customs document administering voyage.
Boat	Name of boat.
Port	Port with which boat is associated in entry.
Merchris	Christian name of person styled Merchant.
Mersur	Surname of person styled Merchant, and their status as senior or junior if given.
Mastchris	Christian name of person styled Master.
Mastsur	Surname of person styled Master, and their status as senior or junior if given.
From	Port of departure stated or implied.
To	Port of destination stated or implied.
Margin	Marginal notation to entry.
Other Date	Date stated other than coquet date.
Miscellanea	Data stated for which there is no standard attribute, in particular occupation and residence of merchant, burthen of vessel, information about duties paid. Also indication of association with another entry if relevant.
Othchris	Christian name of person other than master or merchant.
Othsur	Surname of person other than master or merchant.
Cargo Quantity	Numerical value associated with cargo item.
Cargo Measure	Unit of measurement associated with cargo item.
Cargo Commodity	Cargo item or indivisible group of items.
Cargo Additional	Additional information associated with cargo item, about packing, duties, or status.
Check	Person who has checked transcription.

Figure A.3 *Data item list for the Portbooks Database*

Faithfulness to the original has been maintained wherever possible. With regard to the transliteration of words, spellings have been standardised only where the meaning is certain; where there has been doubt, words have been accurately transcribed. Ports, for instance, are standardised and abbreviated to facilitate transcription (though they are automatically extended in the database itself), but surnames are transcribed following the original and highly variant spellings. The aim has been that no data should be simplified in ways which would prevent analysis of their most detailed meanings. Thus the temptation has been resisted to record cargoes by a classification instead of the original terminology. The order of the commodities in the cargo description has also been preserved, in case this proves of significance. It was decided to normalise the *spelling* but not the *phrasing* of commodity descriptions: for example 'Kidderminster' is always translated to modern spelling, but 'Kidderminster ware' and 'Kidderminster goods' are distinguished even though they might prove to be the same. The transcription methods have been extremely faithful to the source by comparison with most earlier computer-based research projects. Since classification was not used in entering commodities, words whose meanings were not known have been included, and specialist classifications tailored to particular needs can be applied without distorting the data.

The time and resources employed in the project have been considerable. A network of over 60 volunteers was established to transcribe records on to data entry forms for processing by data preparation staff. The volunteers were supplied with Xerox copies from microfilms of the Books, and supported by a comprehensive set of instructions, word lists and frequent visits from Programme staff. Some problems arose, principally concerned with the laboriousness of administering such a large group and the varying competence of transcribers. However, extensive manual and mechanical checking of blank, inaccurate or invalid data has reduced false transcription to a minimum, and blank items to the core which are genuinely illegible. While it has not been possible to check all 37,614 forms, for example by double transcription, contributions by new or less reliable transcribers were checked in detail, all forms were read to look for implausible information, and transcribers were encouraged to highlight any doubts or queries. At the data entry stage, automated validation compared all words with dictionaries for each field, for example listing all ports encountered, all surname spellings, or all commodities. Data thus identified as invalid were manually corrected or added to dictionaries as new terms. Thorough sorting and searching of the data subsequently has shown occasional anomalies which have been logged and investigated. While it must be accepted that any large transcription project will introduce errors, these are now, after some years of using the database, at a minimum.

The completed Gloucester database contains 37,614 individual records with almost 2 million data attributes. This occupies about 50 megabytes (uncompressed) of storage. The database was created using the INFORMATION database management system, with PACE front end software, on the University's PRIME mini computer. This has now been largely replaced by a copy of the database converted for use with the FoxPro2 database management system operating on networked PCs. It is hoped that the database will become more widely available in this form using CD-ROM. A copy of the data has been deposited with the History Data Unit of the ESRC Data Archive.

The richness of the source in database form has already fed a wide variety of investigations. The earliest of these have been concerned with the evaluation of the sources itself, and have shown its inherent accuracy as well as its particular limitations. Armed with such assessments, the database has demonstrated much about the scale of trade on the River Severn. In the first quarter of the eighteenth century, probably as much tonnage passed on river vessels through Gloucester as on all long-distance road services from London put together; and the voyages were regular and diverse in their cargoes. The growth in trade can be indicated: voyage numbers grew at least 50 per cent between 1666 and 1722 and the quantities of goods grew even more.

Quantification of recorded trade in particular commodities has helped to refine knowledge of the regional economy in ways which would have been prohibitively difficult by manual methods. For example, the geographical limit of the Shropshire coal market has been identified as Gloucester, less far downstream than might have been expected; in field crops the region's great surplus of exports over imports can be illustrated; and the radical shifts in the salt trade have been revealed. Figure A.4 is a graph of recorded downstream salt shipments. It shows the lack of outward trade from the region until the 1690s, except for a short-lived boom when the Second Anglo-Dutch War of 1664–67 interfered with salt supplies from overseas. It provides some measure for the first time of the remarkable transformation which occurred from the 1690s as the Droitwich salt industry became markedly more productive, and then the impact of competition from the Cheshire salt field in restricting further expansion. The application of a system of classification to the commodities dictionary has made it possible to study the percentages of any selected group of voyages carrying each class of goods, analysis which would be impossibly time-consuming in any other way. The results help to characterise the economies of exporting and receiving regions: for instance showing Bewdley's prominence in mineral, metal and craft trades compared with other leading ports, but its lesser importance in agriculture and food.[5]

Free searches can be made, and the data can be sorted in many productive ways. Some of the most valuable have been consecutive sorts of the data to divine historical patterns not previously perceived. Tabulated analysis of the destinations of voyages according to home ports of vessels or the merchants named has shown the nature of specialisation in different routes: the leading role of the Jacksons of Bridgnorth in trade between Shropshire and the Wye Valley, or the importance of Tewkesbury as a trans-shipment port for traffic venturing beyond the Bristol Avon.

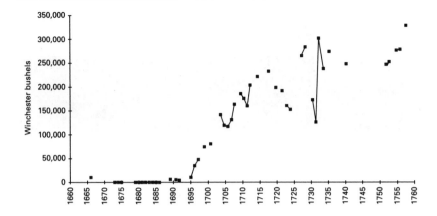

Figure A.4   *Recorded downstream salt shipments from Gloucester, 1660–1760*

The data have also been used at a micro scale to study the careers of individual merchant families or industrial enterprises, for example to provide new evidence of Abraham Darby's experiments in using coal to smelt iron.[6] Data about commodities are being used as a main source for the compilation of a Dictionary of Traded Goods.[7]

The comprehensiveness with which the data have been computerised mean that analyses at many different levels can be carried out: to study places, people, goods, vessels, events, and many other themes. The database will permit new applications of the source for many years to come.

■ *Chapter 2* ■

Database Concepts and Terminology

The idea of managing large sets of research data using a computer might seem a straightforward one, yet there is no doubt that database systems are conceptually much more sophisticated than other popular computer applications like wordprocessing and spreadsheets. Indeed, given the high-level theoretical work on which they are based, and the very considerable R & D effort required to develop them, modern systems may justly claim to be at the 'leading edge' of computer technology. Almost inevitably, the development of database systems has spawned a whole new set of terms and concepts, often competing or ill-defined. Although the more arcane and technical aspects of database systems – such as the mathematical reasoning that underpins modern programs, or the way that the software physically stores the data – can safely be passed over,[1] the essentials must be understood before effective use can be made of the technology.

■ 2.1 Database Concepts

□ *What is a database?*

To begin, it is important to distinguish between three related and frequently encountered terms: *database, database management system*, and *database system*.

The term *database* is often used loosely to indicate a large collection of related data of one or more types (numbers, text, images, speech) held on computer file(s). For some purposes this description is sufficient. However, a sharper, more technical, view is generally taken by computing professionals and database designers. In their terms, *a database is a collection of interrelated data organised in a pre-determined manner according to a set of logical rules, and is structured to reflect the natural relationships of the data and the uses to which they will be put, rather than reflecting the demands of the hardware and software.* An important perspective is embraced by this definition. This is that a 'true' database is designed to meet a particular set of operational requirements. Database designers engage in requirements planning, and they proceed by applying rules and criteria to create a *conceptual database model* (design) which is developed independently of hardware and software considerations. Only when this has been fully considered and documented is attention turned to the implementation of a *physical database design*, using a suitable database management system.

A *database management system* or *DBMS* consists of the software programs required to create, maintain and use the database. The DBMS (which is sometimes called the DB manager) organises the structure of a database and handles all requests from users for access to the database, thus shielding the end user from hardware-level details. In the commercial world, many different software packages, with widely differing features and characteristics, are advertised as DBMSs. We will differentiate between the major types on the market in Chapter 3.

A *database system* is more than just the database and DBMS. It is in fact all the elements that combine to make a computer-based system for collecting, recording, maintaining and retrieving data. The elements are threefold: the database; the hardware and software needed to support and manage the database; and the personnel, documentation and procedures needed to operate the system.

□ Data and information

In a conventional database, the data are stored in *tables* (files). Some simple databases may consist of a single table; many, however, will consist of a number of tables which have to be conceptually linked together (a multifile database). A column of the table represents a *field*, and contains a single item of data, such as a surname, sum of money, date or address. All data entered into a field must be of the same type (for example, numbers, characters or dates) as specified by the designer or owner of the database. Each field in a table must have a *fieldname* which uniquely identifies it. One or more fields may also be designated as *key fields*; they are used to locate individual records or groups of records, and for sorting records into an appropriate order (e.g. alphabetically). The rows across a table are data *records*. Records may be either fixed or variable in length. With fixed length records, each has the same number of fields and each field has a fixed number of characters. Variable length records might have a variable number of fields within each record, and/or a variable number of characters within one or more fields. Variable length records use storage space more efficiently than fixed length records; the trade-off is that more complex programs are required to organise and access data in variable length fields. Each record contains a collection of fields which describes the *entity* – person, organisation, transaction, event, etc. – which we wish to document. Entities may be tangible objects, such as **Performer** and **Theatre**, or intangible objects such as **Contract** and **Transaction**. It is useful to keep in mind that, when the database is implemented, each entity will be represented by a table in the database. *Attributes* are properties of entities and a set of attributes describes an entity. The entity **Voter**, for example, may be described by the attributes surname, first name(s), address, and occupation (as in some poll books). When the database is implemented, each attribute is represented by a field in a table. The general arrangement of a database into tables, records and fields is illustrated in Figure 2.1, together with some alternative DBMS terminology.[2]

Conceptually, a database may be thought of as an efficient *data storage* method – the electronic equivalent of a filing system with cabinets divided into drawers, and drawers into folders. The database management system offers facilities for entering and checking data – via keyboard entry, file transfer, scanning and the like – and for storing it on hard disk and other electronic media. However, a database management system goes beyond even the best manual systems in its *data processing* capabilities. Data, in its raw, unorganised form, is not particularly helpful to the potential user; it needs to be organised and transformed into meaningful information. In this context, it is helpful to distinguish between the terms *data* and *information*. Data does not mean the same as information, although the distinction between the two is not always clear-cut. Data might be thought of as basic, uninterpreted facts or as input for a computer program; information, on the other hand, might be thought of as being generated through data processing or as the human-useable output of a computer program. As can be seen in Figure 2.2, various data processing activities or operations can be used to transform data items into meaningful information: sorting, classification, comparison, selection, and calculation. The results may be displayed on a visual display unit (VDU), saved to a separate file, or printed out as hard copy.

Information might thus be described as data which has been organised and communicated in a meaningful way. It should perhaps be added that what constitutes information in one situation might constitute data in another. A data item only becomes information when it forms the basis for a human action.

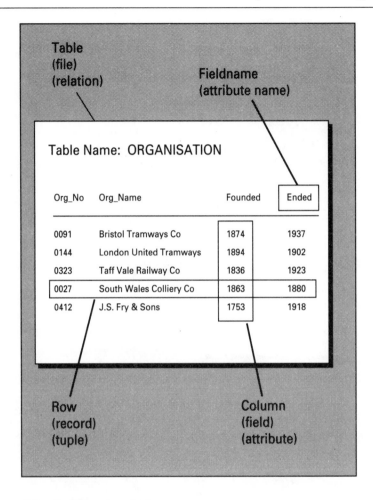

Figure 2.1   *Database terminology*

■ 2.2 Evolution of Database Systems

Before the emergence of mature database technologies, the traditional approach to data storage was to organise computer applications into functional areas, each possessing its own custom-designed files, programs, input, and output. Each computer file was closely coupled with the application which created and utilised it. There are a number of difficulties with this *applications-centred* approach. The most significant are:

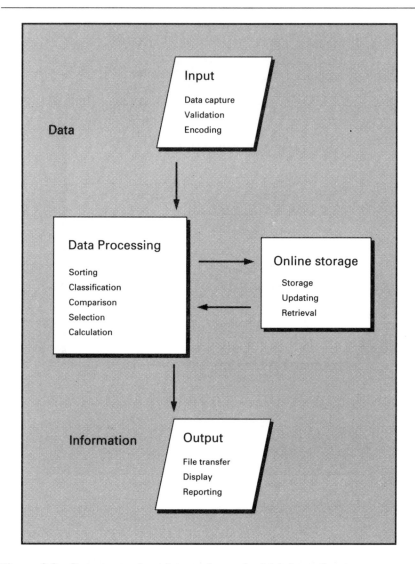

Figure 2.2 *Data processing: data and meaningful information*

- inflexibility
- data dispersion
- data duplication or redundancy
- loss of data integrity

There is a high degree of inflexibility inherent in the approach because files are designed for particular applications. Major difficulties can arise if changes must be made either to programs or data formats. The extent to which the data can be put to new uses which were not

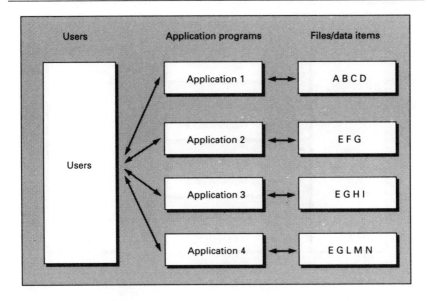

Figure 2.3 *Applications-centred approach to data processing*

envisaged when the application was designed is often limited, unless the data user can afford to have a new specialised program written. Additionally, because data are dispersed between separate applications, it becomes very difficult to connect different data items and make cross-references. This leads to under-utilisation; there is little sharing of data between different users. Most serious of all, this dispersion of data leads to problems of data duplication or redundancy. In Figure 2.3 it can be seen, for example, that application programs 2, 3, 4 and 5 each require data items E and G, and that these are consequently duplicated in separate files. As a result of data redundancy, extra clerical effort and storage space is required to capture data and maintain files, and retaining data integrity (consistency) between files becomes a major headache.

In order to remedy the problems inherent in 'traditional' approaches to data storage and retrieval, computer scientists and software developers began in the late 1960s and early 1970s to design various methods of storing and retrieving data in a more flexible, speedy and efficient manner. The result was the emergence of a *database philosophy* rather than an applications-centred philosophy; a view of data processing that proposed the use of a single database – a logically structured collection of related data – that could be accessed and manipulated by a variety of different applications. This is illustrated in Figure 2.4.

The fundamental idea was that in such an integrated system each item of the data should be entered and stored only once, and that any

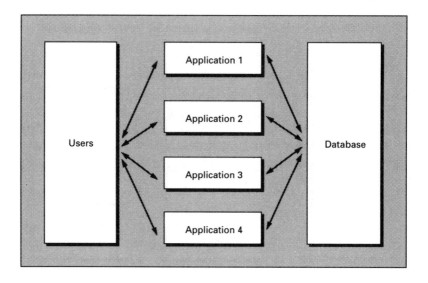

Figure 2.4 *The database-centred approach*

authorised user would have quick and speedy access to any data item. Thus, in contrast to the traditional approach to data processing, the database-centred approach offers the following advantages:

- data integrity and consistency
- data sharing
- data independence

The concept that applications programmers and users should draw upon a common set of data files is of crucial importance because the best way to reduce the occurrence of inconsistent data is to avoid unnecessary duplication. When data are entered, updated or deleted in a properly designed database system this entails a single operation, as any action is exploded across all files to ensure integrity and consistency. This integrated approach also makes for more efficient use of the database; users may access, combine and cross-reference different subsets of the data to perform many different tasks. Moreover, programs and data are made independent of each other. Different application programs share the database, operating unaware of each others' existence. With data independence, programmers are freed from the responsibility of deciding how the data are to be stored. Thus applications can be changed, and new ones developed, without requiring modifications to the data files; and, *vice versa*, altering data structures does not necessitate modification of application programs.

Such concepts were confined for some time to theoretical and academic circles – partly because business users had already made major commitments to older methods, and partly because the database approach does have some disadvantages. DBMS routines have large memory requirements, both in terms of main memory and data storage, and processing speeds can be slow. The use of magnetic tape and other sequential methods of secondary storage had to give way to hard disks, and processors and main memory had to become fast and cheap, before the implementation of sophisticated database management systems became a practicable possibility. Such problems have declined considerably in importance as hardware costs have fallen and capacities risen, but have not entirely disappeared. Database systems will always be demanding in terms of processor power and data access times.

Database systems also require considerable design effort, and complex systems need trained staff to maintain them. Although the fundamental principles are quite straightforward, database systems demand more of their users than many popular types of software. The learning curve is steep, and often there is a need for special training to maximise benefits. In the early years, these costs often proved more than had been anticipated by those commissioning database systems. However, recent developments – ever-improving DBMSs and the emergence of structured design methodologies – have led to considerable reductions in development and maintenance costs.

All database systems can be classified according to the type of *logical model* supported by the system. The words logical model refer to the way in which the data items are organised, and to the relationships which can exist between them: i.e. the logical structure of the data. Above all, it is differences in the form of the conceptual model that distinguish database systems. Over the years, three principal approaches to data organisation have been developed: the *hierarchical* model, the *network* model, and the *relational* model. (It should be said, however, that there are many variant and hybrid types; additionally, we will discuss newer approaches such as hypermedia and object-oriented models in later sections of this book.)

The hierarchical model was developed in the 1960s, and until quite recently predominated in the world of large mainframe applications. As the name suggests, it is well suited to data which can readily be organised into some sort of hierarchy. In a hierarchical database system, data items are organised as a series of inverted trees, and the different levels are often referred to as 'parents' and 'children' (Figure 2.5). Each 'child' item can have only one 'parent' above it, but a 'parent' can have many 'children' dependent upon it. Thus, a hierarchical database may be said to consist of a number of *one-to-many relationships*.

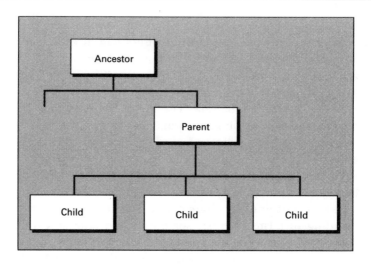

Figure 2.5   *Representation of the hierarchical model*

The hierarchical model is simple in structure, and relatively easy to understand and use. But unfortunately it lacks flexibility compared to more recently developed approaches. Data which do not fall into some kind of natural hierarchy can be difficult to handle, and may lead to unnecessary duplication. In addition, querying can be slow, because searching involves moving up and down the hierarchic paths; records can only be accessed through their parents and ancestors. To make a connection between two data items, it may be necessary to move up several levels before descending down a different branch.[3]

To solve some of the difficulties inherent in hierarchical systems, the network model was developed. It is less restrictive, and permits a wider variety of relationships to be represented. Unlike hierarchical database systems, networks can cope with *many-to-many relationships* – for example, the relationship that would exist between **Investor** and **Company**, where one person holds shares in many companies and one company has many shareholders. Networks consist of records (or nodes) and links (associations) between them (Figure 2.6). Links not only exist between parent and child, but can also connect a record to several records at a superior level, or to other records at the same level, as well as to children at a lower level. Although network database systems have often been used on mainframes and minicomputers, they have rarely been developed on micros – largely because the power of micros was limited until relatively recently, and because the network model is more complex than the hierarchical one. However, although more complex, it does possess the advantage of being more applicable to the 'real world'. Additionally, the existence of sideways links speeds

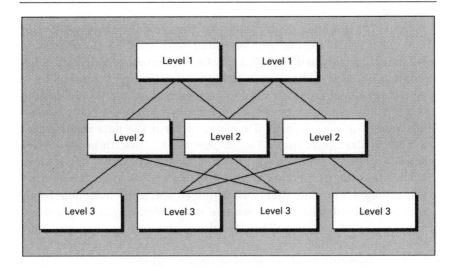

Figure 2.6   *Representation of the network model*

up access to the data since links do not have to be made through parents.

But network systems also have their drawbacks. Although the interconnecting links in a network database allow quick and fairly flexible access to information, the insertion and deletion of records is complicated by the fact that new or broken links must be correctly updated. Changing the structure of the database is often tricky and time-consuming. This means that network database systems are most effective when relationships between records are likely to remain relatively stable.[4]

The most significant problem with the hierarchical and network models, however, is not that they cannot handle data structures adequately, but that they require complex programming to query them. The programmer or end user has to know how the data are actually structured, and has to define the navigation paths between records. The complexities of managing large hierarchical and network structures led in the early 1970s to the development of the relational model by a mathematician at IBM, E.F. Codd. Codd noted that hierarchical and network systems were not founded on the basis of previously defined theoretical work: instead, the conceptual models were identified *post facto*, being drawn from systems which were already in operation. The relational database, on the other hand, rested from the outset on a sound mathematical base and a set of theoretical principles which have since been further developed in numerous books and learned papers.

The great strength of relational database management systems (RDBMSs) lies in their apparent simplicity. In the relational model, all data are organised into simple two-way tables made up of rows and columns. These tables, which are also known as relations, are manipulated by the DBMS in storing and accessing data, and all the operations that can be performed on them can be mathematically defined. Many people who have difficulties conceptualising complex hierarchies or multi-dimensional arrays are used to organising data into two-dimensional tables. Additionally, users are able to retrieve data from many tables at one time to answer a particular query or meet the data requirements of a particular application. This is possible because links are created between tables by the use of repeated fields. However, in relational tables, there are no parents or children. This means that the ability to connect data items in different tables is not predetermined by the structure of the database; users are free to specify their data requirements at the point of retrieval. Thus relational database systems provide a high degree of flexibility and data independence. The creator of the database does not need to try to anticipate all the questions that will be asked of the data; instead, data files might be used for purposes not considered when they were originally designed and set up. Thus relational systems, unlike network and hierarchical systems, are well suited to situations where the users' queries cannot be precisely specified in advance. The advantages of this to historians, who frequently want to ask new questions of their data, will be obvious.[5]

The relational model was slow to gain acceptance, and the relative merits of competing approaches have been fiercely debated by computer professionals. From the early 1980s, however, the relational model has been widely accepted as a *de facto* standard, and it has come to dominate the DBMS market, both for mainframes and micros. Some of the claims made by its advocates might seem hyperbole or special pleading, were it not for the fact that the operations which RDBMSs perform on data are all defined in strict mathematical terms, based on the theory proposed by Codd and his fellow-researchers. Many older, non-relational, products have been extended to give some kind of relational support – with, it has to be said, varying degrees of success.[6]

Database management systems have become commonplace only in the last few years, and in many respects such systems are still in their infancy. It can be predicted with confidence that DBMSs will continue to evolve and that the subject of database systems will continue to grow in importance during the course of the next few years. Particularly significant is the extension of database management systems in new directions – often by building upon a relational core – to facilitate the incorporation of sound and images as well as numbers and text. Since the early stages of their development, database management systems have excelled in the handling of numeric data. Gradually, their ability to cope with textual data items has also improved, and powerful facilities have been provided for manipulating 'strings' of text. ('Text' in this context is defined as groups of any alphanumeric characters or special characters – #, \, *, [, etc. – within the standard character set.) It is not surprising, therefore, that the vast majority of historical database projects – and commercial databases too – have involved the storage and manipulation of text and numbers. This emphasis seems set to continue for some time at least, and this book concentrates upon the planning and management of such projects.

However, in planning future projects, researchers would be well advised to consider whether opportunities exist for the integration of sound and images into databases. Binary fields can hold digitised sounds and pictures captured with scanners and digital cameras like Canon's Ion. Such applications seem set to grow rapidly in the future. In certain areas, such as art history and historical geography, the integration of visual material is already occurring.[7] The physical requirements for the storage and display of high-quality full-screen graphical images are substantial, although costs are expected to fall sharply. The term 'multimedia' has been coined to describe integrated systems of various types, and behind the marketing hype there undoubtedly lie some exciting opportunities (see section 7.2).

■ 2.3 Features of Database Systems

In section 2.1, we defined a database as:

a collection of interrelated data organised in a pre-determined manner according to a set of logical rules, which is structured to reflect the natural relationships of the data and the uses to which they will be put, rather than reflecting the demands of the hardware and software.

We can now further refine our definition. A database may be a resource for many programs in several application areas, and many people may be interacting with the data. However, it is under central control, and consequently it involves little data redundancy; a data item is held once and shared rather than being duplicated. Additionally, we can note that although the logical structure of a database is of great importance, and is the responsibility of the researcher or database designer, he/she does not need to be concerned with the way in which the data are physically stored by the DBMS. The result is a powerful, flexible system that meets the requirements of the 'end user'. It allows sophisticated interrogation of the data in ways which allow end users to meet their specific needs while shielding them from the technicalities of data storage.

Whilst the DBMSs available commercially may differ considerably in appearance and ease of use, the range of features and facilities which they offer are fundamentally similar. These include:

- Data definition facilities
- Data manipulation facilities
- Help facilities
- Reporting facilities
- Data control features
- Other advanced features

□ *Data definition facilities*

Data definition facilities enable the user to describe the structure and characteristics of the database. They comprise *data description languages* (DDLs), and *data dictionaries*. A data description language provides 'a set of commands with a formal syntax that enables users to create logical descriptions of the contents of a database.'[8] As well as creating tables, DDLs provide restructuring facilities. Changes to field lengths and the addition and deletion of fields are obvious examples. Whilst good design will make frequent restructuring of the database unnecessary, restructuring is a vital activity when a database is retained in use over a long period of time. Sooner or later even the most carefully planned database will need some modification.

As the database is created by the data description language, its essential characteristics are recorded in the data dictionary. Thus the data dictionary is at the heart of a DBMS; it is a table that contains *metadata* (data about data), and is consulted by the database system before actual data are read or modified. For each data field it will give vital details as to what the field represents, the fieldname, the type of data it can contain (numeric, text, etc.), and its maximum length. It may also contain a variety of other information, such as the edit mask (the number of leading zeros and decimal places of numeric fields, etc.); the maximum and minimum values which the field may contain; pointers to lookup tables (special tables which contain a list of all the values or text strings which may legally be entered in the field); and information about passwords and other security features.[9] Data dictionaries become more important as the number of people who need to access or update the database increases.

An associated task is the creation of data entry forms (also known as entry screens or screen forms) to allow records to be created, amended or deleted. There is usually a special 'form creation' mode, which allows the screen designer to move about the screen, indicating the location and appearance of fields, and typing headings, fieldnames, and instructions for data entry, in a free manner. In some packages, such as ORACLE, the creation of data entry forms follows on from the definition of the database structure. In others – including the majority of micro-based packages – database definition, the creation of the data dictionary and screen design are closely connected events. As the user creates a screen form for each table in the new database, the underlying structure of tables and fields is also established. In such instances, of course, it will be necessary to define data types, field lengths, etc., as well as identifying their location on the screen.

☐ *Data manipulation facilities*

As well as providing for data definition, DBMSs offer a *data manipulation language* (DML) which enables the user to manipulate the data in various ways. These include inserting data into tables, updating existing data in tables, deleting data from tables, and querying the data. In fully-featured DBMSs, the DML provides features to enable programmers to write programs in languages like COBOL, C or Pascal which can access the database for purposes of data entry, modification and retrieval. This facility, however, is strictly for computer professionals interested in building applications which will remain relatively stable over the course of time. Researchers and other end users will be more interested in the provision of *query languages*. A query language is an integral part of a DBMS. It is an end-user facility which allows the retrieval of data without the need for a custom-written program. The very presence of a database means that queries will arise for which neither time nor economic justification can be found for special programming. Query languages are at a very high level, allowing the user to input simple criteria (conditions) about the data to be retrieved. An example is given in Figure 2.7; it uses a language called Structured Query Language (SQL) which has emerged as the industry standard for relational DBMSs. SQL is discussed further in Chapters 5 and 6.

This is of course a simple example; in multitable database systems, it is also possible to use a single query to link together data held in several different tables. It should furthermore be noted that the term 'query language' is somewhat inaccurate: as well as retrieval *per se*, it also allows the user to update, delete, add and sort data.

Another common query method is known as *query-by-example*, or *QBE*. This is very easy to use. Instead of writing an instruction like the SQL statement given above, the user simply gives the DBMS an example of

```
SELECT  *                              select all the fields
FROM Person                            from the table Person
WHERE Last_Name = 'Robson'             where the person's last
                                       name is Robson
AND Age >11                            and his/her age is greater
                                       than 11.
```

Figure 2.7   *A query in Structured Query Language (SQL)*

the result he or she is looking for. The examples are entered in a *query form*, and all the records which meet the search criteria are copied to an **Answer** table. For instance, if we were using QBE to formulate the query in Figure 2.7, we would simply enter *'Robson'* in the *Last_Name* field of the query form, and >11 in the *Age* field. Not all queries can be answered in this way, but it is very useful for simpler types of queries. QBE is discussed further in section 6.1.

☐ *Reporting facilities*

Most DBMSs provide a 'quick print' facility to allow the user to print out all the data in a table in a single continuous list. This is sometimes sufficient, but for many purposes more sophisticated presentation is required. Report generators allow users to present retrieved information in a readily usable form. A report generator essentially is an extension to a query language, oriented to paper rather than the screen. Reports list data in the specified order, giving sub-totals, totals, averages, and headings as required. The standard of reporting facilities varies between DBMSs. They are usually flexible enough to meet the needs of all but the most demanding of users, but often lack the advanced text and page formatting needed for really attractive printouts. An important feature, therefore, is the ability to 'print to file' rather than sending the output to the printer; the user can then import the file into his or her preferred wordprocessor or desktop publishing program for further formatting.

☐ *Help facilities*

Early mainframe DBMSs provided relatively little in the way of on-screen guidance to users. Similarly, early PC-based products were often 'user-unfriendly'; dBase II's 'dot prompt' – a blank screen with a single full-stop to 'prompt' the user – was justly notorious. As time has gone by, however, and DBMSs have moved out of the realm of computer professionals, suppliers have recognised the need to provide on-screen advice and explanations. Some of the more modern systems may have *context-sensitive* or *hypertext*-type help support. Context-sensitive help attempts to provide assistance which is relevant to the task currently being performed. For example, if the user asks for help whilst creating a query, the help screen should describe querying, and indicate how to move to help screens about related topics like sorting data. Hypertext-type systems are particularly associated with Macintosh, Windows and other graphical user interfaces. Here, the help information is arranged like a stack of index cards. The front card may provide a relatively brief summary of the feature, whilst the cards behind it provide progressively greater levels of detail. Users navigate around the stack by clicking their mouse pointer on buttons which appear on the screen or on keywords in the text, which are usually underlined, italicised or in reverse video to indicate that they are 'doorways' to further information. Unlike other types of help facilities, where the user has to move from screen to screen in a sequence determined by the programmer, hypertext thus allows access to assistance in a particular sequence, and at a level of detail, appropriate to the needs of the individual user. Hypertext is discussed further in section 3.5.

☐ *Data control*

Data control refers to the provision made for data *recovery, security* and *integrity*. The significance of this will be readily apparent in major research applications, where it is vital to ensure that user program failure, system hardware failure, or disk media failure do not irretrievably corrupt the database.

Most good quality DBMSs provide a range of recovery routines to cope with hardware, software and disk media errors. At the simplest level, this involves automatically backing up the files – either at regular intervals of time, or whenever a file is updated. However, this is insufficient with many database applications. Other type of software, such as wordprocessors or spreadsheets, generally involve single files which are relatively small and not in continuous use, and hence can be regularly backed up as described above. Database systems, on the other hand, may use a wide range of interrelated files, some of which can be extremely large, and it would not be practicable to take the whole database out of commission whilst it is backed up. Moreover, editing a particular data item may mean that several related tables have to be updated; if the computer were to crash before all the updates had been completed the database could be irretrievably damaged. More sophisticated techniques are therefore needed. The usual procedure is to define a group of inter-related updates as a single *transaction,* and to keep a log of all transactions which modify the database. In the event of a major failure, this *recovery log* can be used to reconstruct the database up to the point of failure. A transaction will either be completed or entirely ignored. If there is a hardware or software failure, the database can automatically be restored by *rolling back* (undoing) all the transactions being processed at the time of failure to their starting points. Alternatively, if there is a disk media failure, the most recent archive (backup) copy can be reinstalled, and the DBMS will then bring it up to date by *rolling forward* (redoing) all changes made to the database since the archive copy was saved.

An essential requirement of a DBMS is the provision of sophisticated facilities for ensuring the security of the database. It will readily be appreciated that data has to be protected from unauthorised users. Permission to use certain data items or records may be provided in various ways. Passwords may be provided for individual users or groups of users. There may also be different levels of security, allowing specified users full or limited access to the data: for example, there may be 'read only' access for researchers who only need to browse through the records; 'read and query' access for those needing to interrogate the data; and full 'read-write' access for those empowered to modify the structure of the database, add or delete records, and so on. The quality and range of security features provided is a major factor in distinguishing between DBMSs.

Data integrity features are also needed. Data integrity means ensuring that the contents of the database are not corrupted. The most common cause of data corruption is user error, such as mistyping or misunderstanding what should be entered. Most modern DBMSs therefore include a range of error-checking features. These range from the very straightforward – ensuring that text is not entered in a numeric field, for example – to the more sophisticated, such as ensuring that a particular value cannot be entered in a field unless it has already been listed in a *lookup table.*

☐ *Other advanced features*

Besides the generally available DBMS features which have been described above, some of the more advanced DBMSs offer additional features and facilities. One feature which is becoming of increasing importance as a growing number of PCs are linked together by networks is *multiuser capability*. This is obviously desirable where several researchers are engaged on a project, for ensuring that everyone is working on the same version of the database can be a major headache if standalone PCs are used. However, problems can occur in multiuser environments when two or more users try to gain access to the same record to modify its contents. The problem is solved by locking certain parts of the database whilst they are undergoing modification. Handling clashes in this way is called *concurrency control*, and the sophistication with which this is done varies considerably between DBMSs. Ideally only the records(s) actually being modified are locked to other users – locking larger units, such as the whole table involved, would degrade database performance and seriously impede user access.

Another, even more advanced, feature is the concept of *distributed systems*. It will be recalled that one of the benefits of modern DBMSs is that the user does not have to know where or how the data is physically stored. As a logical development, a distributed database is one that is not stored entirely at a single location, but is spread across a network of computers. Some DBMSs provide tools that allow the system to be used as a distributed database system, but at present this remains relatively uncommon.

■ 2.4 Conclusion

The technology of database systems has evolved quite dramatically over the course of the past twenty-five years, driven by the requirements of the business world. Relational databases, in which data are organised in a set of related two-way tables, have emerged as the *de facto* industry standard. Historians have responded enthusiastically to the opportunities afforded by the technology to the point that we might speak of a 'database revolution'. But any such notion should be strictly qualified. There is dissatisfaction with the limitations of relational databases both in academia and industry. Critics of the relational model point out that the rigid compression of data into tabular form is 'unnatural' and that there are many forms of naturally occurring data that cannot be tabulated – free text, sound and images are generally cited. They make the argument for more flexible and accommodating database systems, as does Frank Colson in Case Study C in this volume. In the following chapter, we examine relational database management systems and their fast-emerging competitors in greater detail. We take the view that the historian should select the software for a project which has the characteristics, features and functionality best matched to the task in hand.

Case Study B
The Register of Music in London
Newspapers, 1660–1800

Catherine Harbor
Royal Holloway, University of London

Traditionally, musical scholarship has tended to concentrate more upon musical style and biography rather than on the economic and social factors that activate the growth of music as an industry. Newspapers have often been used as a source of information on the musical life of London in the eighteenth century. Advertisements for, and reviews of, concerts, operas, plays with music, ballets and other musical performances have enabled scholars to draw up calendars of the musical events which took place there.[1] Publishers' advertisements have also facilitated analyses of music publishing.[2] However, newspapers can yield much more information and are indispensable for an understanding of music's exact role in London society.

In the spring of 1977, Professor Rosamond McGuinness of Royal Holloway, University of London, began to work chronologically through the late seventeenth- and eighteenth-century newspapers held in the British Library, extracting all references to music. By the beginning of 1983 it had become obvious from the quantity and diversity of information that the computer was the most appropriate tool with which to organise the material and make it accessible to scholars. It was decided that a computer database, 'The Register of Music in London Newspapers 1660–1800', should be developed.

While concentrating upon the most logical way to order the data she was collecting, it became apparent to Professor McGuinness that patterns were emerging in the ways a number of the musical references appeared in the newspaper sources. From experiments analysing these patterns and relating them to each other, it became obvious that with rigorous scrutiny they could provide a key to the variable characteristics of the newspaper press, aspects elusive because of the absence of essential documents. They could also give an insight into the important ways in which the newspaper press, the public, commerce and music interacted, and could suggest a mechanism for the formation of taste in the metropolis. A systematic analysis of the material about music in the newspapers would facilitate a methodical study of the devices and techniques used at the time to stimulate demand and to determine more specifically who the entrepreneurs were who exploited these techniques. It would allow scrutiny of the language and the patterns of advertising in relation to the structure and ownership of the press, management policies, political stance, production and distribution methods, readership, circulation figures, costs and profits, and relationships with coffee houses, postal services, theatres and other institutions. It would enable scholars to relate the musical references in the newspapers to those in other sources, and to analyse the newspapers themselves as a system of information about music in London's culture and commerce.

The Register of Music in London Newspapers aims to collect items relating to music which appear in newspapers published in London between 1660 and 1800. The project's range of interest is broad and includes:

- advertisements for concert performances, operas and plays with music, for printed music or books about music, for the sale or repair of instruments;
- news items in which music plays some part;
- puff-reviews;
- reports, commentaries, etc.

References to dance are also included.

The Register of Music in London Newspapers uses the ORACLE relational database management system. The information is stored in a number of tables which can be searched either alone or in combination. Conceptually, the Register is divided into two parts: a textbase containing information about the location of the musical references and the texts themselves; and a Newspaper database which contains information about the newspapers.

Within the textbase, sufficient detail is recorded to locate the musical reference exactly and to describe it to some extent:

- newspaper title (codes are used to reduce input errors);
- date;
- page number;
- nature of the reference: advertisement, news, review, commentary, puff or miscellaneous;
- classification of the content as prose, verse or letter; combinations are also provided for.

The text is transcribed in its original spelling but without indication of font changes or original line length. Pictorial devices in the original are represented by codes. Normally items are transcribed in full but occasionally they will be abbreviated, for example, when the reference to music occurs within a largely non-musical news item, enough detail will be given to identify the item and give a context for the musical reference, but much of the rest will be omitted.

The textbase consists of a single table, **Register**, which stores the location and text of the musical references.

Field Name	Null?	Field Type	Field Length
TEXTNUM	NOT NULL	NUMBER	7
NEWSCODE		CHAR	4
DAY		NUMBER	2
MONTH		CHAR	3
YEAR		NUMBER	4
PAGENUM	.	NUMBER	2
NATURE		CHAR	13
PROSE		CHAR	1
VERS		CHAR	1
CORRS		CHAR	1
TEXT		LONG	

Technical limitations at the time the database was first implemented meant that it was impossible to carry out searches on a field of type LONG. Thus, in its original form, the **Register** table contained a large number of fields of type CHAR (maximum length 240 characters) in which the actual text was stored. This meant that searches of the text were possible, but were rather inefficient. It was also felt that the multiplicity of detail within the texts would require more sophisticated searching techniques than simple string searches. Initially it was planned to construct an index to the textbase. This single table would act as an independent database, containing information extracted from the full texts. The material transcribed into the Register being of the utmost variety, it was felt that no single format would encompass all the items included; the only way to index such heterogeneous information was to fragment the text into discrete details and index them separately. While providing an immensely flexible and sensitive research tool, this system of indexing would have been enormously time-consuming to set up manually, involving as it does the review of every single record, and entry into the index of every single relevant detail.

The development by Oracle Corporation of SQL*TextRetrieval, a free-text retrieval and search module, provided the means to solve the problem of creating an index to the texts in the textbase. The text could now be stored in a single field of data type LONG. When loaded into the SQL*TextRetrieval module, each word in each text is indexed and its exact location recorded, thus making searches much quicker. Moreover proximity searching is also enabled, so that one can find all occurrences of a certain word within a specified distance forwards or backwards from another word. Thus one could find occurrences of the word 'violin' within a fixed proximity of the word 'concerto', and in this way focus in on violin concertos, whether they were described as 'violin concerto' or 'concerto for the violin', etc. However, the real power of a free-text system lies in the range of thesaurus-based facilities provided. For each word on the word index list one can build up a group of synonyms, broader terms and more loosely-related terms. Thus for the names 'Haendel', 'Hendel', 'Hendl', 'Handl', and 'Handel', the thesaurus would provide the synonym 'Handel' as the standardised form, with 'composer', 'performer', and 'person' as broader terms. The process of editing the thesaurus once for each music-related term, however many times it occurs within the textbase as a whole, is much less time-consuming than that of entering the required three- or four-part code for each and every occurrence of every music-related term which would have been necessary with a manual indexing method. There is, however, some loss in terms of precision, in that it is not possible to specify that one musical reference mentions Handel in his capacity of composer and another in his capacity as performer.

The Newspaper database contains information about the newspapers themselves:

- their title and any changes of title;
- date when publishing commenced and ended;
- frequency of appearance;
- information in the colophon about printers, publishers, editors, etc.;
- location of the source in the microfilm collection *Early English Newspapers* (Woodbridge, Connecticut: Research Publications Inc., 1983); other location if missing from *EEN*.

The Newspaper database consists of several tables: **Title, Papers, Colophon, Newtitles, EEN,** and **Missing. Title** stores the titles of the newspapers and their associated codes.

Field Name	Null?	Field Type	Field Length
NEWSCODE	NOT NULL	CHAR	4
NEWSNAME		CHAR	180

Papers stores information about the newspapers which is current for the whole of their run.

Field Name	Null?	Field Type	Field Length
NEWSCODE	NOT NULL	CHAR	4
STARTDAY		NUMBER	2
STARTMONTH		CHAR	3
STARTYEAR		NUMBER	4
ENDDAY		NUMBER	2

ENDMONTH	CHAR	3
ENDYEAR	NUMBER	4
FREQUENCY	CHAR	35
COMMENTS	CHAR	80

Colophon stores in information contained in the colophon of each news-paper. This is recorded whenever the colophon changes, the date of the first and last appearances of a particular item of information being given. Certain names may appear for a period, then be absent, then reappear; each appearance and reappearance will be noted separately. Each colophon may generate more than one record, depending on the number of names and associated addresses given.

Field Name	*Null?*	*Field Type*	*Field Length*
NEWSCODE	NOT NULL	CHAR	4
STARTDAY		NUMBER	2
STARTMONTH		CHAR	3
STARTYEAR		NUMBER	4
ENDDAY		NUMBER	2
ENDMONTH		CHAR	3
ENDYEAR		NUMBER	4
NAME		CHAR	60
TOWN		CHAR	6
STREET			60

Newtitles stores information on title changes, linking together titles which are in reality one newspaper which has undergone successive changes in title. These title changes may only be a matter of slight changes in spelling, or may be quite radical.

Field Name	*Null?*	*Field Type*	*Field Length*
NEWSCODE	NOT NULL	CHAR	4
NEWNEWSCODE	NOT NULL	CHAR	4
NEWDAY		NUMBER	2
NEWMONTH		CHAR	3
NEWYEAR		NUMBER	4

EEN stores information about the newspaper which changes from year to year; the reel number in the *Early English Newspapers* microfilm collection for the year in question is also given.

Field Name	Null?	Field Type	Field Length
NEWSCODE	NOT NULL	CHAR	4
YEAR	NOT NULL	NUMBER	4
PRICE		CHAR	8
PAGES		NUMBER	2
EEN_NUM		NUMBER	4

Missing stores information on the location of issues of newspapers which are not present in the *Early English Newspapers* microfilm collection.

Field Name	Null?	Field Type	Field Length
NEWSCODE	NOT NULL	CHAR	4
DAY		NUMBER	2
MONTH		CHAR	3
YEAR		NUMBER	4
ALT_SOURCE		CHAR	60

The Register is now substantially complete for the years 1660–1720. 13,272 references in some 31 different newspaper titles have been entered into the textbase; Figure B.1 shows the chronological spread of the references.

The final product of the project will be a very large database. Exactly how the data will be made available is now being investigated. There are three possibilities:

- On-line, mounted on the VAX 6430 at Royal Holloway, University of London and accessible through national and international networks. This would entail development of a custom-designed data query module.
- Written request: research reports to be supplied at cost in response to individual requests for information. This is the method used at present.
- Publication on CD-ROM.

Informal publicity alone has already brought a steady stream of requests for information from Australia, the British Isles, Denmark, Finland, France, Germany, Italy, Japan, the Netherlands, New Zealand and the United States. Those writing have included scholars from the fields of dance, education,

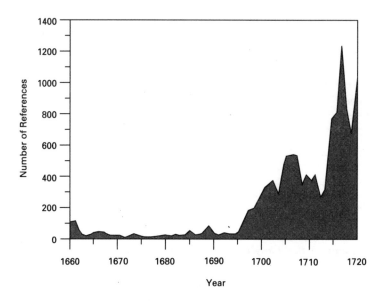

Figure B.1 *Numbers of references, 1660–1720*

economics, the history of literature, music, printing, publishing, society, theatre, and those involved in the use of the computer in the organisation of large quantities of varied data.

■ Chapter 3 ■

Database Management Software

One of the most important factors influencing the success or otherwise of historical database projects is the choice of software. The research team must ensure at an early stage that a DBMS is selected which has the functionality to cope efficiently with the nature, form and volume of the data to be stored and accessed. Many types of software package are advertised as DBMSs, though they vary widely in their general characteristics, and some at least do not really qualify as such. It is worthwhile to differentiate between the major types of data management programs on the market. To begin, we can differentiate between software packages in terms of the *type of platform* required and the *range of facilities* available.

Until quite recently, systems offering extensive facilities ran only on mainframe or mini computers, such as large IBMs, Primes, or DEC's VAX range. Moreover, little attention was given to *connectivity*; for example, a database implemented using INFO (a Prime minicomputer DBMS) could not easily be ported across to other machines and systems. Virtually any historical database project of any size, therefore, meant having recourse to the central computing facilities of a university or college and becoming committed to a particular machine and program. However, the rapid advance of microcomputer capabilities has meant that full versions of many of the most advanced data management programs have become accessible through standalone or networked PCs. The number of platforms supported has also increased, and systems are now available which will run on whole ranges of machines that use different processor chips and operating systems. These software systems are said to be *portable*. For example, ORACLE is a leading RDBMS which was originally developed in the late 1970s as a mainframe product. Recent versions have been written in the programming language C to make porting to different systems a fairly straightforward exercise. Today, ORACLE can be run on IBM PCs, various workstations and minis, and mainframes from all the leading suppliers, including VAX and IBM, and data transfer between any of these machines is problem-free. Other powerful packages have been developed

47

specifically for the Macintosh and the IBM PC and its clones. Well-known examples include Omnis (Macintosh), dBase IV, Superbase, Paradox and FoxPro (PC). Here too attention has been paid to the question of connectivity. Most leading commercial DBMSs now provide good import/export facilities to enable data and tables to be transferred to and from a variety of well-known formats – such as dBase, Paradox and Lotus.

Not surprisingly, there has been a tendency to add extra features and facilities to established programs. Commercial DBMSs are the products either of specialist software houses such as Borland and Microsoft or of major hardware manufacturers like IBM, DEC and ICL. The products of these firms are under development all the time. They pass through a series of releases as new features are added or modifications made, and competition ensures that a good idea on the part of one DBMS supplier will quickly be taken up by others. This is sometimes described as 'creeping featurism'. It is not always a desirable phenomenon, as it can lead to unwieldy programs which are difficult to learn and make excessive demands in terms of hardware requirements. For this reason, a demand still exists – and doubtless will continue to exist – for straightforward and easy-to-learn packages which provide relatively limited facilities. The major software suppliers have recognised this, and alongside their 'leading edge' programs they offer packages whose facilities are constrained not by the power and size of the machine on which they run, but by marketing considerations and perceptions of end-user needs. Frequently encountered system limitations are:

- maximum number of fields in a record;
- maximum number of characters in a field;
- maximum number of fields within a record that can be indexed;
- no support for variable length fields;
- limited ability to retrieve data from separate files with a single query;
- limited ability to restructure a database;
- limited security facilities;
- lack of multiuser capacity.

Powerful DBMSs have few such limitations.

It should be noted, however, that, whilst there is often a trade-off between comprehensiveness of features on the one hand and 'user-friendliness' on the other, the two are not necessarily mutually exclusive. Some powerful and fully featured systems are nevertheless easy to use. Packages which run on the Macintosh and take advantage of its graphical user interface (GUI), mouse support and pull-down menus are held to be more user-friendly than their non-GUI rivals. Similarly, in the PC world, the development of a new generation of Windows-based programs is helpful, in that the new user is presented with a familiar interface (layout of screen and menus) rather than an unknown proprietary one. The quality of the manuals is also an important factor. Software houses have invested large sums of money in manual writing; the results are not always as user-friendly as one might desire, but clearly written, well-structured manuals can make even the most powerful DBMS more accessible.

As well as differentiating between software packages on the basis of type of platform and range of features, we can also distinguish between *flat file managers* (FFMs), *database management systems* (DBMSs), *textual information management systems* (TIMSs) and *integrated* or *multimedia systems.*

■ 3.1 Flat File Managers

FFMs possess the major advantage of being simple to understand and easy to use. Examples of FFMs are PC-File and Q&A for PCs and FileMaker Pro for the Macintosh and Windows. They are often rather like spreadsheets in appearance, and may employ spreadsheet-like functions for data manipulation. The emphasis is on fast querying and reporting; some packages also offer useful graphing facilities. They are often aimed at the lower end of the market, and consequently there may be some limitations on the features offered – such as the maximum length of a field, or the number of records that can be accommodated. However, a powerful and up-to-date FFM like Symantec's Q&A will include the following features:

- A range of field types, including logical fields (Yes or No) and currency fields in a variety of formats, as well as the common text, numeric and date fields.
- Error checking methods to ensure that the wrong type of data cannot be entered into a field.
- Functions to enable calculations to be performed on data in one or more fields, and the results stored in a summary field (totalling, averaging, counting, percentages, standard deviation, and so on).
- A range of *data views* to permit browsing through or editing existing records and adding new ones. The most common are *form view* – a single record on the screen at a time, with a list of fieldnames down the left hand side of the screen, accompanied

by suitably sized boxes into which data can be entered – and *list or table view* – like a spreadsheet, with a record to each line, and the fields in columns. Also important are *cross-tab views* – to provide summation, averaging, etc. of a pair of fields – and *graphing views*.

- Methods to automate data entry (for example, allowing data from the corresponding field in the previous entry to be copied automatically to the new record being inserted).
- Straightforward searching and selecting facilities.
- Sorting and indexing routines to reorder the whole database or a subset of it.
- Speedy and flexible reporting features to allow data to be printed out in a variety of formats.
- Macro-writing facilities to speed up repetitive tasks.
- Flexible import and export facilities to allow data files to be moved to and from various well-known formats.
- Support for networking.

As the name suggests, FFMs support the creation of single-file (or flat-file) systems. Whenever there are only one-to-one relationships between data items, and the data can be stored in a single table, with each row representing a record and each column a field, then a flat file manager is an appropriate solution. Consequently, FFMs can be very useful research tools, particularly for smaller jobs, such as the computerisation of a membership list.

However, whilst FFMs of various kinds may play an important part in *supporting* historical research, there are but a few database projects which can be implemented using a FFM. This is because of the multiple relationships which frequently exist between data items. As noted earlier, FFMs provide a suitable software solution where the relationships between data items are one-to-one, and the data fit neatly into a two-dimensional matrix of rows and columns. It *is* possible to use them to handle data sets where there are one-to-many or many-to-many relationships, but not without duplicating data. This may be acceptable where the data set is relatively small, but generally is to be avoided because of the data integrity problems which result. Thus, for most sophisticated database projects, the complexity and extent of the data demands the use of a multifile DBMS.

■ 3.2 Database Management Systems

As noted in Chapter 2, a database management system is a generalised software package that is used to create and maintain a database. It may be thought of as a layer of software lying between the physical database and the user, so shielding the user from hardware level detail. The core work of a DBMS is file creation, manipulation and updating. Collectively, the many advanced technical features possessed by DBMSs provide the flexibility and power needed to operate at the centre of a corporate information system. These same features have been identified by researchers in the humanities and social sciences as valuable for storing and manipulating research results.

The basic qualification for a DBMS is that, unlike a FFM, which allows the user access to a single file at a time, the software handles multiple files of data as an integrated database. Multifile databases are the best way to store and link one-to-many relations. Most modern database management systems support the relational methodology pioneered in the 1970s by E.F. Codd (see Chapter 2). Relational database management systems (RDBMSs) establish relationships between related files, and allow them to be interrogated as though they were a single file. Thus data can be entered into multiple tables via a single data entry form, and data from multiple tables can be displayed or printed in a single report. This is possible because:

- links between tables are maintained by the use of fields which are common to each table.
- to facilitate the linking of tables, there is a *primary key* – either a single field (simple key) or group of fields (composite key) – which uniquely identifies each record in each of the tables to be linked.
- the records stored in a particular table are not just any collection of data items, but a special grouping of data. Typically, each table stores data about a single entity in which we are interested.

It should be noted that the process of identifying primary keys and arranging data in special groups is not a trivial matter; it requires careful thought and a deep understanding of the data. Several methodologies have been developed to assist in this task. They are discussed at length in Chapter 5.

As noted earlier, there are a large number of relational database packages on the market, and in some instances it has to be said that the term 'relational' is used rather creatively by marketing executives. A valuable survey of leading systems is provided by Valduriez and Gardarin.[1] A leading commercial RDBMS, and one widely available to the academic community, is ORACLE. When it was released by the ORACLE Corporation in 1979, it was the first commercial RDBMS to feature the query language SQL. It was also one of the first complete database management systems to be designed from the outset as a relational system; many of its rivals are descended from earlier designs which have subsequently had relational elements added. ORACLE is now available on a variety of platforms, ranging from IBM mainframes to DEC minis and PC-compatible microcomputers. Because it is available in many university computer centres, it has been used to implement a number of important historical research databases, including the Westminster Historical Database (see Case Study F) and the Register of Music in London Newspapers, 1660–1800 (Case Study B). It will also be referred to in section 6.2 on SQL, and section 8.2 on record linkage.

As can be seen from Figure 3.1, ORACLE consists of an integrated set of computer programs. At its core is the relational database management program itself, together with the SQL query language. If the data are to be readily available without the aid of expert technicians, then applications should be easy to build and use. So ORACLE surrounds its RDBMS kernel with an integrated suite of development tools. These are described in turn.

The SQL*Plus component, as the name suggests, provides extensions to standard SQL, as defined by the American National Standards Institute (ANSI) and the International Standards Organisation (ISO), such as the ability to modify the structure of database tables after they have been created. SQL*Plus allows commands to be entered and executed directly from the keyboard, or run non-interactively from batch files (see Glossary at the end of this volume). It also provides facilities to link a PC user to ORACLE systems on other machines on a network. Data from a remote machine can be accessed, processed locally, and then sent back to update the remote database. It offers a basic 'command line'-type interface, and lacks menus, windows and function key facilities.

The ORACLE RDBMS provides an integrated data dictionary, CASE*Dictionary, which holds all the information about tables, users, programs, access rights and so on. Being fully integrated, the dictionary can be updated on-line. As new tables or users are added to the database, the dictionary is immediately updated. The dictionary is held as standard data files, and may itself be queried in the normal way. For those creating major applications, CASE*Dictionary goes even further, providing a structured system for monitoring and controlling the design and documentation of database applications at all stages of their development, from initial analysis to implementation and maintenance. It provides a definitive record of the system's aims and operations. CASE*Dictionary can highlight inconsistencies in the analysis of the system's functions and makes preliminary assessments of database layout, size and performance.

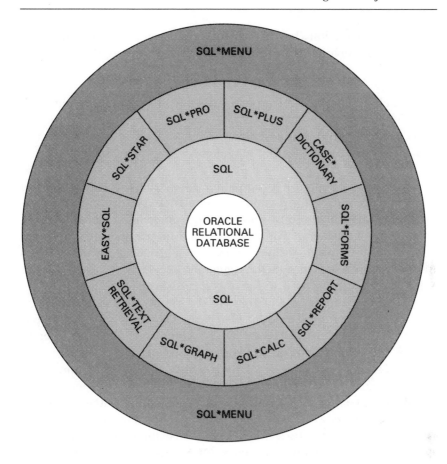

Figure 3.1 *The ORACLE relational database system*

SQL*Forms is an interactive screen designer, and is one of the most useful of ORACLE's software tools. Without a screen forms generator, data entry and modification would have to be done through raw SQL and SQL*Plus commands. This would be feasible for a skilled programmer, but it would be inappropriate for less skilled users running ORACLE applications. In practice, data entry and updating is generally achieved through screen forms designed with SQL*Forms. It uses pull-down menus, windows and screen painting to help users build and modify the screen forms they need.

SQL*Report is a powerful report-formatting package that allows the application developer to create single and multi-query reports using a number of complex and versatile reporting formats. It automatically transforms the result of any SQL query into a report, using default column headings and data formats taken from the data dictionary. The user can then add page headers and footers, specify that totals and other calculations be performed on sub-groups of data and override any of the dictionary defaults. SQL*Report has the following features:

- Quick development of reports with no programming required.
- Easy report maintenance.
- Context-sensitive online help.
- Interactive browse facility for quick viewing of reports.

SQL*Calc is a Lotus 1-2-3 compatible spreadsheet. It can be used to build models and perform complex calculations on data held in database tables. This is done by entering SQL commands into cells, prefaced by the $ character. For example, data from a specified table can be loaded into the spreadsheet, starting at a given cell, by using SQL's SELECT command. Other SQL commands like UPDATE, DELETE and INSERT can also be used within the spreadsheet.

SQL*Graph automatically converts the result of a database query into a graphical representation. Pie-charts, bar-charts, and line-graphs can all be drawn in full colour. Graph commands allow the user to change the colour, pattern, size, orientation, etc. of any element.

SQL*TextRetrieval is a set of tools which add fully-functional text retrieval capabilities to the ORACLE RDBMS. A set of special commands for querying free text is provided. Relational systems have traditionally worked with structured data, and the ability to store and manipulate both structured data and unstructured text in the same database is a considerable advance. ORACLE's SQL*TextRetrieval is discussed further in section 6.3 below. Historical projects which exploit its capabilities are described in section 5.2, and in Case Study B.

Facilities are provided for end users with widely differing levels of technical skill. Easy*SQL is a mouse-driven program which allows inexperienced users to exploit SQL by selecting what they want to do on-screen. Rather than learning the language's syntax and typing in commands, they simply point at what they want to do. In short, it offers a much more 'user-friendly' way of accessing the database than the SQL*Plus command-line interface. Like SQL*Plus, however, it allows an ORACLE user, typically on a PC, to link to the ORACLE system on another machine in the network, usually a mainframe. He/she can extract data from the other machine, process it locally, and then send it back to update the database on the other machine. SQL*Star goes one step further, and gives network users transparent interactive access to data on any ORACLE system in the network, regardless of the host system on which it actually resides. This can be of major benefit to a research team using a variety of different platforms. Pro*SQL is for professional programmers, allowing them to embed SQL routines into procedural ('third generation') languages like C, COBOL, Pascal, etc. Finally, surrounding and integrating ORACLE's various software tools is SQL*Menu, a flexible and easy-to-use menuing system which structures the way in which tasks are carried out and prevents unauthorised use of the database.

Modern RDBMSs like ORACLE have much to offer the researcher. However, it should be remembered that RDBMSs were conceived at a time when most databases consisted solely of numbers and short, fixed-length text fields. In recent years, they have also been used for an increasingly wide variety of data types. ORACLE's SQL*Text Retrieval has been mentioned, and other up-to-date packages like FoxPro, Access and Paradox provide memo and binary fields which can often hold data of any size and type. This makes them well-suited to storing information which varies in size, like descriptions, comments, letters and even binary data like digitised sounds and images. Nevertheless, it remains generally true to say that the essential characteristic of RDBMSs is that they handle *structured* data. They do not offer an ideal solution for projects which involve loosely structured data or free text. In such cases, text or document management systems may be more appropriate to the historian's needs.

3.3 Textual Information Management Systems

RDBMSs have risen to the fore in recent years because of their flexibility, ease of use, and the ability to link tables together when retrieving information from a multifile database. However, they have not had the capacity to handle long strings of text efficiently. In such cases, the original source(s) cannot be neatly divided into a set of short, structured fields. Moreover, we are dealing here with data where some of the meaning is embedded within the text itself. Much of the meaning comes from the context within which the characters exist, and individual words and even phrases may be meaningless in themselves.

Those with a need to manage and analyse large collections of text have to make use of another class of software. Programs designed specifically to handle unstructured data are known as textual information management systems (TIMSs). Examples of leading TIMSs are BASIS (Batelle Automated Search Information System), developed by the Batelle Memorial Institute and distributed in the UK by Information Dimensions Ltd., and STATUS, marketed by Harwell Computer Power Ltd.

Both are available on a range of platforms, including IBM mainframes, MS-DOS, VMS (DEC VAX) and Unix.[2] TIMSs were developed to facilitate access to the wide variety of documents which large organisations need to conduct business – contracts, proposals, memos, planning documents, patents, research data and the like. The potential value of TIMSs for historians, who likewise need to access a wide range of document types in their research, is obvious.

In comparison with structured databases, textbases have developed relatively slowly. The first difficulty is that of size. Many large databases require less than 10Mb of storage, whereas textbases of 100Mb or more are by no means unusual. A second problem is the apparent lack of structure within textbases. In fact, this is less of a problem than it might seem. Text is divided by spaces into words (or into characters in ideographic languages like Japanese or Chinese), and into sentences and paragraphs. At a higher level (i.e. document level) a structure can also be identified in many instances: division, for example, into author, subject, date of creation, abstract, body text, etc. The task, therefore, is to deal efficiently with variable length records while allowing speedy, straightforward querying. A third difficulty is that text retrieval is essentially probabilistic, unlike database querying, which yields definite answers. With textbases, there is always a trade-off between high accuracy and high recall. Both high accuracy *and* high recall are desirable, but may be theoretically as well as practically impossible. A final difficulty is that many documents contain line art, tables and images as well as text, sometimes in colour as well as black and white. All these problems are now being overcome by increased computer power, improved searching algorithms and falling hardware costs, and the number of textbase applications looks set to grow rapidly in the coming years.

TIMSs share many features of a good DBMS – data integrity, security, data independence, ease of access, and so on. But, unlike standard DBMSs, TIMSs support the storage and searching of large individual documents, and large collections of documents. Textual documents are often of large size and have unpredictable structures; thus TIMSs impose few restrictions on textbase size or layout. Documents retain their original formatting, and TIMSs permit the user to treat documents according to their natural divisions rather than arbitrarily dividing them into fixed-length records. In addition to the 'long text field', however, TIMSs do enable the user to create some structured fields for the manipulation of recurring elements within the document, or for data about the document itself. Once created, it should be possible to query and display these structured fields, as required. Thus, as well as searching the documents for words or phrases, it is also possible to search for documents by specified authors, date of creation, type, and so on. Indexing data are also stored in fixed formats to permit fast updating and retrieving.[3]

Most commercial systems work with three main files: the *text file*, containing the actual data, together with any related structured fields; an *inverse file* (also called a *word list* or *concordance*), which contains an indexed list, in alphabetical order, of all the useful words in the text file; and a *pointer file*, which points to each occurrence of an indexed word in the text file.[4] The user can determine not only the number of categories in the index, but also the complexity of index structure. Researchers can settle for simple (flat) index systems, or create conceptual 'trees' with numerous subcategories. The results of any search can be stored as a new category in the index system.[5] Such indexes can readily be modified, expanded and updated as the research project develops. Indexes are often very large – sometimes as large as the text to which they refer. The pointer file ensures that the index can track the document section and context unit (sentence, paragraph, etc.) in which terms occur. The system can also recall the order in which the terms occur within the context area. This ensures that the user moves immediately to the exact location where the searched-for term occurs, regardless of the document's length. Users can then scroll through the text, move to the next occurrence of the search term in the document, or, if the document is of no interest, move to the first occurrence of the search term in the next document.

The essence of the TIMS concept is that the entire contents of the database should be searchable. In a TIMS, the idea of keyword searching is extended to include the text of the whole document. This is called *context indexing*. (However, words like 'the', 'and', 'but', and so on are not indexed; it is unlikely that anyone would wish to search for them, and because they occur so frequently they would greatly increase the size of the index. The TIMS should be capable of eliminating these *stopwords* or *common words* from the index, thus saving disk space and speeding retrieval times.) The principal benefit of context indexing is the elimination of the labour costs involved in manually developing a list of keywords, or search terms. Instead, the software performs the task automatically by indexing all the important words in the document. This distinguishes TIMSs from other types of document retrieval systems which require users to attach predetermined keywords or identifiers to the text. TIMSs may in fact permit the addition of such descriptors to indicate the text's structure, appearance or significance, but they do not depend upon them. (STATUS, for example, adds markers to indicate the start of a chapter, article, named section or paragraph. These categories are clearly defined in the documentation, and are a useful means of narrowing down the scope of a particular query.)

Perhaps the important characteristic of a TIMS, however, is ease of use. Once the textbase is set up, it can be queried by end-users who have no detailed knowledge of computers. The user does not need to remember predetermined keywords or document filenames to retrieve a particular item, and changes to the data can be made without requiring the user to run a program to update the index. Instead, changes lead to automatic rebuilding of the index – a process which is transparent to the user.

TIMSs make use of a variety of content-based techniques for retrieving textual information. There are numerous options which enable users to search for the entire contents of a field, phrases, individual words, numbers, or repeating strings. As in DBMSs, TIMS software supports *truncation, reverse truncation* and *wildcard searching*. Truncation helps to ensure that plurals and other inflections are retrieved together, while reverse truncation (sometimes called *left-hand truncation*) handles words with different prefixes. Wildcard searching copes with search terms for which there are alternative spellings. The use of a thesaurus is another feature essential to text retrieval. The TIMS thesaurus contains a list of words or concepts, and information on the relationships between them. Some systems, such as BASIS, offer automated thesauri. For example, searching a thesaurus-controlled field for the term 'USA' would retrieve all documents containing the terms 'US', 'America' and 'United States' as well as 'USA', with a single search. More important to the researcher, however, is the ability to modify the thesaurus to meet his or her specific needs. This helps to ensure that synonyms or near-synonyms of the chosen search words are also retrieved – thereby providing conceptual associations which would be missed through conventional automatic database indexing. Thesauri also provide an opportunity to clarify ambiguous word meanings, and include relevance ranking and 'sounds like' facilities. As well as searching for words, numbers or phrases, the user can define the positional or logical relationships that are required between them. A good system will also have sophisticated facilities for *proximity searching*. Proximity searching enables the user to find all occurrences of a certain search term within a specified distance forwards or backwards from another search term. Querying a textbase is considered further in section 6.3.

While this section has focussed on describing the many useful features for the analysis of free text which are provided by sophisticated TIMSs, it should be noted that other, related, types of software can also be useful for handling unstructured data. Generally, though, they lack the power and flexibility of TIMSs, as may be gauged from Figure 3.2.

Database management systems	Can be used to store document descriptors and keywords, and may include a 'long text' or 'memo' field. However, most have difficulty in coping with the unstructured text of an entire document. DBMSs in addition often have problems with variable length descriptors, requiring fields of fixed length.
Document retrieval systems	Like TIMSs, document retrieval systems archive documents and their locations. However, to retrieve a document the user must know the name, date or some other descriptor assigned to the document when it was created or loaded into the system.
Keyword systems	Allow users to search a document by entering keyword descriptors. Keyword systems involve considerable labour because the initial selection of keywords must be performed manually. Additionally, there is the problem that the user may not find the information required because his/her search criteria do not exactly match those used during the initial indexing.
Records management systems	Require data to be entered into a structured format, and the user defines fields for author, date, title, subject and text. They are of value for cataloguing, but are not suitable for large files or unstructured text.
Document image processors	Store scanned (bit-mapped) images of documents, often using optical disks because of the large size of the resulting files. Like record management systems, structured fields can be added to record author, date and other descriptors which can be used in retrieval; with the same disadvantages.

Figure 3.2 *Other types of text retrieval systems*

In this context, reference should also be made to on-line biblio-graphic retrieval systems which, like TIMSs, are designed to handle loosely structured text. Early systems were *batch processing* (*off-line*) systems. Because they were usually dependent upon slow magnetic tape for data storage, queries were processed in batches. All the records would be scanned in turn, and any that matched the search criteria would be copied to a second tape, together with the relevant query number. The matching records would then be sorted into sets for each query, printed, and sent off to the person who had originated the query. There would be a considerable delay between the submission of a query and the receipt of the hard copy. In the later 1970s and early 1980s, with the improved performance of processors and storage media, came the widespread introduction of *on-line* information retrieval systems, which allow users to search a database *interactively*. Improved data communications have enabled users to access databases from remote terminals, and download the results of a search in machine-readable form rather than awaiting hard copy.

To perform a successful online search, the researcher must learn the system's query language, and something of the database's contents and structure. In some cases, this means that expert assistance is needed to access online systems. Problems can result. There may be some delay before a query is run, and while the intermediary may be expert in online searching, he or she will lack the specialist knowledge of the researcher. If the resulting communication gap is to be bridged, the researcher must take care to define the queries fully and precisely. Nevertheless the process is far swifter and thorough than manual searching. Many historians will be familiar with the use of computerised bibliographic citation lists such as the British Library Automated Information Service (BLAISE) and American equivalents like DIALOG. These systems are able to process search requests and return printed lists to the originator of the query. They are much swifter and more comprehensive than searching manually through citation lists. DIALOG is particularly useful because each entry includes, together with the usual bibliographical details, an abstract and a list of keywords for cross-referencing. Invaluable too is the ability to log on to the online information retrieval systems of academic libraries via the Joint Academic Network (JANET) or the Internet, which enable researchers to search library holdings from their own offices.

Finally, reference should be made to a number of hybrid programs which attempt to provide the best features of competing approaches. One example is Idealist, from Blackwell Scientific Publications. Idealist is particularly interesting in that, whilst all the records fit into a single file, as in a conventional flat file manager, they do not necessarily have the same structure. Instead, the user can define a variety of different structures, and select whichever is appropriate when entering a new record. Idealist is also unusual in that it can handle free text as well as the structured fields of more traditional FFMs. Long text fields can be added to hold abstracts and research notes. In short,

Idealist is intended to provide an uncomplicated way of capturing, storing, retrieving and outputting loosely structured or even unstructured collections of data, and this gives it the character of a simple textbase management system rather than a conventional FFM. Idealist has been marketed as a bibliographic tool, though it does lack important features one would expect: connectivity to online bibliographical databases like DIALOG and BLAISE, for example.[6] Its best use, in fact, is as a 'research notebook', and historians have recognised that it can be used very effectively when a combination of text and structured data, or a variety of record formats, is required.

Thus a considerable variety of programs have evolved to store and manipulate free text or loosely structured data. Some, like BASIS and other fully-featured TIMSs, offer great flexibility and power to the user, and refinements are constantly being made to enhance the range of features offered. However, such programs have not taken over from conventional DBMSs. They represent an alternative approach not a universal solution, and, in fact, TIMSs and DBMSs are often run side-by-side to meet different project needs. The result has been a tendency for the distinction between the two to become blurred, as leading DBMS suppliers have added text-processing modules to their products.

■ 3.4 Integrated Systems

The ORACLE Corporation has been one of the front-runners in this process, with the addition of a text management module to its suite of software tools. SQL*TextRetrieval is designed to add fully functional text retrieval and manipulation capabilities to the ORACLE RDBMS. This means that both structured data and unstructured text may be held in the same relational database framework. Typically, structured fields may be used to describe the text (`Author`, `Location`, `Creation_Date`, etc.), while the text itself is held in a single long field. Originally, texts had to be in sections of no more than 32K each, though this limitation has been removed in the latest releases. Text may be loaded from flat ASCII files, or, with structured data, from specially formatted files. It may also be entered from within the package itself. Standard SQL queries cannot be used on the long text field, but a set of special commands for querying free text is provided. Queries on the text can be constructed using truncation, reverse truncation, and wildcards. Additionally, proximity searching enables the user to find all occurrences of a certain word within a specified distance forwards or backwards from another word. As with a TIMS, however, the real strength of ORACLE's SQL*Text Retrieval lies in the range of thesaurus facilities provided. For each word in the word index list, the user can build up a group of synonyms, broader terms, narrower terms, and a variety of more loosely related terms. The use of ORA-CLE's SQL*TextRetrieval in historical research projects is discussed further in sections 5.2 and 6.3 below.

Other RDBMSs are following similar routes, often developing the concept of the memo field as a means of coping with the storage of text. It seems likely that the distinctions between software categories will become increasingly blurred as several RDBMSs and TIMSs converge on a general integrated model.

■ 3.5 Multimedia and Hypermedia

The term *integrated systems* has been used to describe packages which offer facilities for the storage and manipulation of both structured and unstructured numeric and textual data. An increasing number of projects also demand the integration of graphics and sound. The term *multimedia* has been coined to describe this tendency. It is often abused in marketing circles and undoubtedly means different things to different people. It is sometimes applied to conventional DBMSs which extend the concept of the memo or general field to handle binary large objects (BLOBS) – types of data such as pictures or sound samples – as well as more or less free text. Examples of this are provided by FoxPro (especially the Windows version), Paradox and Superbase. None of these, however, is a multimedia product in the fullest sense of the word. Essentially, multimedia means the extension of a graphical user interface to enable the integration of digital sound, still images and real-time video (either windowed or full-screen). The hardware requirements are considerable. Fast processors, fast video RAM and video cards are essential, and the storage requirements are very demanding. For this reason, CD-ROMs, videodisks, WORM (Write Once, Read Many) disks or erasable magneto-optical devices are used for data distribution and storage, as well as very large hard disk drives. The peripherals required, like digital cameras, scanners and camcorders for input and stereo sound equipment, colour page printers and compression equipment for output, are also expensive. The level of technical expertise required is likewise high. Multimedia is at the leading edge of technical development. For example, the incorporation of real-time full-screen video depends upon the continuing advances being made in data compression techniques; without effective compression, the data would occupy a massive amount of storage, and could not be displayed at normal speed. Apple's Macintosh computers are at the forefront of the multimedia boom, and other major players like Microsoft, Sony, IBM and Phillips are all bidding for substantial shares of the market.

An interesting multimedia application is Art Gallery, developed by the National Gallery in association with Microsoft. Art history archives and catalogues are obvious potential beneficiaries of the multimedia approach; the applications being developed often use specially written software to capture and manage images, and to control the sophisticated hardware required. Art Gallery is a computerised information system which contains background information on every painting in the National Gallery, and allows the user freely to explore his or her particular area of interest, whether painting, artist, period, subject or genre. In the version available at the National Gallery, the information is presented on colour screens with touch controls. At the heart of the system is a complete illustrated catalogue of the Gallery's holdings, divided into four sections. The 'General Reference' section contains entries and examples for key terms and subjects, such as 'Cartoon', 'Chiaroscuro', and 'Christ Crowned with Thorns'. The 'Artists' section contains a biography and visual index of the works of all the artists represented in the National Gallery. The 'Picture Types' section provides a visual classification of the collection by type of painting. There are six main categories, 'Still Life', 'Religious Imagery', 'Portraits', 'Views', 'Everyday Life' and 'Stories and Allegories', which are then further subdivided. Finally, the 'Historical Atlas' presents the collection by time and place, using a series of maps and example paintings. Visitors to the National Gallery can use Art Gallery free of charge, though a nominal charge is levied if the user wishes to print out pages of the catalogue, and the package is now published by Microsoft on CD-ROM.[7]

A convenient entry into the world of multimedia is provided by *hypertext* and *hypermedia*. Hypertext is an approach to information management which, in recent years, has begun to generate a good deal of interest. Its intention is to allow the user to break away from the notion of linear text, and develop associative referencing of information; in other words, information can be accessed in different sequences according to the needs of the individual researcher, rather than in the manner prescribed by its original author. The term hypertext is somewhat misleading in that such techniques are not solely confined to the manipulation of text. Text can be supplemented by still pictures, video and sound; indeed, one of the potential benefits which it brings to the research process is the way in which it encourages the use of graphic imagery and visual modes of thinking, and this has led to the use of the more accurate, if somewhat pretentious, term *hypermedia*.

A hypertext has been defined as 'an electronic document which is essentially a database with "live" cross-references. This document may be read in a non-sequential manner, because the computer enables the reader to follow conceptual links between items, thus removing some of the constraints we all experience when reading conventional linear documents (such as books). . . . The entire structure of a hypertext is actually a network of nodes with links to other nodes, and a reader "browses" or "navigates" through the network.'[8] Nodes can contain information in a variety of formats. In the case of text, they may be words, phrases or whole documents. They may also be graphics, sound, still images, video sequences, or a combination of these. Nodes are connected to each other by links, which are selected with the mouse pointer. The existence of links may be indicated on the screen by buttons or icons. Additionally, rather than being represented by a visual symbol, the link can be embedded in the text. For example, a word in reversed video might signal that it is a text button which can be selected to provide more information. Associated with each button is a set of instructions, or script, which defines what will happen when a button is selected. It may be a simple 'goto' message, which displays another screenfull of data. It can also be used to perform more complex operations – perhaps depending upon the route through the data previously followed by the user. Alternatively, the path to be followed may not be predetermined; instead, it may require some input from the user – perhaps to enter the criteria for a string search before executing the search and displaying the results on screen.

The hypertext concept was pioneered by HyperCard, which Apple provided free with all Macintosh computers. HyperCard is based on a card-to-card relationship, rather than a text-to-text one; it follows the metaphor of a *stack* of index cards. Each card can contain *fields* and *buttons*. A field is an area of the card into which the author can type text. A button is a small rectangle or icon which initiates a particular action – such as jumping to another card in the stack when the mouse is clicked on it. The action is controlled by a *script* – a program written in HyperCard's authoring language, HyperTalk. Cards may also contain graphics created using other programs, and digital sounds. The user may browse through the stack sequentially, or jump to a remote location by clicking on a button. It is the ability to link non-adjacent cards which is HyperCard's greatest strength. Placing several buttons on a field enables users to navigate their own paths through the data set.

HyperCard's principal rival on the Macintosh is SuperCard. SuperCard is an expensive program; to justify its price, it offers a wealth of features not found in HyperCard. Notable amongst them are its superior range of painting and drawing tools, its rich programming environment, and its animation features. SuperCard offers its own scripting language, SuperTalk, and most commands are available by way of pop-up or pull-down menus which can be scrolled to locate the appropriate command. The basic unit in SuperCard is the project. This consists of windows, cards, menus and resources, together with the scripts to make it all work. Each window is equivalent to a HyperCard stack, and a SuperCard project can contain multiple windows, several of which can be displayed on screen at any one time. When setting up a project, the developer creates standard Macintosh pull-down menus to allow the user to navigate through the data. After organising a menu structure, a SuperTalk script is written for each menu item to trigger the required operation. The button palette provides options for creating a full range of Mac-style buttons. Icons can be created and stored, and are used to illustrate buttons. SuperCard readily allows the user to import text, graphics and sound from other programs.

Other packages emanating from the commercial world include Guide, which is available for both the Macintosh and the PC. Guide allows users to investigate documents by creating individually determined routes. However, considerable care must be taken when setting up documents. Any routes which may be followed have to be set up in advance before the user can browse through the finished document. Guide allows the user to create new documents and link existing ones together through the use of text and graphics buttons. Other buttons may be used to activate external programs, or drive peripherals like modems or CD-ROMs. There are substantial differences between Hypercard and Guide. HyperCard is really an application-building environment. Guide, on the other hand, is a computer-based information publishing system, and its strengths lie in its ability to create, link and cross-reference multiple documents. Guide tries, as far as possible, to emulate the paper-based document systems with which users are familiar, and it has found favour with many large organisations which need a 'natural' searching and cross-referencing system.

It is evident that hypermedia goes beyond conventional approaches which access text and other data types in linear or sequential ways. Applications can be designed to enable users to find their own way through the data, perhaps resulting in fresh insights and different perspectives. Additionally, hypermedia plays to the strengths of graphical user interfaces by encouraging the integration of pictures, maps and graphs. Images can be captured via video recorder or digital camera, and annotated through the use of buttons. Similarly, sounds can be integrated with visual information. Hypermedia approaches encourage the development of systems which bring together image manipulation with more established types of text-based research and information systems. It is for these reasons that of late there has been a good deal of interest in hypermedia for both the teaching of history and historical research.

However, it should be noted that the promise of hypermedia has yet to be fully realised. Whilst HyperCard and related packages are flexible and relatively easy to learn, the time and trouble involved in the development of hypermedia applications should not be underestimated. Constructing a hypertext document is a demanding design problem. As with any sophisticated medium of communication, considerable attention must be devoted to the design phase before implementation begins. A particular problem with many systems is the need to predefine links. This means that the designer must consider carefully how the finished structure might actually be used by researchers to inform their work. The usability of an application may be seriously reduced if insufficient or inappropriate links are established, and debugging a system to ensure that users cannot get lost as they navigate around it can be an onerous task. Another, related, problem is the need to modify source documents by the insertion of markup codes to define the links.[9]

One hypermedia package which offers innovative solutions to these difficulties is Microcosm, which has been developed by a team of researchers at the University of Southampton's Department of Electronics and Computer Science. An important feature is Microcosm's ability to generalise links. Like other hypermedia packages, it allows the user to make *specific* links, which can be assigned to buttons, between particular instances of keywords. (The term *anchor* is however preferred to the term keyword, as the objects being linked may be sound or images rather than text.) In addition, Microcosm provides *local* and *generic* links. Local links enable the user to follow the link after selecting the anchor at *any* point in the current document. Generic links, on the other hand, allow the user to follow the link after selecting the given anchor at *any* point in *any* document. This means that whenever a new document is added to the system it will immediately have access to all the generic links which have previously been defined. The benefits to a historical research project, where the document set will be in a process of continual development, will readily be appreciated.

Microcosm also differs fundamentally from most hypermedia systems because of its ability to integrate information using a variety of third-party applications. Video and sound objects, as well as text and pictures, can be linked in this way. Microcosm includes tools to view data held in standard formats, together with the ability to link with other Windows applications, such as Lotus 1-2-3, MS Word and Autodesk Autocad, which become viewers for their own data. To facilitate this, the source documents are not marked up in any way, but remain in the native format of the program which created them. Information about links is held separately in *link databases* (or *linkbases*). A major advantage of this approach is that is is possible to create different sets of links for the same data. For example, workgroup members may share a 'public' set of links, and also create a 'private' linkbase for their own annotations. Another important benefit is that it becomes poss-ible to create links to documents which are held in read-only formats like CD-ROM.

To enable the user to navigate around the system, Microcosm pro-vides a variety of filters. They include the History filter, which records the documents which have been visited and enables the user to return to a particular document, and the Mimic filter, which enables the user to follow a predefined path, branching off and returning to it as he or she wishes. The whole is managed by a Document Management Sys-tem (DMS), which keeps track of the documents in the system and their attributes. The DMS provides an efficient method for moving the physical location of documents without having to change all the links, and also provides a variety of library catalogue-like features, such as searching for keywords. Microcosm currently runs under Windows 3.1, OS/2 and Windows NT, and UNIX and Macintosh versions are under development.[10] The case for using Microcosm in historical research projects is considered by Frank Colson in Case Study C, and hypermedia databases are considered further in section 7.2.

■ 3.6 Conclusion

In this chapter we have provided a review of the main software alternatives available to those embarking upon an historical research project. We have demonstrated that research into database technologies continues to proceed apace, challenging the dominance of market-leading relational database management systems. In recent years, as the demands and expectations of users have become more sophisticated, the limitations of relational systems have become more apparent. Perhaps most notable is the fact that data about an entity (a real world 'object' or 'event' in which we are interested) may be scattered over several tables, and only connected when a multitable query is run. It is for this reason that *object-oriented* database ideas are being taken increasingly seriously and incorporated into both newly-designed and long-established systems. In an object-orientated database, all the data about an object can be stored in one place and accessed via a single command, and thus can be retrieved more rapidly and more naturally. (Object-orientated databases are considered more fully in section 7.3.) At the same time, it has become clear that in the future databases will have to accommodate all types of information, including graphics, images and sound, as well as text and numbers. New retrieval methods will be needed to organise and retrieve this increased variety of data – much of which will be unstructured. Such developments in database software, coupled with the latest graphical tools and storage techniques, may well trigger an explosion in the use of databases in historical research projects.

Case Study C
A Hypermedia Database Management
System: Microcosm as a Research Tool[1]

Frank Colson
HiDES Project, University of Southampton

The analysis and interpretation of complex historical events requires the historian to explore and link together a wide variety of evidence in the form of text, numbers, sound and images. It is this requirement that makes Microcosm, an 'open' hypermedia database management system developed at the University of Southampton, an ideal tool for historical research.

Many fields of historical investigation remained untouched by the early phase of the database revolution: conventional database systems had obvious applications for historians concerned with numbers, quantities and trends, but for the majority concerned with the qualitative – with so-called 'thick description' – they had much less to offer. As late as the mid-1980s, historical computing still seemed irrelevant to large numbers of scholars. Perhaps the best way of describing their predicament is to take a particular example: how best could an historian describe a particular conjuncture – a 'day in the life' of a man whose activities may well have been peripheral to a major event? To what extent could the available software aid in the delineation of the event so as to incorporate contemporary perceptions while conveying an understanding of the *longue durée*? The answer was, only to a very limited degree. The early phase of the database revolution emphasised order, structure and leanness, when what was needed by those interested in multifaceted explanation and full contextualisation was rich unstructured databases encompassing a variety of materials which often possessed no discernable structure.

My own work on the Brazilian political crisis of 1889 may be used to illustrate the point. In this case there are good time-series data on prices, currency values, commodity production, imports, exports and demographic structure which provide a context for understanding a 'day in the life of a Rio de Janeiro trader in 1889'. We can readily make use of powerful computing tools of the most traditional kind to enable us to identify and assess patterns of economic growth, and to understand something of the structural changes occurring in Rio de Janeiro in 1888–90. Yet there is a sense in which this precision is spurious. It tends to define an event in terms which may not have been recognised by the economic actors of the day. Traders concerned with short-term profit-taking were super-sensitive to short-term fluctuations, and may well have been relatively impervious to more profound changes in the economy. The tenor of their incessant gossip on the Rua do Ouvidor (the Palais Royale of Rio de Janeiro) has to be captured if the local 'market' is to have its say. The scholar, concerned to understand the prevailing political mood of the city, will want to consult a variety of historical materials beyond those immediately available to the local trader. Newspapers, political pamphlets, speeches, photographic images, and even music, are useful in identifying the extent and sources of dissatisfaction with the government. It is apparent that all these forms of evidence might be brought to bear on the central question: what inspired the shift in political mood in May 1889 which led to a series of devastating attacks on the Brazilian Cabinet and its resignation early in June?

Perhaps we might take a step backwards, and revisit the evidence upon which the historian might draw in order to gauge the extent of the crisis of 1889. The identification of mood in Rio de Janeiro demands an understanding of the contents of popular music, newspapers, official and private correspondence. With half a dozen broadsheets supported by commerce and the major political parties, an active 'alternative' press, a vigorous industry of pamphlets, a continuous stream of government publications, the daily debates of Parliament, a lively theatre, and a flamboyant, noisy and highly visible social life subject to acid commentary by one of the country's outstanding writers, Machado de Assis, the historian is faced with a substantial archive – a plethora of data of considerable quality, all of which might be deployed.

Marshalling this data in a database system is a distinctly non-trivial task. Three principles should be born in mind. First, the original format of each document should be retained for future reference. Secondly, copies of documents should also be available in a form which may readily be analysed and manipulated. Finally, it is necessary to establish links between the various entities (people, places, events, etc.) referenced in different sources. The 'shape' and location of a text on a page of the *Jornal do Commercio* (the country's leading newspaper), for example, was dictated by custom, but certain sections frequently carried commentaries which were widely seen as indicative of mood. The contents and images of letters and official correspondence similarly carry their own encoded messages. The lesson is that each document must retain its native format and be processed as such. Without this rule, the database may well be unacceptable to colleagues for the simple reason that the evidence contained therein has been fundamentally distorted.

It was the severity of these requirements that created the imperative for an open hypermedia system. As late as 1989–90 they could not be met through the use of commercial software. At this stage, I was fortunate in gaining the support of colleagues in a computer science department who had become equally dissatisfied with the limitations of conventional database systems. Their interest lay in the design and implementation of open hypermedia systems which could cope with the requirements of non-structured data. Their labours led to Microcosm. From the outset, Microcosm was able to cope with the demands posed by the historian's need to cope with the complexity of 'thick description'. Moreover, since it was expected that very large datasets (defined as in excess of 20,000 files) would, sooner or later, be held on remote systems and manipulated via a network, Microcosm was designed to cope with a variety of networked hardware platforms. And since no historian could ever be sure of exhausting all forms of data, the capacity readily to add new modules to the system was an essential design feature. Links between entities in the database are stored in a separate and identifiable linkbase. In this way Microcosm serves as a completely integrated information system which acts like an umbrella, extending the working environment of the user. It might properly be described as a 'link service system', underpinning hypertext database structures which emerge as the historian develops an understanding of the interplay of events recorded in sources as diverse as sound recordings, photographs, newspapers, pamphlets, diaries and speeches.

Microcosm has proved invaluable to my research on the Brazilian political crisis of 1889. My discussion of the crisis has been crucially informed by the various hypertext links which it provides. As an example, let us consider the events of 7 May 1889, when the Chamber of Deputies had opened and the fate of the abolitionist ministry hung in the balance. Newspaper references to the comings and goings of various deputies and senators noted in the *Jornal do Commercio* are linked by static hypertext links to references contained in back numbers of the *Jornal* from the previous seven days. These images are stored in the Bitmap Viewer as 'links' located at specific points on the images. In other words we can 'map' the references to various newspaper items, not only indicating their provenance, but delineating the position on the image of the relevant page. These buttons serve three purposes: to enable a scholar to reference the text; to designate the reference; and to chart the location in the newspaper page at which the text item occurs. This last is crucial, for it enables us to decode the spatial language of the *Jornal*: Brazilian politicians were accustomed to 'reading' the long closely-typed language of the *Jornal* very carefully. All reportage was published anonymously, but they could trace the hand of the Ministry through the ability of government officials to 'place' items on the front page. Since Microcosm allows us to store and designate the links between these maps as separate objects, all reference to members of political groups can be collected together so that the historian can more accurately identify the skeins of alliances and political movements as they appeared to the politically-aware reader of the *Jornal*. We can therefore marshall evidence on political groupings of radicals and reformists which would previously have had to be inferred through allusion or inference.

We can further deepen the analysis by linking newspaper references to individual politicians with prosopographical data managed by the DBMS κλειω (kleio)[2] and accessible through Microcosm. The repeated identification of certain family names lays bare various interrelated networks of interests and alliances. Senator Antonio Prado, for instance, did not merely represent the Province of Sao Paulo. He was also a powerful entrepreneur, banker and *fazendeiro*, heading a family whose interests were deeply entrenched in that Province. A Conservative, he was widely regarded in May 1889 as the man most likely to wreck the current administration. Mention of his name in the Rua de Ouvidor between 7 and 8 p.m. of an evening in early May conjures up an image of power which might be fully investigated using Microcosm and κλειω. Since we are attempting to delineate the crisis through the perspective offered by the *Jornal do Commercio* and related textual references, a generic link established in Microcosm enables us to invoke congeries of interests through the multiplicity of texts and bitmap links available within the dataset.

Described in this way, Microcosm and ancillary applications provide the 'research desk' which enables the historian to delineate the many-faceted crisis which shook Brazilian politics in 1889, capturing the essence of the interplay between perceptions creating a sense of 'unease', of the deep dissatisfaction with existing institutions which remained a component of politics well into the following decade.

Without Microcosm, we would simply be able to document this crisis by allusion and inference. With it, we can depict the crisis, and thereby understand the threat felt to established property and power: explaining perhaps the long conservative reaction which shaped twentieth-century Brazil. With Microcosm, the 'metaphorical' element implicit in our attempts to define the interplay of interest and power becomes just a little more visible, multimedia are wholly incorporated into our argument.

■ *Chapter 4* ■
The Database Project Life-Cycle

■ 4.1 Project Management

We are concerned in this chapter with simple yet valuable techniques for bringing a database project to a successful conclusion. Without adequate planning and management, projects can become excessively costly, and worse still may not properly support the research. A disciplined and systematic approach to database planning and development, therefore, should pay a handsome dividend. It may not be necessary for researchers handling small, unified data sets to trouble too much about the intricacies of database design: common sense and the support of a good database management system will probably suffice to ensure the success of the project. However, this is unlikely to be so if the projected database is large in scale and scope, perhaps involving complex data relationships. There are many reasons why the planning of historical projects might prove difficult. It is not always easy to define a precise set of project aims and objectives; it is often hard to specify the precise form of the data and its volume; the reconciliation of available resources and project aims can be problematic; and the researcher may have little or no knowledge of the technology best suited to the project, beyond a general awareness that a computer solution is likely to be desirable.

If the intention is to develop a major resource, then these hurdles must be overcome, and historians should not hesitate to make selective use of the techniques which have been devised for defining and managing projects. The methodologies of systems analysis and design (SAD) and project management have been developed in recent times to help plan, direct and track projects. A review of the literature may well lead to the adoption of techniques and working practices which will prove of enduring value.[1]

In recent years, structured SAD methodologies have been widely adopted to handle the common problems of designing advanced information systems. These methodologies take a data-oriented view of a system through the analysis of its *data structure* (the form of the data),

data flows (who uses the data), and *processes* (what is done with the data). The approach involves the division of projects into stages – for instance, *strategy* (determining what needs to be done, and how much it should cost), *analysis* (specifying user requirements), *design* (deciding what the system should look like, and what tools and components should be used), *construction* (developing and prototyping the system), and *implementation* (going live with the full system, preparing documentation, and maintaining the system). At each stage, certain well-defined tasks are undertaken and the foundations laid for further work. A good deal of effort is put into project management, documentation, and the monitoring of progress. Experience has shown that substantial benefits stem from the adoption of structured SAD methods: better information systems result, with efficiently-structured databases at their core.

To assist in the tasks of designing and implementing databases, project management techniques can usefully be applied. In accordance with the stage approach outlined above, most of the competing methodologies emphasise the importance of taking a top-down approach (progressively breaking the work down), modularity (breaking the work into discrete modules), defining the project structure (around which the work is organised), documenting the project, and reviewing it to test for correctness and completeness. Some of the key features of project management methodologies are *hierarchical decomposition, project modelling,* and *project review.* These are described briefly in the next few paragraphs.

Hierarchical decomposition is a simple technique for analysing the scope and components of a project. Project components are of two types: compound (involve many tasks) and unitary (involve a single task). We begin by listing the most compound components. Typically, for instance, these are research design, hardware and software selection, data collection, application development (programming), data analysis, and publication. Next, we decompose the main components of the project into sub-components, and, through repetition of the process, we arrive at a full list of tasks. These can be imagined as the leaves on an inverted tree; and, indeed, it is useful to sketch out the project in this way. Hierarchical decomposition leads to the identification of tasks which often would have been neglected or postponed to the detriment of the project. For example, it may become apparent that the project will require the application of sophisticated multivariate techniques for the analysis of nominal data. Arrangements can be made for researchers lacking such skills to receive training at the appropriate point. Similarly, attention may be given to ensuring that project members are properly trained in the use of the DBMS as the project progresses; the effort required to gain a good working knowledge of a powerful DBMS should not be underestimated.

Project modelling takes as input the goals of the project, the task list resulting from hierarchical decomposition, and estimates of the resources needed to complete each task. Two sets of constraints are imposed: resource constraints and time constraints. The aims of project modelling are to schedule tasks, match resources to tasks, and effectively limit the duration of the project. A project network diagram shows tasks placed in a logical order – i.e. sequentially and/or in parallel, with minimum and maximum durations fixed for each task. These diagrams, known as PERT (Project Evaluation and Review Technique) charts, are most easily generated using specialist project management software such as Project for Windows, TimeLine and Harvard Total Project Manager. The diagrams are used in matching resources to tasks, in ensuring that the resource budget is not exceeded, and in highlighting a critical path through the project. The critical path draws attention to tasks to which a high priority must be given if the project as a whole is to be completed on time. One tool frequently used to diagram time spans and deadlines is the Gantt chart – a bar chart with time as the *x*-axis. The scheduled duration of each task and phase can be displayed, and compared to actual. Slippage is thus highlighted – and prompt action can be taken to deal with it.

Project reviews are an essential feature of project management. Reviews take place at milestone events (recorded on the PERT chart) which generally lead to greater or lesser adjustments in the project. Reviews may be minor, involving part of the project team, or major, involving the whole of the project team. Discussion papers or reports are considered at review meetings, the decisions made are recorded and action steps indicated. Regular project reviews not only help with quality assurance; they also ensure that understanding and expertise are shared amongst the members of the project team, rather than being confined to a few key personnel. Since there is ample opportunity for the sharing and refining of ideas, individuals come to identify more closely with the project, and those offering technical support feel that they are contributing to the creative process. It also means that support comes to be viewed as a continuing process, rather than being called in at, or after, a moment of crisis.

Techniques such as those briefly outlined in the preceding paragraphs are readily applied to historical projects. A good development methodology for historical projects will embrace the stages set out in Figure 4.1. Stages 1–3 essentially represent the analysis and design phase; stages 4–6 refer to the implementation of the database. It should of course be added that in practice the process is iterative – feedback and looping are essential at all stages. In the following sections, we will consider each stage described in Figure 4.1 in turn.

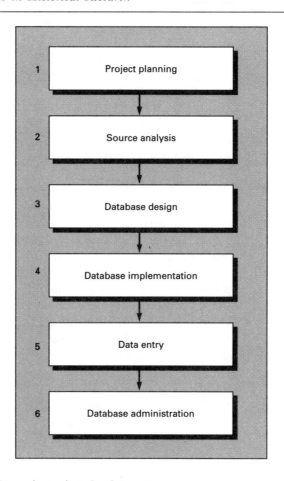

Figure 4.1 *Stages in project development*

■ 4.2 Project Planning

It is something of a truism to assert that the planning phase is of critical importance to the success of a research project. Time spent on planning avoids costly mistakes. As an example of what can happen without adequate project planning, one can cite the case of a PhD student who began the creation of a large database whilst on an ESRC research studentship. No effort was made at the outset to estimate the time needed for data collection and entry, with the result that more than three person years were devoted to this effort. So much for the 3–4 year PhD! Other mistakes are commonly made at the data entry stage, and these can subsequently prove very costly. The lesson is simple: a sound research design which equates goals with resources is an asset worth investing in. Project management methods assist this process by forcing thought at an early stage when it is a simple matter to revise goals and schedules. The objective is to arrive at a project specification which can then be used as a guide for the research team and associated staff, and as a basis for funding applications. This specification must define, as precisely as possible:

- Aims, objectives and feasibility of the project.
- Estimated volume of data.
- Scheduling and likely duration of the project.
- Estimated resource requirements and costs.

The logical way to begin a major project is to specify its aims and objectives. It is important that the goals of the project, its boundaries, and its broad structure are clarified at an early stage. As Cipolla has remarked, 'the quality of the answer depends to a considerable degree upon how clearly the problem has been formulated.'[2] Professional systems analysts emphasise the importance of effective communication between the project team members, for many errors result from misunderstandings at the specification stage, and the user later says 'that's not what I said – or meant – or need'. The result is delay and dissatisfaction, and the expenditure of scarce time and resources putting it right. Moreover, the later the problem is identified, the higher the cost of rectification. The statement of aims and objectives which results from this activity should specify the type of project, the extent of the database, the means by which the database will be accessed, and the size and diversity of the user community. Enough should be said to make evident the value of the work to be undertaken. A description should also be provided of the end-products which will be deliverable.

Once the project's goals have been accurately identified – itself by no means an easy task – it is important to consider the feasibility of the project, and the desirability of adopting a computer-based solution. Some form of cost-benefit analysis is essential. Computers should not be used simply because the technology is available, nor as a means to impress. Nor is there much point in simply studying the non-computer methods formerly used and designing a means of imitating them. If such manual systems were sufficient, we would not be trying to improve upon them. This activity should be as wide-ranging as possible, but should also focus in on the detail of specific processes or requirements. If the project is fairly straightforward but involving a large number of researchers and assistants, then some form of survey may be desirable to determine what use is likely to be made of the database.

In order to estimate the scheduling and resource requirements needed to build a large historical database, it is necessary to make a preliminary assessment of the extent and characteristics of the available data. Data entry, staffing, hardware and software are all affected by data considerations, so close scrutiny of original sources is a vital task. Matters are usually complicated by the tendency for the amount of data to vary between years covered by the project. Some form of estimation procedure is usually required. A case in point is the Register of Music in London Newspapers, 1660–1800, described in Case Study B. Stage one of the project covered the period 1660–1745 when the number of newspapers, frequency of publication and number of musical items per edition were all on the increase. An estimate of the total number of characters relating to music in a given period (year n to year m) is given by the following:

$$N = \sum_{i=n}^{m} \bar{\rho}_i \cdot P_i$$

where $\bar{\rho}_i$ is the average number of characters per musical item and P_i is the total number of items in each year i through the period. Estimates for both $\bar{\rho}_i$ and P_i have been made following examination of the newspapers for selected years. A representative subset of all newspapers has been used to determine the average number of characters per item. Estimates were also made of the number of items concerned with music in each of the sample years. These are presented in Figure 4.2.

A continuous function Pnm (year) has been obtained by fitting a curve to the sample data. If we assume that the variation in the average number of characters per item is small over the period, such that ρ_i may be regarded as a constant $\bar{\rho}_o$, the estimate for N can be obtained from:

$$N = \bar{\rho}_0 \cdot \int_{year_n}^{year_m} P_{nm} \ (year) \ d \ year$$

For the entire period, 1660–1745, the total number of characters in London newspapers spent on musical matters is estimated to be nine million (18,000 items with an average number of characters per item of 500).

Some form of scheduling is an essential part of the planning process; this is often achieved using the PERT and critical path analysis techniques described in the introduction to this chapter. The application of these techniques to historical projects cannot be fully explained here,[3] but the basics may be quickly summarised:

- Identify tasks.
- Identify sequence and dependencies.
- Estimate timespan.

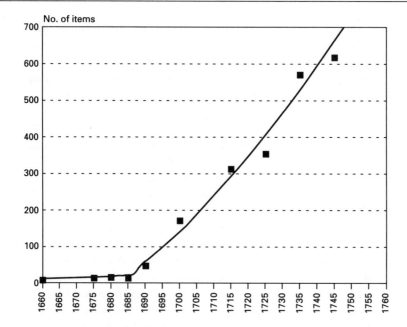

Figure 4.2 *Music-related items in London newspapers, 1660–1745*

- Identify resources required.
- Iterate until acceptable in timescale and resource usage.

Many of the variables in computerised historical research are quantifiable, and thus timetables and schedules can easily be produced. First, a task list is drawn up, using hierarchical decomposition. Each activity or major part of the project is identified, and broken down into a number of individual tasks. Second, these tasks are linked together by establishing logical relationships and dependencies – the ways in which tasks depend upon each other. These dependencies may be of three types:

- Finish to Start (one task must finish before another can start).
- Start to Start (where related tasks must start, but not necessarily finish, together).
- Finish to Finish (where related tasks must finish together, regardless of starting time).

Estimates can then made of the time and resources required to complete each task. Hardware and software needs are not difficult to evaluate; research and data entry needs are more problematic. Keying in data, for instance, may be a simple process, but account must be taken of operator speed, training and fatigue. Attention must also be given to the fact that the relative costs of different data entry strategies are volatile. Until recently, for example, many large commercial enterprises employed large numbers of data entry clerks; this is now changing fast as improved scanning and optical character reading technology is adopted as an alternative means of capturing data. Historians planning large projects would do well to consider the merits of each approach.

The resulting information may be entered into a project management program which will produce a visual overview of the project, showing all the tasks in a logical order, together with the estimated duration and resource needs of each task. Once this is done, it is often found that the project's objectives cannot be fulfilled in the anticipated timespan, or with the resources which are likely to be available. If this occurs, the model may be interactively modified until an acceptable compromise is achieved. As a general rule, there is a trade-off between time and resources; additional resources may enable the timespan to be reduced, while inadequate resourcing may mean extending the life of the project. An alternative strategy may be to prune the project, both in time and scope; this may be frustrating, but the trade-off should be a better degree of success. Moreover, the successful conclusion of a first phase may well lend impetus to a fresh drive for funding.

Thus project management makes researchers more aware of resource requirements and constraints, with beneficial results. Another advantage of using project management software is the ease with which schedules can be monitored and modified; as the project progresses, it will be possible to compare the actual progress of each phase with the original plans, and refine the estimates in an iterative manner. The output of this planning stage will be a comprehensive plan of the proposed project, which may provide the basis for funding bids to major grant-awarding bodies. The production of a detailed and accurate specification will provide very effective support for the narrative. Grant-awarding bodies are not always provided with clear specifications – and this must tell against the proposer when competition for funding is so fierce.

■ 4.3 Source Analysis

One of the most important aspects of applying formal project management techniques to computer-based or computer-aided projects is that it obliges researchers to think more clearly about their data and its possibilities. This is an extremely constructive activity. In our experience, data analysis is vitally important to computer-based historical research. This process builds upon preliminary examination of data at the preceding planning stage.

A good example is provided by Adman, Baskerville and Beedham's research into parliamentary elections in Cheshire between 1681 and 1734. They note that a large amount of time had to be spent during the early months of the project discovering 'just how little we (or anyone else for that matter) knew about many of the record sources we were using.' Although some of the document categories they used, such as early land-tax assessments, had received a good deal of scholarly attention, others, like different types of estate records, were less well-known. Their experiences led them to remark that 'those who would link their data must first understand its peculiarities.'[4]

The difficulties which they encountered included dealing with inconsistencies in documents written in several different hands; changes in administrative practice over the course of time; acquiring an accurate and unambiguous understanding of the terminology employed; coping with the shortcomings of second- or third-generation copies; and so on. Given that these difficulties are common to many historical research projects, it might seem something of a truism to assert that historians should know their sources. Nevertheless, Adman, Baskerville and Beedham are undoubtedly to be applauded for devoting sufficient time at an early stage in their project to investigating the nature of the sources being used. There are a number of reasons why computer-based projects can run into trouble at the design or implementation stage, but by far the most common reason is that the provenance and content of the sources being used have been incompletely understood.

One useful technique for analysing source material is data decomposition. It is often possible to extract different data items from a particular source, and these may be organised into logical types or groupings, where each item shares a common structure and purpose with other items in the same set. Figure 4.3 shows how this may be done for the contents of newspapers. The text may be subdivided into a number of categories, including news items and advertisements. Advertisements may, in turn, be subdivided into such categories as entertainment, services offered and employment opportunities.

The outcome of the source analysis stage will be a detailed statement of the character, consistency and quantity of data to be processed. This detailed statement should facilitate the process of database design.

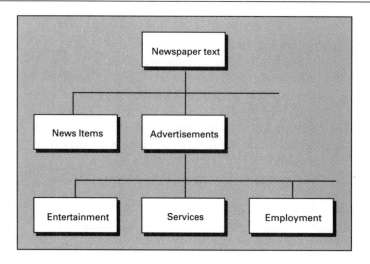

Figure 4.3   *Newspaper content analysis*

■ 4.4 Database Design

Once source analysis is complete, the process of database design may begin in earnest. Here, the objective is not to begin the construction of the database, but to have a clear written version of how it should work, and what its features are. Specifications are developed which reflect the goals and scope of the project.

The first task is to prepare and document a conceptual database design (or *conceptual schema*) for the project. As noted in Chapter 1, the approach to database design will depend upon the type of data and the data model (e.g. relational or hierarchical) which is most appropriate. As this stage is so critical to the success of a project, it will be considered in detail in later chapters. The relational approach will be set out in Chapter 5 before turning to source-oriented approaches. The idea of an *implementation-independent* approach is essential to the process of database design: it is important to avoid becoming too concerned about hardware or software before logical requirements have been thoroughly analysed. It is all too easy to design a database which fits the features of a specific DBMS with which the designer is familiar rather than developing data models which satisfy the full requirements of the project.

Nevertheless, once the conceptual schema has been prepared it will of course be necessary to implement the design using an appropriate DBMS. At this point, the conceptual schema is refined and modified using the concepts of the chosen database model. The result may directly

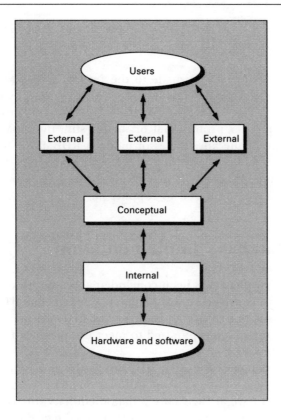

Figure 4.4 *Schemas*

correspond with the conceptual schema, but it may differ to some extent.
There are three principal reasons why such differences may come about.
First, the exact construction of the conceptual schema may not be
supported by a particular database theory – for example, a schema
which requires an entity to have two or more 'parent' relationships
cannot readily be implemented in hierarchical data structures. Second,
the designer may decide to depart from the conceptual schema for
operational reasons: for example, to provide simplicity and easy of use,
or flexibility to meet changing user requirements. A third factor is
that commercial DBMSs all have their own strengths and limitations –
many are not fully relational, for instance, despite their suppliers' claims
– and consequently some software-specific modifications may be necessary.

Next, in large projects, we may go on to define the *external schema*,
which describes how each user, or group of users, sees the data in
which they are interested. Each user's view of the data is kept as simple
as possible, and as the data in which they are interested normally make
up a subset of the data stored in the database such external schemas

are also referred to as *sub-schemas* or *user schemas*. They are especially useful in maintaining database security and limiting access to authorised users.

Finally, reference may be made to the *internal schema* (also referred to as the *storage schema*). Here we are dealing with physical storage strategies and access strategies. For the most part, this process can be left to the computer professional or, better still, the DBMS: as noted elsewhere, one of the advantages of modern RDBMSs is that the user does not need to know anything about where and how the data are physically stored. However, it may be desirable to define the indexes and other elements required to support particular access strategies.

■ 4.5 Database Implementation

Once the design phase has been concluded and a tightly-defined specification agreed, construction of the database can begin. The first stage of this process is to prepare a prototype (or first-cut) implementation, which can be tested and optimised to meet the specification set out by the researcher.

A major advantage of leading RDBMSs is the provision of facilities for the rapid development of operational database systems. All fully-fledged DBMSs have at their core a data dictionary for recording data about database systems (such data are often called metadata). Definitions of tables, attributes and other items are held in the data dictionary and are used in creating a prototype database. This facility, and others, make it possible to move swiftly from conceptual modelling to the implementation phase of a project. As noted above, the details of mapping from a conceptual model to a tangible design are DBMS-specific. With the ORACLE RDBMS, the database designer is offered a set of guidelines. The following are examples:

- Each entity identified during data analysis becomes a table in the database.
- Each attribute in the primary key is specified as NOT NULL.
- Each attribute in the primary key is indexed.

By following such guidelines it is quite easy to take the conceptual model embodied in entity description forms and create the tables of a prototype database. ORACLE stores table and attribute definitions in its data dictionary and these are called by its applications generator to build default data entry/query screens. Little difficulty is experienced in moving from conceptual model to prototype database system. The actual process of constructing a database is considered further in section 5.4.

Prototypes are used to test the underlying logic of a conceptual model. Test data, selected to include the extraordinary as well as the ordinary, are entered into the system. The database is then systematically queried and its performance assessed. Trials of this kind, which vary considerably in length and sophistication, provide the feedback needed to correct, improve or modify the database design. The technique is essentially one of refinement through a cycle of test–observation–modification–test. It might be thought that countless iterations could result, but experience shows that a refined system usually emerges after very few cycles. Rapid implementation is made possible by the existence of a sound conceptual model. An equal measure of success is not likely to accompany database development on a purely trial-and-error basis.

Prototyping, of course, is not always an appropriate technique. If, for example, the project is relatively small and straightforward, and can be implemented relatively quickly, there seems little point in extending development time by adopting a prototyping approach. But in larger projects, involving considerable timespans and/or considerable risks, it is generally to be recommended.

The testing of a database is followed by all-out data entry and release to the user community. A database may be made available through a single release or a number of staged releases: the more onerous the task of data entry, the more appropriate the staged approach.

■ 4.6 Data Entry and Validation

Data entry can be a major bottleneck in the process of converting sources to machine-readable formats. In this section, a variety of issues and methods relating to capturing, entering and checking historical data are explored.

□ *Data capture*

Historians are normally concerned with the transcription of existing data, rather than the direct data entry techniques common to many business situations, such as banking transactions and airline booking. Methods of data entry include:

- Keyboard entry.
- Scanning technologies.
- Secondary use of electronic files.

Large amounts of data still have to be keyed in the traditional manner. However, as keyboard entry is error-prone and very labour-intensive, a good deal of attention has been paid to the development of alternative methods of data capture. These include scanners, optical character readers (OCRs) and digital cameras.

Scanners are photosensitive devices used for capturing printed text and graphics. There are hand-held and flatbed types – the latter is generally to be preferred – and they are usually provided with software for image enhancement, cropping, etc. They offer a variety of resolutions, typically 100 to 400 dots per inch (DPI), and can capture colour or greyscale images. Greyscale scanners are capable of resolving either 64 or 256 shades of grey. There is a tradeoff between resolution on the one hand and cost of hardware and size of data file on the other – high resolution images can require enormous hard disks. Scanning results in a bitmapped image, which is sufficient for capturing drawings, photographs and other graphical data, but scanned text needs to be processed by optical character recognition (OCR) software to translate it from individual dots into characters. The accuracy of OCR systems has improved considerably in recent years with the development of pre-processing techniques and more sophisticated character recognition algorithms. However, it remains true to say that whilst they generally work well with typewritten text they still leave much to be desired in their ability to cope with manuscript sources.[5]

Another type of photosensitive device for capturing digital images is the digital camera, such as Canon's Ion camera and Logitech's Fotoman. Whereas a scanner captures flat documents, a digital camera can create images of three-dimensional objects. An alternative to this approach is to use a conventional video camera and video digitising software to translate analogue video (stills or moving images). It is claimed that some of the more recent packages can work from almost any video source, and display TV-quality pictures, together with sound. The use of real-time, full-screen video is still limited for most applications, however; vast amounts of data have to be pulled off the hard disk or CD-ROM and image quality is limited by the speed of data transfer, though this problem is gradually being overcome by the development of more sophisticated data compression techniques.

It should be noted that data are increasingly available electronically, though not always in the appropriate format. For example, the ESRC Data Archive at Essex holds a complete machine-readable set of election results for Imperial and Weimar Germany. This resource is an excellent starting point for research into regional variations in political support. It is, however, in an 80-column 'punched card' type format suitable for analysis with the statistical package SPSS, and might need reformatting before it could be imported into a DBMS. There are, of course, a number of other problems which can arise when using other people's data: in particular, documentation may be incomplete, and thus the degree of accuracy achieved will be unknown, and any prior decisions which have been made about the data format may be unclear. In the example given above, in fact, the format is fully documented, and the meaning of the data unequivocal. Other collections in the ESRC Archive, however, are much less satisfactory for secondary use – especially where data has been collected and/or coded for a specific task. For this reason, one of the principal objectives of the History Data Unit which has recently been set up by the ESRC Data Archive is to ensure that historical datasets are adequately documented and catalogued so as to encourage secondary use.

□ *Stages in data preparation and entry*

The activities involved in data preparation and entry are described in Figure 4.5 below.

Several of these stages are concerned with ensuring the accuracy and completeness of the data being captured. The inevitability of errors means that careful checking is essential at all stages of the data preparation and entry process. Many different types of error can occur. In declining order of frequency they are:

- Transcription.
- Transposition.
- Omission.
- Addition.
- Random.

Random errors are in fact surprisingly rare – which is just as well, as they are the most difficult to pick up.

Because of the frequency with which errors may occur, the *validating* and *auditing* of data are important considerations. For the purposes of this discussion, validation refers to *preventative* methods – ensuring that data with incorrect or illegal values are not added to the database. Auditing, on the other hand, refers to *detective* methods – identifying rogue data items after they have been entered. Manual methods are

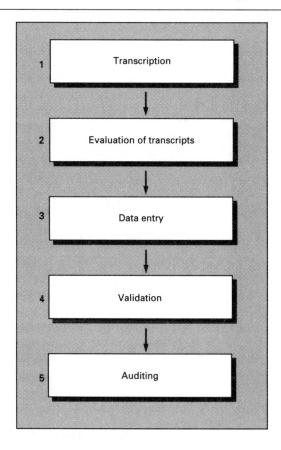

Figure 4.5 *Stages in data preparation and entry*

far from infallible, and they need to be supplemented by a variety of automated controls. Controls are intended to cope with inaccurate or incomplete entry of data, and may also be designed to prevent data entry by individuals without the appropriate authorisation. Various issues relating to error avoidance and error trapping are considered in the following sections.

☐ *Transcribing data*

As noted above, errors most commonly result from inaccurate transcription of the original data. Sometimes these can result from the illegibility of the original source – always a potential problem with historical data. At other times, errors will result from the inevitable tendency when keying in data to make assumptions about what the source says rather than transcribing it literally, character by character.

The likelihood of errors is compounded by the fact that it is often necessary to copy the original data on to a transcription form for subsequent entry by other people. There may be advantages in this approach where the source is difficult to read or would present difficulties to a keyboard operator who is not a trained researcher, or where some data is to be transformed by coding before entry (but see section 8.1 on issues relating to data coding). However, because transcription involves an intermediate stage between original source capture and data entry, the opportunities for human error are increased. Strategies are required to deal with this problem.

In the Genealogical Society of Utah's 1881 Census project, each batch of records from the enumeration books is transcribed twice by different people, and then evaluated by a third. This will identify many of the more obvious errors or omissions. Only when the evaluator is sure that the two transcriptions are as accurate as possible are they submitted for data entry. Because transcription errors are by far the most common, the strategy adopted by the GSU has much to commend it. It is, however, a very time-consuming and costly approach, which would be impossible if large numbers of volunteers did not give their time for free.

Another project which has addressed the question of transcription methods is Wolverhampton University's Portbooks Programme which was described in Case Study A, and its approach may usefully be described in some detail. The Portbooks Programme has been in existence for more than a decade. It has computerised the Coastal Port Books for Gloucester and neighbouring ports between 1575 and 1765, thus providing a comprehensive record of well over 35,000 voyages. The project has a vast potential for shedding light upon the economy of the Severn Valley in the era before the Industrial Revolution.

Considerable attention was given to transcription and data entry when the database was being planned and implemented. To assist with the work of processing such an enormous volume of data, about 60 volunteers were recruited to transcribe records on to data entry forms which could then be keyed in by staff at the University's Computer Centre. This necessitated the creation of an administration system capable of overseeing the work and ensuring that accuracy was maintained. Definitive rules for the transcription of data had to be devised and communicated to all concerned. All 170 Port Books were photocopied from microfilm and then bound into volumes resembling the originals. The folios and entries were numbered, and the books given to the transcribers, together with detailed instructions covering every conceivable eventuality. Sample transcriptions were provided, together with word lists to help the transcribers read the documents and use approved abbreviations. Word lists were provided for such fields as boats, ports, firstnames, lastnames, units of measurement and commodities carried. Where volunteers were uncertain of any entry, they put three crosses in place of the doubtful word. Listings of records containing these blank items were regularly printed out for checking against the originals by members of the research team. Follow-up visits were made to all volunteers to check queries, and ensure that the work was being done in a consistent fashion. When collected, all the forms were examined to check for obvious inaccuracies by members of the research team before being keyed in by Data Preparation staff at the University. The authors of the database insist that the adoption of rigorous methods of transcribing and checking data is essential if the database is to provide a sound foundation for analysis and interpretation.[6]

☐ Screen form design

Though data entry screens are often automatically created as part of the process of table creation, screen form design is worth careful consideration. Properly-designed screen forms can speed the data entry process and reduce errors. Screen forms generally display field names and prompts. When a record is filled in, there is normally an opportunity to check it before adding it to the database. When it has been checked, it is entered into the database, and the same prompts reappear on the screen ready for typing in the next record. A highly sophisticated forms generator is ORACLE's SQL*Forms, briefly described in sections 3.2 and 6.2.

Forms should include titles and clear and accurate captions for each data item. Fieldnames should be given in full and should be unambiguous – for example, 'Income' is susceptible of several interpretations. Guidance notes for data entry may usefully be included, perhaps in the lower part of the form. If more than one screen is used, this can be made clear with phrases like '<PgDown> for more', or 'Screen 1 of 4'. Because data entry tends to be tedious, it is best to keep screen layouts simple and consistent. It is distracting and fatiguing if data items are placed differently on related forms. The useability of input screens can be greatly enhanced if the following factors are also borne in mind. First, the sequencing of fields is important. Data should be entered in the order in which they are usually received, whether this is direct from the original source, or from transcription sheets. Secondly, it is beneficial if data items are logically grouped on the screen. Thirdly, the frequency of use is another consideration; it is generally beneficial to group the most frequently used data at the top of the form. Where these three objectives clash, the order of priority given here should be followed.

□ *Approaches to data entry and validation*

Some data entry problems are specific to historical data, or, at least, particularly acute in such cases. Examples are the difficulties associated with handling nulls, and poor quality and illegibility of many hand-written sources. Nevertheless, many of the techniques used in commercial database environments can usefully be applied. A wide variety of control techniques have been developed over the years; some may be applied to batches of data, others to individual transactions.[7]

Batch data entry and validation is the more 'traditional' approach. For example, a widely used technique is to divorce data entry from the master files in the database proper (the operational data, as it is called). One historic reason is that older systems required that data be held in a particular sequence. Data was therefore input to a data entry program for storage in a temporary file. This could then be sorted and transformed into a sequential file ready for addition to the master files. Now that relational DBMSs have become increasingly prevalent, this is less important, for a key characteristic of a RDBMS is that data can be entered and stored in any order. However, separating data entry from the master files remains a very valuable technique of data validation, for it permits a variety of checks and balances to be performed in batch mode before the database itself is updated. Techniques which are specific to batch methods include:

- Transaction or item counts. A manually derived count of each record or item to be entered is provided along with each batch of trans-actions. The item count is entered as a data field in a header record which is keyed in before the batch of documents to which it refers. The batch itself is then entered, but is not added to the database unless the number of entered records matches the count held in the header record.
- Control totals can be applied to any numeric fields. Again, the usual procedure is to supply manually derived totals for each batch of records. This total may be added to the header record. When processing the batch, the computer repeats the calculations. If there is any discrepancy between the manual and computer-generated totals the batch is not added to the database, and an error message is sent to the operator. The batch has to be re-entered and the control total re-calculated.

Another valuable technique for ensuring the accuracy of input data is double entry. This approach is associated with batch entry methods, and is now considered to be fairly old-fashioned in the world of commercial applications, but is still highly applicable to inputting historical data, and is very reliable. Input rates may be measured (and remunerated) on the basis of keystrokes, number of fields entered, or (where records are of fixed length) number of records keyed in. Many systems will gather such data automatically, and, by reference to the user's password ID, assign it to the appropriate entry clerk. The usual approach is for one operator to go flat out, and the data are then entered a second time by another operator who stops on a mismatch. This type of approach is taken by the Genealogical Society of Utah with the 1881 Census Project. As noted in Case Study D, the second operator types over the original entries (whilst being unable to see them); discrepancies are flagged, and the second typist is able to override the initial entries, or bring them to the attention of a supervisor.

A newer and less cumbersome approach is to make use of front-end validation (i.e. at point of data entry) controlled by the software. A variety of front-end validation methods are summarised below. The challenge is to devise different types of controls to ensure correct input in every field of each record.

- *Field type checks.* If a field should contain alphabetic data only, a control can be applied which will reject or flag input which includes numbers or special characters. Similarly, a control can be applied to ensure that a number field contains only the numeric characters.
- *Field length checks* are useful whenever entries should be of similar lengths. Maximum field lengths are set when creating the database, but it can also be helpful to set fixed or minimum field lengths.
- *Date checks* are often used by businesses to ensure that transactions refer to the correct accounting period, but the technique is readily applicable to ensure that historical data relate to the right century, decade, etc.
- *Range controls* (also called limit or reasonableness checks) are used to safeguard against the input of values which are unreasonable or outside the boundaries of a normal range of values. They can be relative as well as absolute: for example, a range control could specify that a date entered in a person's `Year_Died` field cannot be earlier than the entry in the same person's `Year_Born` field.
- *Unique value.* The data entry software can be set to reject any entry which duplicates an existing value. This approach is used where a particular field must have a different value for every record in the database table. This is often a record number or reference number field, though it can also be a character field. In relational databases, the primary key used to join different tables must con-

tain unique values (see section 5.3 for further explanation).

- *'Must Match'*. The Must Match attribute allows a field value in one table to be matched against a corresponding value in another table, thus ensuring that all values are entered correctly. In some cases, this will be another base table in the database; at other times, however, it will be a separate lookup table, whose only function is to store a list of legal values which the Must Match field may take. If a value is entered which does not occur in the other table, an error message is generated. Depending upon the program, the user may be offered a list of acceptable values, from which to choose. In some situations, of course, it will be necessary to add new entries as data entry proceeds.

- *Must Fill' fields* are also called 'mandatory data present', 'required' or NOT NULL fields. They are used to ensure that essential data is always entered – such as in a primary key field, which must not be null (see section 5.3).

- *Duplicate and autoincrement.* These are not really checking methods, though they may help to ensure accuracy of data input. The use of a Duplicate attribute can help to reduce entry errors where fields in a record are frequently the same as the corresponding entry in the previous record. During data entry the previous record's value for that field is carried forward. This default value may be overwritten at any time, with the new value becoming the default. The drawback of this approach is that if an inputter is distracted whilst entering a new record he/she can leave an incorrect value rather than overwriting it. Autoincrement fields are filled in automatically by the system, reducing the amount of typing and consequently the likelihood of error. A typical example where autoincrementing is useful would be a unique reference number field.

☐ Auditing

Data validation, however, cannot identify or eliminate all errors. Some will remain, and may only be spotted by the researcher who has a deep understanding of the historical period and context to which the data refer. It is for this reason that auditing – post-entry checking – will always remain an important part of database construction. Traditional proof-reading techniques remain an invaluable part of the auditing process. As noted in Case Study D, the Genealogical Society of Utah believes that the best way to trap residual data entry errors is for one person to read out each entry to someone else. In general, however, it has been found that proof-reading tends to be more effective when working from a hard copy rather than on-screen. Transcription forms should be retained to provide a permanent, physical record which can be used for auditing.

When large quantities of data are involved, it may not be practicable to carry out a manual check of each record. In such cases, it is necessary to devise sampling procedures. For example, the 1881 Census Project team selects a 10 per cent random sample from each batch for checking. Any errors found will be corrected, and if the number exceeds a pre-determined figure the whole batch will be rejected and submitted for re-entry. As with data entry, manual methods may usefully be supplemented by a variety of automated controls, including checking algorithms and programs.

Auditing procedures should also be applied to scanned input. The accuracy of OCR systems has improved considerably in recent years, but this should not lead the researcher to assume that it is unnecessary to check the results of the automatic process. Manual comparison of the originals with the machine-readable version is beneficial, but still prone to error. This has led some researchers to propose the development of automated methods to check the results of the OCR process against the original greyscale document image. A string-matching algorithm for assessing the results of an OCR process has been described by Concepcion and D'Amato.[8]

■ 4.7 Database Administration

A database is a resource shared by a community of users, and, like any shared resource, it must be managed to prevent degeneration. The guidelines needed to regulate a database should be established well before a project is completed and following consultation with potential users.

To begin with, it is essential to devote some thought to the nature of the end-product, and how it may best be made available to the community of users. A variety of methods are possible, including on-line access, CD-ROM, microfiche and printed editions. Each has its own advantages. For example, CD-ROM technology may be appropriate if the dataset is large but relatively stable; though regular (perhaps monthly or quarterly) updates may be required. The costs of origination and distribution will require careful consideration: what level of initial and recurring costs will the user community be prepared to bear?

The existence of a community of users also means that other issues require consideration. How is access to be regulated and the security and integrity of the database maintained? What measures need to be taken to ensure that there is appropriate technical support? What type of documentation is required? Underlying all these issues is the question of ownership, which must clearly be determined. Historically, the person responsible for creating the database has been considered its owner, with complete control over issues relating to access and modification of the data. But, whilst this might seem easy to justify in the case of small, single-person projects, it does not always work. In a large project, with numerous contributors, it may not be possible to identify a single individual as the owner. Increasingly, a group of researchers may be drawn from different institutions – in such cases, the locus of responsibility for administering the database needs to be particularly clear. The question of ownership is also raised where a database project has been funded by a grant from one of the funding councils. There are often rules and regulations about the ownership and accessibility of the research data. An additional consideration is the relationship between the research team and the Computer Centre responsible for the hardware, which also needs to be defined. The solution which is often adopted in large database projects is twofold: first, a written agreement is drawn up at an early stage which precisely defines ownership of the product; and secondly, ownership is separated from administration for operational purposes. A database administrator (DBA) is appointed, who assumes responsibility for maintaining and running the resource. Typical responsibilities of the DBA are:

- Advising researchers on database design.
- Implementation and modification of the database structure.
- Keeping the data dictionary and any other documentation up to date.
- Overseeing database security and granting rights of access to users as agreed with the database owner(s).
- Database recovery in the event of a hardware or software failure.

Additionally, one may note the value of a supervisory board for large projects. The project then can be divided up into a number of small, discrete projects, all under the guidance of the supervisory board. The board may play a key role in reviewing project goals. Regular reviews – sometimes called *quality assurance reviews* – are an essential part of project development, ensuring that the project gets back on track if there are slippages or deviations. They should not be used to criticise individuals involved; the objective is to review project goals, data models and documentation, not people. It is important that mistakes be rectified as early as possible; it is estimated that the cost of rectifying errors rises exponentially over the lifespan of a project.

One of the key tasks of the DBA is ensuring that proper documentation is maintained. Proper documentation ensures understanding on the part of users. Part of this function will be met by the data dictionary defining the structure of the database. But this needs to be supplemented by additional documents such as technical reports, database specifications and discussion papers. In many cases, it will also be necessary to preserve paper copies of source documents, details of their archival location(s), and the transcription forms used, so that subsequent researchers can trace records back to their original source.

Another key role for the DBA is regulating access to the database. A number of important questions should be addressed. Who is to have direct access to the database and what restrictions should be placed upon each class of user? How can the data be made accessible whilst protecting the database as a whole from unauthorised copying? If reasonable answers to questions such as these are not found, a database, however well constructed, may still fail to meet the needs of its community of users. The first task is to define a set of rules describing what access is permitted. Secondly, enforcement mechanisms must be implemented to make sure the rules of access are obeyed. Authorisation rules specify what actions a user is allowed to perform on the data. The facilities offered by a DBMS generally allow the database administrator to restrict access to various levels (file, record, data item) and in many different ways. This is important because sometimes the concern is not to limit access *per se*, but to limit what specific users can do with the data. There may be open access for browsing, but more restricted access for copying data to the user's own file or directory, or for modifying the data in some way. Thus the user may be restricted to a particular *view* or subset of the data which may be appropriate to his or her needs. The use of views is considered in section 6.2 below.

The level of access is usually set when assigning a unique ID and password to each user. This is relatively easy to implement, but often suffers from poor reliability. This is not due to the activities of the computer hacker, as the popular press might lead us to believe, but to the fact that people are notoriously lax about giving details of their passwords to others, writing them down, or choosing something obvious like their initials. The problem should be borne in mind by researchers when giving access to large numbers of users, though there is little that can be done about it, beyond restricting access to those people who really need it. The objective is always to strike an effective balance between ease of access and maintaining the safety and integrity of the data.

Finally, the DBA has a crucial role to play in recovering from disaster. In the life of a project, the odds are that major difficulties will be met at some point along the way, either through technical or human causes. Ensuring that routine tasks like backing up are properly carried out is a vital function. The data of an operational database system must be kept secure against corruption, whether malicious or inadvertent.

■ 4.8 Conclusion

Historical database projects are resource-intensive. They require a substantial commitment by the research team, often over long periods of time. Large-scale projects should be properly planned so that researchers understand their aims and fully recognise the implied resource requirements. The importance of thorough documentation at every stage of the project must also be emphasised. This is particularly crucial in large projects, where personnel changes may occur during the project lifecycle. The general advantages of applying project management techniques to research projects are:

- They make it much easier to understand complex problems and plan in the face of uncertainty.
- It becomes easier for project teams to arrive at a mutual understanding of key issues and co-ordinate their efforts.
- Resource constraints have to be acknowledged, forcing prudent changes in project goals and aspirations.
- Progress can be monitored and changes made to help performance match the plan.

Historical database projects are often critically dependent upon a successful bid for research funds. As those involved know well, applying for major grants and administering the funds so obtained are demanding tasks. A careful and systematic approach to project development can greatly assist in the preparation of a convincing and fully documented application; maximise the use of resources and time as the project progresses; and guarantee that it is completed successfully within the anticipated timespan and budget. It is in the interests both of project proposers and grant-awarding bodies that database projects are carefully planned and successfully brought to fruition. The intention of this chapter has been to make historical researchers aware of concepts and techniques which might help in bringing database projects to a successful conclusion.

Case Study D
Creating a Machine-Readable Version of the 1881 Census of England and Wales[1]

Matthew Woollard
University of the West of England, Bristol

The Genealogical Society of Utah (GSU) was founded in 1894 by the Church of Jesus Christ of Latter-day Saints with the aim of collecting and making genealogical material available. Motivated neither by altruism nor curiosity but by a belief in retroactive baptism,[2] the GSU has undertaken to create a machine-readable database of the whole of the 1881 Census of England and Wales – 1881 then being the most recently available census. The project aims to produce various indexes relating to all 26,603,097 people enumerated.[3] The project, which commenced in 1987, has neither fixed financial nor fixed time limits for completion, the requirements being only that it should be accomplished as quickly and as cheaply as possible without consequent debasement of quality. Whilst the project is unique in its immensity, it is also remarkable for its use of project management techniques to ensure that resources are not squandered, that goals are achieved and that completion will be in as short a time as possible.

The census enumeration books, held at the Public Record Office (PRO), are the project's source. Hard copies of these were made and divided into batches, each batch corresponding to an original enumeration district or part of one and allotted a unique identifier.[4] There are 49,113 batches. A batch transmittal form, which contains relevant information (including the unique identifier) about the batch, is attached to it and remains with it for the entire project. All batches were ready by late 1989 for subsequent distribution to the Family History Societies (FHSs) which would be responsible for their transcription. Some batches are of such poor quality that transcriptions will be made directly from the enumeration books. Transcription of all 26.6 million records was completed in May 1995.

Detailed instructions were provided for transcribers indicating the correct procedures to follow, along with transcription forms.[5] Generally, data is transcribed exactly from the original enumeration books. However, some material is standardised: schedule numbers are omitted; deleted matter is enclosed within double brackets; data in another hand is enclosed within single brackets; but no proper names are altered.[6] To ensure accuracy each batch is transcribed twice; the results later being collated to produce a definitive version.

Evaluation follows transcription. Evaluation ensures the accuracy of transcription and prepares data for entry. During evaluation both transcriptions are collated and the batch transmittal form is checked, for precise indexing depends on the accuracy of the parish name. Parishes are identified using a contemporary gazetteer. Parishes may be enumerated in one county but located in another. As individuals will be indexed by county, these records need moving to their correct county. Some parishes are in two counties – these batches are divided with reference to contemporary maps. Evaluation also involves checking the transcription for uniformity of data. It should also be noted that data entry operators are instructed to make no qualitative decisions about the accuracy of the data. This is vital, as transcription rules have altered slightly since inception. With smaller scale source-oriented projects it is possible to examine the complete source, devise rules for standardisation and transcription and proceed to data entry. With 26 million records it was considered impossible to devise rules to cope with all the idiosyncrasies of the data. Originally, miscellaneous material was not carefully considered, but today if there is any descriptive material in a field which should not contain it the information is noted on the back of the transcription sheet to be included within another field.

The decisions involved in this process are often subjective, which may be detrimental to data integrity.[7] A requirement of creating a machine-readable source is that the data should be as similar to the original as possible. For this project, where the aim is only to provide indexes of people in the Census, it may be acceptable to standardise parish names, 'correct' county boundaries and 'change' family relationships. But if the results are to be made available for other research these factors will need to be borne in mind.[8]

Once evaluation is complete, batches are entered onto computer.[9] Data entry is performed in two stages. The first stage is copy typing, and the second verification – simply a repetition of the preceding process. The second operator types over the original entries (whilst unable to see them); if there are discrepancies, the second typist is able to over-ride the initial entries. Unresolved mis-matches are brought to the attention of a co-ordinator. Output in the early 1990s averaged approximately 450,000 entries per month.

Once complete batches have been entered, the first checking process takes place. The aim of auditing is to ensure that the records (but not the batch headings) have been transcribed correctly and to correct further residual errors. A sample of about 10 per cent is chosen randomly for auditing. Records are compared with the original for the last time. This process is oral – one auditor reading the machine version aloud to another inspecting the original. If more than a specified number of errors is found, the batch may be rejected so that evaluation can take place again. It may be argued that this process is flawed. If transcription, evaluation and data entry have been reliably performed the machine-readable version would be accurate – auditing would only introduce new errors into the data. However, the GSU feels that the procedure of reading to one another is proven to be the best method for correcting residual transcription errors.

Verification is the second checking process, and is performed using DataEase and a program called UDE.[10] The structure and added material may be altered, but not the original data. The process checks, among other things, whether a batch has the right number of records – as each record in a batch is numbered sequentially, each record number should correspond with its numerical position within a batch. It also checks that no field is empty and no page has more than 25 records. If errors are brought to light, they are manually corrected with reference to the transcription forms. Originally verification and auditing took place in England; now it is performed at Salt Lake City, where batches are also aggregated to produce indexes. Automatic data verification was tested, but considered too time-consuming with regard to the very small number of errors picked up.

In a linear description of the project, it is impossible to describe the rôle of the most interesting process of the project. Tracking affects all stages of the project and is necessary because of the project's staggering size. Imagine having to know where, among approximately 200 locations, any of the 49,000+ batches is located.[11] DataEase is used to keep track of the whereabouts of every batch at any particular time, and the stage of the project it is at. This means that each transcribing Family History Society is monitored; if it is working quickly more batches can be sent to it and if it is working slowly some batches can be reallocated. Tracking is vital for the indexing process; before any indexing can take place, counties must be completely transcribed and made machine-readable. No indexing could take place if every county was only partially transcribed. In project management terminology, tracking determines, at any particular moment, which tasks are slack and which are critical.[12] An example of the favoured technique of this project, 'just in time', is that no computers for data entry were bought before enough transcription had been achieved for them to be used to their maximum potential.

The aim of the project, as mentioned earlier, is to produce indexes of the Census. County indexes, by surname, by surname and birthplace, by surname and as enumerated, and simply as enumerated will be produced first. Lists of miscellaneous notes, vessels and institutions will also be published. Once all county indexes have been completed two national indexes are envisaged, one for England and Wales and one for Scotland, by surname and by surname and birthplace. Under the licence agreement, copies of the indexes will be made available in microfiche form to the FHSs that assisted and deposited with Her Majesty's Stationery Office, the Public Record Office, ESRC Data Archive, and copyright libraries. Further copies will be made available to other libraries and academic institutions. By the end of 1995, all the counties had been published on microfiche. To facilitate the use of the data, the complete Census may be made available on CD-ROM. However, as the original project manager has pointed out, the use of the project for other research is only a by-product of the original plan; additional money and time would be needed from GSU to generate a CD-ROM index, 'and must', therefore, 'be viewed in terms of its many projects and priorities commensurate with costs.'[13]

Everything that can be done to make the project successful has been done. The initial projected level of accuracy was 95 per cent, plus or minus 5 per cent, but the eventual accuracy rate will certainly be much higher than this. The error rate for the completed project will be so small as to be entirely insignificant when considering the total Census. The criticisms of the project come mainly from genealogists. Some suggest that some people will be given surnames they never bore in life because of mis-transcription. A few FHS members have complained about the over-efficient nature of the tracking department; others have complained of the workload and potential inaccuracies which may result. Minor errors are of course a problem particular to genealogists, as they are concerned with individuals, unlike historians, whose interest is rather with populations as a whole.[14] The project is not yet complete; and, whilst it is too early to predict whether it will be an absolute success or not, the indications are favourable. Those interested in the methodology of historical computing can judge for themselves now; genealogists, historians, demographers and others will have to wait until they can use the data.

■ *Chapter 5* ■

Database Design and Implementation

■ 5.1 Approaches to Database Design

Database management systems offer powerful tools for the storage, organisation and retrieval of historical data. However, the benefits they offer are only attainable if the data are properly organised. All too often little thought is given to issues of database design, with the result that more complex types of queries cannot be answered and the desired information retrieved from the system. This danger is often acute in historical research because of the inherent complexity of the data and the circular nature of the research process. *Database design* describes the two related stages of *data analysis* and *data modelling* essential to the creation of correctly structured databases. Over the years, computer professionals have devoted much attention to the development of structured methodologies in order to reap the theoretical benefits of modern database management software and cope with the practical problems of database design. The general purpose is to produce a *conceptual model* that can be implemented using a database management system. It must be developed according to correct principles, otherwise the resulting system will not function efficiently in terms of either data entry, storage and update, or speed and quality of information retrieval. A conceptual model, and the techniques used to devise it, are general purpose tools, independent of the particular software used to implement the database. Additionally, the model does not describe the way in which data are physically stored. It is a *logical view* taken by the database designer, and it should be capable of supporting many *external views* of the database. An external view is a partial view of a logical data model taken by an individual user or application. In supporting many such views, the needs of different specialists within a user community can be accommodated.[1]

It would not be appropriate to consider the full range of techniques employed by systems analysts and database designers. However, consideration will be given in this chapter to two important techniques which are widely used to design database systems: entity-relationship

102

modelling (ERM) and relational data analysis (RDA). The main distinction between them is that ERM takes a top-down approach to data modelling, beginning by taking a wide view of the subject under consideration, and progressively adding fresh levels of detail. RDA takes a bottom-up approach, starting with a close examination of the raw data and progressing towards a general design. Each technique will be discussed in relation to an historical research project.

■ 5.2 Entity-Relationship Modelling

□ *Introduction*

ERM is a graphical method of data modelling. It results in the production of an *entity-relationship diagram (ERD)* which serves as a conceptual model for the database. The conceptual model is described in terms of logical components known as *entities, attributes* and *relationships.* Entities are the objects in which we are interested, and about which we hold data. They may be tangible objects, such as **Performer** and **Theatre**, or intangible objects such as **Contract** and **Transaction**. It is useful to keep in mind that when the database is implemented, each entity will be represented by a table in the database. Attributes are properties of entities and a set of attributes describes an entity. The entity **Voter**, for example, may be described by the attributes surname, firstname(s), address, and occupation (as in some poll books). When the database is implemented, each attribute is represented by a field in a relational table. Relationships exist between entities, and each relationship may be classified as one of three types: *one-to-one, one-to-many* or *many-to-many.*

One-to-one relationships exist when one occurrence of an entity *A* can be related to only one occurrence of an entity *B*. Under the existing British electoral system, for example, a Member of Parliament represents a single constituency. In Figure 5.1, the entities **MP** and **Constituency** are represented by rectangular boxes and the straight line between the two boxes indicates a one-to-one relationship.

In a one-to-many relationship, one occurrence of an entity *A* can be associated with many occurrences of an entity *B*. An example of a one-to-many relationship is described in Figure 5.2: a father may have many children, but each child has only one father. A 'crow's foot' is used to indicate the 'many' end of the relationship.

Many-to-many relationships exist when one occurrence of an entity *A* can be associated with many occurrences of an entity *B*, and vice versa. For example, consider the relationship set out in Figure 5.3:

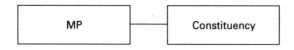

Figure 5.1 *One-to-one relationship*

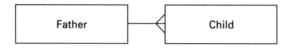

Figure 5.2 *One-to-many relationship*

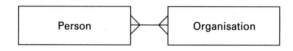

Figure 5.3 *Many-to-many relationship*

many individuals are members of an organisation, and an individual may be a member of many organisations.

It should be noted that these are all *direct relationships*. An *indirect relationship* can also exist between two entities *A* and *B* where they require a third entity *C* to support the relationship. For example, **Parent** is not directly related to **School**. The relationship is indirect, through a **Child**'s attendance at school. Where indirect relationships exist, they must be identified, and the data structure modified to eliminate them. This is done by explicitly defining the linking entity in the data model.

In the following sections, the ERM technique is illustrated with reference to a database designed for a project on the business elite of Bristol in the period 1870–1914.[2] The objective is to provide a step-by-step guide through the database design process, providing sufficient detail for readers to make practical use of a powerful and widely applicable data modelling technique.

☐ *Aims of project*

The initial step in developing the database is the specification of the aims and scope of the project. This defines the universe we are interested in, and helps determine the design of the database. Three main factors recommended the model-driven approach adopted for our project. The first was that we had only a relatively small amount of research time available and thus wished to restrict and direct the data gathering process. Data modelling helps clarify thinking on two key questions: what are the main historical issues raised in the project? and what data are required before these issues can be tackled? Secondly, from earlier work we had a good knowledge of several of the main sources that would be used in the project and what data these might yield. We thus had the opportunity to design a database that reflected to some degree the potentialities of the sources. Thirdly, we wished to create a database that would be self-documenting, easy to use, and would readily yield meaningful information on individuals and groups of individuals. These properties can readily be achieved if a database is founded on a logically correct data model and implemented using a highly functional database management system.

Our interest in the business community of Bristol stems from a wider interest in British business and entrepreneurial history. We take the view, shared by others involved in the study of provincial business communities, that many of the general accounts of economic and social change in modern Britain are flawed by a failure to recognise the importance of local and regional differences in patterns of development. This is certainly the case for the period 1870–1914, about which all sorts of generalisations – often contradictory – are made in the effort to find the root causes of the more recent decline in Britain's relative economic standing. We believe that more robust explanations of national economic performance than those currently on offer must be founded on research into the operation of the business system at grass-roots level. It was the general idea that capitalist economic development is complex and multi-dimensional, varying in form not only over time but also over space, that gave rise to the proposal for a set of parallel studies into the composition and operation of provincial business communities between 1870 and 1914.

In our earlier work on Bristol, we observed that the enduring prosperity of the region was a product of industrial diversity and economic flexibility.[3] In the years between 1870 and 1914, a number of large enterprises did grow up, but small and medium-sized enterprises continued to predominate. Yet, although these enterprises were independent under the law, and highly diverse in terms of their operations, they frequently had partners, major shareholders, directors, professional advisors and managers in common. On working through the sources, the same names repeatedly occurred – sometimes in identical, sometimes in different, groupings. We recognised the possibility that the activities of networks of businessmen may have been important in determining investment patterns and business organisation in the Bristol region. Moreover, certain of the most prominent businessmen were very active in local politics, and were involved in many of the burning issues of the period at the interface between politics and business. These observations in turn suggested the need for a more systematic examination of the background, connections and activities of leading members of the business community.

We decided that the best way forward was to create a prosopographical database that would help us examine:

- the activities and social attributes of leading businessmen and relationships between them;
- the relationship between politics and business in Bristol;
- the validity of the concept of the provincial business community.

Before constructing any database of this type, it is necessary to limit the scope of the enquiry; it is impossible and indeed undesirable to collect data on all and any entities that might be related to a project. This involves deciding upon selection criteria for inclusion in the database. In this case, we decided to confine attention to people whose place of business was the City of Bristol for some time between 1870 and 1914, and who satisfied one or more of the following conditions:

Member of the Society of Merchant Venturers of the City of Bristol. The Society, which was founded in 1552, had about 250 members at any one time, and was one of Bristol's most prestigious organisations. Its members were not just merchants; they were leaders of the business community who identified themselves with the City of Bristol and its economic interests;

Officer of Bristol Chamber of Commerce and Industry. The Chamber of Commerce was a newer (dating from the 1820s) and more open organisation than the Merchant Venturers. It sought to represent the city's manufacturing and retailing interests rather than its commercial elite;

Board Member or **Senior Manager** of a listed company with its headquarters in Bristol, or of a Bristol firm or mutual society known to have employed a capital of £25,000 or more, or with a labour force of 100 people or more.

Membership of Bristol's business elite is thus defined operationally by the test of whether or not a candidate satisfies one or more of these conditions. There is clearly scope for debate in matters of this kind, as much depends on the judgement of the researcher, but there is virtue in the fact that the selection criteria are made explicit.

☐ *Database specification and selection of software*

Having decided to gather data on leading Bristol businessmen active between 1870 and 1914, and on how to select these individuals, the next stage in the project was to specify more fully the content of the proposed database and the requirements of the software needed to create, manage and query it. The intention was to store materials gathered from a large number of sources in both structured and unstructured data formats.

Structured data may be thought of as a conventional set of records; as lists or tables wherein the data are presented as a matrix of rows and columns. Structured data records with a fixed number of fields are useful for storing important data on subjects of particular interest to the researcher. In our case, we wished to store biographical data on the business elite of Bristol, data on the personal connections of members of the elite, and data on the organisations to which members of the elite belonged. We also wished to document the research process by keeping records in a structured format on the sources used to construct the database. Many of the sources available to us already exist in a structured or implicitly structured format, and the data contained in them are easily captured in machine-readable form. The volume *Bristol Lists* of 1899, for instance, contains many lists, some dating back as far as the sixteenth century, relating to the Corporation and officials of the City, Members of Parliament, professional people, and leading businessmen who were members of the Society of Merchant Venturers or officers of the Chamber of Commerce.

Valuable research material is also contained in many other sources in the form of unstructured blocks of textual or free-form data, as in obituaries and other items found in newspapers and similar publications. *Work in Bristol,* for example, published by the *Bristol Times & Mirror* in 1883, provides a series of sketches of the City's largest employers in the chocolate, tobacco, footwear, sugar refining, coal mining, cotton textiles and carriage building industries. It would be possible to extract details from these texts and store them in a structured data format, but this would be very costly and would almost certainly lead to a loss of valuable information. It is potentially much more useful to have complete texts available in machine-readable form.

It followed from the above that the software used to create, maintain and search our database would have be able to handle data in both structured and unstructured formats in an efficient and integrated manner. The database would consist of a number of data files, some of which would contain conventional structured records, and others of which would contain a collection of texts of varying length. Our need for the Bristol project was for a database management system which could offer the advantages of both a RDBMS and a TIMS: a system which had successfully integrated both approaches. At present, few systems are available which offer all the facilities we required, although, as noted in Chapter 3, several RDBMSs and TIMSs are beginning to converge on a general integrated model. The ORACLE RDBMS provides a text management module as part of its suite of programs, and this, combined with the other facilities offered by the system, recommended ORACLE as the right software for our project.

☐ *Design of database*

An ORACLE database consists of a set of tables. Some tables might contain conventionally structured records; others might contain tables with a number of fields for structured data plus a single long-text field suitable for the storage of unstructured texts. As is usual with RDBMSs, records within one table may be joined with records in another table because the two tables share one or more common fields. Providing that the design process ensures that tables in a database are correctly structured – conceptually linked together on the basis of common fields – the database forms an integrated whole, and it is possible to navigate freely between tables in the database, linking records as necessary, to retrieve logically related data from many tables (involving many joins) with a single query.

The approach to ERM taken by the authors is outlined in Figure 5.4. This suggests that the designer works through six well-defined stages, but in practice the data modelling process is an iterative one: repeated backtracking is often required as a model is refined.

The first stage in the process involves the identification of entities of primary interest to the researcher. Definitions of entities should be unambiguous. To achieve this, the data must be fully understood, and the names assigned to entities must be clear.[4] The process of definition is especially valuable in helping expose the underlying nature of implicitly structured data. Once entities have been defined it is a fairly easy matter to group the attributes associated with each. A further advantage is gained when projects involve researchers from different specialisms:

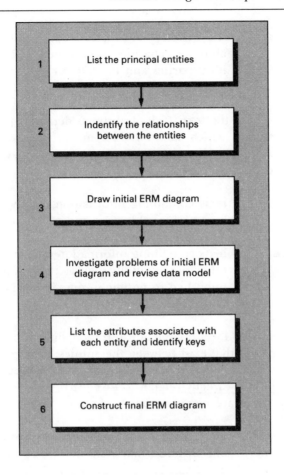

Figure 5.4 *Six-stage approach to entity-relationship modelling*

the effort taken to define entities produces a higher degree of common understanding and fewer conflicts of interest. In our Bristol project, we began by identifying the entities about which we wished to hold just a few key details in a structured format. These were:

Source	details of the sources from which texts originate relating to members of the business elite and organisations to which members of the elite belonged;
Person	personal details of members of the business elite;
Residence	details of the places where members of the business elite lived;
Connections	details of family and other close personal relationships of members of the business elite;
Organisation	details of the organisations to which members of

the business elite belonged, including schools, churches, charities, professional associations, political parties and the like, as well as business enterprises.

We decided to hold the texts (full or abstracts depending on the quality of the material) which would yield some of the data describing these entities, and provide a wealth of other information, in two tables, **P_Notes** and **Org_Notes**:

> **P_Notes**   texts containing information mainly on business-
> men such as obituaries and profiles in newspapers
> and other publications;
>
> **Org_Notes**   texts containing information mainly on firms and
> other organisations such as the company profiles
> published from time to time in local and national
> newspapers.

The second stage in entity-relationship modelling is to identify the direct relationships that exist between the entities. Each pair of entities is investigated in turn (except **Residence** and **Connections** which we only consider as directly related to **Person**). Six relationships are one-to-many; three are many-to-many; none are one-to-one:

One-to-many   one **Source** may yield many **P_Notes**;
                     one **Source** may yield many **Org_Notes**;
                     one **Person** may have many **P_Notes**;
                     one **Organisation** may have many **Org_Notes**;
                     one **Person** may live in many **Residences**;
                     one **Person** may have many **Connections**;

Many-to-many   A **Source** may yield data on many **Person**(s)
                     and data on a **Person** may be contained in many
                     Source(s);
                     A **Source** may yield data on many **Organisa-
                     tion**(s) and data on an **Organisation** may be
                     contained in many **Source**(s);
                     An **Organisation** may have many **Person**(s)
                     as members and a **Person** may belong to many
                     Organisation(s).

In the third stage of ERM, we proceed to draw an initial ERD combining the binary relationships previously identified. The initial ERD for the Bristol project is reproduced in Figure 5.5. The data model

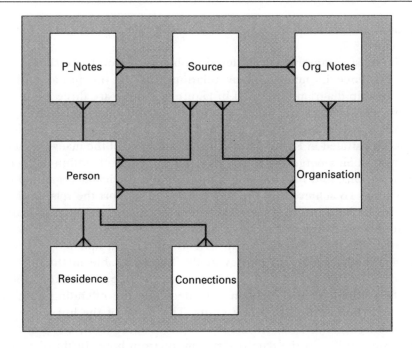

Figure 5.5　*Initial entity-relationship diagram*

represented in the diagram is not sound and needs to be refined, as is usual at this stage in the ERM process. It is very unusual to achieve a correct data model without first having to resolve various technical problems.

The fourth stage in ERM is to investigate and rectify any problems that may be associated with the initial ERD. Three types of problem are commonly encountered. First, the relationships between entities may be inappropriate. In a correctly structured ERD, the relationships between entities are always one-to-many. If a one-to-one relationship exists between two entities, the entities may be combined without loss into a single entity; if many-to-many relationships are found, they need to be dissolved through the creation of a new linking entity. Secondly, *redundant relationships* may exist. There are costs involved in maintaining links between entities (additional data storage) and, if there is more than one way of linking two entities, it is important to determine whether both links are actually necessary – usually they are not. Redundant relationships are shown diagrammatically in Figure 5.6. Thirdly, there may be *redundant link entities*. Redundant link entities occur when there are multiple paths between a pair of primary entities. Redundant link entities are costly in terms of data storage and make the database design unnecessarily complex. The solution is to select the most appropriate pathway and abandon the others, or to *combine* the pathways, as is shown in Figure 5.7.

The most commonly encountered problems, however, are caused by the existence of many-to-many relationships. In the initial entity-relationship diagram illustrated in Figure 5.5, there are three many-to-many relationships. In order to sustain many-to-many relationships, identical attributes must be attached to each of the paired entities. This is illustrated in Figure 5.8 which refers to some of the many business interests of Sir George White. We wish to identify his role within different organisations, and his changing status within a particular organisation over time. To achieve this, the data needed to support the relationship have to be held in two places. Thus the consequence of many-to-many relationships is data redundancy. Storage space is wasted and a risk is created that inconsistencies may arise as entries are updated, deleted or modified: changes to entries in the **Person** table might not be matched by changes to their counterparts in the **Organisation** table.

The solution to the problem is to decouple the offending entities through the insertion of a link entity. The name of the link entity is determined either from the nature of the data content, or from the purpose it fulfils in the database system, or from both. In this case we decided to create a linking entity called **Membership**. The result is a pair of one-to-many relationships. Data relating to the individual's role in the organisation are removed to the link entity. The Sir George White example is continued in Figure 5.9, from which it can be seen that data redundancy has been eliminated.

The next task was to consider how the many-to-many relationships between **Person** and **Source** and between **Organisation** and **Source** could be dissolved. One solution would have been to create two linking entities – **P_Source** and **Org_Source**. But these entities would have been redundant, as pathways between the two pairs of entities already existed: by way of **P_Notes** and **Org_Notes**. Evidently, the original many-to-many relationships were actually redundant and could simply be deleted from the ERD.

Once problems of this kind have been resolved, the database designer has a final set of entities, each of which will be represented by a table in the database. The next stage in the process is to identify the precise contents of each database table by determining the attributes that will be associated with each entity. In the Bristol case, we took a minimalist approach to the entities associated with purely structured data; limiting the fields in each table to 'vital statistics' which would be available for most businessmen and organisations. The judgements made in each case depended on historical rather than technical considerations.

However, there are important technical points to bear in mind at

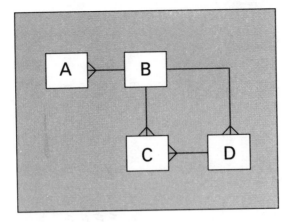

Figure 5.6   *Redundant relationships*

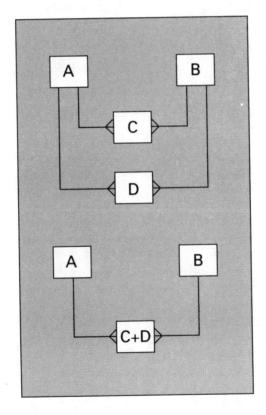

Figure 5.7   *Redundant link entities*

Entity: PERSON

P_Number	P_Name	Born	Died	Estate	Org_Number	Org_Name	Role	Began	Ended
0035	Sir George White	1854	1916	185579	0091	Bristol Tramways Co.	Secretary	1874	1894
0035	Sir George White	1854	1916	185579	0091	Bristol Tramways Co.	Director	1894	1900
0035	Sir George White	1854	1916	185579	0091	Bristol Tramways Co.	Chairman	1900	1916
0035	Sir George White	1854	1916	185579	0145	Great Western Steamship Co.	Director	1891	1896
0035	Sir George White	1854	1916	185579	0233	British & Colonial Aeroplane Co.	Chairman	1910	1916

Entity: ORGANISATION

Org_Number	Org_Name	Org_Type	Founded	Ended	P_Number	P_Name	Role	Began	Ended
0091	Bristol Tramways Co.	Company	1874	1937	0035	Sir George White	Secretary	1874	1894
0091	Bristol Tramways Co.	Company	1874	1937	0035	Sir George White	Director	1894	1900
0091	Bristol Tramways Co.	Company	1874	1937	0035	Sir George White	Chairman	1900	1916
0145	Great Western Steamship Co.	Company	1881	1896	0035	Sir George White	Director	1891	1896
0233	British & Colonial Aeroplane Co.	Company	1910	1919	0035	Sir George White	Chairman	1910	1916

Figure 5.8 *Tables before dissolution of many-to-many relationship*

Entity: PERSON

P_Number	P_Name	Born	Died	Estate
0035	Sir George White	1854	1916	185579

Entity: MEMBERSHIP

Org_Number	P_Number	Role	Began	Ended
0091	0035	Secretary	1874	1894
0091	0035	Director	1894	1900
0091	0035	Chairman	1900	1916
0145	0035	Director	1891	1896
0233	0035	Chairman	1910	1916

Entity: ORGANISATION

Org_Number	Org_Name	Org_Type	Founded	Ended
0091	Bristol Tramways Co.	Company	1874	1937
0145	Great Western Steamship Co.	Company	1881	1896
0233	British & Colonial Aeroplane Co.	Company	1910	1919

Figure 5.9 *Tables after dissolution of many-to-many relationship*

this stage. These relate to the idea of the keys used to identify and link records in database tables. A *primary key* is formed by the data in one or more fields in a table and is used to identify uniquely an individual record. It is important to identify the primary key fields and designate them because only in this way can we be certain that no duplicate records exist. (If duplicates exist, then we cannot be sure whether we are dealing with one occurrence of an entity – person, organisation, event or object – or another, and thus we cannot effectively link records in different tables.) A *foreign key* is a primary key from one table which is replicated in another so as to enable the two tables to be joined together. When a set of tables can be linked together on the basis of common fields, the researcher is able to *navigate* between them and retrieve any logically related data as a single unified record.

Often, as in the Bristol case, it is impossible to find any natural entity attribute(s) which might identify uniquely the records in a table. In **Person**, for instance, we might think of identifying individuals on the basis of the *composite key* formed by a person's name and date of birth. The problem with this, however, is that we are unlikely to have date of birth details for every individual. The preferred solution, therefore, was the creation of an *artificial identifier*; a new field containing a discrete reference number for each person. Likewise, we opted for artificial primary keys for the **Source** and **Organisation** tables. The tables used to connect these three entities together have composite keys formed from the primary keys of the tables they link.

Once the problems of the initial data model have been investigated and resolved, we can proceed to the last stage in database design: constructing the final ERM diagram. In Figure 5.10, the complete diagram for the Bristol database is redrawn, with attributes listed against each entity. Primary keys are italicised. It should be noted that a certain amount of redundancy has been allowed. Strictly speaking, *Org_Name* and *P_Name* are unnecessary in **Membership**, given that linking can be achieved through the unique identifiers *Org_Number* and *P_Number*. The same applies to the insertion of *P_Name* as well as *P_Number* in **Residence** and **Connections**. The redundant attributes, however, here serve a useful purpose by facilitating browsing and querying of the database; without them, even the simplest query requires linking between separate tables, because the researcher will want to know names rather than reference numbers. This underlines the point that while the data modelling process helps to guide the database designer, it should never be pursued in a slavish and restrictive fashion.

☐ *Implementation of database*

Once the final entity-relationship diagram has been drawn up, implementation of the database can begin. The precise details will depend upon the software used, but, in general, each entity identified during modelling becomes a database table. To assist in this process, an *entity description form* may be prepared for each table. It provides detailed information about the characteristics of each attribute. The field length and type will be identified, and the form may also record decisions which have been taken about handling missing or ambiguous data, as a guide to those responsible for data entry. It will thus become a vital part of the documentation which should accompany the development of every project. An example of an entity description form is provided in Figure 5.11 for the entity **Membership**.

Once a prototype set of tables has been constructed, it can be used to test the underlying logic of the data model. Test data, selected to include the unusual as well as the ordinary, are entered into the system. The database may then be systematically queried, and its performance assessed. The results of these trials provide feedback which is used to correct, modify and improve the database design. This is an iterative technique, involving a cycle of testing, observation and modification.

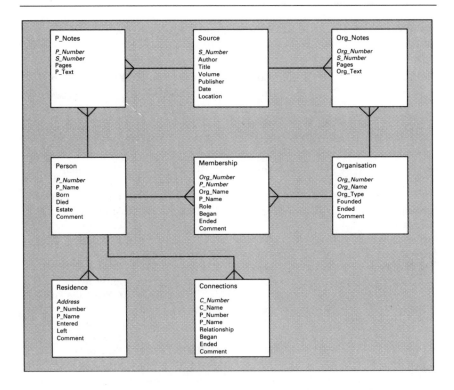

Figure 5.10   *Final entity-relationship diagram*

A stable system usually emerges quite rapidly, and data entry proper can then begin.

□ *Conclusion*

Entity-relationship modelling is a formal method of database design, well-suited to the production of model-driven databases which integrate structured and textual data. It is not an intellectual straitjacket, but a set of tried and tested guidelines. From the outset, it encourages the researcher to think clearly and logically about the problems and issues at hand – precisely defining the project's aims and objectives, and resolving ambiguities in the data. Thus whilst ERM can usefully be employed in the early stages of many types of historical research project, it is particularly suited to sharply focussed applications with well-defined goals, rather than more open-ended, source-driven projects.

A database founded on ERM has two main virtues. First, each record in the structured part of the database is unique. The absence of duplicate records is vitally important, because it ensures that the integrity

PROJECT: The Business Elite of Bristol
DATE: 5 August 19xx
ENTITY NAME: MEMBERSHIP
ENTITY DESCRIPTION: Link entity, describing a PERSON's role
                      in an ORGANISATION.

DATA ITEM	NULLS ALLOWED?	MUST MATCH	FORMAT	WIDTH	COMMENT
Org_Number	No	Yes	NUMBER	6	Must match entry in ORGANISATION
P_Number	No	Yes	NUMBER	6	Must match entry in PERSON
Role	No	No	CHAR	25	
Org_Name	No	Yes	CHAR	50	Must match entry in ORGANISATION
P_Name	No	Yes	CHAR	40	Must match entry in PERSONS
Began	Yes	No	NUMBER	4	Year only
Ended	Yes	No	NUMBER	4	Year only

Note: Primary key in italics.

Figure 5.11 *Entity description form for the entity* **Membership**

of the database is maintained, and allows the researcher to navigate efficiently between tables to search and retrieve data. Second, the application of logical rules results in a database which is structured to reflect the natural relationships of the data and the uses to which it will be put, rather than reflecting the demands of the hardware and software; only when the logical design is fully worked out does the developer turn to the physical implementation of the database.

In offering a strategy for the integration of structured and unstructured data, the approach set out here also points a way to the future. To date, the vast majority of historical databases have involved the storage and manipulation of text and numbers within structured fields. This is beginning to change, as historians come to recognise and exploit the opportunities offered by the integration of relational database management systems with textual information management systems. The number of historical database projects which involve the integration of structured data with text, sound and images is now set to multiply rapidly.

■ 5.3 Relational Data Analysis

Relational data analysis (RDA), or *normalisation* as it is sometimes called, is another key technique for analysing and organising data which can usefully be applied in many historical research projects.[5] RDA's bottom-up approach is particularly suitable when the task facing the researcher is the computerisation of a set of source materials; most usually already organised in structured lists, records or tables. The method is rule-driven, and if the rules are applied correctly, the same data model will always emerge from a given set of data items. In this section, we begin by outlining the theory of RDA before providing a worked example based upon the authors' own research. Readers who have difficulty with the theory may elect to read the worked example first and then backtrack to read the whole section.

The aim of RDA is to produce an outline specification for a relationally organised database in what is known as *third normal form* (*3NF*). In a table in 3NF, each data item in a record is identified by a unique *primary key* consisting of one or more of the data items in the record. Each data item in the record is identified by the whole key and not just part of the key. No data item in the record is identified by any other data item in the record which is not part of the key. A number of operations are required in order to ensure that all the tables in a database are in 3NF. We begin with a list of unnormalised data items (extracted from the sources) and reduce it, consecutively, to first normal form (1NF), second normal form (2NF), and 3NF. This procedure is summarised in Figure 5.12.

1NF refers to a collection of data organised into records which have no *repeating groups* of data items within a record. By avoiding repetition the amount of redundant data in a database is sharply reduced. The transition to 2NF eliminates *partial dependencies* to ensure that all the data items in a record depend for their identification on the whole of the primary key. In a similar fashion *indirect dependencies* are eliminated in the transition to 3NF to ensure that none of the data items in a record can be identified by a non-key data item in that record. The removal of partial and indirect dependencies is beneficial in simplifying the structure of the database by identifying and separating out distinct entities. In this way, data redundancy is again avoided and problems with modifying, inserting and deleting data are eliminated.

RDA rests upon two crucial procedures. One is the progressive sub-division of the data into a set of related two-dimensional tables. This begins with the transformation of an unnormalised data item list into a set of table headings in 1NF. In the example given in Figure 5.13, data items *E* and *F* can take multiple values. If a separate record is

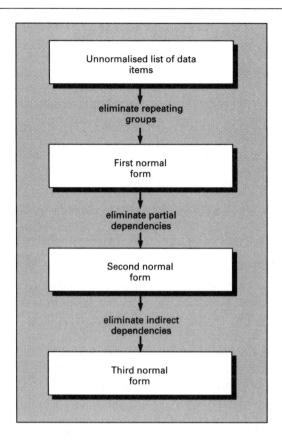

Figure 5.12 *Normalisation*

created for each occurrence of *E* and *F*, then it will be necessary on each occasion to key in identical data for the data items *ABCD*. As a result of this data redundancy, extra clerical effort and storage space will be needed to capture data and maintain files, and retaining data integrity (consistency) between files becomes a major headache as entries are updated, deleted or modified. The solution is to remove the *repeating groups* to a separate table.

The subdivision of the data set, however, requires a means of linking the related tables. This involves the other crucial procedure: the identification of *primary keys*. The question of primary keys was considered earlier in this chapter, and it may be recalled that the purpose of a primary key is to provide a unique identifier for each record or row in a table, and facilitate the linking of related tables. A *foreign key* is a primary key from one table which is replicated in another so as to enable the two tables to be joined together. When a set of tables can be linked together on the basis of common fields, the researcher is

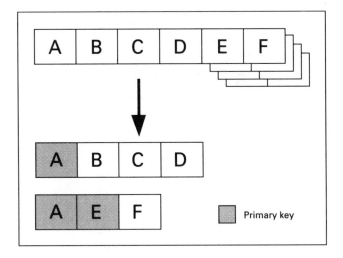

Figure 5.13   *Removal of repeating groups*

able to navigate between them and retrieve any logically related data as a single unified record. Two integrity rules ensure that linkage can be achieved. The *entity integrity* rule states that once the primary key is established, no change may be made that destroys its ability uniquely to identify a record. (For instance, no primary key (or any part of the primary key) shall have a null value.) This ensures access to all data. The *referential integrity* rule states that the value of a foreign key in a table must be null or correspond to a primary key value in the associated table. To ensure that these rules are followed, many RDBMSs use 'Must Fill' or 'Must Match' features to ensure that illegal entries are rejected.

When the repeating groups have been dissolved and a primary key chosen for each table, the unnormalised list of data items has been converted to a set of table headings in 1NF.

> **Definition:** *a table is in 1NF when for each value of the primary key there is no repetition of groups of non-key data items.*

Further checks may then be made for *partial* and *indirect dependencies.* When a table in 1NF has a primary key consisting of more than one data item, there is a possibility that some non-key data items do not depend upon the whole key. The upper part of Figure 5.14 is a dependency diagram, which shows the relationship between non-key data items and the primary key. The dependent end of the relationship is indicated by a short bar. In this example, data items *C* and *D* depend

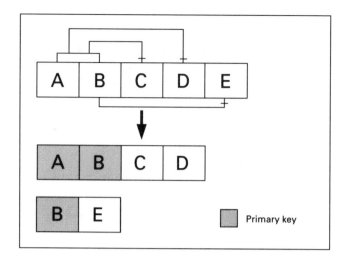

Figure 5.14   *Removal of partial dependency*

upon *A* and *B*, but data item *E* only depends upon *B*. This is partial dependency, and should be removed as shown in the lower part of Figure 5.14. The resulting tables are in 2NF.

Definition: a table is in 2NF if each non-primary-key data item depends upon the whole of the primary key for its identification.

Indirect dependency (sometimes called transitive dependency) is illustrated in Figure 5.15. Here, data item *C* does not directly depend upon the key *A*, but indirectly via another non-key data item, *B*. This should be resolved as shown to produce tables in 3NF.

Definition: a table is in 3NF when all the non-key data items depend for their identification directly upon the primary key, and not indirectly through some other non-key data item.

Thus we can summarise the normalisation process by stating that: *in fully normalised tables, each non-key data item depends upon the whole key, and nothing but the key*. The normalisation process might be taken still further, but for most purposes such refinements are not necessary.[6]

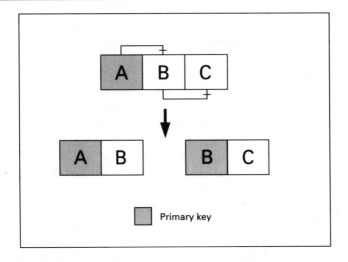

Figure 5.15   *Removal of indirect (transitive) dependency*

□ *Illustration of RDA*

The main product of RDA is a logical data model which might be implemented using a RDBMS. A data model of this type consists of a set of table names, the data item (field) names for each table, and primary and foreign key designations for each table. The practicalities of generating a model may be demonstrated with reference to a simplified case study based upon our own research on the shipping industry.

Amongst the most valuable sources for nineteenth-century maritime history are the Crew Lists and Agreements held by the Public Record Office (BT98 and BT99), which provide a record of every foreign voyage. At the end of the voyage, the master had to supply documents listing the vessel's name, tonnage and destination, the name, age, date and place of birth, the rank and wages of every crew-member, the date on which they signed on, and their last ship. The rations provided and any deaths or desertions which occurred during the voyage were also noted.[7] Here we have a typical database problem: each ship makes many voyages, and on each voyage many seamen are employed.

It should be emphasised that the dataset is considerably simplified for the purposes of exposition: the objective here is to explain the methodology rather than describe a specific research project. Data relating to the rations provided, intermediate ports of call, deaths and desertions, and the place where seamen signed on and were discharged are all omitted. It is assumed that we are working on the post-1854 period when an official number (unique identifier) was allocated to all newly-registered ships, and seamen were required to carry a Registry Ticket. It is further assumed that we want to record occupational groupings (officers, foremast hands, specialists, etc.) as well as describing each mariner's exact rank.

The starting point in a project of this type is a close examination of the data and the extraction of a list of data item names and characteristics. The preparation of this *data item list* may seem a fairly straightforward task, especially when the data are already in tabular form. However, it is most important to ensure that nothing is missed, that each data item is tightly defined, and that suitably descriptive data item names are chosen. Our example data item list is given in Figure 5.16.

The next stage in RDA is to choose an initial primary key. The general idea is to select the key which most appropriately identifies the remaining items in the data item list. This is partly a subjective matter, and partly a matter of establishing how in reality one data item stands in relation to another. In this case the obvious choice is *Ship_No* which uniquely identifies the values of the data items *Ship_Name*, *Regd_Date*, *Regd_Port* and *Burden*. It may be said that these values *depend* on *Ship_No*. More generally, when selecting between possible initial primary keys, known as *candidate* keys, the following guidelines should be followed:

- Choose the candidate key with the fewest components.
- Where candidate keys have the same number of components, choose the one which uniquely identifies the largest number of non-key data items.
- Where there is a choice between an alphanumeric field and a numeric field, make the numeric field the primary key.

Once the primary key has been selected, we can begin to normalise the data. If for a given value of primary key there is more than one potential value of a non-primary key data item, then the data are said to be unnormalised. When we examine our data item list, it will immediately be seen that for a given value of primary key (*Ship_No*), there will be many potential (and actual) values of *Voyage_Start*, *Crew_Name*, and the other data items which describe voyages and crew-members. This is shown diagrammatically in the top part of Figure 5.17. As noted earlier, the existence of these repeating groups of data items means that there will be large amounts of redundant data stored in the table. This is inefficient, and may well lead to problems with insertion, updating and deletion. Once the data items which are capable of containing repeating groups have been identified, the next step is to transform the unnormalised data into 1NF by eliminating these repeating groups. This can be done by moving them to separate tables

Data Item	Description
Ship_No	Number of ship in register: uniquely identifies each ship
Ship_Name	Name of ship
Regd_Date	Date on which the ship was registered
Regd_Port	Place at which the ship was registered
Burden	Notional figure of tonnage according to formula
Voyage_Start	Date of commencement of voyage
Voyage_End	Date voyage ended and Crew List and Agreement were submitted
Depart_Port	Port of departure
Destin_Port	Port of destination
Crew_No	Mariner's Registry Ticket number (unique identifier)
Crew_Name	Name of mariner (forename(s) and lastname in full)
Date_Birth	Full date of birth: day, month, year
Place_Birth	Town, county or country of birth (country if foreign)
Age	Age given by mariner at date of joining ship
Rank	Mariner's exact rank (third mate, able seaman, etc.)
Occupation_Group	Group of workers to which mariner belongs (officer, foremast hand, etc.)
Wage	Mariner's wage per calendar month
Last_Ship	Name of last ship in which mariner served

Figure 5.16 *Unnormalised data item list*

(Figure 5.17). A new primary key must be created for each table. It is formed by the addition of a further data item (or data items) to the original primary key; so forming a new key by which the non-primary-key data items in the table may be uniquely identified. We now have separate tables in 1NF for the entities **Ship**, **Voyage**, and **Seaman**, each with a primary key.

The next step is to transform the tables into 2NF by identifying and

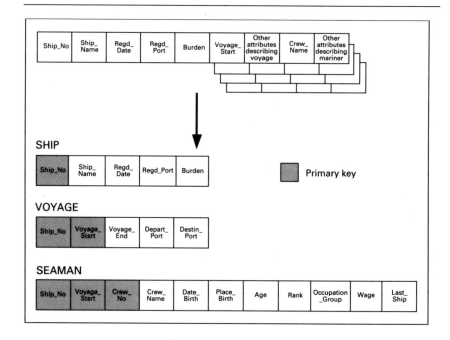

Figure 5.17   *Transformation to first normal form through removal of repeating groups*

removing partial dependencies. All composite keys must be examined to determine if each non-primary-key data item could be uniquely identified by knowledge of part rather than all of the primary key. Problems do not exist with the table **Ship** since its primary key consists of a single data item, *Ship_No*; thus the non-key data items *must* depend upon the whole key, and the table is already in 2NF. The other two tables, however, require consideration, as they have composite keys. Analysis of **Voyage** reveals that in fact *Voyage_End*, *Depart_Port* and *Destin_Port* all depend upon the whole key. Their values can only be determined when we know both the ship (*Ship_No*) and the particular voyage (*Voyage_Start*) involved.

However, as Figure 5.18 shows, the table **Seaman** does contain partial dependency. The *Age*, *Rank*, *Occupation_Group*, *Wage* and *Last_Ship* of a seaman may change from one voyage to the next, and thus are dependent upon the whole key. However, the seaman's name and date and place of birth do not depend upon the ship and the voyage, but only on *Crew_No*. The solution once again is to subdivide the table, removing the partially dependent data items to a new table with a primary key consisting of the data items upon which they *were* found to depend. In Figure 5.19, where the tables are set out in 2NF, **Seaman** has been dissolved into two tables, **Seaman_Personal** and **Seaman_Voyage**.

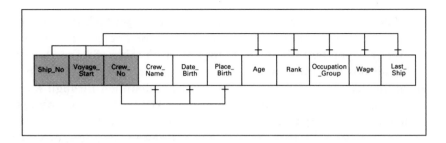

Figure 5.18 *Dependency diagram for the Seaman table*

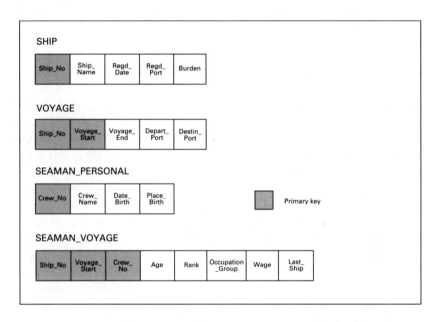

Figure 5.19 *Transformation to second normal form through removal of partial dependency*

The 2NF tables may now be examined for indirect (transitive) dependency. It may be recalled that this occurs when the identification of a non-key data item is indirect through another non-key data item which *is* dependent upon the primary key. In our example, **Seaman_Voyage** needs to be examined closely for indirect dependency. *Age*, *Rank* and *Last_Ship* will change from one voyage to another, and from one seaman to another; thus they all depend directly upon the whole of the primary key. It might be thought, however, that *Wage* depends on *Rank*, and if this were the case then it would be an example of indirect dependency. But in fact wages varied with time, within ranks and by voyage. Thus *Wage* too is directly dependent upon the primary key. The same is not true of *Occupation_Group* which *does* provide an example of indirect dependency. This is because *Occupation_Group* is directly dependent upon *Rank*: for any given value of *Rank* there is only one possible value of *Occupation_Group* (Figure 5.20). It is apparent that *Occupation_Group* may be identified through *Rank* rather than any component of the primary key to **Seaman_Voyage**. A new table, **Occupation**, is therefore created, with *Rank* as the primary key. *Rank* is also a foreign key in **Seaman_Voyage**, enabling records in the two tables to be linked together when necessary. The tables are now in 3NF (Figure 5.21).

The logical data model thus created can be used as the design for an operational database system.

□ *The advantages of RDA*

The advantages of applying RDA are both technical and academic. The first important technical advantage is that conversion to 3NF almost always reduces the amount of backing storage required for the database because of the elimination of data redundancy. This fact, along with the logical ordering of the data, yields a second advantage: a reduction in the amount of processor time required for routine database operations (searching, sorting, etc.) and consequently improved times for information retrieval. A third technical advantage is that database operations like updating and deleting are greatly simplified since there are far fewer redundant values. Finally, if the data are not well structured, it may be very difficult, or even impossible, to answer more complex database queries. A query might appear to be valid yet contain subtle illogicalities. This is referred to as *semantic disintegrity*, and it may be minimised through putting the data in 3NF.

The main academic benefits of RDA are twofold. The first is that the process of identifying entities and relationships between them, which is integral to RDA, should greatly assist the historian in developing an accurate representation of whatever aspect of the past he or she is interested in. The discipline of data modelling helps bring to the fore those objects (people, organisations, etc.) and processes that were significant in the past in much the same way that it brings information systems specialists to understand what is significant in the present. In other words, RDA can help the historian refine an old skill: the rigorous and systematic analysis of data sources. The second main academic benefit stems from having a database in 3NF. No duplicate records exist in 3NF tables, and thus a basic condition for record linkage – that of *list uniqueness* – is satisfied. This is a valuable property which

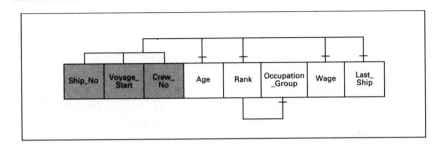

Figure 5.20   *Dependency diagram for the* **Seaman_Voyage** *table*

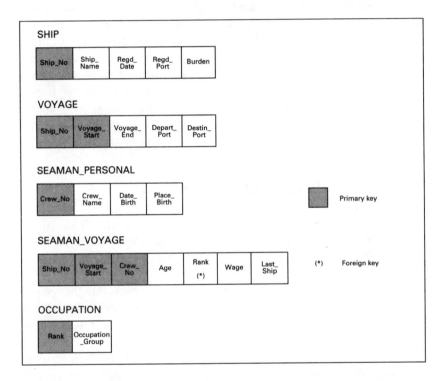

Figure 5.21   *Transformation to third normal form through removal of indirect (transitive) dependency*

might be exploited in the increasing number of multi-source projects for which record linkage is a critical operation.

☐ *Conclusion*

RDA is one of the most valuable techniques available to the database designer. It may usefully be employed whenever an historical researcher is faced with the task of creating a database from one or more existing sets of structured data. Data in this form are to be found in many types of records – electoral, production, employment, health, and demographic, to name just a few. In applying the technique, a discipline is imposed which helps create a database representative of objects and relationships in the real world. It obliges the researcher to think carefully about semantics – what the data actually mean – and provides a set of simple procedural rules which ensure that every data item is associated with the right entity. Databases designed in this way are stable yet flexible and easily modified. A database may be designed intuitively, and at times this might prove satisfactory, but at other times effort might be lavished on the creation of a database whose structure is logically unsound, and consequently incapable of yielding answers to many of the questions which might interest researchers. Even an elementary knowledge of RDA should help avoid such disasters.

■ 5.4 Creating a Database

With the completion of the design phase, attention can turn to implementing the database. Provided that the design has been adequately documented, it is quite easy to take the conceptual model embodied in entity description forms and data item lists and use it to create database tables and fields. In this section, we describe the physical creation of the maritime history database which was designed using RDA in previous paragraphs. The DBMSs used are ORACLE and Microsoft Access.

ORACLE uses a high-level language called SQL to create, modify and query databases. SQL – usually pronounced 'Sequel', but originally an acronym for Structured Query Language – was first defined in 1974 by D.D. Chamberlin and others at the IBM Research Lab in San José, California. Commercial products came in the late 1970s and early 1980s. More recently, it has become established in the microcomputer world, with leading products like dBase IV, FoxPro, Paradox, Rbase and Access all adding SQL facilities. By the end of the 1980s, there were already more than 50 products in the marketplace which supported SQL, and it had become established as the *de facto* standard in the relational database world, running on machines ranging from the largest mainframes down to relatively cheap micros.[8]

Despite its name, SQL not only provides querying facilities; it is a complete language for data definition, access and processing. SQL commands can be embedded in programs, and sent from one program, and one platform, to another. This makes it a powerful data interchange language. One program can request from another complete data files, subsets, or individual records which meet complex searching and sorting criteria. Thus data can be exchanged independent of the hardware, program or operating system. The benefits of this should be obvious. Because SQL is a standard interface, users can migrate from one platform to another without difficulty.

SQL carries out its functions through a relatively small but powerful command set. There are three categories of SQL command – *data definition, data manipulation,* and *data control.* We are concerned here with the first of these. The term data definition refers to the construction of the tables which make up the database, and their modification and deletion. To create and modify tables, SQL uses the verbs CREATE and ALTER. Before any data can be entered into the database, the empty tables must be created. This is done with the CREATE TABLE command, which is used to specify:

- the name of the table;
- the name of each field;
- the type of data to be stored in each column;
- the width of each column;
- other optional information.

Thus, to create the **Ship** table, we would enter the following:

```
CREATE  TABLE  Ship
     (Ship_No  NUMBER(6)   NOT  NULL,
     Ship_Name  CHAR(18)   NOT  NULL,
     Regd_Port  CHAR(12),
     Burden  NUMBER(5));
```

The first line assigns the name **Ship** to the table. Tables must have unique names. Subsequent lines each describe a field (column) within the table. The *Ship_No* field is used to assign a unique reference number to each entry. NUMBER(6) specifies two things: the data type is NUMBER, which means that only numbers may be stored in this column, and the size of the number is limited to six digits. Additionally, we want to ensure that all records have a reference number; and so the instruction NOT NULL ensures that this field must always be filled in. Thus the creation of the table permits a degree of validation, in that neither alphabetical characters nor numbers over 999999 can be entered into the field, and it cannot be left blank. The next line of the instruction creates a field to contain the *Ship_Name*. This is a character field that can accept the letters of the alphabet, numbers, or special characters like hyphens, with a maximum length of 18 characters. Again, we want to ensure that it is NOT NULL. *Regd_Port* is another character field, and finally, we have a field to record the *Burden* (tonnage) of the ship. This is another NUMBER field, with a maximum length of five digits. If the tonnage figures included fractions, we might alter this to *Burden* NUMBER(6,1), which would allow numbers up to six digits long, including one digit after the decimal point. The final semi-colon closes the command and executes it.

The validation features available when creating tables in SQL, though relatively limited, are very useful. The ability to set primary and foreign keys to NOT NULL ensures compliance with entity integrity and referential integrity rules. In some SQL dialects (though not the basic ANSI/ISO standard) it is possible to ensure values entered into a field have a unique value, or fall within a specified range. More sophisticated validation facilities are usually provided by the RDBMS's screen forms generator, such as ORACLE's SQL*Forms, which is discussed overleaf.

ALTER TABLE is used to add a field to the table, or modify an existing field. In the following example, a date field is added to store the date of registration:

```
ALTER  TABLE  Ship
     ADD  Regd_Date  DATE;
```

Since our example database only requires the year of registration, however, we may prefer to make *Regd_Date* a number field:

```
ALTER  TABLE  Ship
     ADD  Regd_Date  NUMBER(4);
```

It is sometimes necessary to alter the specification of a field once data have been entered into it. For example, we might find that 12 characters is insufficient to store every port of registration, and decide to increase it to 15 characters. We would change the structure of the *Regd_Port* field by using the command:

```
ALTER  TABLE  Ship
     MODIFY  Regd_Port  CHAR(15);
```

When the table has been created, its structure can be displayed by using the DESCRIBE command.

```
DESCRIBE Ship;
```

produces the following result:

```
Name                Null?            Type
---------           ---------        ---------
Ship_No             NOT NULL         NUMBER(6)
Ship_Name           NOT NULL         CHAR(18)
Regd_Date                            NUMBER(4)
Regd_Port                            CHAR(15)
Burden                               NUMBER(5)
```

Once an empty table has been created, data can be entered into it using the INSERT command.

```
INSERT INTO Ship
    VALUES (125,'Martha Jane',1841,'Sunderland',274);
```

will enter values into the first row of the table. The *Ship_No* on the Register is 125, Martha Jane is the *Ship_Name*, 1841 the *Regd_Date*, Sunderland the *Regd_Port*, and the *Burden* is 274 tons. It should be noted that, unlike numeric fields, the contents of character fields must be enclosed in inverted commas.[9] The command can be repeated to add more records to the table. Records can be added one at a time, or in batches.

This method of data entry, however, while acceptable for small quantities of data, is far from user-friendly. In practice data entry and updating is generally done via screen forms designed with the DBMS's forms generator. As noted in Chapter 3, ORACLE users are provided with a set of programs called SQL*Forms. They provide pop-up menus, windows and screen painting to help users build and modify the screen forms they need.

A simple form can be set up to enter data into a single table in a couple of minutes. The user only has to specify names for the form and the table it is to access, and accept a default layout. The system then automatically designs the form, defining the areas where the data will actually appear and providing appropriate screen prompts for the user. In the default layout, each field will normally be on a separate line, with the fieldname flush left. Once the default form has been created, it can immediately be used for data entry. Alternatively, it can be customised to meet the user's needs. The range of features offered by SQL*Forms is very comprehensive. Complex forms can be spread across several pages if the quantity of data is too great to fit on a single screen. Forms can be multi-table, permitting data to be inserted into two or more related tables from the same form. In such instances, forms can be split into 'blocks', where each block handles a separate table. Forms can also be multi-record, with a number of records tabulated on separate rows beneath the column headings.

For each field there is a Field Definition menu which provides great flexibility. Some of the most obvious features are those for modifying the layout of the screen form. The sequence of fields on the form can be modified (perhaps to match the structure of the document being transcribed), and the field length and display length can be adjusted. A format mask can be set up to display dates, numbers and currencies in the desired format.

Other modifications to the basic screen form help to speed up data entry and improve accuracy. For example, default values can be entered into fields to reduce the amount of typing involved. These can be accepted or overwritten as necessary. The screen form can accept text as entered, or force it all to upper case, as desired. Whilst forcing all text to upper case does not improve readability, it does reduce typing errors and facilitate querying. SET HINT can be used to provide the entry clerk with an example of an acceptable entry – which can be made visible all the time, or only when help is requested. Data entered into a field can be checked to ensure that it falls within a specified range. This may be achieved by reference to other fields. For example, the entry in a *Last_Year* field must be a later date than the entry in the corresponding *First_Year* field, or an error is returned. A field can be specified as REQUIRED to ensure that it is not left blank by mistake, or set to AUTOINCREMENT, so as to create a unique reference number for each record as it is entered.

The way in which databases are implemented varies considerably from one DBMS to another, though the underlying processes are largely the same. ORACLE is essentially a command line database which uses text screens; Microsoft Access, on the other hand, is a graphical DBMS which uses mice, icons and pulldown menus, and is fully compliant with the Windows philosophy. The procedure which we would use to create the **Ship** table in an Access database is described in the following paragraphs.

When Access is loaded, the user is greeted with the *database window* (Figure 5.22). It lists the principal categories of objects which can be created and used in Access: tables, queries, forms, reports, macros and modules. Tables are used to define the actual data structures and store the data. They may also be used for directly entering, updating and deleting records, though this is usually done via screen forms. Queries may be run on their own or used as the basis for forms and reports. Macros provide facilities for automating tasks without the need to use

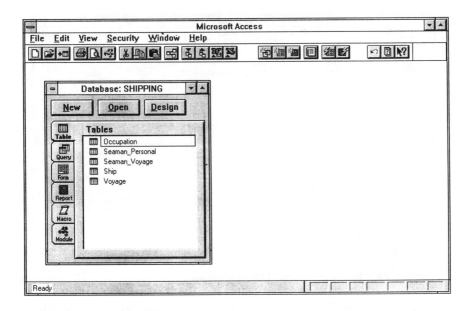

Figure 5.22 *Microsoft Access: the database window*

a programming language; modules, on the other hand, provide a powerful database programming language, Access Basic, which can be used for more complex automated processing.

To create the **Ship** table, we click on TABLE and then NEW in the database window. Access offers two options: tables can be automatically created with Microsoft's Table Wizards feature, or set up from scratch. Table Wizards allow the user to choose from a wide range of sample tables and fields, but are not particularly useful for the historian as most of the specified table types are business- or household- related. However, constructing a table from scratch is a straightforward task. Figure 5.23 shows the *design view* which is used for table definition.

The fields are specified in the upper half of the window. The fieldname and data type are inserted, together with an (optional) field description; this will appear at the foot of the screen to prompt the user when data are being entered in the field. Unlike many DBMSs, Access is relatively generous in its handling of fieldnames. They can be up to 64 characters long, and may consist of spaces and a mixture of upper and lower case letters. This allows the use of clear, descriptive names which can easily be recalled when viewing or querying records. The data types provided are Text (alphanumeric characters, with a maximum length of 255 characters); Number (integer or fractional values); Date/Time; Currency; Yes/No (Boolean); OLE Object (graphics or other binary data up to 1 gigabyte); Memo (a long text field with a maximum

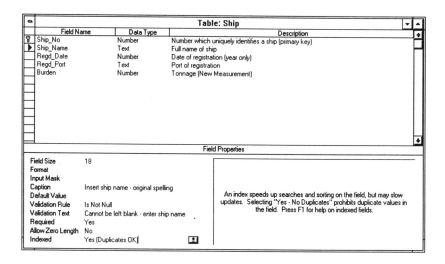

Figure 5.23 *Microsoft Access: table definition*

length of 64,000 characters); and Counter (a numeric value which is automatically incremented for each record which is entered). In our **Ship** example, the fields are either text or numeric. Additionally, *Ship_No* is identified as the primary key; Access adds a key icon to mark each primary key field. Fields can be moved around by clicking to the left of the fieldname, and then dragging the field to its new position. In a similar fashion, a field may be deleted by clicking to the left of the fieldname and typing DEL.

The lower half of the screen is used to set field properties. In Figure 5.23, the field properties of *Ship_Name* are displayed. Field Size defines the maximum size of the field. Format is used to determine the way in which dates and numbers will be displayed – for example in Long Date (e.g. 19 June 1884) or Currency (£0.00) format. Input Mask may be used to force all input data into a particular format. Caption is used to provide a caption for the field when it is used in forms and reports. It is not essential to do this, however, as the field name would be used by default. The Default Value property is left blank in this example because not many ships share the same name. When the field frequently contains the same entry, however, it is advisable to enter a default value which will automatically be inserted each time a new record is created. It can of course be overwritten by the user where it is incorrect. The Validation Rule may contain an expression that limits the values which can be entered in the field. Is Not Null ensures that the ship's name cannot be omitted. In a numeric or date field, the validation rule is often used to ensure that values fall within a specified range. The Validation Text box is used to enter the error message which appears whenever the validation rule is contravened. The remaining properties are self-explanatory: the Ship_Name field is required, cannot have a zero length, and is indexed. Because *some* ships had identical names, duplicate values are allowed. In the primary key, however, each entry must be list unique; Ship_No is therefore indexed with duplicates prohibited. Fields which are unlikely to be searched and sorted are not indexed to speed updating.

This completes the creation of the **Ship** table. It can now be saved ready for data entry. However, in a multitable database, it is also necessary to define the relationships between tables. This is done by opening the RELATIONSHIPS window and specifying the tables to be linked, the linking fields and the nature of the relationship (typically one-to-many) between them. Access also permits the user to enforce referential integrity rules for the relationship.

Another task which is generally an important precursor to data entry is the creation of screen forms. As noted earlier, forms provide a more 'user-friendly' means of entering and viewing data. Forms in Access are very powerful because they can provide attractive formats with special fonts, colour and shading; mimic the paper records which are being input; perform calculations on the data entered and insert the results into calculated fields; present data in alphabetic or numeric order; and manipulate data from more than one table. Many different layouts are possible, but the most common formats are single record on a page (screen), or tabular, displaying each record as a row of fields. Access' Forms Wizards are rather more useful than the Table Wizards. They prompt the user to select the data source and the required fields, and then automatically create a useable form. A data entry form for the **Ship** table is given in Figure 5.24. Forms – and indeed the underlying tables too – can easily be printed out. However, for more sophisticated print-outs, reports are used. We consider report generation in section 6.4.

■ 5.5 Conclusion

Entity-relationship modelling and relational data analysis are alternative ways of producing a conceptual data model which might serve as the basis for a computer database. As one might expect, there is much discussion as to the relative merits of each technique. Either method can be applied in most cases, but certain types of project lend themselves more readily to one method rather than the other. In projects where the structure of the data is obscure or difficult to disentangle, it is

Ship				
Ship_No	**Insert ship name – original spelling**	**Regd_Date**	**Regd_Port**	**Burden**
10035	Martha Jane	1840	Bridgwater	145
10046	St Michael	1840	Bridgwater	132
10076	Red Rose	1840	Bridgwater	181
10144	Ellerslie	1840	Bridgwater	213
10188	Saxon	1840	Bridgwater	167
10286	Syren	1841	Bridgwater	59
10313	Calder	1841	Bridgwater	181
10315	Garrow	1841	Bridgwater	229
10342	Rover	1841	Bridgwater	204
10367	Jane Dixon	1841	Bridgwater	91

Record: 1   of 11303

Figure 5.24   *Microsoft Access: form definition*

better to apply RDA. One major advantage of RDA is that it obliges the researcher to study the sources very closely before moving to a higher level of abstraction. Another is that the method merely requires the application of a few simple rules. As noted earlier, providing that the rules are applied correctly, the same data model will always emerge from the same data item list.[10] No such assurances can be given with ERM, where much depends on the initial choice of entities and the skill and judgement of the individual modelling the data. Essentially, RDA is a simpler and more natural technique than ERM; it makes few conceptual demands and produces consistent results.

The advocates of ERM, on the other hand, point out that the approach is very positive in obliging project developers to think exactingly about the requirements of a database system. This is true, and the method undoubtedly scores heavily when it comes to scoping and detailing projects that are model-driven rather than data-driven. Moreover, ERM can be applied very neatly in projects where little difficulty exists in identifying the main entities, attributes and relationships. ERM may also be the preferred approach where there may be a large proportion of nulls (missing data), and where the fragmentation into a large number of tables may be counter-productive; its implementation often results in simpler data models with less elaborate data paths than those produced by RDA. It is worth saying, additionally, that ERM is a useful approach to database projects irrespective of whether RDA is ultimately carried out. It is an excellent way of mapping out a situation, clarifying thought and producing a provisional data model that can be understood by non-specialists who may ultimately use the database.

Whichever approach is adopted, data analysis and modelling provides the specification for the database system. It is critical to the success or failure of any system of more than moderate complexity, and hence it is an extremely important part of information systems analysis and design as a whole. Many systems in use today, in both the commercial and academic spheres, are founded on inadequate data models. This situation will hopefully change in the medium term, driven by the spread of better professional practice. Professionalism itself will be aided by the spread of software tools (already available) which make data modelling a much more automated process than it is at present. However, there will always be a need to acquire a clear understanding of the exact nature and meaning of the data if satisfactory results are to be obtained from such procedures.

If database design has been properly carried out, and unambiguously documented, implementation should be a relatively painless procedure. As we have demonstrated, the creation of tables in a relational database is straightforward: each entity defined at the design stage becomes a table and each attribute a field. Nevertheless, as we noted in the previous chapter, considerable attention should be paid to the provision of data entry screens and data validation procedures. These can make a big difference to the ease and accuracy with which data are entered.

Case Study E
Indicators of Regional Economic Disparity: The Geography of Economic Distress in Britain before 1914

David Gilbert and Humphrey Southall
Queen Mary and Westfield College, University of London
Royal Holloway, University of London

The recession of the early 1980s and the return of mass unemployment brought renewed interest in the nature and history of the 'north–south divide' in Britain. This interest has been sustained by the recession of the early 1990s, in which the long-term geography of regional disparities in wealth and economic performance seems to have been altered, with parts of the 'south' now experiencing serious economic problems. A conventional account of the history of regional economic disparities holds that the last major change was a reversal in the fortunes of 'north' and 'south' around the time of the First World War.[1] This view of British regional history seems to come both from a reading of contemporary responses to the inter-war depression and from inferences drawn from patterns of regional growth in employment, rather than from detailed research on the regional and sub-regional patterning of unemployment and other forms of economic distress before 1914. Recent research on the relationship between pauperage and local and regional economic performance,[2] on unemployment among unionised workers,[3] and on patterns of employment,[4] seemed to bring this orthodoxy of a reversal in regional fortunes into question. The central aim of the project funded by the Leverhulme Trust which established the Queen Mary & Westfield (QMW) Labour Markets Database was to provide a systematic empirical basis for the comparison of economic performance between regions and sub-regions in Britain before the First World War. To this end the project sought to gather and computerise statistical series which were national in scope, which were broken down into sub-national spatial units, and which were consistent enough to provide a basis for comparison between regions and localities.

It is no coincidence that widespread recognition of regional differentials in unemployment in the inter-war period came with the availability of relatively comprehensive unemployment statistics which were compiled through the operation of the National Insurance scheme. National Insurance developed directly from earlier unemployment insurance schemes run by individual trade unions.[5] Aggregate returns from these schemes have been used to calculate national unemployment series for the period prior to 1914, but until recently no attempt had been made to produce disaggregated series, not least because of the volume of data involved. An initial study concentrating on the records of the Amalgamated Society of Engineers, and restricted to the statistical returns of a few selected months, suggested that cyclical unemployment before 1914 was concentrated in the industrial north.[6] The database has successfully extended this research, and now contains bi-annual or quarterly details of unemployment payments made by three unions from the mid-nineteenth century until the First World War (see Figure E.1 for full details of coverage). The database holds information for unemployment payments at branch level. This means that unemployment rates can be constructed for different geographical units such as regions, counties, or local labour markets by aggregating the information for individual branches. Given the proviso that unemployment insurance was mainly limited to unionised, skilled, male workers, the three unions with statistics included in the database provide good representative coverage. These unions were the largest providing insurance; in 1880 their members formed nearly 60 per cent of all unionists providing unemployment returns to the Board of Trade, and despite the expansion of these schemes the three unions still covered well over a third of the insured workforce in 1900. The two larger unions, the ASE and the Carpenters and Joiners' Union, represented trades which were found in a variety of industries, and had branches in most towns and cities. While the conversion of the absolute level of unemployment in these unions into a representative rate for all sectors of a local or regional economy is highly problematic, it is not unreasonable to assume that changes in the union rate give some indication of the performance of the wider economy.

Since the inter-war depression, unemployment and economic hardship have been almost synonymous, particularly when regional and local economies are under consideration: hard times are periods of high unemployment and deprived communities are those with above average joblessness. Recognising the complexity of the late-nineteenth century economy, one of the aims of the project was to set the reconstructed disaggregated unemployment series in the context of other indicators of economic distress. Those in unemployment insurance schemes formed a very specific and, in some senses, powerful and privileged minority within the workforce, and unemployment was only one possible labour market response to recession. These alternative or complementary responses are every bit as difficult to reconstruct as pre-1914 local unemployment rates, but two series in the database do give some impression of the geography and history of wage rate changes and short-time working, albeit within a limited number of occupations, and, once again, for the best organised sections of the workforce. Statistical series in the database for pauperage and personal debt provide information about the wider dimensions of economic distress. Poor Law statistics are notoriously difficult to interpret as economic indicators; geographic disparities in pauperage rates reflect differences in the politics and administration of the Poor Law as much as differences in local material conditions. However, some have argued that useful economic information can be teased out from these statistics[7] and their juxtaposition with other statistics within the database provides an opportunity

Figure E.1 **Contents of QMW Labour Markets Database**

Character of material	Source	Years covered	Type and approximate number of geographic units
Membership and numbers on unemployment, sickness and superannuation benefits, Amalgamated Society of Engineers	ASE Monthly Reports	Bi-annual (January and July), 1851–1913	Union branches in Great Britain and Ireland (94 in 1851 to 610 in 1911)
Membership and numbers on unemployment, sickness and superannuation benefits, Amalgamated Society of Capenters and Joiners	ASC&J Monthly Reports	Bi-annual, 1863–1912	Union branches in Great Britain and Ireland (47 in 1863 to 770 in 1912)
Membership and numbers on unemployment and other benefits, United Society of Boilermakers and Ironship Builders	Boilermakers Annual and Monthly Reports	Quarterly, 1873–1914	Union branches in Great Britain and Ireland (135 in 1873 to 326 in 1914)
Numbers of Poor Law relief recipients, by category	Poor Law returns in Parliamentary Papers	Bi-annual, 1858–1913	Union counties in England and Wales (55)
Numbers of Poor Law relief recipients, by category	Poor Law returns in Parliamentary Papers	Annual, 1896–1913	Poor Law unions in England & Wales (630)
Small debt plaints in County Courts	County court returns in Parliamentary Papers	Annual, 1849–1858 1866–1913	Individual County Courts in England and Wales (430)
Number of marriages (includes figures for marriages in established and non-established churches)	Annual reports of the Registrar General	Annual, 1841–1870	Registration districts in England and Wales (627)

Average days and hours worked in British coalfields	*Labour Gazette*	Monthly, 1900–1913	British coalfields (17)
Wages Statistics for 26 trades (usually official union rates)	Board of Trade, Labour Department report (1907)	Annual, various starting dates from 1845; all series end in 1906	Between 22 and 50 towns
Occupational data from Census for male and female employment: 45 to 50 occupational categories	Census occupational tables	1901, 1911	All urban areas with over 5,000 in employment in England & Wales (approximately 450)
Occupational data from Census for male, female and total employment: 27 occupational categories	Lee, C.H., *British Regional Employment Statistics* (1979)	All census years, 1841–1931	Counties and sub-regions in Scotland and Wales (52)
All strikes in England and Wales, with location, industry, cause, outcome, and method of settlement [This data results from a separate project funded by the Nuffield Foundation]	Ministry of Labour strike registers, PRO LAB 34	1903, 1908, 1913, 1918, 1923, 1928, 1933, 1938	Data concerns individual disputes

for further analysis. The database also contains details of the number of small debt plaints submitted to County Courts in England and Wales. These statistics are not as well known as those for unemployment or for the Poor Law, but represent a considerable resource for the economic historian, albeit one which requires careful analysis and interpretation; the number of plaints made exceeded one million in several years, and certainly directly affected a far greater proportion of the population than the Poor Law. The database also contains information from the Annual Reports of the Registrar General about marriage rates in mid-Victorian England and Wales, as the postponement of marriage was another response to economic hardship. A final set of tables in the database contains occupational data drawn from the reports of the Census. The main run of occupational data draws upon Lee's county-level analysis of Census statistics which gives the benefit of a high degree of consistency of both occupational categories and areal units over time.[8] There are also more detailed occupational statistics from the 1901 and 1911 Censuses.

The database started its existence on a MicroVAX minicomputer in the Geography department at QMW, but has been moved to the more powerful ICL DRS 6000 machine run by the College's central computing service. This machine, which runs the UNIX SVR4 operating system, is easily accessible via JANET. The QMW Labour Markets Database uses an SQL-compatible relational database management system called INGRES. Input of the data takes place through an entry system programmed in INGRES' own fourth generation language. So that the data could be used by other researchers, and to make the database as accessible as possible, the tables of the database were designed to mirror as accurately as possible the physical documentary sources. Variable names were chosen which were a literal or obvious transcription of headings on the documents. It is hoped that anyone reasonably familiar with the physical data source would not need a codebook to work with these tables. These source tables or base tables can be thought of as a documentary level to the database. One of the main database management tasks is to convert these base tables so that they can be used for comparative analysis. It is possible to identify two higher levels of tables associated with the database, which can be called a comparative historical level, and a geographically aggregated level.

The comparative historical level consists of tables constructed from the base tables which allow comparisons over time and space. For example, the trade union records used to calculate unemployment rates do not always have figures corresponding directly to the number of members out of work or the total number eligible for unemployment payments. Using the union rule-books, it is possible to convert the figures for different sorts of benefit payments and for different categories of membership to produce a standard measure of unemployment within a particular union. Poor Law records provide another example, where the original categories which are not consistent over time have been boiled down to a set of consistent categories, such as 'all able-bodied men on indoor relief'. Another level to the database consists of tables which are standardised both over time, and aggregated geographically. One of the cornerstones of the QMW database is a large gazetteer in the form of a look-up table. This facilitates aggregation of information at a range of geographic scales including standard regions, counties and local labour markets.

Using a relational database management system like INGRES, it should be possible to maintain the tables in the higher, analytical levels of the database as 'views'. This means that all information which is constructed from the base tables is stored as the result of a calculation (rather like a cell in a spreadsheet which is defined as a calculation on data in another cell).[9] This solves problems of data concurrency as information is not duplicated in the database, and any alteration to the base tables is reflected in the calculated and aggregated views. Unfortunately, this database management strategy has proved to be unfeasible as any calculations involving these views were unacceptably slow, even when the database was transferred to a faster machine. Hence independent tables were created to correspond to the levels of the database described above; these tables exist separately on the computer's storage disks and do not change dependently if the base tables are altered. The relationship between the tables are maintained by a suite of SQL aggregation programs, which have to be run by the administrator of the database whenever changes are made to the base tables.

It has always been one of the goals of the project that the database should be as accessible as possible. To some extent this has been achieved by using an SQL compatible database management system. Anyone with a working knowledge of SQL should be able to interrogate the database and export data from it, although, of course, only those working on the project are able to alter or destroy the tables. However, despite SQL's promotion as a standard for access to databases it is not well-suited to inexperienced users. The QMW Labour Markets Database project has attempted to produce a user-friendly graphical interface, to allow those without knowledge of SQL to extract information from the database. This front-end to the database uses HyperCard, a hypermedia programming environment on the Apple Macintosh, to send SQL queries to the database via a remote link. Rather than interrogating the database using commands, this system allows the user to ask for information by selecting objects or items from lists on menus on the computer screen. Most of the information is presented in the form of maps; a screen from the database system is shown in Figure E.2.[10] There have been some problems in re-establishing the link between the database and the HyperCard system since the database was moved on to its new machine, but a cut-down non-networked version of the system has now been available to researchers by the authors.

The first major publication drawing on the database is an overview of the different dimensions of economic distress in the late Victorian economy.[11] Another paper is in preparation on the relationship between the timing of marriage and the geography of economic distress in the mid-Victorian

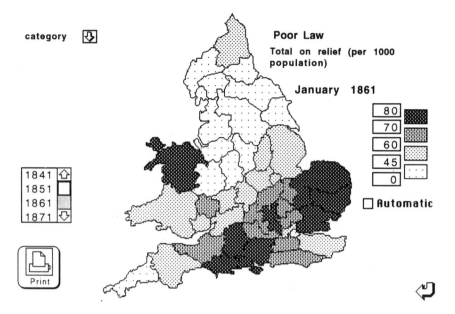

Figure E.2 *A screen from the Labour Markets Database*

period, and a detailed analysis of the relationship between local wage rates and unemployment is planned. The database has also been used to provide background information for a forthcoming study of strikes and industrial conflict;[12] the database includes transcriptions of government strike records for the early part of the twentieth century, as part of a project funded by the Nuffield Trust. Immediate plans for the technical development of the database are centred on the HyperCard information system and its link to the host mainframe computer at QMW. Although the HyperCard system is able to produce a large number of good quality statistical maps quickly and easily, it is not a full Geographic Information System (GIS). When compared with the way that GISs like ARC-INFO handle spatial data, the use of a look-up gazetteer table seems rather simplistic, and medium-term plans for the database involve its implementation within a true GIS environment.

■ *Chapter 6* ■

Information Retrieval

The careful thought needed to design and implement a fully functional database should be considered as an investment which will pay handsome dividends at later stages in the research process. Querying also demands attention to detail in order to ensure that the correct information is retrieved. Some suggested guidelines for interrogating a database or textbase are set out in Figure 6.1.

From the standpoint of the user community, a major factor determining the value of a database is the ease and efficiency with which it can be searched, sorted, and updated. In all good modern DBMSs, selection functions work on the basis of the values which records contain, not their location or other physical characteristics. There are a variety of ways of retrieving and organising information. The simplest method is *browsing* records sequentially. This can be useful when the exact value being searched for is not known, and is also helpful for proof-reading. Once located, a record can be changed, copied, removed or printed. However, the features available whilst browsing are quite limited; searching and sorting, for example, are not possible. For most purposes, there is a choice between using *Query-by-Example* or a *query language*. These are considered in turn in the following sections. We then examine the process of creating and querying a textbase using ORACLE's SQL*TextRetrieval text management module, and conclude the chapter with a description of the use of report generators.

■ 6.1 Query-by-Example

Query-by-Example, or QBE, was initially developed by IBM Research as an alternative to query languages.[1] It provides a quick and straightforward way to retrieve information that does not have to meet too many conditions. It has been implemented in many commercial packages, most notably Borland's Paradox DBMS and, more recently, Microsoft Access. QBE allows the user to enter a set of search conditions through a *query form*. The fields to be searched are displayed on the screen as columns in the query form, and the desired retrieval criteria are typed into the relevant columns.

General

- Employ different angles or perspectives.
- Consider a search as an experimental, heuristic activity, which may well lead to further refinement or modification.
- Before searching, consider how the search may be progressively broadened or narrowed.
- Learn as much as possible about the searching features of the software so as to take maximum advantage from them.
- Learn as much as possible about the data set and the structure of the database in order to identify suspicious results, and be especially suspicious about null returns.

Formulation of Concepts

- Avoid broad or fuzzy concepts if possible.
- Start with the most important concept(s) and then broaden.
- Do not attempt a 'catch-all' approach or too narrow a strategy; match the search to the particular need.
- Use Venn diagrams to help visualise the task.

Language: Describing Search Criteria

- Browse through database or index to identify search terms.
- Make descriptors as specific as possible.
- Use truncation, reverse truncation and wildcards to find word variants.
- When using free text searching, use acronyms and abbreviations as well as full names.

Modifying a Search

- Widening (increasing recall)
  Use OR rather than AND in search criteria
  Add additional synonyms and related terms
  Use truncations, reverse truncations and wildcards
- Narrowing (increasing precision)
  Add additional concepts and use AND to link concepts

Cost Effectiveness

- View a sample or subset before initiating a full search.
- View on the screen before commencing a full printout.
- For general topics, consider whether browsing would be more effective than using specific search criteria.

Figure 6.1 *Guidelines for interrogating a database or textbase*

Source: Based upon S.P. Harter and A.R. Peters, 'Heuristics for Online Information Retrieval: A Typology and Preliminary Listing', *Online Review*, Vol. 9, No. 5 (1985), pp. 407–22.

The technique is demonstrated in Figures 6.2–6.8. The examples are drawn from a greatly simplified version of a database of British Members of Parliament in the early twentieth century, running under Access. It was originally created to investigate the activities of MPs active in the Industrial Group (a backbench pressure group active between 1918 and 1924), and is therefore called **Indgroup**. Figure 6.2 shows the window which greets the user when the database is loaded. Various tables have been created to hold data about the MPs' personal and public lives. Figure 6.3 shows the result of clicking on a form called **Seat** which displays part of the table of the same name. It lists MPs' names and parties, and the elections and constituencies which they contested.

To query the table, the user simply selects QUERY and then NEW in the database window. A blank query form appears on the screen, and the user is prompted to select the table to be queried. This appears in the upper part of the form. The fields required can then be dragged to the lower half, which defines the structure of the query. In the example shown in Figure 6.4, we have selected from the **Seat** table the MP's name and party, the constituency, the date of the election, and whether or not he/she was successful. Additionally, we have specified that the output should be sorted alphabetically by name and that all the fields selected will be displayed. Selection criteria are also inserted here. Suppose that we want to identify those who successfully stood for election in 1918. 1918 is inserted in the *Date_Stood* field, and "YES" in the *Elected* field. Inverted commas are used when specifying criteria for text or logical fields, but not for numeric or date fields. The resulting specification, which Access calls a *design view,* is then saved for future use under the name **Elected in 1918**. Switching from the design view to the *datasheet view* (or opening the query on a subsequent occasion) runs the query. All the records in the database which meet the specified search criteria are output to what Access calls a *dynaset* (called an *answer table* in some implementations of QBE). The output may be seen in Figure 6.5.

The query in Figure 6.4 might have been written as =1918. If a relational operator is not entered, equality is assumed. Other relational operators like <, > , <=, and >= may also be used in QBE. More complex querying is possible too. For example, entering BETWEEN 1900 AND 1918 will retrieve all those who were parliamentary candidates between 1900 and 1918 inclusive. Using LIKE with the asterisk wildcard is an invaluable technique for retrieving similar but not identical records. LIKE 'BIRMINGHAM*' will retrieve all Birmingham constituencies, including 'BIRMINGHAM LADYWOOD' and 'BIRMINGHAM MOSELEY'.

Boolean operators provide additional flexibility. The example in Figure 6.4 uses the AND operator; for a record to be retrieved, a person must

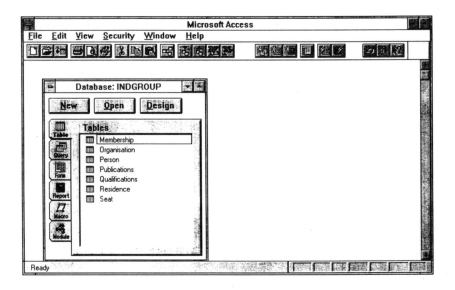

Figure 6.2 *Microsoft Access: the* Indgroup *database window*

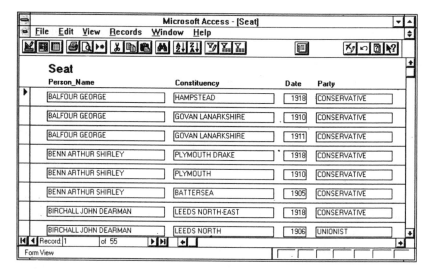

Figure 6.3 *Microsoft Access: the* Seat *form*

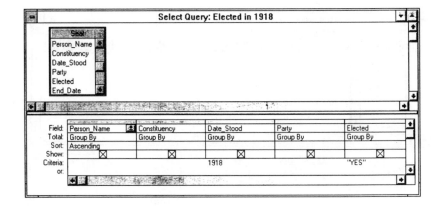

Figure 6.4   *Microsoft Access: single table query – design view*

Person_Name	Constituency	Date_Stood	Party	Elected
BALFOUR GEORGE	HAMPSTEAD	1918	CONSERVATIVE	YES
BENN ARTHUR SHIRLEY	PLYMOUTH DRAKE	1918	CONSERVATIVE	YES
BIRCHALL JOHN DEARMAN	LEEDS NORTH-EAST	1918	CONSERVATIVE	YES
BOWYER GEORGE	BUCKINGHAM	1918	CONSERVATIVE	YES
BRUTON JAMES	GLOUCESTER	1918	CONSERVATIVE	YES
CHAMBERLAIN NEVILLE	BIRMINGHAM LADYWOOD	1918	CONSERVATIVE	YES
CLOUGH ROBERT	KEIGHLEY	1918	DEMOCRATIC UNIONIST	YES
GRATTON DOYLE NICHOLAS	NEWCASTLE-UPON-TYNE NORTH	1918	CONSERVATIVE	YES
HICKS WILLIAM JOYNSON	MIDDLESEX (TWICKENHAM)	1918	CONSERVATIVE	YES
LLOYD-GREAME PHILIP	HENDON	1918	CONSERVATIVE	YES
MANVILLE EDWARD	COVENTRY	1918	CONSERVATIVE	YES
ORMSBY-GORE WILLIAM GEORGE AR	STAFFORD	1918	CONSERVATIVE UNIONIST	YES
RICHARDSON ALEXANDER	GRAVESEND	1918	CONSERVATIVE	YES
ROGERS HALLEWELL	BIRMINGHAM MOSELEY	1918	CONSERVATIVE	YES
SEDDON JAMES ANDREW	HANLEY	1918	LABOUR COALITION	YES
WILLEY FRANCIS VERNON	BRADFORD SOUTH	1918	CONSERVATIVE	YES
WISE FREDERIC	ILFORD	1918	CONSERVATIVE	YES

Figure 6.5   *Microsoft Access: single table query – datasheet view*

both have stood for election in 1918 and been elected. Additionally, OR conditions can be set by placing the criteria on separate lines rather than on the same line. Thus in Figure 6.6, the retrieval criteria are met where the party is either `'CONSERVATIVE'` or `'UNIONIST'`, and the person was elected.

Multitable queries are almost as straightforward. Early implementations of QBE, such as Paradox for DOS, were not particularly intuitive when it came to linking more than one table. Access is a great improvement. The technique is demonstrated in Figures 6.7 and 6.8. In this example, we want to identify the constituency and year of birth of MPs who were members of the Industrial Group. This requires a three-table join. Information about constituencies is held in the **Seat** table; membership of various organisations is held in the **Member-**

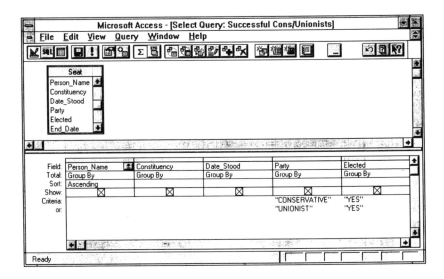

Figure 6.6   *Microsoft Access: using OR in querying*

ship table; and the year of birth is in the **Person** table. As before, a query form is created by selecting QUERY and then NEW from the database window. The three tables are selected and displayed in the upper half of the design view. As well as displaying the tables, Access shows the fields which are used to link them and the relationships which exist. As can be seen, there are one-to-many relationships between the **Person** table and **Membership**, and between **Person** and **Seat**: one person can be a member of many organisations and can stand for many constituencies at many elections. The rest of the procedure is the same as for querying a single table. A refinement is that the information displayed in the lower half of the window includes the table from which each field is drawn; this is a useful reminder when, as is often the case, there are identically named fields in different tables. Finally, the query is saved for future use as **Industrial Group Members**. The output which results when it is run is shown in Figure 6.8.

These simple examples do not demonstrate all of QBE's many features, but they do serve to indicate the essentials of the approach.[2] Transparency and ease of use are the essence of QBE. The limitation is that it is difficult to operationalise complex algorithms of the type common in advanced historical research. Admittedly, complex queries can sometimes be expressed as a series of simple queries. Since the result of the first query is output to a separate table, the answer table can be used as the object of the second query, and so on. One advantage of this approach is that the results of each step can be displayed, and checked to ensure that the expected results have been obtained. However,

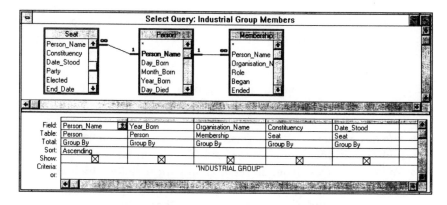

Figure 6.7 *Microsoft Access: query form for the multitable query*

Select Query: Industrial Group Members					
Person_Name	**Year_Born**	**Organisation_Name**	**Constituency**	**Date_Stood**	
BALFOUR GEORGE	1872	INDUSTRIAL GROUP	GOVAN LANARKSHIRE	1910	
BALFOUR GEORGE	1872	INDUSTRIAL GROUP	GOVAN LANARKSHIRE	1911	
BALFOUR GEORGE	1872	INDUSTRIAL GROUP	HAMPSTEAD	1918	
BENN ARTHUR SHIRLEY	1863	INDUSTRIAL GROUP	BATTERSEA	1905	
BENN ARTHUR SHIRLEY	1863	INDUSTRIAL GROUP	PLYMOUTH	1910	
BENN ARTHUR SHIRLEY	1863	INDUSTRIAL GROUP	PLYMOUTH DRAKE	1918	
BIRCHALL JOHN DEARMAN	1875	INDUSTRIAL GROUP	LEEDS NORTH	1906	
BIRCHALL JOHN DEARMAN	1875	INDUSTRIAL GROUP	LEEDS NORTH	1910	
BIRCHALL JOHN DEARMAN	1875	INDUSTRIAL GROUP	LEEDS NORTH-EAST	1918	
BOWYER GEORGE	1886	INDUSTRIAL GROUP	BUCKINGHAM	1918	
BRUTON JAMES	1848	INDUSTRIAL GROUP	GLOUCESTER	1918	
BURN CHARLES R	1859	INDUSTRIAL GROUP	TORQUAY	1910	
CHAMBERLAIN NEVILLE	1869	INDUSTRIAL GROUP	BIRMINGHAM LADYWOOD	1918	
CLOUGH ROBERT	1873	INDUSTRIAL GROUP	KEIGHLEY	1918	
COWAN HENRY	1862	INDUSTRIAL GROUP	ABERDEENSHIRE NORTH	1910	
COWAN HENRY	1862	INDUSTRIAL GROUP	GUILDFORD	1906	
COWAN HENRY	1862	INDUSTRIAL GROUP	ISLINGTON NORTH	1923	
DAWSON PHILIP	1866	INDUSTRIAL GROUP	LEWISHAM WEST	1921	
Record: 1	of 55				

Figure 6.8 *Microsoft Access: result of the multitable query*

complex querying is usually best handled by means of a query language. A variety of query languages have been developed over the years by DBMS vendors. Foremost amongst them is SQL.

■ 6.2 SQL (Structured Query Language)

SQL has emerged as the industry standard for querying RDBMSs. Like other modern, high-level query languages, SQL is non-procedural; the user specifies what is to be done, rather than telling the system how to do it, and the system provides automatic navigation to the relevant data. It is a powerful but easy-to-learn language, with English-like commands and syntax, which allows the user to formulate complex queries. The examples given are based on the simplified maritime history database implemented using ORACLE and described in sections 5.3 and 5.4 above. In this section, we are concerned with SQL's facilities for *data manipulation*.

The most important and most frequently-used SQL command is SELECT. This is used when querying data. Using SELECT enables us to carry out three essential database operations:

- *Selection* retrieves all the records from a table that meet a specified condition, such as *Regd_Port=*'Bristol'.
- *Projection* extracts from all records only those fields which are specified in the query. For example, a query specifying just the *Ship_Name* and *Burden* fields of the **Ship** table does not retrieve or display the other fields in that table.
- *Joining* involves combining two or more tables that contain related data and have a common field or fields. The result of the query may contain any of the fields present in the joined tables, but only a single copy of the common field(s).

The SELECT command consists of up to six clauses which must always occur in the sequence given below:

```
SELECT
FROM
WHERE
GROUP  BY
HAVING
ORDER  BY
```

□ *SELECT and* FROM

Whilst the other four clauses are optional, SELECT and FROM are a mandatory part of every query. The SELECT clause describes which columns (fields) should be retrieved. The fieldnames are listed, separated by commas. The order in which they are given determines how they are listed in the result table; the first field appears in the left-hand column, and so on. The FROM clause appears immediately after the SELECT clause. It defines the table (or tables) that contain the columns specified in the SELECT statement. As in the case of data definition, each query is terminated by a semi-colon.

```
SELECT  Ship_No,  Ship_Name
FROM  Ship;
```

If, as often happens in a multitable database, there is a field with the same name in more than one table, the table name should be given just before the fieldname, and separated by a dot:

```
SELECT  Ship.Ship_No,   Ship.Ship_Name
FROM  Ship;
```

If all fields are to be retrieved, SELECT * can be used rather than laboriously typing in the name of each field. In this case, the sequence in which the field columns are displayed will depend upon the order in which they were created. Alternatively, SELECT DISTINCT <fieldname> (SELECT DISTINCTROW <fieldname> in some dialects of SQL) can be used; in this case, SQL will retrieve only those rows which are not duplicates.

☐ *The WHERE clause and types of search conditions*

Using just the SELECT and FROM clauses, we can retrieve all the data in a table, or all the data in specified fields. However, in most cases we will want to refine our query to retrieve only those records (rows) which meet particular search conditions. The WHERE clause is added immediately after the FROM clause, and is used to select those records which are of interest to us. The values held in each record are tested, and only those which meet the criteria following the WHERE clause are displayed or printed.

```
SELECT  *
FROM  Ship
WHERE  Regd_Port='Bristol';
```

It should be noted that querying is case-specific; querying on 'Bristol' will not retrieve any records containing the text string 'BRISTOL'.

More complex SQL queries can be built by having multiple search conditions. Search conditions can be combined together in a single WHERE clause using the logical operators AND, OR, NOT. SQL provides five different types of search conditions: *comparison tests, range tests, set membership tests, pattern matching tests* and *null value tests.*

Comparison tests use the usual relational operators: =, <, >, <=, >=, and != (not equal to).[3] In addition to comparing a field to a constant value, it is possible to compare the value of one field against another, provided that both fields are of the same type (and in some systems, within the same file).

```
SELECT  *
FROM  Ship
WHERE  Regd_Port='Bristol'
   AND  Regd_Date>=1854;
```

It is also possible to specify range criteria – from 100 to 500 inclusive, between two specified dates, and so on. One way of range testing is to use AND:

```
SELECT  *
FROM  Ship
WHERE  Regd_Date>=1854
   AND  Regd_Date<=1860;
```

However, this can quickly become tedious to type in, especially if several sets of criteria are needed. BETWEEN can be used to simplify range comparisons. We could rewrite the query as:

```
SELECT  *
FROM  Ship
WHERE  Regd_Date BETWEEN  1854  AND  1860;
```

Alternatively, the BETWEEN command can be negated by the NOT operator:

```
SELECT  *
FROM  Ship
WHERE  Regd_Date NOT  BETWEEN  1854  AND  1860;
```

Set membership tests are used when we wish to retrieve records where a particular field contains certain specified values. This could be done using the WHERE clause together with the OR operator:

```
SELECT  *
FROM  Ship
WHERE  Regd_Port='Bristol'
   OR  Regd_Port='Cardiff'
   OR  Regd_Port='Newport';
```

Again, this would quickly become tedious if we were looking for more than a very few values. A better alternative is to use the IN operator:

```
SELECT  *
```

```
FROM Ship
WHERE Regd_Port IN ('Bristol', 'Cardiff', 'Newport');
```

Like BETWEEN, the IN operator can be negated by NOT:

```
SELECT *
FROM Ship
WHERE Regd—Port NOT IN ('Bristol', 'Cardiff',
 'Newport');
```

Pattern matching is a very common type of querying. It is often desirable to retrieve records which fit a particular pattern. For pattern matching, SQL uses an underscore _ to match any single character, and the percent sign % to match any number of characters (including zero). These are equivalent to the ? and * wildcards in MS-DOS and are used in conjunction with LIKE or NOT LIKE. For example, they may be used to group words that commence in the same way but are not exactly identical:

```
SELECT *
FROM Ship
WHERE Regd_Port LIKE 'Bri%';
```

will retrieve 'Bristol', 'Brighton', etc.

This is an example of *truncation*. Additionally, pattern matching can be used in *reverse truncation* to match words with different prefixes – thus '%port' would retrieve 'Newport', 'Bridport', etc. It is also possible to use pattern matching for *midstring searching* to find words or phrases containing a particular string of characters, but with varying prefixes and suffixes. An example of this would be '%ing%', which would retrieve 'Brightlingsea', 'Bridlington', 'Hastings', and 'Lymington'. And since the % wildcard can mean zero characters, it would also match 'Worthing'.

Finally, SQL provides a facility for null testing. Nulls are quite distinct from zeroes or spaces, and are used to show when data are not known or not applicable. As will be seen, this ability to define and identify nulls is important when producing statistical summaries. To select records where a specified field contains a null value, the IS NULL clause is used:

```
SELECT *
FROM Ship
WHERE Regd_Date IS NULL;
```

□ *Statistical functions and the* GROUP BY *clause*

Arithmetic expressions can be included in SQL queries to perform calculations on numerical data. The usual arithmetic operators + – * / are used. For example:

```
SELECT Ship_No+1000
From Ship;
```

would add 1,000 to the value stored in the *Ship_No* field of each record. Additionally, arithmetic expressions can be used to compare the contents of one field with another. If we had a *Date_Scrapped* field in the **Ship** table, we could use the following query to determine the working life of each ship in the database:

```
SELECT Ship_Name,Date_Scrapped-Date_Regd
FROM Ship;
```

Also available are the functions GREATEST, LEAST, ROUND and TRUNC:

```
SELECT Ship_Name,  GREATEST(Burden)
FROM Ship;
```

will display the name and tonnage of the largest ship in the database. Similarly:

```
SELECT Ship_Name,  LEAST(Regd_Date)
FROM Ship
WHERE Regd_Port='Bristol';
```

retrieves and displays the name and date of registration of the oldest Bristol vessel in the database. ROUND and TRUNC are useful where numeric fields contain decimal places. ROUND (*Field_Name*,1) rounds the value in the given field to one decimal point, whilst TRUNC (*Field_Name,*1) simply truncates any digits after the first decimal point.

The arithmetic expressions and functions described above all work on individual records. However, the researcher often needs to obtain summary data rather than voluminous printouts of every record that meets the specified search criteria, and SQL incorporates a number of statistical functions which work on columns of data. These column functions are SUM, AVG, MIN, MAX, STDDEV, VARIANCE and COUNT. FROM and WHERE can be employed in the usual way in such queries to provide a good deal of flexibility.

```
SELECT  SUM(Burden),  AVG(Burden)
FROM  Ship;
```

calculates and displays the total tonnage and the average size of all the ships in the database.

```
SELECT  MAX(Burden),  MIN(Burden),  MAX(Burden)-
   MIN(Burden)
FROM  Ship
WHERE  Regd_Port='Bristol';
```

displays the maximum tonnage, the minimum tonnage, and the difference between them, of ships registered in the port of Bristol.

The COUNT function is a special type of statistical function; unlike the others, its use is not confined to numeric fields. It is often combined with DISTINCT to ensure that identical entries are only counted once. For example, if we wanted to know how many ports of registration are listed in the database, we would need to use the query:

```
SELECT  COUNT  (DISTINCT  Regd_Port)
FROM  Ship;
```

If we omitted DISTINCT, COUNT would return a wrong answer, because many ships were registered in the same port.

In all of these column functions, provision is made to handle null entries. As noted earlier, SQL uses a special value NULL to show when data are not known or not applicable. Obviously, such entries should not be included when averaging, summing, etc. To ensure that spurious results are not returned, all column functions ignore any records with NULL values in the column being summarised.

Column functions will return summary numbers – a single result for all the records selected by the query. However, it is often necessary to produce a more detailed summary, giving totals, averages, maxima and minima, standard deviations etc. for specific groups of records. This is done using the GROUP BY clause. It comes after the WHERE clause, or after FROM if WHERE is not present.

```
SELECT  Regd_Port,  COUNT(*)
FROM  Ship
GROUP  BY  Regd_Port;
```

would calculate and display the number of records (i.e. the number of different ships) registered in each port, as follows:

Regd_Port	COUNT(*)
------------	--------
Bridgwater	35
Bristol	422
Burnham	12
etc.	

As usual, the asterisk in COUNT(*) means 'all fields'.

Whilst SQL's statistical functions are sufficient for many purposes, it does not provide the advanced statistical functions needed for econometric or cliometric analysis. Consequently, it is often necessary to export data to a specialist statistical program like SPSS or SAS.

☐ *The HAVING clause*

Sometimes, after using the GROUP BY clause, we may not wish to display all the groups created. For instance, we may wish to ignore any groups which only contain a few records. The HAVING clause may be used to remove groups of data in which we are not interested. Its function is like that of the WHERE clause, but whilst WHERE operates on rows of data (records), the HAVING clause works on groups of data. It compares a specified property of the group against a constant value. To continue the previous example:

```
SELECT  Regd_Port,  COUNT(*)
FROM  Ship
GROUP  BY  Regd_Port;
HAVING  COUNT(*)>=10;
```

This will ignore minor ports represented by less than ten vessels in the database.

☐ *The ORDER BY clause*

Unless the database is very small, the output generated by a query can easily become unmanageable. Moreover, records will be displayed more or less at random, which is rarely of much use to the researcher. One way of making output more intelligible is to use the ORDER BY clause, which allows output to be displayed or printed in the order selected. It is always the last clause in a SELECT command. If many rows have identical values for the selected field, it will be necessary to select a secondary, and perhaps a tertiary, sort field. Their names can be listed after ORDER BY, separated by commas and with the primary sort field coming first. In the following example, the records will be sorted alphabetically by port, and then according to their size:

```
SELECT  *
FROM  Ship
ORDER  BY  Regd_Port,  Burden;
```

By default, the data are sorted in ascending order (low numbers first, 'A' before 'B', upper case before lower case, earlier dates before more recent ones, etc.). To display the data in descending rather than ascending order, the word DESC can be used in the ORDER BY statement:

```
SELECT  *
FROM  Ship
ORDER  BY  Regd_Port,  Burden  DESC;
```

will ensure that the largest vessels listed come first.[4] However, if a field selected for the ordering process contains nulls, these would always be displayed first, regardless of whether the order selected is ascending or descending.

☐ *Joining tables*

Until now, the queries which have been discussed have all been based on a single table. However, the most powerful feature of RDBMSs is the ability to join multiple tables and retrieve the combined information as a single list. In order to join two tables, there must be at least one key field in the first table that has common data values with a key field in the second table. Using SQL to retrieve data from more than one table is a relatively simple task. First, each table is named in the FROM clause, separated by a comma. Secondly, the WHERE clause is used to make the connection and compare fields in the different tables. For many purposes joining a pair of tables will suffice; however, joins can be made just as easily on three or more tables. Virtually any fields can be joined, provided that they are of the same type and length.

To demonstrate the use of joins, we can query the tables **Ship** and **Voyage** from the maritime history database. To begin, we recall their structures using the DESCRIBE command:

```
DESCRIBE  Ship;
Name                    Null?              Type
-----------             ----------         ----------
Ship_No                 NOT  NULL          NUMBER(6)
Ship_Name               NOT  NULL          CHAR(18)
Regd_Date                                  NUMBER(4)
Regd_Port                                  CHAR(15)
Burden                                     NUMBER(5)


DESCRIBE  Voyage;
Name                    Null?              Type
----------------        ----------         ----------
Ship_No                 NOT  NULL          NUMBER(6)
Voyage_Start            NOT  NULL          DATE
Voyage_End                                 DATE
Depart_Port                                CHAR(15)
Destin_Port                                CHAR(15)
```

Let us assume that we want to retrieve data about ships registered in Bristol which sailed for the port of New York. A join will have to be used because this information is not available from a single table. Ports of registration are listed in the *Regd_Port* field of the **Ship** table, whilst the destination of each voyage is held in the *Destin_Port* field of the **Voyage** table.

```
SELECT  *
FROM Ship,  Voyage
WHERE  Destin_Port  =  'New York'
   AND  Regd_Port  =  'Bristol'
   AND  Ship.Ship_No  =  Voyage.Ship_No;
```

The first and second lines of the WHERE clause specify the criteria for selection. The third line uses the *Ship_No* field to make the join; this is the key field which uniquely identifies each ship. Since fields in the different tables have the same name then the table names must also be specified in the WHERE clause, as shown. It should be noted that the use of the asterisk after SELECT will retrieve all the fields contained in the **Ship** and **Voyage** tables, which may result in the retrieval of a very large amount of data. Consequently we would normally specify only the required fields when making multitable joins.

The example given above is an *equi-join*; that is to say, the join condition includes the equals sign. It is also possible to make joins which do not include the equals sign. These are called *non-equi-joins* or *theta-joins*, and can use any of the following operators: != (not equal), <, >, <=, >=, BETWEEN and LIKE. The following example retrieves data about voyages which did not commence in a ship's registered port. It is a legal query because *Regd_Port* and *Depart_Port* are the same type and length of field.

```
SELECT  *
FROM Ship, Voyage
WHERE Ship.Ship_No = Voyage.Ship_No
    AND Ship.Regd_Port != Voyage.Depart_Port;
```

☐ *Stored queries*

Especially when two or more tables are to be joined, typing in queries can become very time-consuming. Fortunately, queries can easily be saved to a disk file for future use. *Stored queries* provide a convenient way of entering complex queries without typing them in anew each time they are used. When the filename is specified, the database management system looks up the query stored in the file, and executes it. The command SAVE <filename> will save the query to disk with the specified name. If no suffix is given, the default suffix. SQL will be used.

```
SAVE Test1
```

The command GET <filename> will return and display the query contained in the GET statement. However, it will not immediately run the query. To run it, we then need to enter r (which will redisplay the query and run it) or / (which will run it without displaying the query).

```
GET Test1
/
```

As a quicker alternative to using the GET command, we could use @ <filename>, which will recall and run the query without displaying it.

```
@ Test1
```

Stored queries can also be used to speed up the processing of a series of similar but not identical queries. Since the query file is a simple ASCII text file, it can easily be modified with a wordprocessor or screen editor.

□ *Views*

An extension of the stored query is the concept of the *view*. SQL allows the creation of alternative views, or ways of looking at the data. Put simply, a view is a window which restricts the viewer's attention to a selected portion of the underlying data. More formally, a view 'can be considered as a set of instructions to the RDBMS how to extract the required information from the defined tables which constitute the source of the data'.[5] Thus views are *virtual tables* – collections of data which have no independent existence, but which are derived from one or more real tables. If the underlying tables are erased, the view is destroyed as well. In general, though they contain no data of their own, views can be operated on and modified just as though they were real tables.

Views have a number of advantages and uses: most importantly, they simplify data access. Views can be used as filters in order to look at a subset of the data. Alternatively, they may be used to join two or more tables which will frequently be linked. Even if a view is in fact a multitable query, it looks like a single table to the user and can be manipulated as normal. This is of particular benefit if some of the database users are inexperienced and likely to be confused if required to join two or more tables. It must be repeated, however, that the result is a virtual table, not a real one. Each time the view is accessed, the query will be run *ab initio*. This has both advantages and drawbacks. The principal benefit is that if the base tables are updated, the next time they are accessed through the view the updated data will automatically be used. The principal drawback is that using views can be very slow; it might appear to the user that a single table is being used, but behind the scenes there may well be a very complex multitable join which is re-run each time the view is used.

Defining and using views is a straightforward task. The CREATE VIEW command is used to name the view and describe, in the form of a SQL query, what the view is to contain. The following command is used to create a view called **Destination**, which may be used to find out the destinations of ships registered in different ports. It contains the four fields *Ship_No*, *Ship_Name*, *Regd_Port*, and *Destin_Port* which are extracted from the **Ship** and **Voyage** tables.

```
CREATE  VIEW  Destination  AS  SELECT  Ship.Ship_No,
   Ship_Name,  Regd_Port,  Destin_Port
FROM  Ship,  Voyage
WHERE  Ship.Ship_No  =  Voyage.Ship_No;
```

To find out the destinations of Bristol-registered ships, we could then query the **Destination** view rather than performing a join on the **Ship** and **Voyage** tables:

```
SELECT  *
FROM  Destination
WHERE  Regd_Port  =  'Bristol';
```

☐ *Summary*

This section has summarised the powerful features which have made SQL the international standard query language for relational databases. SQL does not require the user to know where and how the data are physically stored. However, it does encourage logical precision. Even the most complex algorithms can be implemented, tested and refined, and the resulting queries saved to disk for future use. The case of record linkage algorithms and their implementation using SQL is considered in Chapter 8 below.

A good deal of effort has been put into making SQL accessible to the casual or inexperienced user. Indeed, users of some modern programs may not always be aware that they are using SQL when manipulating a database. As we have seen, Microsoft Access allows users to insert search criteria into target fields via a query window. Behind the scenes, however, Access is actually constructing an equivalent SQL statement which may subsequently be viewed or edited (Figure 6.9).[6]

There are numerous benefits which result from SQL's establishment as a *de facto* standard for database querying. First, standard languages, and therefore the applications which utilise them, are assured of a reasonably long lifetime – not an inconsequential matter given the rapid rate of technological change in the computing world. Secondly, there are the advantages of cross-platform and cross-system communication. Applications can run unchanged across a variety of hardware platforms and software environments. This facilitates multi-user and multi-site projects. Moreover, if the same language is widely supported, then users can choose the software implementation which best meets their own particular needs. The portability of applications is thus assured. A project which outgrows the micro on which it was initially developed can subsequently be run on a minicomputer or mainframe. Learning costs are kept to a minimum if users can move from one environment to another without having to learn new querying techniques.

Finally, whilst the establishment of SQL as an international standard has been closely associated with the rise to market leadership of the relational model, it is already clear that it will be extended in order to

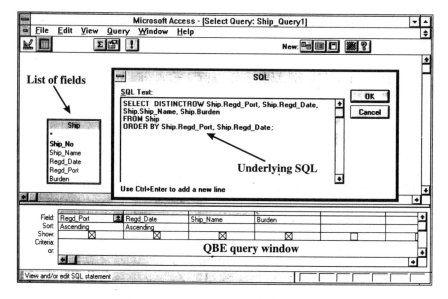

Figure 6.9   *Using SQL in Microsoft Access: the list of fieldnames in the* Ship *table, the query window and the underlying SQL text*

accommodate more recent advances in database theory. One such development is the provision of object-oriented extensions to SQL. The objective here is to facilitate the manipulation of databases which include a variety of non-indexable forms of data such as pictures, sound and animation. When dealing with rich data, the simple record structure which is one of the major advantages of relational systems becomes a disadvantage because of the difficulty of expressing the semantics of complex objects in this fashion. POSTGRES is a research object-oriented DBMS which can handle complex objects and query them using the SQL extension POSTQUEL; it is briefly described in section 7.3. In a similar way, SQL has been extended to deal with the particular problems of textual manipulation and retrieval. This important development is illustrated in the next section with reference to ORACLE's SQL*TextRetrieval module and the Register of Music in London Newspapers project outlined by Catherine Harbor in Case Study B of this book.

■ 6.3 Querying a Textbase

SQL*TextRetrieval consists of a set of tools for textbase creation, maintenance and querying.[7] The first task in creating a new textbase is to define an appropriate table structure. Both structured data and unstructured text may be held in the same table. Structured data are held in CHAR, NUMBER or DATE fields; text is handled by two field types, FTEXT and LTEXT. FTEXT is a fixed length field containing text strings (up to a maximum of 240 characters) which can be indexed as a single phrase, as word tokens or as keyword terms or phrases. There may be as many FTEXT fields per record as are needed. LTEXT is a variable length field containing free text, indexed by words, where a word is a text string surrounded by delimiters such as the space or other non-indexed characters like − or +. The only limitation on the size of the text is the amount of disk memory available. There can only be one LTEXT field per record. The table must also contain a TEXTKEY field, which stores a unique numeric key for each record.

In our example, the main text table of the Register of Music in London Newspapers was defined as follows:

```
CREATE  TABLE  Register
    (Text  LONG,
    Textnum  NUMBER(7)  NOT  NULL,
    Newscode  CHAR(4),
    Published  DATE,
    Pagenum  NUMBER(2),
    Nature  CHAR(13),
    Prose  CHAR(1),
    Vers  CHAR(1),
    Corrs  CHAR(1));
```

The resulting table, called **Register**, has a long text field *Text*, a numeric field *Textnum* to hold a unique reference number, together with a variety of fields for structured data about the provenance and character of each text.

The entries in the textbase are generally quite short, ranging from advertisements and notices to reports on musical events. Most of the entries were transcribed from microfiche copies of original newspapers. Scanning the entries was not possible due to the generally poor quality of the sources, and data entry was therefore by keyboard. It would have been possible to type directly into the system, but it was much easier to use a wordprocessor and then import files into the textbase. This is a simple process and one that is commonly used in projects of this type.

Following importation, all the entries in a textbase must be indexed. Like most commercial systems, SQL*TextRetrieval works with three main tables, which ORACLE calls the *text table*, containing the actual data, together with any related structured fields; the *word list*, which contains an indexed list, in alphabetical order, of all the useful words in the text file; and the *location list,* which points to each occurrence of an indexed word in the text file. One of the advantages of SQL*TextRetrieval is that all indexes, word lists, location lists, retrieved sets, etc. are held as standard tables, and thus are accessible through SQL. Text can be indexed in one of two modes, STOP or PASS. In STOP mode, each word in the text is compared with a *stop list* – words like 'and', 'the' or 'but' which have no significance. If found, the word is skipped. If it is not a STOP word, then it is a FREE word. If the word has not been encountered before, it is added to the word list. Every occurrence of a FREE word is also recorded in the location list. In PASS mode, words are checked against a pass list which has been created previously. Only words on the pass list are indexed. All other words are ignored. Thus the STOP mode provides full text indexing, and is suitable for investigating the textbase in a heuristic manner; the PASS mode, on the other hand, is useful for fast searching on a limited number of predetermined themes. Indexing generates a word list in alphabetical order, each word being marked as a STOP word, a PASS word, or a FREE word. For each PASS word or FREE word, the word list will contain a count of the number of occurrences in the database. The location list contains an entry for each PASS word or FREE word in the word list, giving a table of pointers to each occurrence in the database.[8]

□ *Word lists and thesauri*

The real power of the textbase lies in the range of thesaurus-based facilities available. Within SQL*TextRetrieval word lists and thesaurus links are maintained through a Text Dictionary Utility. The first of its two maintenance screens is shown in Figure 6.10.

The left-hand side of the screen displays the word list table, which can be browsed and modified as required – for example, by adding a new word or changing the type of a very common word from F (FREE) to S (STOP). The right-hand side of the screen handles synonym maintenance. Every *synonym ring* (group of synonyms) in the word list contains a unique list number. Thus, to add a new synonym ring, the user assigns a unique reference number and enters the words in the ring, each with the same list number. A *preferred* word in the ring is indicated by a marker (P). Homonyms are handled by entering the word into two (or more) different synonym rings, each with a distinct preferred word.

Synonyms may be used to standardise the spelling of words and names.

```
SQL*TextRetrieval:        Wordlist Maintenance:Synonym Maintenance
```

word	type	Frequency	ring/pref	word
coreli	F	1	2	correlli
corell's	F	1	2 P	corelli
corelles	F	1	2	corelly
corelli	F	136	2	corelli's
corelli's	F	54	2	corellis
corellis	F	9	2	corello
corello	F	1	2	corelles
corelly	F	1	2	corell's
corey	F	11	2	coreli
corfe	F	1		
corfu	F	10		
coriolanus	F	52		
cork	F	2		
corke	F	2		
corn	F	7		
cornaja	F	1		

```
Count: *11                                              <Replace>
```

Figure 6.10 *SQL*TextRetrieval: using the thesaurus*

Eighteenth-century orthography creates frequent headaches for the historian. As Harbor notes in Case Study B, the name of Handel appears in different newspaper items in many different forms. The word list can therefore be edited to include such variants as Handel, Handell, Handall, Handl, Handal, Haendel, Hendl, Hendal and Hendall, with the synonym 'Handel, Georg Friedrich' as the preferred form (Figure 6.11). Searching on the preferred form would thus retrieve all texts containing a reference to Handel whatever the spelling used.

The second maintenance screen handles other types of thesaurus links. For each word in the list, the user can build up groups of broader and narrower terms. In the example given by Harbor, 'Handel' is linked with the broader terms 'composer', 'performer' and 'person'. This is shown in Figure 6.12.

The left-hand half of the screen displays the word list, while the right-hand side is used to define relationships between words. BT means broader term, and signifies that 'word1' is a broader term than 'word2'. Thus, in the example, 'composer' is a broader term for 'Handel', and 'person' is a broader term for 'composer'. Once these links have been set up, a search for 'composer' and its narrower terms will also produce all texts containing a reference to 'Handel', as well as all the texts which contain other names which had 'composer' defined as their broader term. A search within the word list for all the

```
SQL*TextRetrieval:        Wordlist Maintenance:Synonym Maintenance

word                    type Frequency │ ring/preF word
handel                   F    100      │  1    P  Handel, Georg Friedri
handel'a                 F    1        │  1       Handel
handel's                 F    61       │  1       Handell
handell                  F    38       │  1       Handl
handell's                F    35       │  1       Handal
handels'                 F    1        │  1       Haendel
handesyde                F    1        │  1       Hendl
handle                   F    2        │  1       Handal
handled                  F    10       │  1       Handall
handmaid                 F    1        │  2       correlli
hands                    F    270      │  2    P  Corelli, Arcangelo
handsom                  F    6        │  2       corelly
handsome                 F    36       │  2       corelli's
handsomely               F    12       │  2       corellis
handsomest               F    24       │  2       corello
handsomly                F    6        │  2       corelles

Count: *11          u                                      <Replace>
```

Figure 6.11   *SQL*TextRetrieval: the synonym ring for ' Handel '*

```
SQL*TextRetrieval:  Thesaurus Maintenance

word             type  freq  │ link word 1            word 2
handel            F    100   │ BT   composer          Handel, Georg Frie
handel'a          F    1     │ BT   performer         Handel, Georg Frie
handel's          F    61    │ BT   person            composer
handell           F    38    │
handell's         F    35    │
handels'          F    1     │
handesyde         F    1     │
handle            F    2     │
handled           F    10    │
handmaid          F    1     │
hands             F    270   │
handsom           F    6     │
handsome          F    36    │
handsomely        F    12    │
handsomest        F    24    │
handsomly         F    6     │

Count: *1                                                  <Replace>
```

Figure 6.12   *SQL*TextRetrieval: other thesaurus links relating to
' Handel '*

names which have 'composer' defined as a broader term would produce a list of all the composers, each with all their permutations of spelling.

The thesaurus is vital for indexing and searching. The same word may have different meanings, and a single concept can be represented by different words or phrases, so it is often important to develop procedures for consistent naming of concepts and cross-referencing of entries. The value of a search is greatly reduced if synonyms are not picked up. There should always be a preferred form, with cross-referencing of synonyms, etc. Acronyms must point to the preferred word or phrase. Homonyms need to be separated out and qualified by using a more detailed term or phrase, or cross-referenced to an unambiguous preferred word. Creating a detailed thesaurus is a highly skilled task. It requires extensive knowledge both of the character of the data itself and of the principles of thesaurus construction.[9] It is time-consuming, and therefore costly. Nevertheless, it will readily be apparent that the value and useability of a textbase largely depends upon the care with which the thesaurus is constructed.

□ *Querying*

Once the textbase has been indexed and the thesaurus prepared, the textbase may be queried and edited. SQL*TextRetrieval uses context-based retrieval (CBR) methods for fast, interactive free-form searching and retrieval. All that is required of the user is the entry of search criteria in the form of numbers, words or phrases. The process takes place interactively through a series of menus. SQL*TextRetrieval responds with a *hit list*, identifying portions of the text that match the query criteria. These can then be displayed, printed, saved to a separate file or used as the basis for further searches.

The LIST TABLES command is used to display information on the tables available to the user (Figure 6.13). The upper part of the screen provides the name of each table and its owner. If the cursor is placed on a table name, information about each of its fields will be displayed in the lower part of the screen. Those of most interest will be fields of type LTEXT or FTEXT, since these are the fields containing text. The TEXTKEY field contains a unique numeric key for the table.

Queries are devised using the CREATE QUERY command. They consist of a mixture of standard SQL and proprietary commands and operators. Searching through the word list is handled by the WHERE CONTAINS clause. The syntax is WHERE <fieldname> CONTAINS <expression>. For example:

```
STRRMU Utility:  Table:                        12-SEP-1994 11:20:50

  Table name                 Table owner
  REGISTER                   RML




                                                               Hitlist
  Column name                Type        To lowercase ?  Digits?  size
  TEXTNUM                    TEXTKEY
  NEWSCODE                   not indexed
  DAY                        not indexed
  MONTH                      not indexed
  YEAR                       not indexed
  PAGENUM                    not indexed
  CORRS                      not indexed
  TEXT                       LTEXT       always lower             76


Count: *15                                                  <Replace>
```

Figure 6.13 *SQL*TextRetrieval: using* **LIST TABLES**

```
SELECT  Text
FROM  Register
WHERE  Text  CONTAINS  'Handel'
```

CONTAINS is the principal addition to SQL's standard commands and clauses. The expression can be any Boolean string containing terms and operators. NOT may be used within an expression, but cannot be used to commence it. Running the query results in a list of the number of hits found (i.e. the number of documents containing the word 'Handel'). The user can then display either the hitlist (the first line of each text – assuming the text has been properly indexed) or each text in turn, with the DISPLAY HITLIST and DISPLAY TEXT commands.

SQL*TextRetrieval uses two types of queries, *active* and *stored*. Each active query is numbered and retained in a list so that it can be reused if necessary. Active queries are erased at the end of the current retrieval session. However, they can be saved to disk as stored queries with the command SAVE QUERY <filename>. Stored queries may be recalled and reused in later sessions by using GET.

A common approach to querying is 'broad-to-narrow'. This involves progressively refining a query in a stepwise fashion. This works well, but has two disadvantages: the database has to be repeatedly searched using the same conditions; and the time taken to run the query goes

```
┌─────────────────────────────────────────────────────────────────────┐
│ STRAMU Utility:    DISPLAY HITLIST        Query £: 2    12-SEP-1994 11:03:00 │
│  ┌──────────────extract-from-target-tables──────────────────────────┐ │
│  │ key TEXT                                                          │ │
│  ├──────────────────────────────────────────────────────────────────┤ │
│  │ 7185   NEW MUSICK.  This Day is publish'd, Printed on a good Paper, and co │
│  │ 7277   NEW MUSICK.  This Day is publish'd, THE Favourite Songs in the Oper │
│  │ 7300   This Day is publish'd, The Second Edition of @ THE MODERN MUSICK-MA │
│  │ 7305   To all Gentlemen that are Masters, Judges, or Lovers of MUSICK.  HI │
│  │ 7309   This Day is publish'd, The Second Edition of @ THE MODERN MUSICK-MA │
│  │ 7378   This Day is publish'd, @ THE FAVOURITE SONGS in the Opera of PORUS, │
│  │ 7382   NEW MUSICK This Day publish'd.  THE whole Opera of PORUS in Score, │
│  │ 7383   This Day is publish'd, @ THE FAVOURITE SONGS in the Opera of PORUS, │
│  │ 7389   This Day is publish'd, @ THE FAVOURITE SONGS in the Opera of PORUS, │
│  │ 7398   NEW MUSICK This Day publish'd.  THE whole Opera of PORUS in Score, │
│  │ 7445   NEW MUSICK This Day publish'd.  THE whole Opera of PORUS in Score, │
│  │ 7450   NEW MUSICK This Day publish'd.  THE whole Opera of PORUS in Score, │
│  │ 7622   MUSICK This Day is publish'd.  THE additional Favourite Songs in t │
│  └──────────────────────────────────────────────────────────────────┘ │
│ command==>          ·                                                   │
│                                                                         │
│ Count: *0                                                    <Replace>  │
└─────────────────────────────────────────────────────────────────────┘
```

Figure 6.14   *SQL*TextRetrieval: the hitlist resulting from a query*

up each time extra search conditions are added. SQL*TextRetrieval's
REFINE command provides an effective answer. Rather than running
the initial query again, it simply retrieves the associated hitlist and
uses it to restrict the scope of the latest query condition to the results
of the earlier query. As successive refinements are added, SQL*Text
Retrieval displays the full history of the query. An example is provided
in Figure 6.15, in which our previous search on 'Handel' is narrowed
down to those texts which also refer to 'Messiah':

In text querying, truncation and wildcards are often used to handle
variations in spelling. This is particularly important in the case of
historical texts, many of which come from periods before spelling had
become standardised. Truncation is often used to remove the terminal
characters of words which are essentially synonymous, leaving just the
common stem. SQL*TextRetrieval uses the stem operator * to match
any number of characters at either end of the string:

```
SELECT  Text
FROM  Register
WHERE  Text CONTAINS  'Hand' *;
```

or:

```
STRRMU Utility: REFINE QUERY              Query £: 2   12-SEP-1994 11:06:29
┌─────────────────────────────────────────────────────────────────────────┐
│ Text retrieval SQL statement                                              │
│  SELECT TEXT                                                              │
│  FROM REGISTER                                                            │
│  WHERE TEXT CONTAINS 'handel'                                             │
│                                                                           │
│                                                                           │
│                                                                           │
│                                                                           │
│ additional refinement conditions (start with AND)                        │
│  AND TEXT CONTAINS 'messiah'                                              │
│                                                                           │
│                                                                           │
└─────────────────────────────────────────────────────────────────────────┘
   command==>

Count: *0                                                       <Replace>
```

Figure 6.15   *SQL*TextRetrieval: narrowing down the search*

```
SELECT  Text
FROM  Register
WHERE  Text  CONTAINS  *'ndel';
```

The stem operator can even be used at both ends of a text string:

```
SELECT  Text
FROM  Register
WHERE  Text  CONTAINS  *'ndel'*;
```

will return 'Handel', 'Haendel', 'Handel's', etc.

It is through the thesaurus, however, that the historian may add most value to a textbase. To obviate the need for stem operators and wildcards, the researcher might progressively develop a thesaurus which intelligently captures knowledge and understanding of the past. Appending the synonym operator & to the end of a search string instructs SQL*TextRetrieval to find all occurrences of every word in the synonym ring. For example, all the defined synonyms of Handel will be retrieved by the query:

```
SELECT  Text
FROM  Register
WHERE  Text  CONTAINS  'Handel' & ;
```

To retrieve the search string together with the preferred term for that synonym ring, the ==> expansion may be used:

```
SELECT  Text
FROM  Register
WHERE  Text  CONTAINS  'Handel' ==> ;
```

Unlike &, using this expansion will not retrieve the other words in the synonym ring. When the search string is a homonym which appears in two or more different synonym rings, SQL*TextRetrieval displays a message stating that the string appears in more than one synonym list. The user is asked to select the number of the appropriate list.

As noted earlier, a common querying strategy is to start broad and narrow down. Alternatively, the researcher may begin with a narrowly defined query and widen it as necessary. Using broader and narrower terms requires that thesaurus links have been set up in advance. Example queries are given below, with explanations:

`WHERE  Text  CONTAINS  'composer' <2`	Retrieve search string with broader terms to two levels
`WHERE  Text  CONTAINS  'composer' <<<`	Retrieve search string with broader terms to all levels

Finally, mention should be made of the value of proximity searching: finding all occurrences of a certain word within a specified distance forwards or backwards from another word. It is possible, for example, to find all occurrences of the word `'violin'` within a fixed proximity to the word `'concerto'` and focus on all references to violin concertos whether they were described as `'violin concerto'` or `'concerto for the violin'`, etc. Proximity searching is handled by the syntax `<term1> (n,m) <term2>`, where n defines the maximum number of words which may occur between the terms when `term1` comes before `term2`, and m the maximum number between them when `term1` comes after `term2`. Thus, to follow the example given by Harbor in Case Study B, we would use the query

```
SELECT  Text
FROM  Register
WHERE  Text  CONTAINS  'violin'  (1,2)  'concerto';
```

to find occurrences where 'violin' and 'concerto' can be found
with no more than one word in between and 'concerto' and
'violin' with up to two words in between.

□ *Conclusion*

There are interesting similarities and differences between the factors
governing the utility of conventional highly structured databases and
more loosely structured textbases. In both cases, the power and flexibility
of the controlling software system serves to enhance or limit the potential
for information retrieval. The sophistication of the available query
language is in this sense paramount. However, there is more to it than
this. Historians add value to structured databases through the process
of database design; through planning and thinking ahead. With a
textbase, value is added through the creation of the thesaurus, a live
and necessarily interactive process. A thesaurus is built gradually and
cannot entirely be preconceived. These ways of adding value – of
imparting intelligence to a system – need to be more widely understood.
There remains a tendency to rely too much on the facilities of the
software rather than exploiting fully the potential of a system through
the application of sound technique.

■ 6.4 Reports

The ability to produce printed reports incorporating the results of queries
is fundamental to any information system. The task of describing the
format and layout of the report is known as *report definition*. The two
main ways of presenting the results of a query are one record at a
time (i.e. all the data relating to the record on a single page) or many
records in a table. One record at a time is useful for some tasks, like
error checking, but for most purposes a tabular format is preferable.
The layout of a tabular report may be 'as it comes' or highly complex.
Many DBMSs provide a 'quick report' facility, which provides a simple
tabular format. However, we often want output to be arranged more
meaningfully – grouped in some way, with subtotals and other summary
statistics, and provided with headings, page numbers, and so on. A
report generator is used for this purpose. The essential features offered

- Select the input file (table) containing the data
- Identify fields to be included in the report
- Determine the selection criteria which determine the records to be selected
- Add any level breaks and group summaries required
- Define layout – headers and footers, pagination, etc.
- Save the query
- Test output

Figure 6.16   *Steps in developing a report*

by report generators vary little between DBMSs, but they do differ considerably in their approach and ease of use; some are menu-driven, others require knowledge of a software-specific command language.

As with any other database-related activity, report generation benefits from careful planning; the task is to ensure that the right information is retrieved, and that it is presented in a clear and unambiguous way. The essential steps are described in Figure 6.16.

To demonstrate the preparation of a report, the following example draws upon the simplified maritime history database described in sections 5.3 and 6.2. It is based upon SQL*Plus and the ORACLE RDBMS. For our report, we want to list all the ships in the database, grouped by port of registration, in the order in which they were registered. We also want to calculate and print the total tonnage of shipping registered in each year in each port.

As noted in Figure 6.16, we begin by locating the table(s) containing the data. Using the DESCRIBE command, we can remind ourselves that all the required data are to be found in the **Ship** table:

```
DESCRIBE  Ship;
Name                Null?              Type
--------            --------           --------
Ship_No             NOT  NULL          NUMBER(6)
Ship_Name           NOT  NULL          CHAR(18)
Regd_Date                              NUMBER(4)
Regd_Port                              CHAR(15)
Burden                                 NUMBER(5)
```

The next stage is to specify the fields to be printed in the report, together with any selection criteria which may be required. This is done by a standard SQL query statement:

```
SELECT  Regd_Port, Regd_Date, Ship_Name, Burden
FROM  Ship
ORDER  BY  Regd_Port, Regd_Date;
```

□ *The BREAK and COMPUTE commands*

Having selected the data and the sequence in which they will appear, we can begin to format the report. First, we want to create blocks of data so that they are easily identifiable and comparisons can readily be made between them. The BREAK command identifies a group of data with a common property. In our example, we want to group all records relating to a particular port, and therefore break on the *Regd_Port* field. We then want to sub-group by date of registration (*Regd_Date*), and finally, we want to insert a blank line (SKIP 1) between the groups. The complete command is:

```
BREAK ON Regd_Port ON Regd_Date SKIP  1
```

The use of breaks enables two activities to be carried out. First, the block itself is clearly identified in the mind of the reader by means of the space separating it from the next group. Second, arithmetic group summary functions can now be applied to the members of the group. In this instance, we want to calculate the total tonnage of shipping registered in each port. This is done with the COMPUTE command, which enables the group summary functions described in section 6.2 – AVG, SUM, MAX, MIN, STDDEV, VARIANCE, COUNT – to be applied to groups of records generated with the BREAK command. The COMPUTE command is thus dependent upon the BREAK command, without which group summary functions cannot occur.[10] The command we require is:

```
COMPUTE SUM OF Burden ON Regd_Date
```

This will ensure that for each year of registration the total registered tonnage will be printed in the *Burden* column.

□ *The COLUMN commands*

Having specified the required breaks and group summaries, we can now turn to improving the readability of our printout by adding column headings. Strictly speaking, it is not necessary to specify the headings for each column (field) in the report; as a default, the fieldnames will be used. However, it is often a good idea to choose alternative headings which help to clarify the function of the columns, especially if abbreviations were used when naming fields. This can be done using the COLUMN HEADING command: the syntax is COLUMN <fieldname> HEADING <'column title'>.

```
COLUMN  Ship_Name  HEADING  'Ship  Name'
COLUMN  Regd_Port  HEADING  'Registered|Port'
COLUMN  Regd_Date  HEADING  'Date  of|Registration'
COLUMN  Burden  HEADING  'Tonnage'
```

'Registered Port' and 'Date of Registration' are spelled out in full rather than being abbreviated like the equivalent fieldnames. They are, however, rather long column headings, and the vertical bars ensure that they will be displayed on two lines rather than one. We have also decided that 'Tonnage' is a more meaningful title to the reader than 'Burden' (though, given the peculiarities of nineteenth-century tonnage calculations, a note of explanation will still be necessary).

Readability will also be enhanced by adjusting the column spacing. There are various ways to adjust the width of fields and the spacing between them. (It should perhaps be emphasised that all of the methods described here apply to the way the report is laid out and do not affect the underlying database structure.) SET commands affect default layout values and thus are applicable to all columns in the report. For example:

```
SET NUM 8;
```

will set the default display width of all numeric fields to 8 characters. Similarly, the standard spacing between columns can be defined by:

```
SET SPACE 3;
```

Often, though, we will want to control the width of individual columns rather than assigning a particular default value. Let us assume that in our sample report definition we do not want to alter the default values. However, we wish to reduce the width of the *Ship_Name* column to 12 alphanumeric characters (there are no very long ship names) and cut the maximum size of the *Burden* column from five to four numbers (i.e. we have not recorded any ships of more than 9999 tons). Instead of using SET, this can be achieved with the COLUMN FORMAT command. As can be seen below, the way this is done depends upon the type of data:

```
COLUMN  Ship_Name FORMAT  a12
COLUMN  Burden FORMAT  9999;
```

☐ *The complete report definition*

The report definition is now complete, and reads as follows:

```
BREAK ON Regd_Port ON Regd_Date SKIP  1
COMPUTE SUM OF Burden ON Regd_Date
COLUMN Ship_Name HEADING 'Ship  Name'
COLUMN Regd_Port HEADING 'Registered|Port' FORMAT a12
COLUMN Regd_Date HEADING 'Date  of|Registration'
COLUMN Burden HEADING 'Tonnage' FORMAT 9999
SELECT Regd_Port, Regd_Date, Ship_Name, Burden
FROM Ship
ORDER BY Regd_Port, Regd_Date;
```

Once the finished report definition has been created, the user can specify the file into which the resulting report is placed by typing:

```
SPOOL  <filename>
RUN;
```

Spooling is ended with the command:

```
SPOOL OFF;
```

A sample from the resulting report is provided in Figure 6.17.

As an example of the use of report generators in a Windows-based package, we can consider the creation of the same report in Microsoft Access. It will be recalled that we want to list ships in the database, grouped by port of registration, in the order in which they were registered. We want to calculate and print the total tonnage of shipping registered each year at each port, and substitute more descriptive headings for some of the fieldnames. On selecting REPORT and NEW, the user is asked to select the table or query which will form the basis of the report. In this example, we are using the single table **Ship**. If we wanted to draw upon more than one table, or required data to be selected according to specified criteria, the report would be based upon a query instead of a table.

Access uses Report Wizards to automate report creation. Although it is certainly possible to create a report from scratch, it is often easier

Registered Port	Date of Registration	Ship Name	Tonnage
BRIDGWATER	1840	MARTHA JANE	145
		ST MICHAEL	132
		ELLERSLIE	213
		SAXON	167
		RED ROSE	181
*************			
SUM			838
	1841	SYREN	59
		CALDER	181
		GARROW	229
		ROVER	204
		JANE DIXON	91
		ELIZABETH	167
*************			
SUM			931

Figure 6.17 *Sample printout of the completed report*

to use a Report Wizard and then modify the resulting design as necessary. If the Report Wizard facility is to be used, a variety of report types are offered. AutoReport is the most highly automated; it creates a simple report using all the fields in the source table or query. Other types prompt the user for input about the report's contents and format. Amongst the most useful are the Tabular Wizard, which creates reports that display each record as a row of fields, and Groups/Totals; this groups records together and displays totals for each group.

To prepare the report, we select the Groups/Totals Report Wizard. Two of the prompt screens are shown in Figure 6.18. The first allows us to choose the fields which will feature in the report. The order in which they are selected determines the final layout: the first field selected appears in the leftmost column, and so on. All the fields are selected except *Ship_No*, in the order *Regd_Port*, *Regd_Date*, *Ship_Name* and *Burden*. The second screen is used to determine how the results are to be grouped. In this report, we want to group first on port of registration and then on date. Another prompt screen (not shown) allow us to select the sort order required – such as alphabetical by port of registration. Finally, we can choose the page layout required and save the completed report as **Shipping List by Port, Date**.

Figures 6.19 and 6.20 show the design view of the report and an

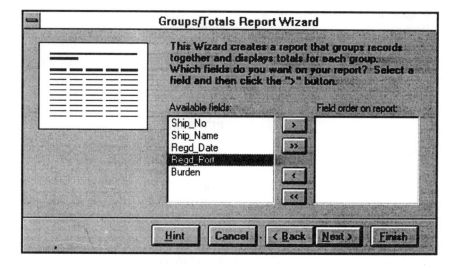

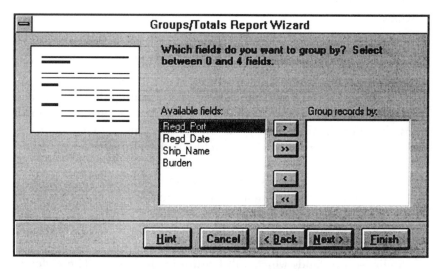

Figure 6.18 *Microsoft Access: prompt screens in the Report Wizard*

extract from the printed version. The report header (printed once at the start of the report) shows the name of the report and the date on which it was generated, and the page header defines the column headings which are to appear at the top of each page. The *Regd_Date* and *Regd_Port* headers are used to set up the group breaks. The detail section contains the fields to be printed in the body of the report. The *Regd_Date* footer prints a total tonnage for each year, and the *Regd_Port* footer a total tonnage for each port. Finally, the page footer prints a page number at the bottom of each page, and the

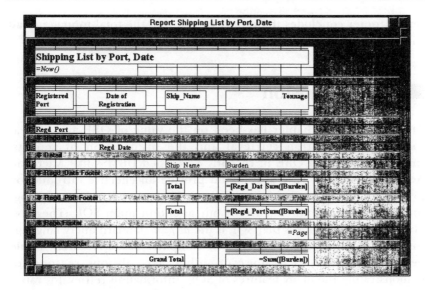

Figure 6.19 *Microsoft Access: the design view of the report*

Shipping List by Port, Date
07–Nov–94

Registered Port	Date of Registered	Ship_Name	Tonnage
Bridgwater			
	1840		
		Ellerslie	213
		Martha Jane	145
		Red Rose	181
		Saxon	167
		St Michael	132
		Total 1840	**838**
	1841		
		Calder	181
		Elizabeth	167
		Garrow	229
		Jane Dixon	91
		Rover	204
		Syren	59
		Total 1841	**931**
		Total Bridgwater	**1,769**
		Grand Total	**136,002**

Figure 6.20 *Microsoft Access: an extract from the printed report*

report footer concludes the report by printing the total tonnage of all ships in the database.

■ 6.5 Conclusion

The focus of this chapter has been on the value of QBE and SQL as tools for information retrieval and the preparation of reports. Implementations of QBE in recently developed DBMSs like Microsoft Access are flexible, easy to use, and provide an effective introduction to querying and reporting for many users. However, we make no apology for concentrating rather more of our attention upon SQL. The most obvious reason for this is that SQL is the *de facto* standard query language with which all historians engaged in computer based research should be familiar. There are, however, other, less obvious reasons for demonstrating the many features of SQL. Information retrieval is rarely a trivial matter. Certainly much can be done using QBE and similarly down-to-earth forms of querying. But most historical research makes more demands than can be met by such simple approaches. The implementation of complex record linkage algorithms in demography and the study of electoral behaviour are examples which come readily to mind. It is important therefore to have a realistic idea of what sophisticated query languages like SQL can and cannot do. We hope to have provided a fair indication of this, but would add that there is much more to learn about the advanced features of SQL than we have presented here.

In our experience, a knowledge of SQL and its text handling extensions is of more than immediate value. The principles which underpin the language have general applicability. Computing historians have much to gain from an understanding of these principles: more than almost anything else, it should enable them to get the most out of the databases to which they devote so much time and intellectual resources.

Case Study F
Analysing Social Structure and Political Behaviour using Poll and Rate Books: The Westminster Historical Database[1]

Edmund Green
Royal Holloway, University of London

Thirty years have passed since the publication of E.P. Thompson's *The Making of the English Working Class* marked a critical shift in the historiography of later Hanoverian England.[2] Where once that historiography seemed dominated by the high political history of interminable ministries, so now it seems dominated by the low political history of interminable thieves. And yet the distinction between the two kinds of history was always artificial, for they remain the opposite sides of the same coin. The central thesis of that vast book, which encompassed metropolitan reformers and Lancashire Luddites, has been the subject of much critical scrutiny. The bold assertion that 'between 1780 and 1832 most English working people came to feel an identity of interests as between themselves, and as against their rulers and employers' invites empirical, local, and above all quantitative examination.[3] Nor is the invitation weakened by Thompson's insistence upon class as relationship as opposed to class as category. But what kind of evidence can be brought to bear on the slippery subject of class consciousness and class relationships?

The Westminster Historical Database was created in the belief that the Thompson thesis may be tested in the light of evidence from parliamentary elections in a large, open, and frequently-contested metropolitan constituency. With up to 10,000 voters participating in twelve contested parliamentary elections between 1774 and 1820, Westminster had the largest and one of the most frequently consulted electorates in the country. Moreover, it had a wide franchise of adult male householders, it was beyond the control of any single patron (although the Court retained some influence there), and its metropolitan location exposed the electorate to the ebb and flow of the tides of public opinion. Indeed, Westminster radicalism is a recurring theme in Thompson's work, from the founding of the London Corresponding Society in 1792 to the challenge of resurgent Whiggism in 1819.

But the crucial distinguishing feature of British parliamentary elections prior to 1872 was that voting was open: the Westminster Historical Database records the political preferences of each voter for whom the evidence survives at each election contest between 1749 and 1820. One part of the database thus consists of many thousands of poll book cases, recording the names, addresses, occupations, and political choices of the voters. The other part consists of rate book cases. These local property-tax assessments record the names, addresses, and tax assessments of the householders who constituted the electorate. Using ORACLE, a powerful relational database management system, to link cases on the basis of common fields of name and address leads to the creation of extended cases. There will ultimately be many thousands of extended cases, each recording a voter's parish and ward of residence, his tax assessment, his occupation, his prior political behaviour, and the dependent variable of his vote at the election in question.

The explanation of electoral behaviour has also been described as a 'shop-window for social science research methods'.[4] There are a number of reasons for this. In the first place, elections in modern democratic societies are one of the few occasions when a large proportion of the population simultaneously participates in decision-making. Secondly, at each election the choice available to each elector is broadly the same. Thirdly, the choice for many electors is distilled by the political process: for some it may even be a dichotomised choice. And finally, for reasons which remain inadequately explained, the electors feel that the choice is sufficiently important to be worth making. The result is to make the explanation and modelling of electoral behaviour much simpler than the explanation and modelling of economic behaviour. And yet whilst liberal democracy has brought widespread participation in the decision-making process, it has also brought the ballot. Reconstructing the relationship between social structure and political behaviour is easier for the period of open voting than for the period between the introduction of the ballot and the rise of public opinion polling. The creation and application of the Westminster Historical Database was inspired not only by the humanistic discipline of history but also by the methodologies of social science.

Historians have made quantitative and computer-assisted studies of English political behaviour based on poll book data for about twenty years. Beginning with Speck's initial analysis of early eighteenth-century county electorates,[5] the central questions have concerned the behaviour of voters at a single election and the turnover and loyalties of voters at pairs of elections. But as others took up the challenge more difficult questions came to be asked, involving complex multitable linkage routines.[6] Thus poll book data may now be linked to other poll book data, to rate book data, to data on religious affiliation, or indeed to all of these, in order to illuminate and explain political behaviour. The urge to comprehend and explain past political behaviour has been facilitated by technological change, in which the development of powerful relational database management systems, with their simple query structures, has supplanted unimaginable reams of FORTRAN programming.

Much has been written about the decline in support for the British Labour Party since 1959. Questions as to whether this is the product of a decline in class voting or the elimination of the old cloth-cap working class have their mirror-image in discussions of the origins of metropolitan artisanal culture. For whilst the full potential of the Westminster Historical

Database remains to be exploited, it is clear already that the twin forces of continuity and change were at work in later Hanoverian London. In terms of continuity, it is found that the greatest single explanation of voting behaviour lies in the voter's prior behaviour, suggesting that an individual's conscience might have been more important than group consciousness in explaining political behaviour. Meanwhile in terms of change, it is found that the years following the French Revolution witnessed a critical shift in the social context of popular political behaviour, when the occupants of lower-rated houses began to vote in a different way from their higher-rated neighbours. Now that the Westminster Historical Database is nearing completion, what remains to be tackled is the complex task of modelling the effect of all of these variables in conjunction, to produce for the first time a truly rounded picture of the electorate of later Hanoverian London.

■ *Chapter 7* ■

Source-Oriented Database Systems

Theoretical neatness, adaptability and ease of use have all contributed to the rise to dominance in recent years of relational database systems and relational thinking. Yet, just at the point when many historians are becoming comfortable with RDBMSs, we can hear a rising chorus of dissatisfaction with the limitations of the relational model. Computing historians at the leading edge have been quick to point out that many historical sources cannot easily be rendered into the relational format of linked two-way tables. They argue that historical sources more often than not consist of text and images – forms of rich data with deeply embedded meanings – whose relation to one another is not transparent. Thus software and techniques which seek to impose a structure on the data at an early stage are deemed to be inappropriate for much historical research. What is needed, they say, is for the structure to adapt to the needs of the data, rather than vice-versa. Similar conclusions have been reached by other users of rich data in areas as diverse as computer-aided design, journalism and software engineering. The fundamental charge that the relational model is restricted, however, is not shared in all quarters. The advocates of the relational approach have published *The Third Generation Database Manifesto*,[1] in which they argue that such needs can all be provided by extensions to the relational model, while retaining the benefits of ease of use and data independence which characterise today's RDBMSs.

There is nevertheless a fundamental problem with extending relational systems in the manner proposed. In a relational database, queries establish links between related tables by means of common fields. This works well with alphanumeric data, but is much less manageable when using sound and image data. It would certainly be possible to use common fields of digitised pictures in order to link tables, but bitmapped images occupy large amounts of storage and it would be inordinately time-consuming to establish links and answer queries. It is for this reason that relational databases which deal with binary data in various forms, such as Paradox, treat it as an extension to data tables rather than as an integral part of them. Thus these 'binary large objects' (BLOBS) can be handled as fields in data tables, but cannot easily be edited or used in queries. The limitations of this approach are apparent. Hence the search for alternative solutions.

The limited ability of relational systems to handle binary images, sounds and the like is not the only cause of dissatisfaction amongst critical computing historians. Researchers have frequently called for software specific to the historian's needs; arguing that software developed for business users does not have the full range of tools needed to conduct historical research. Foremost amongst the critics is Manfred Thaller of the Max-Planck-Institut für Geschichte, Göttingen.[2] Thaller argues that the information contained in historical sources has a number of properties which are not common in commercial environments, and not recognised by conventional DBMSs. Some of these properties are fairly obvious: historical databases may include a variety of structured, implicitly structured and unstructured sources; they do not have fields of fixed length; fields are frequently missing; and many-to-many relationships are common. There are also a number of problems which are highly specific to historical research. At the most abstract level, Thaller argues that the processing of historical sources is different from the processing of present day data because when historians start their research they 'do not really "know" with absolute certainty what their texts mean.'[3] 'Fuzzy data' is a common phenomenon; values, dates, people's ages and occupations and the like are often approximations, or may be defined relatively rather than absolutely. A more practical consideration is the need to handle orthographical variations – especially in the spelling of people's names and place names. This is a major topic which we consider in Chapter 8. Other issues have to be dealt with, such as the use of different calendars in the past,[4] and the existence of non-decimal systems of currency or measurement.

Not everyone agrees with critics like Thaller. The advocates of relational methodologies point out, for example, that they are highly flexible, and explicitly designed to cope with many-to-many relationships and other aspects of 'real world' data models. Nevertheless, various approaches have been taken by historians in response to the perceived shortcomings of RDBMSs. One approach, described in Chapter 3 of this book, is the use of textual information systems like BASIS and STATUS to organise and manipulate unstructured data (i.e. free text), or ORACLE's SQL*TextRetrieval module to handle a mixture of structured and unstructured data. A more ambitious approach has been the development of the Historical Workstation by Thaller and his colleagues at Göttingen. Other important developments are represented by the growing interest in multimedia and hypermedia databases, object-oriented approaches, expert systems and knowledge bases. The uses and potential of these very different approaches are described in this chapter, with reference to a number of pioneering historical projects.

■ 7.1 Source-Oriented Data Processing

Manfred Thaller is one of the most prolific and influential writers on historical computing. He is the leading advocate of what has come to be known as source-oriented data processing. This section provides a summary of his ideas and work.[5] Readers are also referred to Denley's 1994 article in *History and Computing*, which provides a critical assessment of the relative strengths and weaknesses of the source-oriented approach *vis-à-vis* relational methodologies.[6]

Thaller argues that there are two stages in historical research at which a computer may be gainfully employed. The first is extracting and formalising information from a source. This is usually called coding, though with non-quantitative applications the term markup may be preferred. The second is in analysing the data to extract meaning, either through the application of formal methods (statistical and linguistic, for example) or through converting the original into a form which is more useful for human interpretation (such as a thematic map). Thaller makes a further distinction between what he describes as the *method-oriented* approach and the *source-oriented* approach. By method-oriented, he means the approach adopted by historians using relational methodologies like entity-relationship modelling and relational data analysis, where the historical source is converted into a set of strict and well-defined conceptual categories. With the source-oriented approach, on the other hand, the historian always enters the original text into the computer, only later deciding on the categories or classes into which the data should be organised for analysis. The idea here is that data entered in this way may be used for more than a single purpose. It may be reused and if necessary recoded as desired by different researchers. Moreover, a source-oriented data processing system should provide tools specifically for the generation of historical knowledge. For instance, Thaller notes that it should be possible to enter calendar dates like 'on the Thursday after Whit Sunday of the year 1564', or monetary values like '5 Mark 3 Stüber', which will be understood and interpreted by the computer system.[7] Thaller therefore offers the following definition:

> Source-oriented data processing attempts to model the complete amount of information in an historical source on a computer; it tries to administer such sources for the widest variety of purposes feasible. While providing

tools for different types of analysis, it does not force the historian, at the time he or she creates the database, to decide which methods shall be applied later.[8]

To give expression to his ideas on source-oriented data processing, Thaller and his colleagues at the Max-Planck-Institut für Geschichte, Göttingen have progressively developed a DBMS for historians known as κλειω (kleio is the Greek for Clio, the Muse of History). Since its origination on a UNIVAC mainframe in 1978 the software has moved from research-project status to marketed versions for PCs and a variety of UNIX platforms.[9]

κλειω uses a completely different metaphor for database creation to conventional DBMSs. As shown in a previous chapter, the relational approach requires the user to begin by analysing the information to be held in the database; decide what kinds of tables are required to hold the data and how they are to be related to each other; and then construct a system of screen forms for data entry. Finally, the user takes the source document(s) and selects such information as is needed to fill in the data entry forms. Thaller argues that this metaphor of 'creating a database by filling in forms' has serious shortcomings because historians do not control their information in the manner of businessmen or scientists. For example, he asks how a researcher in chemistry uses a computer:

> First an experiment is . . . designed and performed, the information gained by that experiment being submitted to an analysis performed with the help of the machine; if it turns out that some information is lacking, or a relationship cannot be proven sufficiently clearly by the data we have received, the experiment is redesigned and analysis proceeds with the (hopefully) improved data. This is precisely what is impossible for a historian: if our sources do not contain the information we need, we cannot and must not try to rewrite them.

Thaller goes on to assert that what the historian is doing when creating forms and filling them in 'is actually the creation of a reality, which has not existed before.' This is unacceptable. Instead, 'when committing the content of a historical source to the computer, you should think twice before leaving anything out just because there is no convenient slot in the form; this item of information may be just the crucial one, to understand how the various bits and pieces are connected.'

To facilitate this, κλειω uses the metaphor of translating a source into a description of its contents for the computer, which employs a 'descriptive language' developed during data input. All data in the database exist at two levels: as uninterpreted strings of arbitrary characters on the one hand, and as meaningful units (numeric or calendar data, etc.) on the other. A constant translation process takes place between these two levels, based upon a well-defined mechanism for representing necessary knowledge. Thus the database is conceived as a 'machine-readable edition' of the original source. The objective, in short, is to mimic the procedures used in doing historical research without a computer; on the one hand, the historian seeks to transcribe the source as painstakingly as possible; on the other, he or she uses a variety of notebooks, card indexes and the like to keep track of assumptions about the meaning of individual parts of the source. Thus, κλειω allows the user to input the source in its original form, and then provides a wide range of tools for handling such areas as chronology and systems of coinage and measurement. For example, to pursue the example of the date defined in relation to a saint's day, κλειω knows that expressions of the form <day-of-the-week><temporal-direction><feast><year> are legitimate ways to define dates, and can interpret them by referring to the appropriate definitions. Additionally, some saints' days vary from region to region, and κλειω allows the user to create specific rules to define exactly where – and when – the source was written.

Thaller give the following overall definition of κλειω's handling of sources and knowledge about sources:

> In κλειω a historical source is administered by transcribing various parts of a source, assigned to individual elements of a database, as accurately as possible. All knowledge about the meaning of the transcribed items is administered separately in a layer of the system which is specifically dedicated to the administration of knowledge. Any query the user makes, any command that has to access the data which are stored in the transcribed source, is interpreted according to the knowledge stored about the source.

This separation of the data itself from what is variously termed the *knowledge environment* or *logical environment* is a fundamental characteristic of κλειω. It is the knowledge environment which allows the researcher to model the world in which the source was created. And, as this knowledge environment is held separately from the data, it means that different interpretations can be made without affecting either the original structure or form of the data. Schematically, this provides the relationships set out in Figure 7.1.

The usual method of creating a database for use with κλειω is as follows. First, a file containing the rules which define the structure of the database (the *structure declaration*) is created and entered into the system. κλειω databases always have a hierarchical structure (though there may be times when there is only one level in a hierarchy). The highest level of a database is called, in κλειω terminology, the *document*

User
↓
Software
↓
Knowledge Environment
↓
Transcribed Source

Figure 7.1 *Relationship between the user and* κλειω

level. Within a document, the basic building blocks are described thus by Denley (our italics):

> *Groups* are abstract groupings of information – with some similarities to entities in relational databasing – which exist in hierarchical relationship to each other up to an almost infinite level of complexity. Groups contain *elements*, which bear superficial similarities to fields or attributes in conventional databasing, but which are in reality much more complex and flexible. Elements in turn are composed of *entries*, of which there can be any number; multiple occupations, for example, can be listed without effort. Each entry can in turn have different *aspects* (the historian can include original text or editorial comment in this way), *views* (i.e. variants of the text, perhaps Latin and vernacular equivalents of the same data), and *visibility* (a quantitative estimate of the value or reliability of the information).[10]

Next, an ASCII copy of the source document is created and then marked up according to the structure which has been defined. As can be seen from Figure 7.2, which shows an idealised users'-eye view of κλειω, this is generally done with the user's preferred wordprocessor or text editor; although data entry via menus is possible, this is one of κλειω's less than satisfactory aspects. The marked-up data file can then be put into the system, and processed – compiled – with the rules file to create a working database ready for querying.

This simple description implies that the structure of the database is added to the system first and the data second, and this is true to the extent that data cannot be entered until the database has been initialised. But the process can be an iterative one. The fact that κλειω keeps the actual data separate from its administration of the data structure ensures that data can always be re-edited, and even restructured. If any errors are discovered, or the researcher decides to try a different approach, the data file or the rules file can be amended and the working database recompiled as often as is necessary. Consequently κλειω is much more tolerant of an 'experimental' or 'try it and see' approach than most other DBMSs.

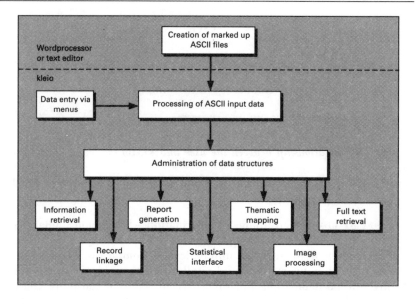

Figure 7.2 κλειω – *user view*

Once the rules and the data have been integrated, further rules, known in κλειω as *logical objects*, are introduced to form the knowledge environment. Logical objects tell κλειω how to interpret the data. Some are made available by κλειω itself; providing a range of tools which are generally applicable to historical projects. They include order (a means of defining different sort orders), chronology (algorithms describing how κλειω should interpret various dating systems), a variety of pre-treatment algorithms for manipulating text strings before record linkage; and tools for producing graphical representations of topographical objects. Other logical objects can be defined by the researcher; often they are specific to the individual project, though this is not necessarily the case, and there is an increasing tendency to make libraries of logical objects available to fellow κλειω users. All logical objects can be updated or deleted as the user requires.

The compiled database and logical objects together allow the user to perform a number of different types of task, including information retrieval, report generation, the linkage of records and databases (akin to the process of linking related tables in a relational database), the production of thematic maps, full-text analysis, and outputting information from source material into files that can be immediately understood by statistical software like SPSS or SAS. As will be seen later, users with sufficiently powerful hardware can also process digital images using the 'high-tech' version of κλειω.

Figure 7.3 provides a representation of the relationship between the

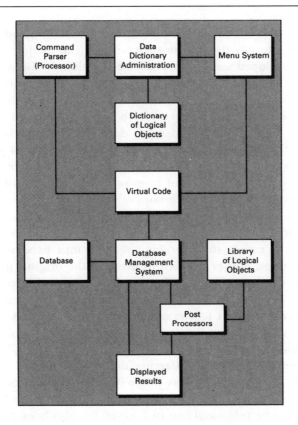

Figure 7.3   κλειω – *technical description*

different technical elements of κλειω. It identifies the main elements
of the system and how they interrelate. The dictionary of logical objects
contains all the relevant default information for the operation of κλειω.
These system-defined logical objects are linked to the data dictionary
administrator, which in turn is linked, either via the menu system or
(more commonly) through a command parser, to the database management system itself. Any number of databases can be interrogated
simultaneously; each database acting in a similar manner to a table
within the relational model. The library of logical objects contains user-
defined rules which κλειω uses, along with the system-defined logical
objects, to interpret the data. When queried, databases yield results
which may be displayed on-screen, or sent to disk or printer. As noted
earlier, this structure means that in κλειω the information is held
separately from both the default rules and the additional user-defined
rules. These three elements only interact when the user queries the
data.

The development of Thaller's ideas has aroused a good deal of international interest, though, not surprisingly, the majority of the applications developed using κλειω have been within the German-speaking world. As an example of a κλειω-based project, we may consider Burkhard Pöttler's work on probate inventories as a source for the history of everyday life. The many projects which have exploited probate inventories have had to collect and input data in a more or less encoded form, and thus have lost much of the potential value of the source. Pöttler's first aim, therefore, has been to develop a flexible data model so as to cover as many different types of inventory as possible. Most of these are divided into different groups of items, such as heirs, documents, immovables, movables, assets, and liabilities. The groups used, however, vary considerably from one inventory to another, as do their contents. Consequently, rather than forcing the data into fixed titles for the different groups, Pöttler decided to preserve the original groupings of data in the database. Classification is subsequently achieved by the use of thesauri. Using κλειω thus allows semantic as well as structural access.[11]

κλειω's confinement to Germany and Austria has, however, begun to change, with growing interest in Eastern Europe,[12] and the release of an English-language version early in 1994. In the UK, work has recently commenced on transferring the Viana database described in Case Study G to κλειω. It was originally developed at Southampton University using SIR (Scientific Information Retrieval), a hierarchical DBMS with some relational features. κλειω has also been implemented by a team of researchers at King Alfred's College, Winchester, which has been working on the History of Winchester Project since 1990. The team, originally led by Martin Doughty and Tom James, commenced work using a relational DBMS before switching to κλειω.

The objective of reproducing all the information in an original source may not, of course, always be appropriate to a historical research project. First, reproduction can be very time-consuming, especially when large and complex documents are involved. Second, there may be legitimate reasons for preferring a heavily interpreted dataset created for a specific purpose. Just as we often rely on secondary works rather than primary materials because of the way a secondary source can synthesise and interpret the raw material of history, so too we will sometimes want to work with a dataset which is an interpretation rather than a reproduction of an original source.

κλειω's advocates would respond that the system is intended to meet both objectives. The general notion underpinning κλειω, therefore, is not that the user is forced to choose between a completely serial transcription of the actual document and a structured representation of it, but that both or either can be developed, as appropriate. Thaller's preference for the former is clear; but he does recognise that the latter continues to predominate because of the conceptual and practical difficulties of creating a 'machine-readable edition'. To overcome this difficulty, Thaller and his colleagues have been working on a set of extensions to the κλειω model. To complement the κλειω working environment, a complete dedicated support system called StanFEP (Standard Format Exchange Program) has been developed to mark up electronic documents in a way which helps manage the various versions of a database needed by the researcher. The objective is to make data preparation for κλειω as easy as for 'traditional' DBMSs. (Textual mark-up is discussed further in section 8.1.)

Thaller's work on κλειω has led to the definition of what he calls the Historical Workstation. A historical workstation is a computer system which responds positively to the historian's needs. Thus it:

- has access to database management software which allows it to handle large collections of sources, keeping as much of the original information and applying as little coding as is economically feasible for the particular project.
- has access to a set of database lookup tables, etc., which contain background knowledge specific to historical research.
- has access to a set of read-only databases, which are the equivalent of traditional printed editions of source material.
- contains artificial intelligence subsystems to make the preceding features transparent to the user.
- provides a highly integrated interface between the database and a desktop publishing system.
- provides a similar interface to statistical software.

The idea of a historical workstation thus embodies all the ideas which underpin Thaller's concept of source-oriented data processing, and which are practically implemented in κλειω. However, while it is true that the emphasis is currently on the transcription of textual documents, the concept of a historical workstation is aimed more directly towards the processing of complex documents. Like many other researchers, Thaller and his collaborators have begun to study the handling of images and their linkage to related texts. Above all, Thaller considers the future to lie in the manipulation of a particular type of image – facsimiles of the original documents themselves. Thus the notion of a 'machine-readable edition' will no longer mean serial transcriptions of historical documents, but high resolution, digitised images of the documents themselves. Once the digital reproduction of any part of the source has been selected and displayed, it may be processed by subsystems incorporating the full power of image processing and pattern recognition. In many cases, as is well-known in the field of art history, this may be used to improve the quality of damaged portions of the document or reveal information which is not readily apparent to the naked eye. Hypermedia features may also be used, to create relationships between part of an image and descriptions of that image.

An example of this type of approach is provided by researchers at the Institut für Realienkunde des Mittelalters und der Frühen Neuzeit of the Austrian Academy of Science who, since the early 1970s, have been building a major archive of images of medieval life and culture in Austria. In this case, the technical option of relatively low cost, high resolution analogue videodisks was passed over in favour of more ambitious digital technology. The attractiveness of digital processing lies in the possibility of immediate retrieval, the potential to link the 30,000 or so images in the collection with structured descriptions, and the availability of a variety of image enhancement techniques from the IMPART image processing library developed by IBM. In collaboration with the Max-Planck-Institut für Geschichte, the Institut für Realienkunde des Mittelalters und der Frühen Neuzeit has developed κλειω IAS (Image Analysis System). It has now been integrated into κλειω version 6. With this, the textual description of an image can be bound to the image itself (rather like hypertext) and simultaneously displayed. Tools are provided for digital image analysis, image enhancement and pattern recognition.[13]

▌ 7.2 Multimedia and Hypermedia Databases

The advent of multimedia platforms provides intriguing possibilities for the historical researcher. But until recently little was done to turn possibilities into realities. High hardware costs, technical limitations and a lack of international standards meant that there were few genuine multimedia projects. The BBC's Domesday Project, undertaken some years ago and distributed on laserdisk, is perhaps the best-known. However, with the establishment of *de facto* standards by big players like Microsoft, Apple, IBM and rapid technical advance and falling hardware costs, the number of historical research projects adopting a multimedia approach is beginning to grow rapidly.

One obvious use of multimedia is the handling of major archival collections. The example of Art Gallery was cited in section 3.5. Another example is the work recently undertaken by the Royal Commission on the Historical Monuments of England on the feasibility of establishing a multimedia database combining computerised data and images which might be interrogated independently of its physical location. The pilot study focussed on the City of York, which is geographically compact and has a wide variety of historic sites. Textual and visual archives were selected from the National Buildings Record, the National Archaeological Record, and the Lists of Historic Buildings, then held by the Department of the Environment. The pilot project has already produced valuable information on how the RCHME's resources could be presented to users. Further work is planned to evaluate in more detail the costs and benefits, user requirements, and the technology. It is anticipated that the application of imaging technologies will reduce the cost of providing public access to RCHME data; eliminate the need to print in excess of 25,000 new photographs annually; reduce wear and tear (and hence conservation costs) on documents; and create revenue by producing CD-ROM-based products for picture agencies, libraries, tourist boards and the educational market.

Such projects often make use of hypertext-type techniques to enable users to navigate the data in non-linear ways. Hypertext – or hypermedia – is now being actively pursued by research historians. It is an approach which readily accommodates the complex data typically found in historical sources. In textual analysis, for instance, it allows links to be made between the primary electronic text and the related scholarly apparatus. As well as the electronic text itself, there may be displays of facsimiles of the original text, and images from it; displays of related biographical and bibliographical information; explanations of selected words, phrases and concepts; and literary analyses and interpretations of the text.

The types of project which might benefit from a hypermedia approach are summarised in Schneiderman's 1989 article, 'Reflections on Authoring, Editing and Managing Hypertext'. He concluded that there were three 'golden rules' which determined whether hypermedia was suited to an application. First, there should be a large body of information, organised into numerous fragments. Second, the fragments should relate to each other. And third, only a small fraction would be needed by the user at any one time.[14] To these rules, a very practical fourth was added by Nielsen: 'do *not* use hypertext if the application requires the user to be away from the computer for appreciable periods of time.'[15]

As will be demonstrated by the following examples, historical geography is an obvious beneficiary of the hypermedia approach. The software particularly favoured by many geographers is HyperCard; it is supplied free with all Apple Macintoshes, and is the product which has done most to popularise the hypermedia concept. It includes its own programming language, HyperTalk, which offers a full range of functions and control structures, and it can be used to create a wide variety of applications. The simplest type of application is the creation of a standalone set of cards. However, more sophisticated applications can also be developed, such as semi-automated cartography. In a straightforward example described by Gilbert, data on mortality rates in different London parishes are entered into one card, while another provides a suitable base map. Scripts are used to look up values from the table of figures, and the map can be appropriately shaded using HyperCard's painting tools.[16]

Gilbert and Southall also describe how HyperCard can be used as a graphical front end for a remote SQL database. The approach uses a SQL communications product called DAL (Database Access Language) which can be used to link Hypercard to a wide range of RDBMSs, including INGRES and ORACLE. For this purpose, DAL has three elements: software for the remote server, which enables the database to interpret and respond to incoming SQL queries; a 'Hosts' file which automates the connection between the microcomputer and the remote server; and a series of extensions to HyperTalk, the developers' language for HyperCard. The 'Hosts' file provides a variety of macros to facilitate logging on to the server (for example, via a local area network, or from a remote site via JANET, the Joint Academic Network). The extensions to HyperTalk enable SQL commands to be sent to the server and allow manipulation of the returning data stream. The user is presented with a standard Macintosh screen and can make decisions in the usual way by moving a mouse pointer around the screen and clicking on appropriate buttons.

This front end was developed as part of a research project on the history of regional economic change in Britain at Queen Mary & Westfield College, University of London. The project is described in Case Study E. The data are held in a centrally managed INGRES relational database, and because the project team wished to make it accessible to other users they created a user-friendly front end which could be queried without requiring a knowledge of SQL. The HyperCard system holds the maps and the basic screens, and its HyperTalk scripts allow the user to move between screens and devise queries.

After logging on, the user is presented with an index screen, which offers the options 'SQL', 'Regions', 'Counties', 'London' and 'Towns'. The SQL option allows the user to interrogate the database directly using SQL queries, though for security reasons they cannot make changes to entries. The other options each provide a base map on which data can be overlaid. For example, 'Regions' gives access to a map of Britain divided into standard regions. Clicking on a button marked 'Category'

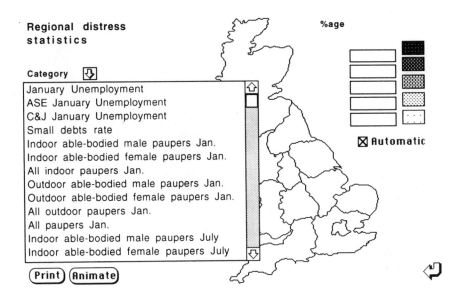

Figure 7.4 *List of datasets which may be mapped on to regions*

Source: David Gilbert and Humphrey Southall, 'Data *Glasnost:* A User-Friendly System for Access to Research Databases across Wide-Area Networks', *History and Computing,* Vol. 3, No. 2 (1992), p. 124.

pops up a menu listing the various categories of data which can be mapped on to the screen (Figure 7.4).

As can be seen, these categories include various measures of economic performance and distress, and occupational categories. When a category is selected, the list disappears and is replaced by a list of the years for which data are available. Economic data are provided for each year between 1850 and 1913, while census data are decennial from 1841 to 1911. Selecting a year launches a HyperTalk script which generates a SQL query, sends it to the mainframe, processes the returned results, and then paints the map. The result is shown in Figure 7.5.

Other facilities are being made available as the database is developed. For example, clicking on a region allows the user to generate graphs of the chosen category over the whole period for which data exist (Figure 7.6). Help screens are being added; rather than offering assistance in using the system, they provide information on the data displayed – its provenance, scope and limitations. This information, like the data it describes, is held in an INGRES database table and accessed via a HyperTalk script.[17]

One characteristic of historical hypermedia projects is that they are

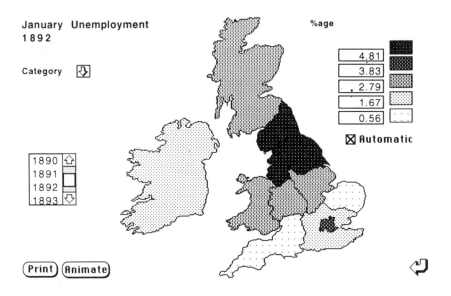

Figure 7.5 *Mapping unemployment data*

Source: David Gilbert and Humphrey Southall, 'Data *Glasnost:* A User-Friendly System for Access to Research Databases across Wide-Area Networks', *History and Computing,* Vol. 3, No. 2 (1992), p. 125.

frequently aimed at both research and teaching. This is the case at the University of Southampton where the intention of one project is to store the entire Mountbatten Archive in electronic form; another aims to access large amounts of archive material relating to Yugoslavia during the Second World War. Both projects utilise Microcosm, an advanced hypermedia package which is being developed at Southampton's Department of Electronics and Computer Science. As noted in section 3.5, one of the disadvantages of using hypermedia-type programs is that the links between data items have to be pre-programmed. Say, for example, it was decided that every occurrence of the word 'Mountbatten' should link to a brief biography. Whenever a new document was added to the database, 'Mountbatten' would have to be manually connected to the biography every time it occurred. As well as being time-consuming and prone to omissions, this would mean that the user could only navigate the documents in ways which the programmer had anticipated. Microcosm, however, supports the concept of generic links; when a word or phrase has been added to the list of links, adding a new document to the system will result in the automatic creation of a new link whenever the word or string occurs. The fact that links are available without being explicitly set up facilitates searching

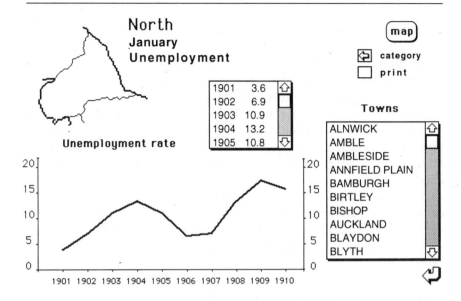

Figure 7.6 *Generating graphs from data held in the underlying database table*

Source: David Gilbert and Humphrey Southall, 'Data *Glasnost:* A User-Friendly System for Access to Research Databases across Wide-Area Networks', *History and Computing,* Vol. 3, No. 2 (1992), p. 126.

the database. The Southampton projects also make effective use of Microcosm's other unique features, such as its ability to manage and create links between documents – sound and video as well as text and still pictures – which are held in a variety of third-party applications and formats.[18]

■ 7.3 Object-Oriented Databases

In the introduction to this chapter, it was noted that, however powerful and flexible they might be, relational databases are unsuitable for some types of project. Increasingly, as databases come to include a variety of non-indexable forms of data (such as pictures, sound and animation), the simple record structures of relational systems have become a major limitation. It is difficult to express the semantics of complex objects in a set of two-way tables. A very different approach to database design has been adopted by a group of experts who specialise in object-oriented (OO) technology. The challenge was laid down in 1989 in a paper entitled 'The Object-Oriented Database System Manifesto',[19] and it has led to a fierce debate as to the relative merits and demerits of rival approaches.[20]

The object-oriented paradigm has its origins in the world of programming. Much of the code being written in the 1960s and early 1970s was unwieldy and unstructured; it was prone to bugs and was a nightmare to document and update. As a result, structured techniques became favoured, and their introduction led to considerable improvements in productivity and quality. However, even structured programming had its shortcomings. Most importantly, the methodologies employed did not encourage the development of reusable components. As Yourdon has remarked, 'people using structured methods as their development paradigm tend to treat each new project as an intellectual exercise never before contemplated; analysis and design literally begin with a blank sheet of paper.'[21] The logical consequence was to move even further towards the idea of free-standing 'modules' or 'capsules' of code. The attraction, of course, was largely that a module could be rewritten if desired without having unexpected consequences on other parts of the program. Modules could be linked together and reused as necessary.

Further impetus towards a new approach came from researchers investigating people's work habits. It was recognised that people are naturally task-centred – gathering together all the data, tools and techniques to enable them to carry out a specific task – but using computers compelled them to adopt a software-centred approach. Even in a multitasking environment, there is something very artificial about switching from one software program to another to manipulate the group of files needed to carry out a particular task. A better approach, it was reasoned, would be to combine the data and processes, so that opening a file would automatically call the software program or tool needed to manipulate it.

A third area of debate has focussed upon the perceived shortcomings of relational systems for some purposes. As well as the problem of handling rich data mentioned earlier, there is the fact that in a relational system data about a particular entity could easily be spread across multiple tables, making it impossible to retrieve without constructing complex queries.

The object-oriented approach, in which data and functions are contained in a single module or package (an *object*), attempts to overcome the perceived limitations of the relational model. Every object has three features: a *name*; a set of *attributes* (which may alternatively be called *fields, properties* or *instance variables*) that hold values of the object; and a set of *methods* (procedures) that act upon the data. As each object contains a definition of itself, it can be distinct from other objects.

This is called *encapsulation*. An object can contain any type of data: text, numbers, sound or images.

Instances are unique objects, such as George_White or Bristol Aeroplane Company, whilst a set of object instances which have similar structure and behaviour, like Person and Company, comprise a *class*. Each object is described by *attributes*. For example:

```
Bristol Aeroplane Company INSTANCE OF Company WITH
     Founded: 1910
     Regd_Office: Bristol
     Capital: 250,000
```

Here, Founded is an *attribute* and 1910 an *attribute value* for the instance Bristol Aeroplane Company of *class* Company. A *relationship* may connect two or more classes. An object may *inherit* some of its structure and behaviour from a parent class, which is called a *superclass* in OO terminology. Thus a *subclass* is a refinement or subset of a generic superclass. Object-oriented systems carry out computations by passing *messages* between active objects.

The potential of the object-oriented paradigm increasingly is becoming recognised. Thus object-oriented programming languages – notably C++ – have been widely adopted to improve code reuse, code maintenance, and modularity. Object-oriented data modelling provides techniques appropriate for the analysis of rich data. One of the most significant features of the object-oriented data model is its ability to represent arbitrary and compound objects, in contrast to the more structured and uniform relational model. Object-oriented database management systems (OODBMSs), which represent the intersection of database and object-oriented programming language technology, are attracting widespread interest both in research and commercial circles.[22] Unlike relational systems, OODBMSs use a navigational model of computation; thus they have been compared with hierarchical and network databases – both have the concept of pointers – and have been seen by critics as a move backwards from the data independence of RDBMSs. In return, the proponents of OODBMSs have argued that 'it is easier to weave your way through objects that model the real world rather than tables, tuples [fields], and records.'[23]

OODBMSs do well with highly complex data with multiple relationships. In a relational database, complex objects have to be split up amongst several tables, which can make for design complexities and difficulties in querying. As a general rule, the more complex the data the greater the performance advantages of OODBMSs over RDBMSs. Thus an obvious application for OODBMSs is the 'document' database – an extension

---

Class: a category of objects with the same attributes and behaviours.

Instantiation: creating an object which is an instance of a class.

Abstraction: the decomposition of a problem into its component levels. The most abstract level describes the components in their most general sense.

Subclassing: the definition of a class hierarchy by defining a class as a more concrete special case of a more general class.

Inheritance: the mechanism for sharing attributes and behaviours amongst layers of a class hierarchy. A behaviour or attribute that is defined at a higher (i.e. more abstract) level can be accessed or have its definition refined at a lower, more concrete, level.

Polymorphism: the ability to send the same command to different objects and achieve the appropriate result relevant to the object. In other words, issuing the same command to different objects may initiate different results.

Encapsulation: the isolation of attributes and behaviours from surrounding layers and structure. The ability to store, with an object, all its attributes and the operations it is capable of performing.

Figure 7.7   *Object orientation concepts*

Source: Based upon Kathy Lang, 'Data Basics', *Personal Computer World* (February 1993), p. 436.

of the textbase, where complex and memory-intensive objects including voice, video and graphics have to be stored as well as text.

The supporters of the relational approach have responded to the object-oriented challenge with *The Third Generation Database System Manifesto*.[24] Its authors argue that data management has undergone an evolution rather than a revolution. The first generation was the hierarchical system, the second the relational system, and the third extensions to the relational approach. Certainly, many recent developments, such as the integration of structured and unstructured data, have been accommodated by extensions to relational systems. According to its proponents, the third generation DBMS will accommodate a broad range of data types, such as still images, video, multimedia documents; have excellent procedures for ensuring data integrity and security; will possess all the good features of second generation DBMSs, such as data independence and support for SQL; and will communicate and be inter-operable with a wide range of programs, applications and software engineering tools.

The manifesto does not explicitly mention the words 'object-oriented'. Yet, as object-oriented systems begin to find their way into the marketplace, the apparent gulf between the supporters of relational and object-oriented systems seems to be narrowing. Some OO design methodologies can be seen as an extension of existing techniques. Kappel and Schrefl, for example, describe an approach for the design of object-oriented databases which is based on entity-relationship modelling.[25] Moreover, some of the participants in the debate argue that a relational system can be provided with object-oriented extensions, thus achieving the best of both worlds. Quite a few of the extensions to relational systems which have recently been proposed are in fact object-oriented 'front ends'. For example, a system described by Premerlani *et al.* allows the user to manipulate the database using both an object-oriented programming language and SQL.[26] Another important development is POSTGRES, a research object-oriented DBMS which is an extension of INGRES, now a commercially successful DBMS. It can handle complex objects, and can query them using the data language POSTQUEL, which, as the name suggests, is an extension of SQL. Its developers argue that it provides all the capabilities of an object-oriented model, but it does so without discarding the relational model and without having to introduce a new confusing terminology.[27]

Other developments, however, owe rather less to the extension of relational database thinking. Notable are extensions to object-oriented programming languages. Operational systems of this type include GemStone, Vbase and ORION.[28] Some OODB researchers claim that object orientation cannot live in the same world as relational DBMSs. ODDESSY, for example, is an object-oriented database design system which is notable in that it uses objects and messages as its database design language; ODDESSY is rule-based, and treats rules as objects.[29]

There are good reasons for believing that object-oriented DBMSs will become of increasing importance in the years to come. As an example of the type of benefits which it promises, readers are referred to Price and Gray's recent article in *History and Computing*. As well as providing a useful introduction to the concepts of object orientation, they describe their use of object-oriented principles for nominal record linkage – a task central to many historical database projects which we consider in section 8.2.[30] As yet, however, the object-oriented approach has not become all-conquering. Though Price and Gray conclude that it has much to recommend it to the historian, since it 'allows the data to be stored and manipulated in a considerably more powerful and realistic way that the relational model,'[31] they do recognise that object-orientation is still at an early stage of development. It tends to be relatively complicated to use compared with the relational model, and is often quite slow in operation. Nor is it underpinned by a single, mathematical theory, as is the relational model: 'object-oriented' means different things to different people. There is also the very real practical problem that at present technical expertise is less readily available to end users. As is so often the case, the question will not be which approach is best, but which best fits the needs of the particular research project. In the shorter term, at least, the strategy of providing extensions to RDBMSs will probably meet many people's needs. The development of object-oriented extensions to SQL seems to be a particularly fruitful approach, holding out the prospect that data objects may be queried alongside conventional relational tables.

7.4 Artificial Intelligence, Expert Systems and Knowledge Bases

Artificial intelligence (*AI*) means the use of computers to undertake tasks which would be considered intelligent if performed by humans. The aspect of AI that appears to have the most far-reaching implications is *heuristic problem-solving.* Traditional methods of programming computers are essential algorithmic, providing a set of detailed steps to be followed, and can respond only to a limited set of predefined situations. They are not suitable, therefore, where very large numbers of variables are involved. Heuristic problem-solving, however, is responsive to encountered situations. Heuristics are general strategies or rules which have been proven by past experience. They select good or adequate solutions from a large and unwieldy set of possibilities.

One of the principal ways in which artificial intelligence is being used to enhance database systems is in the development of *expert systems.* An expert system is one which captures the knowledge and experience of human experts in the form of facts and rules, so as to aid others in the process of decision making in specific subject areas. Expert systems are widely used in disciplines such as engineering, geology and medicine, and are also being applied to business applications where a mixture of knowledge and judgement is needed. Three types of expert system have been identified: those based on design, implementing exact reasoning on highly structured data sets; those carrying out decision support, typically combining database and expert knowledge to explore alternatives, solve problems and make predictions; and those concerned primarily with classification, usually on the basis of large amounts of data.[32]

The major components of an expert system are shown in Figure 7.8:

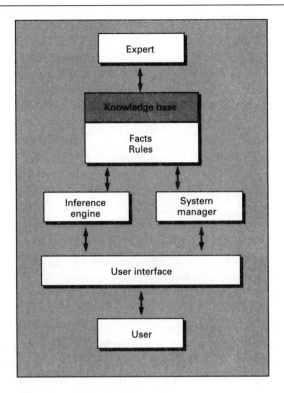

Figure 7.8 *Components of an expert system*

Source: Based upon J.G. Moser, 'Integration of Artificial Intelligence and Simulation in a Comprehensive Decision Support System', *Simulation*, Vol. 47 (Dec. 1986), pp. 223–9; Fred R. McFadden, and Jeffrey A. Hoffer, *Database Management* (Redwood City, CA, 3rd edn. 1991) p. 690.

The principal characteristic of an expert system is that it is supported by a database of knowledge, commonly called a *knowledge base*. To arrive at an appropriate solution, an expert system – just like a human expert – has to make use of an appropriate knowledge base, containing the relevant facts, rules and other information. Unlike conventional databases, this knowledge base must include many different kinds of knowledge about objects and processes, about goals and actions, and about cause and effect relationships.

Facts are representations of knowledge which are generally accepted in the discipline or field. Rules (heuristics) are sets of guidelines which experts typically use to reach decisions, and are usually expressed as IF <condition> THEN <result> statements. Each rule typically contains multiple *antecedents* and *consequents*. Antecedents are part of the IF clause, and provide relation tests: =, <, >, etc. Consequents form part of the THEN clause, and assign particular conclusions to specified facts if the IF part of the rule proves true. For example, a mechanic might say, 'if the car won't start, it might have a flat battery or be out of petrol.' When encoded as a rule, this would read as follows:

```
RULE: Diagnose car not starting
IF        battery_indicator=off OR
          petrol_level=0
THEN  car_starts=no AND
          new_battery=yes OR
          battery_recharge=yes OR
          refill_tank=yes
```

Expert systems can incorporate large numbers of rules, which are connected together to form a problem-solving network.

Sometimes, we need to use probabilities rather than absolute statements. For example, we might have a rule which is true 80 per cent of the time, which would qualify the heuristic. These probabilities can be encoded in rules known as *confidence factors* or *certainty factors* (CFs). These CFs are numbers which measure how sure developers and users are that the rules they use are accurate. CFs are used by expert systems when describing information in constructing or using a knowledge base. For example, we might use the range from $+1.0$ to -1.0 to express levels of confidence ranging from absolutely true to absolutely false (Figure 7.9).

Expert systems also offer the prospect of defining and using fuzzy data sets. A fuzzy set is a means to define partial set membership within a specific context. It is particularly useful when, as is so often the case, subjective or imprecise descriptions are used. For example, consider the question of 'child-bearing age'. For each age value, we can allocate a number indicating strength of set membership (Figure 7.10). We could thus create a graph of set membership, with Age as the *x*-axis and Confidence Factor as the *y*-axis. The attraction of using fuzzy logic and fuzzy sets is that within an expert system they can be used to give probabilistic definitions of knowledge. This is important in history, where knowledge is usually probabilistic rather than absolute (another reason why relational systems can be unsatisfactory).[33]

The expert system also provides some way of inferring new knowledge from the contents of the knowledge base. This is called an *inference engine*. Humans often infer meaning from the context in which a word, image or concept is used. Computer systems, for the most part, can recognise strings of characters, but cannot infer meaning from them through contexualisation. The ability to infer rather than simply recognise is at the heart of expert system applications.

1.0	Absolutely true
0.75	Almost certainly true
0.50	Reasonably true
0.25	Somewhat true
0.0	Unknown
−0.25	Somewhat false
−0.50	Reasonably false
−0.75	Almost certainly false
−1.0	Absolutely false

Figure 7.9 *Confidence factors*

Source: Eric Summers, 'ES: A Public Domain Expert System', *Byte* (October 1990), p. 290.

Value	Strength of Set Membership
8	−1.0 (definitely not member of fuzzy set)
12	0.2 (slightly member of fuzzy set)
20	1.0 (full member of fuzzy set)
30	1.0 (full member of fuzzy set)
45	0.5 (partial member of fuzzy set)
60	−1.0 (definitely not member of fuzzy set)
70	−1.0 (definitely not member of fuzzy set)

Figure 7.10 *Strength of set membership*

The user engages in a dialogue with the system via the *user interface* which prompts him/her to answer a series of questions which define the problem. Rules in the knowledge base are interpreted and processed by the inference engine, which may also make calls to outside programs to perform mathematical calculations or query a database for information. The *system manager* depicted in Figure 7.8 is a control mechanism which manages the system, determining when to start the inference engine, when to ask the user for more specific information about the problem, and when to return and display results.

In responding to a user's query, two principal strategies are employed by the inference engine: *forward chaining* and *backward chaining*. With forward chaining, the program applies a set of IF rules, each consisting of a sequence of conditions which lead to specified actions. The result of applying a rule is to change the contents of working memory, which then triggers another IF rule, and the process continues until the desired goal or result is found. Backward chaining is somewhat akin to the concept of goal-seeking used in spreadsheet software. The user specifies the required goal, and the expert system uses appropriate rules and knowledge to determine if, and how, the desired objective can be achieved. In other words, the idea is to take the result pattern and push it backwards through the rules to see how it might have been generated. Thus, through querying the database, the user can draw conclusions based upon the reasoning performed by the program. Expert systems can usually explain how they arrived at their conclusions, and some high-end packages can graphically display the rules that proved to be true or false.

The development of expert systems has led to the emergence of knowledge engineering as a discipline in its own right. PROLOG is the language currently favoured by most AI researchers. It may be used both to handle information and to define rules for making inferences based on that information. For those who do not want to invest time and effort in learning PROLOG programming skills, there are expert system shells and toolkits. Shells provide a ready-made interpreter and off-the-shelf facilities, which allow rapid development and prototyping. Several commercial expert shell systems are available. However, because they require the user to follow a particular style of representation they can be inflexible to use. As the name suggests, toolkits offer a wide range of different approaches, with sophisticated modelling and graphics features. Though more flexible than shells, they require a longer learning period and tend to be more demanding in terms of hardware.

☐ *Knowledge bases*

Systems which combine artificial intelligence with database technology are known as *knowledge base systems (KBMSs)* or as *intelligent* or *deductive databases*. Intelligent databases represent the latest step in the evolution of database technology. Managing a large knowledge base involves tricky problems, both theoretical and practical; not least amongst them is the need to acquire a good understanding of logic. A definitive discussion of their development and characteristics is provided by Gardarin and Valduriez.[34]

Since a deductive database is first and foremost a DBMS, it will provide the data description and data manipulation languages which conventional DBMSs offer. Additionally, however, it will provide a new interface which is mainly a *rule definition language*. There are various strategies for the development of intelligent database systems. This new interface can be achieved by loosely coupling PROLOG with a relational DBMS or by building a logic programming language inside an extended RDBMS.

For some, intelligent databases go even further. Eventually, the preferred approach may be the full integration of such tools, concepts and techniques as AI, database management, logic programming, information retrieval and fuzzy systems theory into a sophisticated and dynamic system. This is a long-term prospect. It is advocated by those who feel a fresh approach is preferable to 'bolting on' new features to existing systems. They draw upon, and integrate, many of the parallel developments currently taking place in the computer science world, arguing that, to date, such developments have only been tenuously linked to each other, and consequently much of the potential benefit has not been achieved. Thus the intelligent database model created by Parsaye *et al.* is based upon the integration of five information technologies:[35]

- Databases.
- Object-oriented programming.
- Expert systems and knowledge bases.
- Hypermedia.
- Text management.

Within this model, for example, expert systems and knowledge bases will provide the capacity to reason and infer new information. This creates the potential for self-modifying databases, as well as the ability to infer what information a user might be interested in, even if that need was not exactly specified in the original query. Similarly, hypermedia represents an important step towards more dynamic databases by permitting information to be added without concern for the prior structure of the database. This in turn is antithetical to the approach adopted in traditional static database models, and is only made possible by the adoption of object-oriented methods. Parsaye *et al.* state that the three key features of an intelligent database are that it should:

- provide high-level tools for data analysis, discovery and integrity control, allowing users both to extract knowledge from, and apply knowledge to, data.
- allow users to interact directly with information as naturally as if they were flipping through the pages of a standard text on the topic or talking to a helpful human expert.
- retrieve knowledge as opposed to data and uses inference to determine what a user needs to know.[36]

☐ *Historical examples*

A useful introduction to the use of AI in historical research is provided in an article entitled 'Artificial Intelligence, History and Knowledge Representation' by Lee *et al.* It describes one of the earliest attempts to investigate the application of AI knowledge representation techniques to historical research, the RESEDA Project, which was established in the late 1970s by a team of French and Italian researchers. RESEDA's aim was to set up an information retrieval system operating on a historical database which is continuously fed by extracting data from a variety of sources, such as archive documents, scholarly publications and relevant books. This information provides a set of biographical units concerning people involved in the history of France during the later fourteenth and early fifteenth centuries. To cope with the difficulties of handling data which may be incomplete or subjective, specific tools have been designed. First, a 'metalanguage' was developed which is rich and flexible enough to deal with information that might be misleading, contradictory, or false. It allowed a detailed coding of the events which constitute the lives of the individuals concerned. The second feature of RESEDA is its inference procedures, which seek to provide a computational representation of the intellectual processes of a historian. These attempt to isolate information which may provide an answer to the user's question but which is only tenuously linked to the object of the question and therefore would not be found by a simple direct match. A particular feature of the approach adopted by the project team is that, 'rather than considering the database as a closed set in which a certain number of fixed, predefined variables are connected with respect to a limited number of relationships, RESEDA's structure has been designed to record events as they are found in their source, imposing as few as possible preconceived ideas on the associations which will be sought using the system.'[37]

Other important researchers in this field are Caroline Bourlet and Jean-Luc Minel. Since the mid-1980s, they have published a number of articles describing the use of expert system shells in the construction of a prosopographical database of Parisian craftsmen during the reign of Philip the Fair.[38] The database consists of 70,000 records from the Royal Tax Registers of the period 1292–1313, representing about 15–20,000 individuals. The problems which the researchers have faced are typical of medieval history. First, a few common Christian names – Jean, Pierre, Guillaume, etc. – account for the bulk of the corpus. Secondly, individuals are often described differently in the various registers. These variants are due primarily to:

- the absence of certain distinguishing qualities (for example, people might be described by their occupation rather than by name).
- orthographical variations.
- the use of diminutives as Christian names.
- the use of craft names as descriptors as opposed to patronyms.
- the use of different craft names (where the same individual had more than one occupation, or changed occupation over time).

The researchers have concluded that it would be impossible to devise a single procedure which would immediately allow all or the majority of the individuals to be identified. Rather, a variety of techniques must be called upon: identifying equality, compatibility, difference and absence; drawing upon the historian's knowledge as to which crafts were compatible; connecting diminutives with the correct firstname; developing reduction rules to cope with phonetic and orthographic variations; and so on. Thus an initial identification should be considered as a working hypothesis and gradually refined in a stepwise manner, adding some criteria for decision-making and eliminating others.

This seemed a task well suited to AI rather than a conventional DBMS. Bourlet and Minel therefore decided to construct a system containing the classic architecture of the expert system:

- A fact base (description of the individuals).
- A rules base (the historian's expert knowledge in declarative form).
- An inference engine (in this case, the PROLOG language).

An expert shell was used, providing a user-friendly front end for building the knowledge base, a development engine to process the reasoning, and a trace tool to permit the sequence of the reasoning to be displayed. The strength of the system lay in its flexibility. The reasoning could be developed step-by-step under the control of the historian, and the researchers found that about 30 rules allowed the identification of some 60 per cent of the basic corpus. A typical rule (which would link *Guiart le pesier* with *Guiart de Cligny, pesier*) would take the form:

Two individuals may be identical if:

- they live in the same street and the same parish.
- their first names are identical or compatible.
- the craft cited in the surname of one is identical to the craft practised by the other.[39]

The application of AI techniques to historical demography is also a significant and continuing development. In an important article entitled

'Artifical Intelligence and the Historian: Prospects and Possibilities',[40] Schürer examines the areas of historical demographic research where automated techniques akin to the rationale of expert systems are currently being developed in order to facilitate data analysis. In doing so, he seeks to make apparent the potential advantages of such techniques over other research methodologies, and assesses future developments. Schürer suggests that 'it is in the field of historical demography that the greatest use of AI techniques in the form of expert systems is currently being applied to historical research.'[41] The reason is that it involves the analysis of large amounts of data relating to individual events in a person's life history – 'it is the analysis of large amounts of data, measuring the way or detecting the patterns by which various data observations relate to each other, that is central to many expert systems.' Schürer explores two aspects of historical demography in some detail. The first is the application of such techniques to the problems of classifying the structure of residential groupings. A second example of the use of AI techniques in a specific area of historical demography concerns nominal record linkage – the joining together of information from separate documents relating to an individual. For example, facilities such as recursion (the ability to use a rule which can redefine itself) may be employed as a powerful tool to infer kinship relationships from demographic databases.[42] Record linkage is discussed further in section 8.2.

However, Schürer recognises the limitations of such techniques in other areas of historical research. The success of expert systems in the areas which he examines stems largely from the existence of a set of well-defined rules from which inferences may satisfactorily be drawn. The same is not true, however, of other aspects of historical enquiry. 'The ability to define rules of inference is in most cases an impossible task, not only because of the failure to arrive at common interpretations, but also because the historian's search for solutions to problems is infinite, not only changing with the discovery of new "facts", but being liable to constant re-interpretation as the existing facts are viewed from a multitude of different and wide-ranging perspectives.'[43] Thus, the inappropriate application of AI-type techniques can lead to oversimplification or distortion of historical realities.

A similar caveat is issued by Schulte to potential users of PROLOG-based expert systems:

> PROLOG operates on the basis of 'negation by failure to prove', and is thus only designed for a particular kind of problem; a 'self-contained' world of knowledge. In other words, PROLOG users must treat the knowledge representation as a closed system, where *all* the relevant information can be assumed to be present. . . . Moreover, PROLOG

relationships describe this closed logical system in static terms, and take no account of change. Clearly, the real world with which historians concern themselves is not like this.[44]

Schulte concludes that, whilst further advances are continually being made, the benefits of AI depend very much on the type of historical enquiry. Those who 'are addicted to their archival source material, and precise and exacting in their methods . . . will no doubt be attracted by the promise of historical tools that will allow them to find out yet more about highly specialised domains.' However, those who 'wish to survey a far broader panorama of the historical landscape may find that AI cannot, as yet, cope with the wide generalisations and deep underlying causes of which they are so fond.'[45]

■ 7.5 Conclusion

There are many ways in which the database concept has been extended. Sometimes, these extensions are not only desirable but necessary if we are to accommodate all the characteristics of historical data and all the needs of researchers. However, it must be emphasised that there is no single best solution. As McFadden and Hoffer have remarked, psychological research on human information organisation reveals that 'people are able to use a variety of data organisations effectively, as long as they are not forced to use a structure incapable of capturing the true meaning of data. Thus, it would appear that the "natural" structure of data, more than individual, personal, preferences, is what matters.'[46] The guiding principle in selecting a suitable strategy must always be fitness for purpose.

Case Study G
Community Reconstruction and the
Viana Do Castelo Database

Jean Colson
Southampton University

Since the beginning of the 1980s, a team of researchers at the University
of Southampton have been working on a major project to reconstitute
the population of the Portuguese city of Viana do Castelo and investigate
secular demographic trends, including migration to and from the New
World. The successful development of the project has led to a number of
PhD theses and publications. The first thesis using the Viana data was
that of Elizabeth de Azevedo Reis: it was entitled 'The Spatial Demography
of Portugal in the late Nineteenth Century: Evidences from the 1864 and
1878 Censuses' (University of Southampton, 1987). It was swiftly followed
by that of Arno Kitts: 'An Analysis of the Components of Migration: Viana
do Castelo, Minho, 1826–1931' (University of Southampton, 1988). Kitts
and Reis have collaborated with Doulton to publish a detailed description
of their methodology in *The Reconstitution of Viana do Castelo* (Association
for History and Computing, London, 1990), which is essential reading
for anyone embarking upon a project of this nature. Viana's importance
in the period has meant that other writers have drawn on their findings
to discuss such diverse topics as the Portuguese migration to the Amazon
between 1870 and 1910 and the impact of the War between Absolutists
and Constitutionalists, 1827–34.

Data collection began in the summer of 1981, and a database was designed and implemented using the SIR (Scientific Information Retrieval)
DBMS. SIR was chosen because it was available on the ICL mainframe of
Southampton University's Computing Service, and would allow us to create
what was then considered to be a substantial file housing a considerable
amount of data in each record. Another important advantage was that,
although SIR was a hierarchical database system in its physical form, it
also possessed some of the features of network and relational systems.
Thus, for example, it was possible to move from any one point in the
hierarchy to another, whilst retaining a pointer to the original location.
The data were drawn from five document types: muster rolls, electoral
rolls, passports, cemetery lists and marriage certificates. These data were
taken from the records of two parishes, Santa Maria Maior and Nossa
Senhora de Monserrate, as well as the Archive of the Camara of the Villa
of Viana do Castello, Province of Minho, Portugal. The records chosen
spanned approximately 1770–1931, from the dictatorship of the Marques
de Pombal to that of Salazar.

At first glance these manuscript documents appeared to consist of struc-

218

tured data with short fields, which easily lent themselves to the simple alphanumeric representation of variables such as age, sex, and marital condition of the population, which could be handled by SIR. Nevertheless, the Viana project typified many of the problems which have to be confronted and resolved in any large-scale historical database, particularly when it has a lifespan of a decade or more. For example, we encountered the classic problems of nominal record linkage, and spent considerable time standardising names. A second name field was added to provide for the many variations in spelling. Nominal record linkage algorithms were developed by Arno Kitts and Dave Doulton, which matched variant forms of a name and linked by estimating the probability of the properties of other fields; these were age, sex, occupation. The record linkage strategies used in the project are discussed in detail in *The Reconstitution of Viana do Castelo*. Other difficulties have emerged as the project has developed and the demands made upon the database have become more diverse and sophisticated. For example, the study of kinship and family alliance requires a lower level of error than was deemed acceptable for the aggregate data analysis which was the original objective of the project. Other investigations have been hampered by decisions taken early in the project to omit certain data items from the database. Many of these decisions were determined by the limitations of SIR and the hierarchical model on which it is based. At the beginning of the 1980s, SIR was regarded as a powerful and sophisticated DBMS. In the perspective of the mid-1990s, it appears cumbersome and outmoded, placing many restrictions upon the format in which data can be entered and stored. The hierarchical model has been superseded by relational and object-oriented models.

A consideration of each type of source document used in the project provides further evidence of the kind of difficulties encountered. Of the five documents, the muster rolls could be entered almost in their entirety. The electoral rolls, on the other hand, contained much information about different types of taxes which had to be ignored at the original entry. The reason was that SIR required the standardisation to base 10 of the various currencies, weights and measures used in Viana in the period 1750–1931, and this proved impossible. Prior to the 1820s, the cruzado, castilian or even English sovereigns were exchanged at local rates. The Brazilian and Portuguese mil-reis, introduced in the 1820s, were used interchangeably but had different and constantly altering values, and were variously quoted in gold, silver or paper. After 1827, when Brazil finally broke away from Portugal, as many as five different currencies were in use at any one time. Similarly, local, Galician, Minhoto, Portuguese and Brazilian weights and measures were all in use for local commodities such as maize or wine. All this meant that tax records could not be handled by SIR without substantial re-interpretation in which layers of meaning would have to be discarded. It was so difficult to correlate the taxable values contained in the records with other indications of social class that demographic historians showed little interest in financial or monetary questions or the issues of kinship and alliance which pertained to them.

Some of the data available from the passports, which were sometimes held jointly, also had to be omitted because of the limitations of the data model. The name of the passport-holder's sponsor was consistently ignored, so that it later proved impossible to link the names of apprentices going to Brazil with commercial families who were sponsoring them. Similarly, cemetery lists provided the names of the next of kin or the sponsor and wet nurse of foundlings (who were frequently to be found in the conscription records of nineteenth-century Viana) but these could not readily be integrated into the database. Funerary customs, which included the removal of the corpse to a second or third location, were also indicated on the cemetery records but could not be recorded. Another drawback was all too evident; SIR was developed to handle dates after 1900. Various devices were used to take account of this, but it was impossible to enter the various ways in which dates might be recorded, such as 'Festa de Sao Joao, 1794', which would have needed to be entered as a unique text string.

The marriage certificates seemed a great find – for they were far richer than their English equivalent. At their most extensive they not only contained the names of the bride, groom, and their parents, but often those of the grandparents, godparents and tutors: such documents might contain details of the location of the marriage (in private chapels) as well as the social relationships of the priest, and the many dispensations of canon law which might be required. The sheer scale of data meant that on occasion SIR entries numbered more than 50 fields. Other marriage certificates for the same parish, however, might amount to just 20 fields, and contained the skeletal data to be expected in an English register. Such variety meant that SIR coding did not readily express the complex relationships inherent in the material, and this effectively vitiated its use for the study and reconstitution of kinship and alliances in the nineteenth-century society of Viana do Castello.

One aspect of this problem should be noted. Portuguese names draw upon a very limited repertoire, but reflect the substantial changes in orthography which occurred between 1750 and 1931. Consequently naming rules had to be identified and expressed in the design of the database management system. The rules themselves were complex, and varied with social class. It was, for example, certainly not uncommon for grandfather and grandson to possess the same combinations of names, but the same rule might not apply to father and son. At the same time mothers and daughters did not necessarily take their father's/husband's names. The development of algorithms to deal with spelling variations was complicated by the fact that, in SIR, modelling the complex set of relationships which adhere to an individual person required the user to create redundant and duplicate data flagging and data information. Moreover, the repertoire of tags which indicated discrete units of information was too limited. Proximate clusters of data in the document could not be easily represented in SIR as such. At the same time short field lengths often truncated data entries. This meant that another database management system had to be used which allowed for regular recompilation of names and associated elements, so that an acceptable record-linkage algorithm could then be employed.

By the early 1990s, therefore, it was becoming apparent that the project has outgrown the database management software on which it was originally developed, and a fresh look was required. Attempts at codification of more complex types of information led to the conclusion that a more subtle yet rigorous analysis could be achieved by using a flexible and source-oriented database management system. For the greater part of the best data on families and their alliances was unstructured; contracts, probate inventories, newspaper articles and private correspondence needed to be interpolated with the materials culled from structured data such as electoral and military censuses as well as the parish records. This would enable scholars to query and model the structures of kinship within the city and its hinterland, since these were far more extensive and important than had been suspected.

These concerns led to the choice of κλειω for the Viana data. κλειω is source-oriented, and, as described in Chapter 7, it allows the user to provide an accurate representation of the original document rather than one de-termined by the limitations of the database management system. κλειω possesses many attractions for the Viana Project. The fact that the integrity of the original document is retained is of considerable benefit. It ensures that questions can be asked which were not anticipated or allowed for earlier in the project. κλειω's powerful facilities for full text retrieval, cataloguing and codebook creation are extremely useful. Calculation of currencies and their equivalents, and calendar dates expressed in multiple forms, as both text and numbers, are easily accommodated. Thus the user may analyse data contexts requiring both the ecclesiastical and secular calendars, and calculations made in the eighteenth century. Similarly, variations in the spelling of names are no problem, as κλειω is capable of administering an orthography defined by the users. One-to-many and many-to-many relationships, which on occasion created difficulties in SIR, are easily managed in κλειω. So too is the existence of large numbers of nulls – a common feature of historical data.

Additionally, data may be output to other systems (including mapping and geographical information systems) for further analysis. For the Viana Project, an important benefit was that the data administered by κλειω could be compared in a consistent and systematic manner with another data set consisting of free text and images, which is currently administered by Microcosm, a hypermedia program developed at the University of South-ampton. These data include photographic images, maps and plans, and oral evidence on the life of the city and its commercial connections in the nineteenth century.

■ *Chapter 8* ■

Coding and Record Linkage

One of the greatest joys of modern database systems is that they make straightforward what was once complicated. Before the database revolution, the manipulation of large historical datasets generally required the writing of customised computer programs. Days and weeks of hard work were needed to achieve substantial results, and, correspondingly, even small mistakes could prove very costly. This, of course, is no longer entirely true. Database technology is remarkably tolerant of error. Mistakes can quickly be rectified and changes of mind readily accommodated. The potent combination of generic data structures and powerful query languages frees the historian from tedious programming to concentrate on the real task at hand: that of working with data to extract meaningful information.

In this chapter, we focus upon two core historical research techniques – coding and record linkage – and examine how database systems have led to improvements in method. These improvements relate to both speedier implementation and superior technique.

■ 8.1 Coding

Organising historical data into a form suitable for analysis is a task of critical importance. Over the years a great deal of attention has been given to devising appropriate methods for handling historical data, and the solution has often been found in the development of a data coding scheme. Coding has come to be regarded as 'one of the necessary evils of historical research.'[1] It achieves four principal objectives:

- Reducing data storage requirements.
- Standardising the way entities are described.
- Increasing the speed with which data may be queried.
- Organising data items into analytical categories.

In the early days of historical computing, on mainframe and mini-computers, coding was an essential precursor of data entry because of the limitations on data storage. Many programs restricted records to a maximum of 80 characters – the maximum which could be viewed on-screen and stored on the Hollerith 80-column punched cards used for data entry. Moreover, storage media were expensive, and the rate at which data could be transferred and accessed was limited. In recent years, such restrictions have largely disappeared with the advent of sophisticated software and mass storage media.

But while the desirability of limiting data storage requirements has diminished in importance, the classification of data remains an essential part of the process of historical enquiry, no matter what the topic being researched. Even in a highly structured source, the original entries are often variable in form. The recording of marital status provides an obvious example. There are only a few possible categories – unmarried, married, or widowed – yet each might be recorded in one of several different ways. A unmarried person might be entered as 'Single', 'Unmarried', 'Unmarr' or simply 'Unm'. The historian will know that these are as one, but to the computer they are discrete strings of characters. Accurate analysis of the data depends upon the allocation of a code to standardise the entries, regardless of the variant spellings or abbreviations used. There is an immediate gain in clarity and it is much quicker to search for records:

```
WHERE  Marital_Status  =  'U'
```

rather than:

```
WHERE  Marital_Status  =  'Single'
OR  Marital_Status  =  'Unmarried'
OR  Marital_Status  =  'Unmarr'
OR  Marital_Status  =  'Unm'
```

Besides ensuring that data are handled in a systematic way, coding is often used to group data into categories desired by the historian. The main aim is to impose a structure on the data which render them amenable to systematic analysis. Statistical tests, for instance, may not be reliable if there are too many classes containing too few cases.

However, whilst the benefits of coding may seem obvious, there are serious pitfalls for the unwary researcher. First, it is important to avoid what Schürer has called the 'punched card mentality': the tendency for researchers to squeeze their data to fit the software, 'rigorously collapsing fields of information into bands of numeric codes.'[3] He lays part of the blame at the door of software manuals. A recommended text for SPSS, which is one of the most widely-used statistical packages in the social sciences, encourages users to adopt coding schemes which consist of numbers only, even though the program can readily handle alphanumeric strings.[4] Schürer urges that it is time to break away from the punched card legacy.

Secondly, problems may result if a coding scheme is imposed at an early stage in a research project. These are usually most serious when the original data are completely discarded in favour of alphanumeric codes; a technique known as pre-coding. Difficulties arise when the researcher has failed to anticipate all eventualities. The emergence of fresh hypotheses and unanticipated questions is part and parcel of historical research, and in such circumstances the existence of an inadequate coding scheme will limit the capacity for informed analysis.

Thirdly, coding often results in the selective recording of data; as Morris has noted, 'coding at heart trades comprehensibility for loss of information.'[5] The result is not a transcript of the original source, but an adaptation of it. It might be argued that this is not a problem in the marital status example given above, where the categories are few in number and mutually exclusive, but not many types of historical data are as clear-cut as this. The standardisation of names and occupations, for example, inevitably leads to a loss of information which cannot easily be recovered. In this regard, experience has shown just how difficult it is for historians to make use of datasets created for purposes other than their own. As Greenstein has remarked, 'data once coded were lost forever to the secondary analyst whose assumptions and research interests might very well be different than those of the original author.'[6]

The solution to these difficulties lies, to a considerable extent, in abandoning pre-coding in favour of post-coding. Rather than imposing a coding scheme at the outset, the original data are transcribed in full and codes added at a later stage. This creates the possibility for a variety of coding schemes of differing levels and complexity to be implemented as required. As Schürer has noted, the principal advantage is that 'the process of post-coding, rather than pre-coding, enables the researcher to re-structure the codes, or allocate an entirely different coding schema, since the original values from which the codes are derived are retained within the data structure.'[7]

This advice is echoed by researchers working on Wolverhampton University's Portbooks Programme. In this case, a dual policy was adopted during the early years of the project with regard to the transliteration of words from manuscripts. Standard abbreviations (codes) were used when the meaning of a word was certain, as in the case of port names.

But whenever the meaning was in doubt every effort was made to transcribe the word in full and as accurately as possible. However, the original strategy has more recently fallen into disfavour, and with the benefit of hindsight the Project's Directors now recommend that original spellings should be captured at all times.

Thus post-coding may help to ensure that decisions taken at an early stage in the project's development cycle do not irremediably damage the database. Even so, careful attention needs to be taken when selecting a suitable strategy for data coding, to ensure that the project's aims and objectives can be achieved.

☐ *Types of codes*

There are many types of coding scheme in existence. Some are single level; others are hierarchical in structure. Single-level codes are the simpler type, but their uses are limited. For example, they are appropriate for appending unique reference numbers to records and for standardising a set of placenames, but they are not always capable of accommodating the complexities of historical data. Hierarchical codes (also known as nested codes) are arranged as trees. They serve both to classify data and to indicate relationships between data items. A typical example of a hierarchical coding scheme is the UK's Standard Industrial Classification (SIC). As can be seen from Figure 8.1, a broad industrial sector – in this case, metal goods, engineering and the vehicles industries – is subdivided into two increasingly specific levels, ensuring that all industrial undertakings can readily be assigned to an appropriate category.

The SIC is an example of a block code in which the numbers and characters making up the code are *non-significant.* This is often the case. In simple, sequential coding schemes, for example, each new record in a series may be allocated the next available number or alphanumeric character(s) in a rising sequence. The code serves as a unique identifier for the record and has no meaning in itself. In other coding schemes individual codes are *significant.* This is the case with the familiar two-character abbreviations used to represent the names of American states (NY, NJ, CA, etc.). Historians frequently generate codes of this kind – the first four letters of names, names with the vowels removed, etc. – as a precursor to data manipulations like record linkage. The important points are that the coding scheme should be appropriate to the task, and that codes should be easy to use, assign, transcribe and check.

What sounds easy in theory, however, is frequently more difficult in practice, as the long-running debates on occupational coding and

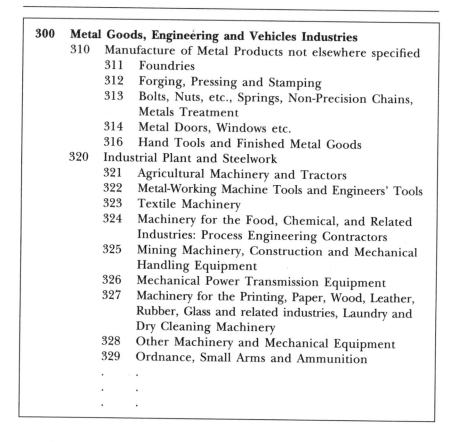

300   Metal Goods, Engineering and Vehicles Industries
    310   Manufacture of Metal Products not elsewhere specified
        311   Foundries
        312   Forging, Pressing and Stamping
        313   Bolts, Nuts, etc., Springs, Non-Precision Chains, Metals Treatment
        314   Metal Doors, Windows etc.
        316   Hand Tools and Finished Metal Goods
    320   Industrial Plant and Steelwork
        321   Agricultural Machinery and Tractors
        322   Metal-Working Machine Tools and Engineers' Tools
        323   Textile Machinery
        324   Machinery for the Food, Chemical, and Related Industries: Process Engineering Contractors
        325   Mining Machinery, Construction and Mechanical Handling Equipment
        326   Mechanical Power Transmission Equipment
        327   Machinery for the Printing, Paper, Wood, Leather, Rubber, Glass and related industries, Laundry and Dry Cleaning Machinery
        328   Other Machinery and Mechanical Equipment
        329   Ordnance, Small Arms and Ammunition

Figure 8.1   *The United Kingdom Standard Industrial Classification System (extract)*

standardising nominal data (people's names) make plain. These debates illustrate very clearly the main issues which must be addressed when designing coding schemes.

☐ *Coding occupational data*

The semantic problems involved in describing occupations are well known; some stem from inconsistent description, others from the fact that the reasons for classifying occupations have changed with time. Nowadays it is common to use occupation as an indicator of social status. This is problematic enough for the late twentieth century; occupation is at best a convenient proxy for a variety of status indicators such as education, skill, income, and relationship to the means of production. The problems of interpretation are compounded when analysing historical data. In the mid-nineteenth century, for example, the census classified occupations according to the raw materials a person worked with. This reflected the belief that disease was a chemical process, and that working with particular materials determined life expectancy. Later in the century, with the emergence of the germ theory of disease and a growing interest in economic and social research, occupational classifications placed more emphasis on skill levels. They also began to distinguish between manufacturing, distributive and administrative occupations.[8]

Yet despite the evident difficulties, the systematic analysis and comparison of occupations and related economic and social issues would not be possible without coding and classification. This is the theme taken up by Morris in his insightful article on the main principles of occupational coding for historical research.[9] The first and most basic principle is that the historian should always proceed in a *scientifically correct* manner. By this, Morris means that only one type of information should be coded at a time; that occupational categories should be mutually exclusive; and that in the classification scheme a place should be found for each and every occupational title. Only if these basic rules are observed can true comparisons be made over time and space.

The second characteristic of a good coding scheme, according to Morris, is *fitness for purpose*. It is unlikely, for example, that a scheme devised for the southern counties of England would have the same categories as a study of the mill towns of Lancashire and Yorkshire. Morris notes the merits for comparative purposes of having 'standard' occupational groups, as in the popular Booth–Armstrong classification,[10] but there are costs involved in slavishly following others: 'such a decision often introduces rigidities, an inability to serve the detailed needs of the project. The apparent consistency of using the same code may conceal differences of judgement that derive from the nature of the document or economic context.' Thus, while he recognises that 'comparability is a desirable and welcome aspect of any analysis', he concludes that 'it should not be purchased at any price. It should be entered into with a full awareness of the risks involved.'

Morris exalts *flexibility* in coding and the avoidance of any form of rigidity. Accordingly, multiple-level – hierarchical – coding schemes are recommended in preference to the simple and unidimensional. This approach has two advantages. First, it encourages sophisticated analysis of a database at various levels of detail. Secondly, it makes it relatively easy to recombine categories in new ways as the historian's original thoughts are refined and reformulated.[11] For example, in a recent large-scale investigation into the social origins of twentieth-century members of Oxford University, coding some 75,000 occupational records took half a person-year. However, those 75,000 records could readily be organised into 700 codes. 'Recombining the 700 distinctive code combinations to create new analytical categories is a job which takes at most a long morning; and it is at this level in the data that any re-coding should take place.'[12]

Know thy sources is the final principle put forward by Morris. He is at pains to point out that any occupational coding scheme worth its salt must take full account of the origins, content, peculiarities and limitations of the sources upon which a database is founded. It is especially important to bear in mind the provenance of a source: 'The purpose of the document is the likeliest guide to the risks being taken in making an inference about occupation from occupational title.' Very often, entries describing an individual's occupation will vary from source to source, and this reflects a search for status and recognition. In nineteenth-century Leeds, for example, Morris found approximately 70 per cent consistency between entries in poll books and trade directories. However, variations in occupational title do not necessarily mean that one is right and the other wrong. Rather, 'they give different aspects of an individual's claims on the economy. They were different presentations of self to the world in which the document was created.'[13] This confirms Morris in his belief that multidimensional coding schemes are the best way to accommodate such differences in representation.

☐ *Coding nominal data*

The standardisation of surnames is a second important activity which falls under the banner of coding. It is a vital first step in the process of record linkage; of establishing with some degree of certainty that someone named in one source is the same as a person named in a second source. Unfortunately, what might seem a straightforward matter is made complicated by the high frequency of discrepant spellings in historical documents. These arise from phonetical and orthographical errors, and actual changes of name. With people's names, the problems with Smith/Smythe or Mac/Mc are well known; even more problematic are the dozen or so ways to spell Mohammed, or the tendency of Portuguese males to use up to five names in any combination.[14] What this means is that a pair of records which on the surface contain substantial discrepancies may in fact, at a deeper level, refer to a single individual. A method of dealing with this problem must be found.

The most obvious strategy is to standardise. It is not necessary that names be standardised to a known name which exists somewhere in the sample; it is sufficient if every version of a name is standardised to the same combination of characters, which is distinct from the combination of characters used for any other name. In general, this involves changing or removing certain letters or letter combinations. One of the best-known solutions is the Soundex code, devised to deal with phonetic variations. The written form of names was derived from the way they were spoken, and so Soundex attempts to 'reverse the name recording process, so that different forms of the same spoken word are coded identically.'[15] To achieve this, Soundex retains the initial letter of a name and replaces the remaining character with three numerals, chosen so that the same number replaces phonetically similar consonants (Figure 8.2). Examples of Soundex coding are given in Figure 8.3.

Soundex does have its shortcomings. Essentially, what it does is to remove the least reliable elements of Anglo-Saxon names, and thus its effectiveness depends upon the proportion of Anglo-Saxon derived names in a sample. It also gets less reliable when applied to older records. Thus many studies have employed modified versions of the Soundex code.

A second type of code – Viewex – was developed to cope with the visual confusions which can be result when the data are in manuscript form. Some handwritten letters or combinations of letters are particularly difficult to decipher, such as upper-case F, J and T, and lower-case combinations including m, n, r, u, and w.

Depending upon the character of the sources being used, a researcher may well decide to standardise textual data using a combination of Soundex- and Viewex-type codes. Thus researchers working on the Pennsylvania Social History Project developed a sophisticated coding system to cope with the peculiarities of German and Irish names. This incorporated both Soundex and Viewex properties and included prefix, infix and postfix treatments to standardise certain combinations of letters at the beginning, middle and end of surnames and forenames.[16] Other researchers have produced their own systems to meet particular needs. Phillips, in his 1982 book on unreformed English elections, describes a basic surname coding system which removes the final 'e', 's' and 'es', and all double consonants. Long names were then reduced to seven letters by deleting, first, vowels, then consonants from right to left.[17] Similar codes have recently been used by Bradley in his work on eighteenth-century nonconformity and radicalism, and by Green for the Westminster Historical Database.[18] Another, rather earlier, system is the Henry code, which was specifically formulated for French names. It is based on coding the first letter and the next two consonants instead of the letter and three digits of the Soundex code; it misses out silent or nasal consonants, and treats double consonants as single.[19] However,

---

1. First letter of surname is used in its uncoded form
2. W and H are ignored
3. A, E, I, O, U and Y are not coded, but serve as separators for consonants
4. Other letters are coded as follows, until three digits are used up:

B, P, F, V	= 1
C, G, J, K, Q, S, X, Z	= 2
D, T	= 3
L	= 4
M, N	= 5
R	= 6

5. Letters which follow prefix letters that give the same code are ignored unless they are divided by a separator

---

Figure 8.2 *Soundex coding*

Source: Howard B. Newcombe, 'Record Linking: The Design of Efficient Systems for Linking Records into Individual and Family Histories', *American Journal for Human Genetics*, Vol. 19 (1967), Appendix, pp. 356–7.

Anderson	A536
Bergmans, Brigham	B625
Birk, Berque, Birck	B620
Fisher, Fischer	F260
Lavoie	L100
Llwellyn	L450

Figure 8.3 *Examples of Soundex coding*

Source: Howard B. Newcombe, 'Record Linking: The Design of Efficient Systems for Linking Records into Individual and Family Histories', *American Journal for Human Genetics*, Vol. 19 (1967), Appendix, p. 357.

Canadian researchers working on the Saguenay region of Quebec rejected both the Soundex and Henry codes because they felt that names were compressed too much. Their preference was to build their own codes empirically and then create a program called FONEM which automatically converted the raw data.[20]

It is evident that the choice of which nominal coding scheme to use depends on the particular characteristics of the source data. A modified combination of Soundex and Viewex seems to be the most logical coding system for many cases, but there is no foolproof method which will successfully standardise all names. As Schürer, Oeppen and Schofield have remarked, 'while the computer can provide an invaluable aid in making the standardisation of spelling both less burdensome and more systematic, it is essential that the historian checks the output carefully and takes final responsibility for the result.'[21]

This is particularly true with actual changes of name. Changes of name are not uncommon and can be highly resistant to standardisation rules. People adopt double-barrelled lastnames, and truncate double-barrelled given names. Diminutive forms of baptismal names are also common. Even more problematic are instances where people adopted alternate names. Swedish males often dropped their patronymic on attaining their majority and took on a new surname. Immigrants to the United States anglicised their names (Schwartz to Black; Schmidt to Smith). This last problem is intractable unless the records contain other information which enable reconstruction.

☐ *Marking-up texts*

The emphasis thus far has been on the coding of structured data like names and occupations. Considerable attention has also been devoted in recent years to methods for systematically analysing unstructured data. This critically depends on methods for marking up texts. Within the field of historical computing, two approaches have predominated. The first is based upon the work of Manfred Thaller and his colleagues at Göttingen and other research institutions in Germany and Austria. The second is the work of the Text Encoding Initiative (TEI), an international research project sponsored by the Association for Computers and the Humanities, the Association for Computational Linguistics, and the Association for Literary and Linguistic Computing. Both approaches have been considered by a working group of the Association for History and Computing on standardisation of machine-readable data. The results have been published as a collection of essays edited by Greenstein under the title *Modelling Historical Data*.[22]

Thaller has for long been concerned with the development of standards for textual markup and transfer; this is vital to data sharing and the creation of machine-readable editions of primary sources. His argument is that 'exchanging data between systems of historical data bases may seem almost irrelevant . . . and a subject of purely technical relevance. It is not. Being able to exchange machine readable sources freely, irrespective of the conventions that have been used when they were made machine readable in the first place, will in many cases be the difference between yet another "data graveyard" and a publicly available computer representation of a text.'[23] Of particular importance is Thaller's paper 'A Draft Proposal for a Standard for the Coding of Machine

Readable Sources', first published in 1986.[24] In this, Thaller is concerned mainly with retaining texts in their original form while creating a data structure though the insertion of standard symbols to delimit and classify particular portions of text. To facilitate this, a program known as StanFEP (Standard Format Exchange Program) has been developed. StanFEP is a preprocessor which is intended, in the words of its creators, to make text markup as straightforward as handling highly structured data. Though the latest version comes bundled with κλειω, it is a standalone system. It allows the historian to transcribe a historical source without any change, loading it into databases via structuring symbols integrated into the text. It also facilitates the transfer of 'neutral' exchange formats into formats recognised by the software systems used to process them. An obvious example is the type of processing required to convert text marked up according to the specifications of the Text Encoding Initiative into formats understood by existing software.[25]

The development of techniques for the marking-up of text, of course, are not only of interest to historians. Scholars in the fields of linguistic and literary analysis, for example, took the lead in the TEI because they have a need for electronic editions prepared according to commonly understood conventions.[26] 'The goal of the TEI', therefore, 'is to develop and disseminate a set of Guidelines for the interchange of machine-readable texts among researchers, so as to allow easier and more efficient sharing of resources for textual computing and natural language processing.'[27] These were first published in 1990, and consist of 300 pages of closely printed A4 paper.[28] All TEI-conformant texts contain a header, which describes the document, the way it has been encoded and a history of any revisions made to it, and the transcription of the text itself. One issue which has been hotly debated is whether the exact appearance of texts should be marked up. In general, TEI codes tend to describe the structure and content of the document rather than simulate its appearance. Mark-up codes may refer either to major structural divisions in the text or to interpreted features like <q> for quoted matter, <name> for people's names, <list> and <item> for lists and items within lists, or <abbr> for abbreviations.

Underpinning the TEI markup scheme is SGML (Standard Generalised Markup Language), which has been widely adopted as a standard in the United States and Europe.[29] It provides a method of identifying separate text elements, such as headings, paragraphs, emboldening, and so on, using codes which can be transported across virtually all hardware and software platforms. SGML codes do the same job as tags in DTP programs. For example, instead of having to define the format for each title in a document, the user simply assigns the formatting information to a single code of standard ASCII characters – in this case, <title>. Each title in the document can be tagged. Then, if the author decides to change the appearance of titles, he/she has only to alter the <title> code, rather than re-editing each title in turn. When a document is sent to another user who needs the data to be displayed in a different format, this presents no problems; the new user simply sets up his/her own SGML configuration for <title>, and the format will automatically be converted. Since SGML coding identifies each element in a document, it is very useful when combined with database functions. A SEARCH <title> command will automatically display all the titles in a document; SEARCH <date> would allow the user to search all documents created between specified origination dates.

In recent years, a variety of commercial programs have appeared for creating SGML-compliant texts. One well-established SGML editor is SoftQuad Author/Editor, which runs on PC, Macs and UNIX workstations. It works like a normal wordprocessor, but instead of producing files in its own format it creates SGML-tagged ASCII text. More recently, WordPerfect has entered the SGML market with WordPerfect Markup. Markup takes a WordPerfect text and inserts SGML codes. The program may be run interactively or in batch mode. The interactive mode is preferable as it allows the user to correct any errors or inconsistencies which may be found.

☐ *Conclusion*

Coding is vital to many historical research projects. An increasing number of these claim that the project database will be of value to the wider research community. If these intentions are to be realised, it needs to be borne in mind that no system of pre-coding, no matter how sophisticated, is likely to meet the needs of other researchers. It is for this reason that computing historians like Schürer and Thaller have argued for the development of standard procedures for the coding of various types of information, and have stressed that post-coding, which retains an accurate representation of the data in the original source, is the preferred approach.

It should perhaps be added that careful attention to coding strategies is very much in the best interests of the creator of the database: it is common enough to find that fresh uses are found for the data as the scope of the research project widens, and as new questions and issues are identified. Since coding is an essential precursor to many types of analysis, it need hardly be said that the usefulness of the data, and the accuracy of the results, depends in large part upon the adoption of an appropriate and flexible coding strategy. Coding, for example, is an essential precursor of record linkage; this task, which is a key part of many historical database projects, is considered in the next section.

■ 8.2 Record Linkage

☐ *Historical research and record linkage*

Linking records has always been fundamental to the process of historical enquiry. Whilst some research projects are based largely on a single primary source, such as a collection of personal papers, the historian is usually required to draw together data from a rich variety of materials and locations. Thus, for example, the study of a leading politician like Benjamin Disraeli might commence with a perusal of his own papers at Hughenden Manor but quickly move on to other records, such as the papers of contemporaries; records of government departments and parliamentary proceedings; newspapers and literary reviews; and so on.

Using information drawn from a variety of sources may present difficulties. A person is not uniquely identified by his or her name. Some surnames are very common, and even when combined with forenames may result in a combination which occurs many times in a given population. This does not often matter in the case of the rich and famous. One could hardly confuse William Morris the leading designer and socialist with William Morris the car manufacturer or with a host of lesser-known people of the same name. But even in famous families the habit of naming sons after fathers or uncles is often a potential source of confusion. Four generations of the Quaker Fry family had the first name Joseph, and three generations of another branch bore the first name Francis. Thus the ability to determine when two different records relate to the same person, or, conversely, to discriminate between two people of the same name, is a key element of scholarship. In making such decisions, the historian draws upon a variety of supporting evidence, and the ability to make logical decisions that comes from familiarity with a particular individual or source. In many cases the decision is intuitive, and hardly requires conscious effort.

In recent decades, however, historians have shifted their attention from famous people to populations as a whole. Here the problems of correct identification are much greater, and reliance on intuitive judgement is much less satisfactory. Hence researchers have come to recognise the need to develop formal rules to supplement the use of intuitive judgement. Such techniques were originally developed for linking records by hand; for instance, in the use of parish registers to identify the ages at which marriage, births of children, and death took place. These techniques, known as family reconstitution, enable the researcher to learn a great deal about whole families from records which essentially contain information about individuals.[30] However, manual record linkage is time-consuming, and historians have responded enthusiastically to the advent of database systems which help to automate, speed and simplify record linkage. It is now possible to organise, compare and link data on a much larger scale than was possible by manual methods. The last twenty years or so have seen a host of research projects which exploit record linkage techniques, and the result has been the appearance of a varied and fascinating body of literature on the subject. This section cannot do justice to all the techniques and strategies which have been developed to link historical records, and readers are urged to investigate the many references provided in the bibliography. In particular, valuable introductions to the topic are provided in the works of Wrigley, Schofield, and other demographers associated with the Cambridge Group for the Study of Population and Social Structure.[31] Another useful summary is provided by Kitts, Doulton and Reis, who identify many of the key figures in the development of record linkage.[32] One of these is Ian Winchester, whose 'What Every Historian Needs to Know about Record Linkage in the Micro-Computer Era' provides an up-to-date summary which lives up to the claim made in the title.[33]

☐ *The uses of record linkage*

In the field of historical enquiry, record linkage has perhaps been most effectively used in demographic research. Indeed, modern historical demography could almost be said to have begun with the development of record linkage techniques and family reconstitution. Many of the techniques now available to historical demographers were developed in the 1960s and 1970s, and continue in the 1990s to make a major contribution to our understanding of the past. The use of computer-based techniques in historical demography is now a commonplace; for example, Schürer and Anderson's survey of 618 machine-readable historical datafiles reveals that about 40 per cent of the projects listed utilise nineteenth-century census data.[34] Whilst the computerisation of an individual census for a particular parish or group of parishes is a relatively straightforward task, for many purposes the historian needs comparative data, and is thus obliged to consider how best to link records from two or more census years. Parish registers are another common source of data (13.5 per cent of the projects covered by the survey) which, like census records, may be combined with data from other sources, such as poll books and trade directories, for detailed analysis.[35] Here again a familiarity with the basics of record linkage is essential.

However, the use of record linkage is by no means confined to demographers. There are many fields of application – economic, social, political and cultural. Psephology – the study of elections and voting behaviour – has long been a major interest of historians, and psephologists, along with demographers, have been the pioneers of record linkage techniques. In England, the study of historical elections owes much to the work of W.A. Speck in the 1970s.[36] Until then, poll books had been used in an unsystematic and largely impressionistic fashion. Speck's computerisation of poll books enabled him to address key aspects of electoral behaviour such as loyalty and turnover which continue to dominate historical psephology today. In particular, there has been a shift from the examination of individual poll books towards the linkage of two or more sources, using increasingly sophisticated linkage methods, and thus permitting a more dynamic view of voter behaviour over the course of time. O'Gorman's *Voters, Patrons and Parties*, for example, provides an excellent synthesis of more recent work on local electoral politics, analysing a wide variety of borough constituencies throughout the Hanoverian period.[37] Recent work has also linked poll books with rate books to provide additional information about voters' occupations and social status. One important project, the Westminster Historical Database, is described further below, and in Case Study F.

Prosopography is another important field of study in which formal techniques for record linkage have been employed, though this is a more recent development than in demography and psephology. Prosopography is the study of people's lives, or careers; as Greenstein has remarked, 'it is a means of getting underneath what historical actors have said about themselves and explaining their behaviour with reference to their social, economic and political affiliations.'[38] It may focus on an individual or small family group, or, on the other hand, may be used to develop novel insights into the behaviour of relatively large groups of people who are linked by common educational or cultural backgrounds, or by business or political interests. The investigation of such networks is an increasingly important aspect of research into regional or local communities. Attempting to identify and unravel the closely intertwined relationships – political, social, educational, cultural, and commercial – which existed inevitably involves the researcher in record linkage issues.[39]

Other sources and fields of enquiry are also worthy of note. The survey of databases which was mentioned earlier includes the following projects, which give some indication of the diversity of the work being undertaken:

- The business structure of Lancashire cotton towns, 1807–1831 (Sheffield Hallam University). The project involves cross-linking the Manchester Poor Rate Assessment Books, which provided an indication of the size and type of accommodation, the name of the occupier and patterns of property utilisation, with data from local trade directories, which identify the type of activity carried out at each address.[40]
- The social composition of nonconformist leadership in Lincolnshire, 1764–1870, drawn from Chancery Rolls and nonconformist records (University of Hull).[41]
- An analysis of parish clergy in the Archdeaconry (later Diocese) of Chester between 1500 and 1580, utilising a wide variety of information drawn from episcopal registers and parish records (University of Manchester).[42]
- The creation of a database on Scottish-registered companies engaged in foreign ventures between 1860 and 1914 (University of St Andrews). Data are drawn from memoranda and articles of association, annual reports and returns, and entries in business directories such as the *Stock Exchange Yearbook*.[43]

Finally, it should be noted that while record linkage is usually concerned with people's names – and hence is often known as *nominal* record linkage – the technique is just as applicable to data about other historical entities, such as ships, companies, organisations, and buildings. As an example, if one wanted to build up a comprehensive machine-readable record of the British mercantile marine in the latter half of the nineteenth century, it would be necessary to link Registry of Shipping records, which provide the 'vital statistics' of each ship registered, with the Crew Lists and Agreements in the Public Record Office series BT98, which describe each overseas voyage made by ships of the British Empire during the period.[44] In short, almost any project which draws upon multiple sources is a potential beneficiary of record-linkage methods.

☐ *Record linkage; definition and issues*

When the historian has two or more lists relating to the same persons or objects, then there is much to be gained by merging them. In this way, he or she discovers additional facts about the people or objects which are the subject of a study. The general principle of record linkage is a simple one: we match the data items in one file with comparable data items in a second file, according to a set of rules known as a *linkage algorithm*. But, alas, life is not quite so simple as this, for there are many problems with record linkage that must be approached in a formal manner. There are two kinds of problem: those that concern the actual data; and those that concern the process of linking the records.

The preliminary issues largely concern data standardisation and coding, and were considered in the previous section. Once these have been resolved, the researcher can then turn to the problems of record linkage itself. The first task is the selection of suitable software. A range of different programs have been used for record linkage, on a variety of platforms, from mainframe and micro. The most important technical development has been the emergence of relational database management systems (RDBMSs) which are well suited to many record linkage tasks. Lists of raw data, such as poll and rate books, can conveniently be held as two-way tables (data files) under the control of the RDBMS. Information may be retrieved from any number of tables with a single command. It is this ability to 'join' tables together which makes RDBMSs highly suitable for record linkage. Records in two or more files can easily be matched, and selected data can be exported from the RDBMS for analysis using standard statistical software like SPSS-X or Minitab. There is, however, a continuing debate as to whether researchers should use database programs aimed specifically at the needs of the historian, such as κλειω (see section 7.1), or more generic tools which are commercially available. As we have seen, each have their advocates. Textual information management systems, with their ability to build powerful thesauri, can also be effectively used to establish links between historical data items. Just about the only type of software which is entirely unsuited to record linkage is the flat file manager, which only allows the user to manipulate one two-dimensional table at a time.

Another important preliminary is to decide whether to adopt a fully automated or semi-automated strategy. The relative merits of fully automatic record linkage versus a combination of automatic and manual methods is an issue which has been vigorously debated in a number of important articles. Researchers working on the demographic history of Quebec, for example, have evolved an approach where the computer is allowed to handle the vast majority of cases in which the linkage problems are straightforward, but they resolve the remainder individually by hand.[45] Similarly, Adman, Baskerville and Beedham emphasise the importance of exploiting both automatic and manual methods of record linkage. They argue that 'no systematic algorithm, no matter how sophisticated, can perform this task as well as can a team of experienced researchers assisted by an appropriate set of software tools.'[46] Other researchers, however, have asserted the importance of automated procedures. Kitts *et al.*, for example, have asserted that 'whatever approach is adopted ought to be fully automatic; ensuring both that linkage criteria are carefully defined beforehand, and that those criteria are consistently applied.'[47] Similarly, Schürer, Oeppen and Schofield note that, when faced with the task of disentangling parish register data into the most probable set of individual life histories, the usual response of scholars is to 'abandon any attempt to use the computer, referring problematic cases . . . back to the historian for the exercise of personal judgement.' However, they argue that 'if the historian's judgement has any claim to historical respectability, the principles on which it is based must be capable of being specified in algorithmic form and so be executable automatically by the computer without further human intervention. Moreover, an automatic resolution of indeterminate networks of linked records would have the additional advantage of avoiding the unconscious biases and inconsistencies that can easily creep in when judgements are made for a long series of individual cases over an extended period of time.'[48]

Record matching, as noted earlier, is achieved through the use of an appropriate linkage algorithm. The algorithm may be *slack* or *strict*. For example, we might decide to link records simply on the basis of standardised name fields:

```
SELECT *
FROM Table1, Table2
WHERE Table1.Name
    = Table2.Name
```

Select all fields from **Table1** and **Table2**, establishing links where the contents of the *Name* field in **Table1** match the contents of the *Name* field in **Table2**.

This is a slack algorithm, and whilst it may succeed in matching many records in the two files, some may be false linkages – that is, they may link records describing two or more people of the same name. To resolve this problem, we insist that, when records in two files are linked, the linked records must be *list unique*; that is, each record in a linked file is unique with respect to the fields in the original data files that were used for record matching. For example, if we linked on name fields only, and thus created a linked file with many records for 'John Smith', we would delete all 'John Smith' records as a matter of course. Thus:

```
SELECT *
FROM Table1, Table2
WHERE  Table1.Name
  =  Table2.Name


HAVING  COUNT(*)=1
```

Select all fields from **Table1** and **Table2**, establishing links where the contents of the *Name* field in **Table1** match the contents of the *Name* field in **Table2**, and each name occurs once only.

The problem here, of course, is that, the slacker the linkage algorithm, the larger the number of links lost through insistence on list uniqueness. In other words, because of the frequency with which common names occur, we would lose large numbers of matches – some of which would be false links, but many others might be true. To reduce the number of links lost through insistence on list uniqueness, we might decide to develop a stricter algorithm, using other fields as well as the standardised name. For example, we may decide that if two records match on the common fields *Name*, *Parish*, and *Occup(ation)* (in, say, two files containing poll books entries for the Westminster elections of 1780 and 1784) then the two records relate to the same individual. In selecting *Name*, *Parish* and *Occup* as our linkage criteria we have the basis of a stricter record linkage algorithm.

```
SELECT *
FROM 1780Poll,  1784Poll


WHERE1780Poll.Name
  =  1784Poll.Name
AND  1780Poll.Parish
  =  1784Poll.Parish
AND 1780Poll.Occup
  =  1784Poll.Occup


HAVING  COUNT(*)=1
```

Select all fields from the tables containing records relating to the poll books for 1780 and 1784, establishing links where the contents of the *Name*, *Parish* and *Occup* fields in **1780Poll** match the contents of the equivalent fields in **1784Poll**, and each match occurs once only.

The stricter the algorithm, the more confidence we have that matched pairs represent *true links*. However, confidence is to some extent bought at the cost of failing to match records that *ought* to be matched. Thus the objective is to strike a balance between a slack algorithm which achieves a high proportion of possible matches but fails to discriminate properly between true and false links, and a strict algorithm which eliminates false or dubious links, but also fails to identify some true links.

It follows that when we are dealing with historical data there are likely to be many feasible record linkage algorithms, no matter what the type of project. The researcher must try to select an optimum algorithm which provides the best balance between the *quality* of the links made and the *number* of records linked. Careful thought must be devoted to the specification, testing and selection of algorithms best suited to the task in hand, and this raises questions relating to statistical confidence, historical judgement, and formal methods.

Consider, for example, the strategy adopted by researchers at the Cambridge Group, who have played a leading role in the development of record-matching techniques. Their approach to automatic record linkage is based on two main principles, as the following summary reveals:

> First, an agnosticism about the number and identity of individuals whose life histories are represented by the events recorded in the registers leads us to form all possible links, and to take note of cases where records cannot be linked together. Second, a belief that in situations of uncertainty it is best to prefer the links in which the information content of the records gives one the greatest confidence leads us to adopt a hierarchical, sequential approach to the resolution of ambiguities. In practice this means sorting the links between pairs of records of all types into a descending order of confidence scores, and within each level of confidence score by descending order of ambiguity (i.e. ascending multiplicity). We begin by accepting the linked pair in which we have greatest confidence as correct, deleting all links that compete for, or are incompatible with, either of the two records concerned. When links are deleted, the multiplicity scores of all records previously linked to any of the records involved are revised accordingly. Once the consequences of accepting the link in which we currently have greatest confidence have been worked through, we proceed to deal with the link which ranks next in our confidence, and so on down to the bottom of the hierarchical confidence list. By this stage the clusters of all possible links have necessarily been decomposed into unambiguous life histories.[49]

The linked records comprising the life histories can then be combined into 'family reconstitution' histories, and submitted to other programs which have been devised for the purposes of demographic analysis.

☐ *Linking poll book records: the Westminster Historical Database*

As a more complete example of the strategies and techniques involved in record linkage, the remainder of this section will focus upon the

Westminster Historical Database, which has been created at Royal Holloway, University of London, to facilitate the study of social structure and electoral behaviour in Westminster between 1749 and 1820.[50] The following paragraphs report on an experiment to find the optimum single pass algorithm for linking data from the original manuscript Westminster poll books of 1784 and 1788. We then go on to demonstrate the advantages of multiple pass algorithms both with regard to linkage rates and the quality of the resulting linked records. The case material may be regarded as a specific (though important) instance of the general problem of record linkage, but the methodology employed is original and a number of issues of general significance are discussed. The key practical matters concern algorithm efficiency, selection and relative confidence.

Westminster had a very large number of ratepayers and electors, with 10,000 turning out to vote in many contests. The data held in its poll books are typical of the individual level data from which historians seek to recover useful information. The database derived from Westminster's poll books records the forename and surname of each voter, his parish and street of residence, his occupation or status, and the candidate or candidates for whom he voted. Further information in the poll books, including the date on which the voter polled and an indication as to whether he swore the oaths, affirmed, or that the oaths were not required of him, was not incorporated into the database. Poll books exist for twelve elections in the period, viz. 1749, 1774, 1780, 1784, 1788, 1790, 1796, 1802, 1806, 1818, 1819 and 1820.[51] These data are held as two-way tables under the control of the ORACLE RDBMS.

In a simple analysis of a poll book, voting behaviour may be explained by the two available variables of occupation and parish of residence. More information about the voters is available in other sources. Payment of rates was the theoretical qualification for voting in Westminster. So by linking the poll book data of 1784 to that of 1780, and to the rate book data of 1784, a more sophisticated model may be constructed, of voting being functionally dependent upon occupation, place of residence by the wards into which parishes were divided, prior voting behaviour, and tax assessment. This would further allow exploration of the relationships between variables such as occupation and tax assessment, or occupation and place of residence.

All this depends upon our ability to link records in one table with those in another by matching data items in a table with comparable items in another. Records are linked by *attributes* that define an *entity*. If the entity is a voter, he might be defined by the attributes of *Name (N)*, *Place (P)*, and *Occupation (O)*. The general formula which gives the number of ways keys can be combined to form linkage algorithms is $2^n - 1$. But since matching of names is a *sine qua non* of linkage algorithms relating to voters, the appropriate formula is $2^{(n-1)}$. Thus if we have three keys including *Name*, we have four basic algorithms, N, $N + P$, $N + O$, and $N + P + O$.

For each of these there are several variations. Westminster's poll books contain two levels of the attribute of *Place*, namely parish and street. In the Westminster project the attribute of *Name* was also defined in two ways, either surname or standardised surname, whilst the attribute of *Occupation* was defined in four ways.[52] The linkage keys available to link poll books were thus:

N1 surname + shortened forename
N2 standardised surname + shortened forename
P1 parish + street
P2 parish
O1 economic sector (Booth–Armstrong classification)
O2 economic sub-sector (Booth–Armstrong classification)
O3 trade cluster
O4 stated occupation

The 30 available algorithms correspond to the four original groups as follows:

$$
\begin{array}{llll}
N & & = & 2 \\
N + P & 2 \times 2 & = & 4 \\
N + O & 2 \times 4 & = & 8 \\
N + P + O & 2 \times 2 \times 4 & = & 16
\end{array}
$$

□ *Algorithm selection*

An algorithmic approach to record linkage of large datasets has two advantages over hand linkage of the same data. First, there is a considerable saving in time, since hand linkage is inordinately time-consuming. Secondly there is the advantage that the method used is capable of being specified. This not only increases the intellectual value of the work reported, but it also promotes its replicability and the possibility of comparing the results obtained with those obtained from similar datasets. Given the profusion of ways in which poll books might be linked using 30 single algorithms and an even larger number of multiple algorithms, and operating under the familiar constraints of time and money, it was decided to link poll book data using the optimum single algorithm. The optimum single algorithm would not necessarily deliver the highest number of linked records, nor would it necessarily link those records at the highest level of confidence, but it would provide the best trade-off between these two competing criteria.[53]

The first step was thus to rank the available algorithms according to the confidence that might be placed in the quality of the set of linked records, establishing an index of relative confidence. To do this, it was necessary to list the 30 possible record linkage algorithms. Weights were then applied for each linkage key, and totalled to find the points score for each algorithm. These weights are shown in Figure 8.4. The relative weight given to each linkage key was determined not by any scientific procedure but on the basis of pragmatic judgement. The weighting scheme is logically and empirically defensible and was seen as the best means of progressing the research. A more scientifically precise weighting scheme is currently under development. For the moment, however, it is sufficient to note the reasonableness of the combination of *Surname + Shtname* receiving a higher score than *Stdsur + Shtname*, the combination of *Parish + Street* receiving a higher score than *Parish*, and *Oclv4* receiving a higher score than *Oclv3*.

Having weighted each of the individual linkage keys, it was necessary to decide on the relative levels of confidence that might be placed in algorithms with different numbers of linkage keys (say *N2* versus *N2 + P1* or *N2 + P1 + O4*). Plainly, linking on three keys (name, place and occupation) inspires more confidence than linking on two keys (name and place), which in turn is superior to linking records on the basis of a single key (name only). But what form does the relationship take between relative confidence and number of linkage keys? The logical answer, we decided, was that each additional key (beyond name) would increase confidence by a constant factor but with decreasing marginal significance. This form of relationship implies a considerable rise in confidence in moving from say one to two keys or from two to three keys, but there is progressively less to gain in terms of confidence from adding in further linkage keys. The formula $1+\log 2(n-1)$ (where n = the number of keys used) was therefore applied as a multiplier to the crude points score for each algorithm. This yields the following set of multipliers:

single key = 1
dual key = 1.301
triple key = 1.602

The results of this process are presented in Figure 8.5. The relative confidence attaching to each algorithm was then calculated simply by

Code	Description	Weight
N_1	Surname + Shtname	20
N_2	Stdsur + Shtname	15
O_1	Oclv1	3
O_2	Oclv2	5
O_3	Oclv3	8
O_4	Oclv4	10
P_1	Parish + Street	10
P_2	Parish	6

Figure 8.4 *Weights for linkage keys*

dividing its enhanced points score by 64.08 (the enhanced points score of the 'perfect match' algorithm) and multiplying the result by 100, as shown in Figure 8.6. The algorithms were then ranked from the highest points score to the lowest to yield an Index of Relative Confidence.

Each algorithm was then implemented using SQL to determine the number of links made between the poll books of 1784 and 1788. The example given in Figure 8.7 is for algorithm 16 which links the poll book data by surname, firstname, parish, and street. It was necessary first to create temporary tables (**1784Temp** and **1788Temp**) from **1784Poll** and **1788Poll** containing those records which were list unique at the level of *Surname*, *Shtname*, *Parish*, and *Street*. Next a table (**8488Temp**) was created containing those cases which were common to the tables **1784Temp** and **1788Temp**. Finally, the table **8488Temp** was linked to the original tables **1784Poll** and **1788Poll** which contained data about occupation and voting behaviour. These tables also contained line numbers which, in conjunction with information about the table and parish, constituted the primary key to identify each case. The result of this query was spooled to the file **8488List**.

The results of running the query for each of the algorithms under consideration are presented in Figure 8.8. These require comment and explanation. First, it should be observed that because of the requirement that records in each poll book table should be list unique (only one occurrence) with respect to the linkage criteria adopted, the maximum number of potential links (described as 'at risk') is always less than the total population of voters. In general, however, we can see that the less discriminating the linkage algorithm (lower confidence level), the smaller the number of cases which it is feasible to link. More discriminating (higher confidence level) algorithms ensure that fewer

Algorithm	Description				Points	Multiplier	Score	Rank
1	N_1	+ P_1	+ O_4		40	1.602	64.08	1
2	N_1	+ P_1	+ O_3		38	1.602	60.88	2
3	N_1	+ P_2	+ O_4		36	1.602	57.67	3
4	N_1	+ P_1	+ O_2		35	1.602	56.07	4=
5	N_2	+ P_1	+ O_4		35	1.602	56.07	4=
6	N_1	+ P_2	+ O_3		34	1.602	54.47	6
7	N_1	+ P_1	+ O_1		33	1.602	52.87	7=
8	N_2	+ P_1	+ O_3		33	1.602	52.87	7=
9	N_1	+ P_2	+ O_2		31	1.602	49.67	9=
10	N_2	+ P_2	+ O_4		31	1.602	49.67	9=
11	N_2	+ P_1	+ O_2		30	1.602	48.06	11
12	N_1	+ P_2	+ O_1		29	1.602	46.46	12=
13	N_2	+ P_2	+ O_3		29	1.602	46.46	12=
14	N_2	+ P_1	+ O_1		28	1.602	44.86	14
15	N_2	+ P_2	+ O_2		26	1.602	41.65	15
16		N_1	+ P_1		30	1.301	39.03	16=
17		N_1	+ O_4		30	1.301	39.03	16=
18	N_2	+ P_2	+ O_1		24	1.602	38.45	18
19		N_1	+ O_3		28	1.301	36.43	19
20		N_1	+ P_2		26	1.301	33.83	20
21		N_2	+ P_1		25	1.301	32.53	21=
22		N_1	+ O_2		25	1.301	32.53	21=
23		N_2	+ O_4		25	1.301	32.53	21=
24		N_1	+ O_1		23	1.301	29.92	24=
25		N_2	+ O_3		23	1.301	29.92	24=
26		N_2	+ P_2		21	1.301	27.32	26
27		N_2	+ O_2		20	1.301	26.02	27
28		N_2	+ O_1		18	1.301	23.42	28
29		N_1			20	1.000	20.00	29
30		N_2			15	1.000	15.00	30

Figure 8.5 *Point scoring of algorithms 1–30*

cases are lost through the imposition of the list uniqueness rule. Second, while it holds that, as expected, the slacker the algorithm the higher the proportion of those at risk linked, it does not follow that less discriminating algorithms necessarily lead to higher rates of linkage for the population as a whole. In other words, the effect of algorithm slackening on linkage rates is two directional: on the one hand rates are pulled downward because progressively more cases are eliminated from potential linkage; while on the other hand rates are pulled upwards because less strict conditions have to be satisfied in order to establish a link.

Algorithm	Description				Score	Index of Relative Confidence
1	N_1	+ P_1	+ O_4		64.08	100.00
2	N_1	+ P_1	+ O_3		60.88	95.01
3	N_1	+ P_2	+ O_4		57.67	90.00
4	N_1	+ P_1	+ O_2		56.07	87.50
5	N_2	+ P_1	+ O_4		56.07	87.50
6	N_1	+ P_2	+ O_3		54.47	85.00
7	N_1	+ P_1	+ O_1		52.87	82.51
8	N_2	+ P_1	+ O_3		52.87	82.51
9	N_1	+ P_2	+ O_2		49.67	77.51
10	N_2	+ P_2	+ O_4		49.67	77.51
11	N_2	+ P_1	+ O_2		48.06	75.00
12	N_1	+ P_2	+ O_1		46.46	72.50
13	N_2	+ P_2	+ O_3		46.46	72.50
14	N_2	+ P_1	+ O_1		44.86	70.01
15	N_2	+ P_2	+ O_2		41.65	65.00
16		N_1	+ P_1		39.03	60.91
17		N_1	+ O_4		39.03	60.91
18	N_2	+ P_2	+ O_1		38.45	60.00
19		N_1	+ O_3		36.43	56.85
20		N_1	+ P_2		33.83	52.79
21		N_2	+ P_1		32.53	50.76
22		N_1	+ O_2		32.53	50.76
23		N_2	+ O_4		32.53	50.76
24		N_1	+ O_1		29.92	46.69
25		N_2	+ O_3		29.92	46.69
26		N_2	+ P_2		27.32	42.63
27		N_2	+ O_2		26.02	40.61
28		N_2	+ O_1		23.42	36.55
29		N_1			20.00	31.21
30		N_2			15.00	23.41

Figure 8.6   *Algorithms ranked by relative confidence*

This is an exciting and interesting result. The existence of countervailing tendencies creates the possibility that some higher confidence algorithms may actually yield higher rates of record linkage than some lower confidence algorithms. You can eat your cake and have it! Moreover, it is a relatively straightforward matter to determine the 'best return' linkage algorithm. This, logically, must be the algorithm which yields the 'optimum' trade-off between linkage rate and relative confidence. Simple linear regression is of value here. In this case, the percentage of linked records (*x* axis) was regressed on the index of

```
CREATE  TABLE  1784Temp
AS SELECT Surname, Shtname, Parish, Street FROM
1784Poll
GROUP BY Surname, Shtname, Parish, Street
HAVING COUNT(*)=1;

CREATE  TABLE  1788Temp
AS SELECT Surname, Shtname, Parish, Street FROM
1788Poll
GROUP BY Surname, Shtname, Parish, Street
HAVING COUNT(*)=1;

CREATE  TABLE  8488Temp
AS  SELECT  1784Temp.Surname, 1784Temp.Shtname,
       1784Temp.Parish, 1784Temp.Street
FROM  1784Temp, 1788Temp
WHERE  1784Temp.Surname = 1788Temp.Surname
    AND  1784Temp.Shtname = 1788Temp.Shtname
    AND  1784Temp.Parish = 1788Temp.Parish
    AND  1784Temp.Street = 1788Temp.Street;

SELECT  1784Poll.Parish, 1784Poll.Oclv4,
       1788Poll.Oclv4, 1784Poll.Vote84,
       1788Poll.Vote88, 1784Poll.Lineno,
       1788Poll.Lineno
FROM  8488Temp, 1784Poll, 1788Poll
WHERE  8488Temp.Surname = 1784Poll.Surname
    AND  8488Temp.Shtname = 1784Poll.Shtname
    AND  8488Temp.Parish = 1784Poll.Parish
    AND  8488Temp.Street = 1784Poll.Street
    AND  8488Temp.Surname = 1788Poll.Surname
    AND  8488Temp.Shtname = 1788Poll.Shtname
    AND  8488Temp.Parish = 1788Poll.Parish
    AND  8488Temp.Street = 1788Poll.Street;
```

Figure 8.7 *SQL record linkage query*

relative confidence (*y* axis). The best return single algorithm is that with the highest positive residual. As may be seen from Figure 8.9, algorithm 18 emerges as the optimum single algorithm (*Stdsur + Shtname + Parish + Oclv1*) with a linkage rate of 33.4 per cent at 60 per cent relative confidence.

				Linkages expressed as	
Algorithm	Population	At Risk	Linkages	% Population	% at Risk
1	8,226	8,181	1,666	20.25	20.36
2	8,226	8,173	1,815	22.06	22.21
3	8,226	8,137	2,017	24.52	24.79
4	8,226	8,171	1,880	22.85	23.01
5	8,226	8,177	1,957	23.79	23.93
6	8,226	8,124	2,201	26.76	27.09
7	8,226	8,163	2,005	24.37	24.56
8	8,226	8,169	2,140	26.02	26.20
9	8,226	8,069	2,263	27.51	28.05
10	8,226	8,113	2,347	28.53	28.93
11	8.226	8,166	2,219	26.98	27.17
12	8,226	7,877	2,374	28.86	30.14
13	8,226	8,100	2,570	31.24	31.73
14	8,226	8,158	2,360	28.69	28.93
15	8,226	8,025	2,649	32.20	33.01
16	8,226	8,115	2,272	27.62	28.00
17	8,226	7,999	2,117	25.74	26.47
18	8,226	7,768	2,749	33.42	35.39
19	8,226	7,957	2,302	27.98	28.93
20	8,226	7,228	2,508	30.49	34.70
21	8,226	8,106	2,670	32.46	32.94
22	8,226	7,817	2,356	28.64	30.14
23	8,226	7,926	2,447	29.75	30.87
24	8,226	7,223	2,305	28.02	31.91
25	8,226	7,873	2,664	32.39	33.84
26	8,226	6,959	2,868	34.87	41.21
27	8,226	7,678	2,733	33.22	35.60
28	8,226	6,930	2,620	31.85	37.81
29	8,226	5,984	2,084	25.33	34.83
30	8,226	5,349	2,227	27.07	41.63

Figure 8.8 *Linkage rates achieved*

☐ *Single versus multiple pass algorithms*

The processing power of modern database systems and the ease with which record linkage algorithms may be implemented using SQL opens up the possibility of further improvements in record linkage techniques. The most obvious and natural refinement of the methodology outlined above is to implement multiple-pass rather than single-pass linkage algorithms in order to secure higher linkage rates at higher levels of

Algorithm	Linkages	Relative confidence	Residuals
1	20.25	100.00	−1.43202
2	22.06	95.01	−0.94894
3	24.52	90.00	−0.24540
4	22.85	87.50	−0.95555
5	23.79	87.50	−0.61352
6	26.76	85.00	0.36143
7	24.37	82.51	−0.60408
8	26.02	82.51	−0.00939
9	27.51	77.51	0.31954
10	28.53	77.51	0.68458
11	26.98	75.00	0.02720
12	28.86	72.50	0.59505
13	31.24	72.50	1.44273
14	28.69	70.01	0.43255
15	32.20	65.00	1.47525
16	27.62	60.91	−0.31731
17	25.74	60.91	−0.98531
18	33.42	59.85	1.70714
19	27.98	56.85	−0.35487
20	30.49	52.79	0.37497
21	32.46	50.76	0.99825
22	28.64	50.76	−0.36966
23	29.75	50.76	0.02782
24	28.02	46.69	−0.76254
25	32.39	46.69	0.81141
26	34.87	42.63	1.54900
27	33.22	40.61	0.87033
28	31.85	36.55	0.20415
29	25.33	31.21	−2.45829
30	27.07	23.41	−2.20451

Figure 8.9   *Regression residuals*

relative confidence. The basic procedure is as follows. First, a strict, high relative confidence, algorithm is applied in a preliminary pass. The linked records are separated out and saved. Secondly, a less discriminating linkage algorithm is applied to the remaining records. The additional linked records are separated out and added to the pool of linked records. Thirdly, the process is repeated as often as thought necessary through the application of progressively less discriminating, lower confidence, algorithms. The combined relative confidence score for multiple pass algorithms is computed by multiplying the individual confidence scores by the proportion of total links made and adding them together. For example, the multiple pass algorithm (*N2* + *P2* + *O3*) + (*N1* + *P1*) + (*N1* + *O4*) yielded 39.6 per cent at 70 per cent relative confidence. This triple linkage algorithm gave a much higher return than any single algorithm and was used in the Westminster project to link poll book data for the analysis of consistency in voting behaviour. Note the similarity of this procedure to that of the Cambridge Group demographers which was described earlier.

□ *Record linkage: summary*

No matter how tight the algorithm applied, the researcher can never claim with complete confidence that all the records in a unified data set represent true linkages. After all, the voter may have died and been replaced by another of the same name, address, and occupation. It seems unlikely that any voter from 1749 could have survived to poll in the election of 1818, so links established between these two poll books may be held to be false. Even using the most discriminating algorithm available, links were nevertheless made between the tables **1749Poll** and **1818Poll** for James Baker, a gardener of Neathouses in St. George's parish, Thomas Keene, a coal merchant of Glasshouse Street in St. James's parish, and for Francis Watkins, an optician of Charing Cross in St. Martin's parish. Meanwhile, the less discriminating algorithm of list unique standardised surname and forename established links between 648 pairs of voters in 1749 and 1818, or about 10 per cent of those at risk.

Enough has been said to demonstrate that historians whose research depends crucially upon the application of record linkage procedures should think in terms of *relative* not *absolute* confidence. This is our first important point. Our second point is that through the application of sound technique it is possible to increase both levels of confidence *and* rates of record linkage. Decisions concerning the selection of linkage algorithms should be taken systematically and should recognise variations in the efficiency with which different algorithms perform.

Record linkage techniques can enhance many types of historical research project. As Wrigley has noted, 'record linkage, because of its ability to articulate and structure data, gives greater depth and fuller dimension to pictures of the past that would otherwise be flat and lack perspectives.'[54] Whilst the basic principles have long been an essential part of the process of historical research, the term 'record linkage' is now used to describe highly sophisticated processes which exploit the power and flexibility of modern database systems.

Of course, the techniques described are not universally applicable, and do not always provide the answers to the researcher's questions.

Not surprisingly, they tend to work best with long timespans and stable communities. The rapid urban growth of the nineteenth century, and the greater social and spatial mobility characteristic of the twentieth, present new challenges to the researcher. There also remain issues concerning the representativeness of the 'reconstitutable minority'. Is it representative of the community as a whole? And, in turn, is that community representative of the national picture?[55] Moreover, there is always the risk that the researcher will be diverted from the big historical issues by the technical detail: as Wrigley warned 20 years ago, 'it is easy to grow fascinated by the minutiae of record linkage, the endless series of logical and practical puzzles which arise with each new body of data.'[56] Record linkage is only a means to an end. What is important is not the technique in itself, but the ways in which it can creatively be used to further our understanding of the past.

■ 8.3 Conclusion

At the beginning of this chapter, we observed that, prior to the database revolution, the manipulation of large historical datasets was very demanding of time, effort and technical skill. This fact alone was enough to deter experimentation and engender an attitude of 'one best way'. Researchers necessarily sought solutions which were simple and relatively easy to implement. The now-damned tendency to code data prior to data entry and the patent crudeness of some early record linkage procedures may thus be viewed with some sympathy.

We have seen, however, that there were many things wrong with the 'one best way' approach. It was unnatural in that it did not encourage the historian to experiment, and it was high risk in that all eggs were placed in one basket. Thus potentially superior logical solutions to problems may well have been neglected. Moreover, the rigidities inherent in pre-coding and the close coupling of programs and data meant more often than not that these early machine-readable datasets are unusable by other historians.

What a difference modern database systems have made! The constraints of cost and complexity have been removed, and with them has gone rigidity. Historians may now freely experiment with different (post-) coding schemes and different record-linkage algorithms. The database is drawn upon to serve a purpose, but is no longer coupled with any particular scheme or algorithm. Hence the much sought-after ideal of databases which can serve the various needs of entire research communities has entered the realm of practical reality.

Case Study H
Researching the Population History of England

Kevin Schürer
*ESRC Data Archive, University of Essex, and Cambridge
Group for the History of Population and Social Structure,
University of Cambridge*

When Wrigley and Schofield's *Population History of England* was first published
in 1981, one of its first reviews was entitled 'History Will Never Be The
Same Again'.[1] The decade-long project which culminated in this monumental
volume not only revolutionised the examination of populations in the
past, but also proved a triumph for the use of computers in historical
research. Although the data marshalled and analysed for the project were
quite voluminous for the day, it was not the size of the database that
made the work particularly special.[2] Neither was it that the project was
the first to have utilised computing techniques, for this was not the case.
The real success lay in the way in which computers were used as a tool to
develop new methodologies and to apply these in order rigorously to test
aspects of demographic theory.

The desire to obtain a set of reliable estimates of England's population
in the past was not something novel to Wrigley and Schofield and their
co-workers at the Cambridge Group for the History of Population and
Social Structure. A similar quest had driven John Rickman, the founder
of the national census at the dawn of the nineteenth century, and, to a
lesser degree, Gregory King two hundred years earlier.[3] But despite the
best efforts of these two luminaries, plus a number of other scholars since,
a comprehensive series of demographic indicators was still wanting.

The main problem that stood in the way of achieving this goal – like so
many other historical conundrums – was the availability of source material. As mentioned previously, the decanal national census had been set
in motion in 1801, and in 1837 the General Registry Office was established
to collect and analyse statistics on the numbers of people being born,
marrying and dying. Yet no direct information on the country's population
size or the underlying demographic forces driving it was available spanning
the pre-industrial, industrialising and industrial periods. In order fully to
understand the interaction between demography and the process of
industrialisation, it was vital to construct a long-run time series of appropriate demographic indices. In this respect the only source available covering
the entire period under investigation which offered this possibility was
ecclesiastical parish registers.[4] These, of course, are not without their
problems. Although much-used by historical demographers, it is often too
easily overlooked that parish registers were established to record religious

ceremonies rather than demographic events. Consequently, in using them, the demographer's first task is to map the correspondence between the numbers of baptisms, marriages and burials being recorded into the numbers of births, marriages and deaths taking place in the population under observation. There are many factors which affect this relationship, of which the principal factors are deficiencies in record keeping and religious nonconformity, but it is clear that the ratio is never 1:1, and that the ratio is neither constant over time nor space.[5]

Thus once the data were gathered in – being transcribed on to specially produced *pro forma* tabulation sheets by an army of volunteers responding to calls made on radio and in local and family history journals – much time was spent testing the representativeness of the resulting sample as well as the validation and correction (via weighting) of the data materials.[6] Such work, invariably time-consuming and generally lacking in substantive return, and certainly so in this case, is of course nothing more than good practice in historiography: understanding the possibilities and limitations of one's source material. Yet it must unfortunately be said that it is all too often the case that computer-using historians have a tendency to skimp on this, the most basic of Clio's crafts, concentrating instead on the application of technique. Clearly the use of relevant computer-orientated techniques is important to the advancement of historical interpretation, but employing even the most sophisticated techniques on ill-informed source interpretation is no better than building a house without foundations and will consequently win few admirers or converts from the ranks of traditional history.[7] Wrigley and Schofield's awareness of this point is amply illustrated by the fact that the whole of the first half of *Population History*, 139 pages in all, is dedicated to the validation of the database upon which the subsequent analysis and interpretation is based.

Although there is a tendency for the correlation between the two to be rather negative, despite the concentration on source validation, the *Population History* is far from being technique impoverished. As stated earlier, the use of parish registers in an attempt to chart the course of the population development in the past was nothing new to Wrigley and Schofield, but at the heart of their analyses lay the rigid application of demographic modelling resulting in the generation of a series of population estimates not previously available. A long-run time-series of births and deaths alone may prove instructive in providing estimates of the overall population size, whether it is rising or falling and the rate at which it is doing so, but it does not provide the degree of accuracy or breadth of information that the Cambridge team required. For this reason a new technique, that of back projection, was developed. Building on the initial projection work of Ron Lee, the revised technique works on the basic premise that the size and age structure of any population at a particular point in time, allowing for net migration, is the result of the accumulation of births and deaths over the previous years.[8] For example, assuming net migration to be zero, the size of a population at date t_{10} will equal the population at t_1

plus the intervening births and minus the intervening deaths between t_1 and t_{10}. Equally, the same logic can be applied to age cohorts within a population. Thus, again assuming zero net migration, those aged between five and ten in a census of 1851 will equate to the total number born between 1841 and 1846 minus the number of deaths occurring to that cohort between 1841 and 1851. Clearly, by turning the equation around the population can be projected backwards just as well as forwards, thus if net migration is zero, the population of 1851 will equal the population of 1861 *minus* the births between 1851 and 1861, *plus* the deaths. Working to this basic principle and combining the series of births of and deaths with a family of standard life table statistics indicating the probability of dying at each age (in other words the structure of mortality), the size and structure of the national population in 1871 was back-projected to 1541, the computer program passing through the data several times to determine the optimum resolution for the given input parameters.[9] The result was not only a new estimation of the population at every quinquennial point between 1541 and 1871 but also its age structure and the net migration rate, which in turn lead to the secondary calculation of demographic indices such as the total marital fertility rate, the gross reproduction rate, the intrinsic growth rate and the expectation of life at birth (i.e. the mean age at death).

As a result of harnessing together data and technique, the Cambridge team were able to produce a wealth of new and reliable demographic estimates for a period of over three hundred years from 1541 to 1871, covering, most significantly, the era of dramatic industrialisation. Yet, it would be misleading if this brief account or a reading of the text gave the impression that the research exercise was simply one in historical positivism. Although, because of the uncertainty surrounding the pace of demographic changes in the past and the forces that underlaid them, it was both necessary and desirable to chart the course of various demographic rates, the factors influencing the research effort went far beyond the simple reconstruction of the historical record. The main focus of the enquiry was rather to test the validity of a number of theories concerning the nature of demographic and economic change.[10]

Chief among these was the desire to evaluate the model of demographic development proposed by Malthus in his various essays on the *Principle of Population* at the turn of the eighteenth century.[11] The Reverend Malthus is, of course, well-known for his postulation that if the population and economy of a nation failed to develop in parallel – for example, with population growing at a geometric rate with the output of food and other economic resources growing at an arithmetic rate – the former would be liable to curtailment due to the intervention of increasing mortality as a result of increased food prices, pestilence and even the possibility of war, in other words a series of *positive* checks. Yet he also proposed an alternative scenario. If population and economy came out of synchronisation then the rate of population growth could also be slowed by individuals reacting to the inevitable decline in real wages by reducing overall levels of fertility, either directly by having fewer children or indirectly by delaying entry into marriage or remaining unmarried. This secondary series of *preventative* checks, although producing the same net result, differ in a fundamental way from the first in that the population controls its growth in a self-regulatory fashion, as opposed to being controlled by external or exogamous factors.

Determining which course was taken by England's population in the late eighteenth and early nineteenth centuries, if indeed it followed either of the two routes mapped by Malthus, was high on the theoretical agenda of the project.[12] Equally, research by others on European marriage patterns and the relationships that existed between the timing of marriage and the establishment of new households made it especially desirable to test the interactions between population development and economic growth, measuring the strengths and weaknesses of the linkages in the Malthusian chains of event.[13] It is of course the case that the *Population History* was important for breaking new technological ground, but the real strength of the volume lies in the harnessing together of technique and theoretical methodology.

■ *Chapter 9* ■

Conclusion: Databases and the Future of Historical Computing

The number of database projects undertaken by historians is set to grow dramatically in the immediate future. Scholars with all kinds of specialist interests are aware of the tremendous potential of database-centred research, both in terms of their own needs and those of a wider historical community. The emerging vision is one of the historian having ready access to a host of databases and electronic editions by way of networks and mass storage media like CD-ROM.

That historians perceive great possibilities in this area is confirmed by the sharply rising number of applications for database-centred projects received by grant-awarding bodies. Typically these point to a primary source or collection of sources whose potential is understood but which has hitherto been neglected because of the daunting scale or complexity of the data involved. The answer, it is proposed, is to exploit modern technology to construct a database which will serve both the immediate needs of the project and, subsequently, scholars working in associated fields. What is plain is that the rate of discovery of fresh research opportunities is positively related to the ever-increasing availability of powerful hardware and versatile software. As the scope and functionality of database systems continues to grow, so too will interest in historical databases.

But while awareness of the potential of database systems is high and rising, it is not matched by a corresponding awareness of how to make the most of available research opportunities. Herein lies the value of this book. Our purpose throughout has been to emphasise good practice. Six key points emerge.

First, it is essential to have a good general understanding of the key characteristics and functionality associated with competing database approaches. Without this, significant mistakes may be made; most obviously, a project may become wedded to software which cannot meet all of its needs.

Secondly, it is important to recognise the importance of methods and standards in database design whether through the application of formal design procedures or source mark-up conventions. All too often, the historian rushes to implementation without considering issues of design. Resources are then squandered on the production of a poorly specified, inaccessible and ill-structured database. At this point, the dream of creating a general purpose resource for the wider community begins to crumble. It is better to seek expert advice at an early stage rather than proceed in a state of ignorance.

Thirdly, time spent on gaining a deep knowledge of the project software generally yields a good return: data may be entered more easily and held more securely; the database is less likely to contain errors; more and better quality information may be retrieved; superior reports may be generated. Generally speaking, it is better to know one or two powerful systems well than it is to know many superficially.

Fourthly, the application of sound project management methods and techniques is highly recommended for all but the smallest projects. Of all the causes of project failure, a lack of project management skills is perhaps the most common. Historians frequently fail to make the most basic calculations: how much data does a source contain? What rate of data entry can realistically be achieved? How long will it take to complete key tasks – project planning, source analysis, database design and implementation?

Fifthly, the flexibility and versatility of modern database systems makes it much easier to apply advanced research techniques within a project. All necessary data may be recovered with ease, and manipulative algorithms encoded through the use of generic querying facilities like SQL and other high-level languages. Data manipulation is a neglected art; one in which it pays dividends to become expert.

Finally, if the goals of data sharing and transportability are to be achieved then common standards must be applied and data archives must be properly resourced and maintained. As Green has observed,

> The enormous investment of resources in databases has major implications for future historical research and scholarly practice. The corollary of the commitment of public funds, together with the need for access to the database for the verification of assertions which in traditional scholarship are made through footnotes, is that the database must ultimately pass into the public domain. The intellectual property of the database must, subject to controls, cease to be vested exclusively in its creator or creators. That this implies a new practice in scholarship has hitherto been only dimly perceived in terms of public access, co-operative research, intellectual property and the principles of verification.[1]

The History Data Unit based at the ESRC Data Archive at the University of Essex was set up in 1992 to address the challenges noted by Green. The Unit's objective is to provide a comprehensive service to the historical community, comprising:

- *Acquisition.* A programme of acquiring selected historical datasets.
- *Processing and preservation.* Dealing with the particular problems presented by historical datasets.
- *Documentation and cataloguing* all historical datasets, and establishing an online information database.
- *Dissemination.* Encouraging secondary analysis of datasets through the provision of data and documentation to the historical community.
- *Information and liaison.* Liaising with data depositors, other archives, data users and the historical community at large.

The Unit's founders believe that one of its most vital tasks is to promote a 'culture of secondary use' of machine-readable historical data: 'it is evident that growing numbers of the historical community are fully committed to the use of computers for primary research. However, it is far from evident that a culture of secondary use of historical data exists in any significant fashion. If the time and resources employed in the creation of historical datasets are to be fully utilised it is essential that exploitation of these rich data sources continues beyond the analysis of the original data compiler.'[2]

The ideals of the History Data Unit are shared by colleagues at other data archives around the world with whom they exchange information and resources. They are part of a wider information network which exists among computing historians. Within that network there are some who believe that computer-based research methodologies will progressively displace more traditional ways of creating historical knowledge. The long-term vision is of the 'new historian', equipped with an advanced historical workstation, freed from the tedium and time-consuming restrictions of archival research and documentary analysis. The historical workstation is more than just a computer: it is a means of gaining access to a vast array of primary sources in the form of electronic editions managed by data archives around the word. The new historian will, according to this conception, be a regular rider on the information super-highway. Moreover, the historical workstation – as specified by Manfred Thaller and others – will have a full range of tools for the systematic analysis of historical sources and state of the art facilities for the writing of history.

The vision which has underpinned this book is much less revolutionary.

We believe that computers generally and database systems in particular are best applied to support rather than displace the dominant paradigm of historical research.[3] We do not counsel perfection, nor do we seek to divide the historical community into computer-literate modernists and dyed-in-the-wool traditionalists. The central message of this book is that good historical practice matters, just as it has always done. Nowadays, and for the foreseeable future, good practice requires familiarity with database systems. Much has been achieved in recent years. Much remains to be achieved. We hope that this book will further promote the cause of higher technical standards in computer-based historical research.

Notes and References

☐ **Preface (pp. xi–xvi)**

1. K. Schürer and S.J. Anderson (eds), *A Guide to Historical Datafiles Held in Machine-Readable Form* (London, 1992).
2. Peter Denley and Deian Hopkin (eds), *History and Computing* (Manchester, 1987); Peter Denley, Stefan Fogelvik and Charles Harvey (eds), *History and Computing II* (Manchester, 1989); Evan Mawdsley *et al.* (eds), *History and Computing III: Historians, Computers and Data* (Manchester, 1990).

☐ **1 Databases in Historical Research (pp. 1–13)**

1. R.G. Collingwood, *The Idea of History* (Oxford, 1946) p. 242.
2. C. Harvey and P. Taylor, 'Mineral Wealth and Economic Development: Foreign Direct Investment in Spain, 1851–1913', *Economic History Review*, Vol. XL, No. 2 (1987), pp. 185–207; C. Harvey and P. Taylor, 'Computer Modelling and Analysis of the Individual and Aggregate Capital, Stocks, Cash Flows and Performance of British Mining Companies in Spain, 1851–1913', in Peter Denley and Deian Hopkin, (eds), *History and Computing* (Manchester, 1987), pp. 115–21; C. Harvey and P. Taylor, 'The Measurement and Comparison of Corporate Productivity: Foreign and Domestic Firms in Spanish Mining in the Late Nineteenth Century', *Histoire et Mesure*, Vol. 3 No. 1 (1988), pp. 19–51.
3. E.A. Wrigley and R.S. Schofield, *The Population History of England, 1541–1871* (revised edition, Cambridge, 1989), p. xiii.
4. *Ibid.*, p. xvi. Since the publication of the *Population History of England*, the technique has been further refined, leading to the adoption of the term 'generalised inverse projection' instead of 'back projection'. See Kevin Schürer, Jim Oeppen and Roger Schofield, 'Theory and Methodology: An Example from Historical Demography', in Peter Denley, Stefan Fogelvik and Charles Harvey (eds), *History and Computing II* (Manchester, 1989), pp. 130–42.
5. R. Floud, K. Wachter and A. Gregory, *Health, Height and History: Nutritional Status in the United Kingdom, 1750–1980* (Cambridge, 1990), p. 28.
6. *Ibid.*, p. 325.
7. Peter Denley, 'Models, Sources and Users: Historical Database Design in the 1990s', *History and Computing*, Vol. 6, No. 1 (1994), pp. 33–43.
8. This quotation is from a paper by Manfred Thaller entitled 'What is "Source-Oriented Data Processing"? What is a "Historical Information Science"?' which has not been published in English. A Russian language version is in Leonid I. Borodkin and Wolfgang Levermann (eds), *Istorija i komp'juter: Novye informacionnye technologii v istoricheskich issledovanijach i obrazovanii* (St. Katharinen, 1993), pp. 5–18.

261

☐ **Case Study A: Investigating Regional Economies: The Gloucester Portbooks Database (pp. 14–21)**

1. Initial work on the source at Wolverhampton was undertaken by Malcolm Wanklyn, Jeff Cox and Nancy Cox and led to the appointment of Peter Wakelin as a Research Assistant in 1984. Dr Wakelin was the founding Director of the Portbooks Programme, from 1988 to 1990, since when this post has been filled by David Hussey. The Programme incorporates several projects in addition to the Gloucester database: to study the coastal trade of the Bristol Channel, 1695–1704 and undertake other case studies of particular regions and trades; to develop a national standard for computerising coastal Port Books; to prepare an analytical guide to the interpretation of the source; and to prepare a statistical summary of the trade of Gloucester.

2. See G.N. Clark, *Guide to English Commercial Statistics, 1696–1782* (London, 1938); N.J. Williams, *Descriptive List of Exchequer, Queen's Remembrancer, Port Books: 1565–1700* (London, 1960); T.S. Willan, *The English Coasting Trade* (Manchester, 1938), pp. 1–11; Peter Wakelin, 'Pre-Industrial Trade on the River Severn: A Computer-Aided Study of the Gloucester Port Books, *c.*1640–*c.*1770' (unpublished PhD thesis, University of Wolverhampton 1991), pp. 51–8.

3. Most notably by Willan, *English Coasting Trade.* Other examples are J.H. Andrews, 'The Port of Chichester and the Grain Trade', *Sussex Archaeological Collections*, Vol. 92 (1954), pp. 93–105; R.W.K. Hinton, 'The Port Books of Boston, 1600–1640', *Lincoln Record Society*, Vol. 50 (1956); G. Jackson, *The Trade and Shipping of Eighteenth-Century Hull* (York, 1975); G.A. Metters, 'The Rulers and Merchants of Kings Lynn in the Early Seventeenth Century' (unpublished PhD thesis, University of East Anglia, 1982); W.B. Stephens, 'The Cloth Exports of the Provincial Ports, 1600–40', *Economic History Review*, 2nd series, Vol. XXII (1969), pp. 228–48; N.J. Williams, *The Maritime Trade of the East Anglian Ports, 1550–1590* (Oxford, 1988); D.M. Woodward, *The Trade of Elizabethan Chester* (Hull, 1970).

4. Peter Wakelin, 'The Comprehensive Computerisation of a Very Large Documentary Source: The Portbooks Project at Wolverhampton Polytechnic', in Peter Denley and Deian Hopkin (eds.), *History and Computing* (1987), pp. 109–15.

5. All of the above findings are drawn from Wakelin, 'Pre-Industrial Trade on the River Seven'.

6. N. Cox and P. Wakelin, 'Data Derived from the Gloucester Coastal Port Books, 1695–1725', Appendix pp. 136–44 to N. Cox, 'Imagination and Innovation of an Industrial Pioneer: The First Abraham Darby', *Industrial Archaeology Review*, Vol. XII (1990), pp. 127–44.

7. N. Cox, 'Objects of Worth, Objects of Desire: Towards a Dictionary of Traded Goods and Commodities, 1550–1800', *Material History Review*, Vol. 39 (1994), pp. 24–40.

□ 2 Database Concepts and Terminology (pp. 22–39)

1. Issues such as these are examined in considerable detail in the standard literature, to which reference may be made if desired. See, for example, works by E.F. Codd, C.J. Date and James Martin in the bibliography.
2. Computer professionals may object that these are not strict synonyms; the terms table, relation and tuple, for example, should only be used to describe relational DBMSs. However, a lesser degree of accuracy will suffice for end-users.
3. On the hierarchical model, see C.J. Date, *Introduction to Database Systems* (Reading, MA, 1986), Vol. I, pp. 505–6.
4. On the network model, see Date, Vol. I, pp. 542–3.
5. It should perhaps be noted that this discussion refers to the *logical* view of the data; it may *physically* be stored in a quite different format. The advantage of a good RDBMS is that the researcher does not need to be at all concerned with issues relating to physical storage.
6. It should be noted that the term 'relational' is used to describe a number of commercial products which do not fully comply with the principles of the theoretical model. Indeed, there are still many problems in fully implementing Codd's 12 rules in commercially viable systems. Even the most powerful RDBMS deviate to some degree, and 8 or 9 is a very good score. A higher score is possible in laboratory-type systems, but such systems make excessive demands on resources, and performance levels are inadequate for commercial use.
7. See, for example, Case Study E, Indicators of Regional Economic Disparity: The Geography of Economic Distress in Britain before 1914 (David Gilbert and Humphrey Southall).
8. D.L. Slotnick, *et al.*, *Computers and Applications: An Introduction to Data Processing* (Lexington, MA, 1986), p. 387.
9. In recent years, there has been considerable work on extending the role of the data dictionary; rather than simply being used to document the creation and modification of the database by the DDL, it may be used as a design tool, generating data structures automatically. See, for example, M. Vetter, *Strategy for Data Modelling* (Chichester, 1987) pp. 299–330.

☐ Case Study B: The Register of Music in London Newspapers, 1660–1800 (pp. 40–6)

1. Michael Tilmouth, 'A Calendar of References to Music in Newspapers Published in London and the Provinces, 1660–1719', *Royal Musical Association Research Chronicle*, Vol. 1 (1960); William van Lennep *et al.* (eds), *The London Stage, 1660–1800* (Carbondale, IL, 1965).
2. William C. Smith and Charles Humphries, *A Bibliography of the Musical Works published by John Walsh: Volume II, 1721–1766* (London, 1968).

□ 3 Database Management Software (pp. 47–68)

1. For an in-depth analysis of leading relational database management systems, including ORACLE and INGRES, see Patrick Valduriez and Georges Gardarin, *Analysis and Comparison of Relational Database Systems* (Reading, MA, 1989).

2. Numerous other text management programs are also available, though, as will be discussed below, they sometimes vary considerably from the fully featured TIMS described here. See R. Kimberley, *Text Retrieval: A Directory of Software* (Aldershot, 1987–), which provides a regularly updated listing of more than 100 programs, with information on the hardware and operating system requirements, the features provided, any limitations on the textbase structure (e.g. maximum number of records or fields), and the price.

3. This is not to say, however, that a TIMS possesses the attributes of a fully-featured relational DBMS; rather, its structured fields are usually more akin to an FFM.

4. A number of alternative strategies are also being researched. They include best match searching, which calculate a measure of similarity between a query and each document in the database, and then sorts the documents into an order of decreasing similarity to the query, and knowledge-based systems, which attempt to model the actions of a human intermediary using techniques originally developed for artificial intelligence research. See John Ashford and Peter Willett, *Text Retrieval and Document Databases* (Bromley, Kent, 1988), pp. 64–100.

5. See Lyn Richards and Tom Richards, 'The Transformation of Quantitative Method: Computational Paradigms and Research Processes', in N. Fielding and R. Lee (eds), *Wordworking: Using Computers in Qualitative Research* (London, forthcoming).

6. Researchers looking for a bibliographic tool are recommended to investigate Papyrus, a program which can print out references in many of the standard formats used by academic publishers. Other formats can be defined by the user.

7. For a discussion of the special needs of art historians, see Michael Greenhalgh, 'Databases for Art Historians: Problems and Possibilities', in Peter Denley and Deian Hopkin (eds), *History and Computing* (Manchester, 1987), pp. 156–67. Also see Greenhalgh, 'Graphical Data in Art History and the Humanities: Their Storage and Display', *History and Computing*, Vol. 1 No. 2 (1989), pp. 121–34; A. Hamber, J. Miles and W. Vaughan (eds), *Computers and Art History* (London, 1989).

8. Gill Russell, 'Hypertext', *History and Computing*, Vol. 3, No. 3 (1991), p. 184. For useful introductions to hypertext and hypermedia, see Jeff Conklin, 'Hypertext: An Introduction and Survey', *Computing*, Vol. 20 (Sept. 1987), pp. 17–41; Ray McAleese, *Hypertext: Theory into Practice* (London, 1989); Jacob Nielson, *Hypertext and Hypermedia* (San Diego, CA, 1990).

9. On this theme, see Deborah M. Edwards and Lynda Hardman, ' "Lost in Hyperspace": Cognitive Mapping and Navigation in a Hypertext Environment', in McAleese (ed), *Hypertext: Theory into Practice*, pp. 105–25.

10. For an introduction, see A.M. Fountain, W. Hall, I. Heath and H.C. Davis, 'MICROCOSM: An Open Model for Hypermedia With Dynamic Linking', in A. Rizk, N. Streitz and J. André (eds), *Hypertext: Concepts, Systems and Applications* (Cambridge, 1990). Other articles and papers by the developers include H. Davis, W. Hall, I. Heath, G. Hill, and R. Wilkins, 'Towards an Integrated Information Environment with Open Hypermedia Systems', *ECHT' 92: Proceedings of the Fourth ACM Conference on Hypertext* (Milan, 30 November – 4 December 1992), pp. 181–90; Z. Li, H. Davis and W. Hall, 'Hypermedia Links and Information Retrieval', British Computer Society 14th Information Retrieval Colloquium, Lancaster University, 13–14 April 1992; W. Hall and H. Davis, 'Hypermedia Link Services and their Application to Multimedia Information', *Journal of Information Technology*, Special Issue on Multimedia (1994).

☐ Case Study C: Hypermedia Database Management Systems: Microcosm as a Research Tool (pp. 69–72)

1. Microcosm runs under MS Windows 3.1, and requires a PC with i386SX or higher running a minimum of 4Mb of RAM. A new version (3.0) of Microcosm is now available through CHEST. Various research projects are currently being developed using Microcosm as a platform, spanning a wide range of countries in the European Union. Widely used as a teaching tool, it is also proving a formidable research platform.
2. κλειω is discussed in section 7.1 and Case Study G.

☐ 4 The Database Project Life-Cycle (pp. 73–97)

1. On systems analysis and design and project management techniques, see S.A. Bergen, *Project Management: An Introduction to Issues in Industrial Research and Development* (Oxford, 1986); I.T. Hawryszkiewycz, *Introduction to Systems Analysis and Design* (London, 2nd edn. 1991); H.R. Hoare, *Project Management using Network Analysis* (Maidenhead, Berkshire, 1973); Dennis Lock, *Project Management* (London, 1989); Jack R. Meredith and Samuel J. Mantel, Jr., *Project Management: A Managerial Approach* (Chichester, Sussex, 2nd edn. 1989); J.A. Senn, *Analysis and Design of Information Systems* (New York, 1985); Don Yeates, *Project Management for Information Systems* (London, 1991). On the use of such techniques in academic projects, see K. Howard and J.A. Sharp, *The Management of a Student Research Project* (Aldershot, 1989); Matthew Woollard, 'Project Management and the 1881 Census' (unpublished MA dissertation, University of London, 1991).
2. Carlo M. Cipolla, *Between History and Economics* (Oxford, 1991), p. 14.
3. A detailed description of the application of PERT to a student research project may be found in Howard and Sharp, *The Management of a Student Research Project*, pp. 49–64. Also see Woollard, dissertation, pp. 7–10.
4. Peter Adman, Stephen W. Baskerville and Katharine F. Beedham, 'Computer-Assisted Record Linkage: Or How Best to Optimise Links Without Generating Errors', *History and Computing*, Vol. 4 No. 1 (1992), pp. 2–15. Also see *idem*, 'Manuscript Poll Books and English County Elections in the First

Age of Party: A Reconsideration of their Provenance and Purpose', *Archives*, Vol. 19 No. 86 (1991), pp. 384–403.

5. For a discussion of the use of scanning and OCR in historical research, see René van Horik, 'Optical Character Recognition and Historical Documents: Some Programs Reviewed', *History and Computing*, Vol. 4, No. 3 (1992), pp. 211–20; René van Horik and P.K. Doorn, 'Scanning and Optical Character Recognition of Historical Sources', in Hans J. Marker and Kirsten Pagh (eds), *Yesterday: Proceedings of the 6th Annual Conference of the Association for History and Computing, Odense 1991* (Odense, 1994). Also see P. Robinson, *The Digitization of Primary Textual Sources* (Oxford, 1993).

6. The authors are grateful to Peter Wakelin and David Hussey for their assistance in the preparation of this section. In particular, reference is made to Peter Wakelin, 'Pre-Industrial Trade on the River Severn: A Computer-Aided Study of the Gloucester Port Books, *c.*1640–*c.*1770' (unpublished PhD thesis, University of Wolverhampton 1991), Chapter 2, 'Port Books and Computer-Aided Analysis'. For a brief published account of the project, see Wakelin, 'Comprehensive Computerisation of a Very Large Documentary Source: The Portbooks Project at Wolverhampton Polytechnic', in Peter Denley and Deian Hopkin (eds), *History and Computing* (Manchester, 1987), pp. 109–14.

7. A particularly valuable introduction for historians is A.G. Darroch and M.D. Ornstein, 'Error in Historical Data Files: A Research Note on the Automatic Detection of Error and on the Nature and Sources of Errors in Coding', *Historical Methods*, Vol. 12, No. 4 (1979), pp. 157–67.

8. Vicente P. Concepcion and Donald P. D'Amato, 'A String-Matching Algorithm for Assessing the Results of an OCR Process', in Francesca Bocchi and Peter Denley (eds), *Storia & Multimedia* (Bologna, 1994), pp. 694–701.

☐ Case Study D: Creating a Machine-Readable Version of the 1881 Census of England and Wales (pp. 98–101)

1. This paper is an updated and condensed version of part of my MA dissertation, 'Project Management and the 1881 Census Project' (University of London, 1991), for which I was in receipt of an ESRC postgraduate studentship. In that work I thanked Dr Philip Hartland, Mr Jack Hoare (then project manager of the project) and the authors of this book for their assistance. I would also like to thank Mr Stephen Young (the current Production Co-ordinator) for his timely assistance.

2. Mormons believe that people who died without 'hearing the gospel can have ordinances performed for them vicariously in the temples'. This act is not performed without thought. Living people must stand in as proxies and these acts are only performed on dead ancestors of these proxies if they have adequate identification of those ancestors. Leonard J. Arrington and Davis Bitton, *The Mormon Experience: A History of the Latter-day Saints* (London, 1979), p. 303; Robert Mullen, *The Mormons* (London, 1967), pp. 194–6. (The Mormons believe that the dead have a choice in deciding whether to accept these ordinances or not.)

3. Work also began on indexing the 1881 Scottish census in late 1992. Transcription, evaluation and data entry for Scotland is complete and all county

indexes will be published before the end of 1995 with the exception of Lanark.

4. The Public Record Office had previously divided the census into 'pieces' for stock control purposes.

5. Tabulated details of what the 1881 enumeration books contain can be found in Edward Higgs, *Making Sense of the Census: The Manuscript Returns for England and Wales, 1801–1901* (London, 1989), p. 111 and Genealogical Society of Utah, *How to Transcribe the 1881 British Census* (Salt Lake City, 1988). There are, in addition, photocopied updates to this manual and supplemental handbooks which describe how to transcribe data from institutions and vessels.

6. Other rules apply; see GSU, *How to Transcribe the 1881 British Census*, pp. 7–13.

7. Alternative spellings of family surnames, if in the original, are added to the transcriptions at this stage. For genealogical purposes it is necessary for each household to have a head. This creates a relationship in the 'As Enumerated' index. If this is not mentioned in the enumeration books, normally when more than one family live together, a putative head is created. Secondary heads of households can also be created if married children live in the house. This would be unnecessary if all the relationships in the enumeration book were correct to the head of household.

8. Limitations of space preclude mentioning all of the various changes made to the data in the project. All of the changes are elucidated in GSU, *How to Transcribe the 1881 British Census*, the various supplementary guides available from the 1881 Census Project, and the Evaluation Go-By Information.

9. The GSU has devised its own data entry software, Universal Data Entry (UDE). The main advantage of using its own software is that it does exactly what the GSU wants and requires no licence fee to be paid.

10. Verification is normally defined as the act of checking data at the stage of input by comparing copies of the data before and after transfer, often by repeating the keyboard operations. Verification in this project refers to the process of automatically checking data input and its manual correction.

11. Over 8,000 volunteers from 116 Family History Societies are either transcribing batches or have completed transcription. Around 7,000 people at 70 locations have been involved in data entry. The new Management Centre in Birmingham has 15 staff and volunteers.

12. This is not the place to launch into a description of project management techniques. Suffice it to say that a slack task is one that can overrun (by a specified amount of time) without affecting the estimated duration of the project, while a critical task is one which must be completed within the allotted time for the project to take place. An excellent introductory study on the subject is Don Yeates, *Project Management for Information Systems* (London, 1991).

13. Letter from Jack Hoare, 26 September 1991. A note by Michael Armstrong in *Family Tree Magazine* (Feb. 1991), p. 40, suggests that the Church of Jesus Christ of Latter-day Saints will hold the copyright to ensure that the project is not exploited and 'used *only* for sensible genealogical studies' (my emphasis).

14. Letters to *Family History Magazine* (Dec. 1990), p. 39; (May 1990), p. 18; *Family History Magazine*, 'Genealogical Miscellany' (April 1991), p. 47. The project hopes to establish a register of errors found by users. These errors will be rectified before the national indexes are made.

☐ 5 Database Design and Implementation (pp. 102–39)

1. C.J. Date, *An Introduction to Database Systems* (Reading, MA, 4th edn. 1986), Vol. 1, pp. 29–30.
2. An earlier version of this section was published as 'The Business Elite of Bristol: A Case Study in Database Design', in *History and Computing*, Vol. 3 No. 1 (Spring 1991), pp. 1–11.
3. C.E. Harvey and J. Press, 'Industrial Change and the Economic Life of Bristol since 1800', in *idem* (eds), *Studies in the Business History of Bristol* (Bristol, 1988) pp. 1–32.
4. The names adopted should accurately describe the entities, and be clearly understandable to the casual user. This is not a trivial matter; misleading names can often lead to muddled thinking at the design stage, while cryptic names can mean much time wasted as users refer to the documentation for an explanation. However, it should be noted that there are advantages in succinctness once the database is operational; querying can become time-consuming and tedious if over-long names are used. Moreover, most database packages place some restrictions on legal names – usually they must be between 8 and 18 characters long, must begin with a letter, and must not contain any spaces.
5. An earlier version of this section was published as 'Relational Data Analysis: Value, Concepts and Methods', in *History and Computing*, Vol. 4 No. 2 (1992), pp. 39–50.
6. Database professionals have also identified *fourth normal form* and *fifth normal form*, which deal respectively with multivalued dependencies and join dependencies. However, these conditions – particularly the latter – are sufficiently rare to be excluded from further discussion here. For further information, see Date, *Introduction to Database Systems*, Vol. I, pp. 381–92; Georges Gardarin and Patrick Valduriez, *Relational Databases and Knowledge Bases* (Reading, MA, 1989), pp. 165–74. It should perhaps be added that, whilst this section describes all the stages involved in transforming unnormalised date into third normal form, they are not all required in every instance. For example, data taken directly from the source are already in 1NF if there are no repeating groups. More rarely, they may already be in 2NF or even 3NF.
7. For an earlier treatment of this data, using a hierarchical methodology, see L.R. Fischer and E.W. Sager, 'An Approach to the Quantitative Analysis of British Shipping Records', *Business History*, Vol. XXII (1980), pp. 135–51.
8. C.J. Date, *A Guide to the SQL Standard* (Reading, MA, 1987), pp. 2–3.
9. As a general rule, these 'string constants' should be enclosed in single quotation marks. Some SQL dialects allow strings to be enclosed in double quotes, though this can make for portability problems.
10. This can be demonstrated by returning to the beginning of the shipping database example, and choosing a different initial primary key from the possible candidate keys. Working through the example will result in the same 3NF model as that set out in Figure 5.21.

☐ Case Study E: Indicators of Regional Economic Disparity: The Geography of Economic Distress in Britain before 1914 (pp. 140–6)

1. N. Von Tunzelman, 'Britain, 1900–45: A Survey', in R. Floud and D. McCloskey (eds), *The Economic History of Britain since 1700, Part 2: 1860 to the 1970s* (Cambridge, 1981); R.C.O. Matthews, C.H. Feinstein and J.C. Odling-Smee, *British Economic Growth, 1856–1973* (Oxford, 1982).
2. M. MacKinnon, 'Poor Law Policy, Unemployment, and Pauperism', *Explorations in Economic History*, Vol. XXIII (1986), pp. 299–336.
3. H.R. Southall, 'Regional Unemployment Patterns in Britain, 1851–1914: A Study of the Trade Union Percentages of Unemployment with Special Reference to Engineering Workers' (unpublished PhD thesis, University of Cambridge, 1984); Southall, 'The Origins of the Depressed Areas: Uunemployment, Growth, and Regional Economic Structure in Britain before 1914', *Economic History Review*, 2nd series, Vol. XLI (1988), pp. 236–58.
4. C.H. Lee, *British Regional Employment Statistics* (Cambridge, 1979).
5. W.R. Garside, *The Measurement of Unemployment: Methods and Sources in Great Britain, 1850–1979* (Oxford, 1980).
6. Southall, 'Regional Unemployment Patterns in Britain, 1851–1914'.
7. MacKinnon, 'Poor Law Policy, Unemployment, and Pauperism'; H.R. Southall, 'Poor Law Statistics and the Geography of Economic Distress', in J. Foreman-Peck (ed.), *New Perspectives on the Late Victorian Economy: Essays in Quantitative Economic History, 1860–1914* (1991).
8. Lee, *British Regional Employment Statistics*.
9. For a discussion of views, see section 6.2.
10. Technical details of this front-end and the database more generally are discussed in section 7.3 and in D.M. Gilbert and H.R. Southall, 'Data *Glasnost*: A User-Friendly System for Access to Research Databases across Wide-Area Networks', *History and Computing*, Vol. 3 No. 2 (1991), pp. 119–28.
11. D.M. Gilbert and H.R. Southall, 'Dimensions of Distress: Manifestations of Economic Hardship in Late Victorian Britain', in R. Salais and N. Whiteside (eds), *Unemployment and Labour at the Turn of the Century: An Interdisciplinary Study of Britain and France, 1880–1914* (forthcoming).
12. A. Charlesworth, D.M. Gilbert, A. Randall, H.R. Southall and C. Wrigley, *An Atlas of Industrial Protest* (1993).

☐ 6 Information Retrieval (pp. 147–84)

1. A key description is provided by M.M. Zloof, 'Query-by-Example: A Data Base Language', *IBM Systems Journal*, Vol. 16 No. 4 (1977), pp. 324–43.
2. For further consideration of QBE, see ibid. Also see C.J. Date, *An Introduction to Database Systems* (Reading, MA, 4th edn. 1986), Vol. 1, pp. 297–301.
3. Some dialects of SQL use <> instead of != for 'not equal to'.
4. It should be noted that the use of DESC in an ORDER BY statement is quite different from its use as a command in its own right. The latter is an abbreviation for DESCRIBE, which, as noted earlier in this section, is used to display the structure of a table and the fields which it contains.

5. Michael Bronzite, *Introduction to ORACLE* (Maidenhead, Berks, 1989) p. 141.
6. On a cautionary note, it should be stated that Access' implementation of SQL, though sufficent for nearly all end-users, does not include the full range of commands which a professional database administrator would expect to find.
7. Key texts on SQL*TextRetrieval are Oracle Corporation UK Ltd., *SQL*TextRetrieval Administrator's Guide* (Chertsey, Surrey, 1990), and J.H. Ashford, 'Text Storage and Retrieval in the ORACLE Relational Database System', *Program*, Vol. 21 (1987), pp. 108–23. On the use of SQL*TextRetrieval in a historical database project, see C.E. Harvey and J. Press, 'The Business Elite of Bristol: A Case Study in Database Design', *History and Computing*, Vol. 3 No. 1 (1991), pp. 1–11.
8. It is also possible to define words or phrases as KEYWORDS. For the sake of clarity, these are not described here. For further information, see Oracle Corporation UK Ltd., *SQL*TextRetrieval Administrator's Guide*, pp. 3.3–3.5.
9. Guidelines are provided in British Standards Institute (BSI), *Guide to Establishment and Development of Monolingual Thesauri* (BS 5723) (1987). Also relevant to the task of thesaurus construction is BSI, *Examining Documents, Determining their Subjects and Selecting Index Terms* (BS 6529) (1984).
10. It should also be noted that the ORDER BY statement must be used in the query if BREAK and COMPUTE are to work properly.

Case Study F: Analysing Social Structure and Political Behaviour using Poll and Rate Books: The Westminster Historical Database (pp. 185–7)

1. The database described in this case study was created during the preparation of my PhD thesis. See E.M. Green, 'Social Structure and Political Allegiance in Westminster, 1774–1820' (unpublished PhD thesis, University of London 1992). I am grateful to Charles Harvey for his patience and wise counsel during the preparation of the thesis, and to the Economic and Social Research Council, the Central Research Fund of the University of London, and Royal Holloway, University of London for financial support.
2. E.P. Thompson, *The Making of the English Working Class* (1963, revised edn. Harmondsworth, 1968).
3. Thompson, p. 12.
4. M.N. Franklin, *The Decline of Class Voting in Britain: Changes in the Basis of Electoral Choice, 1964–83* (Oxford, 1985), p. 2.
5. W.A. Speck and W.A. Gray, 'Computer Analysis of Poll Books: An Initial Report', *Bulletin of the Institute of Historical Research*, Vol. 43 (1970), pp. 105–12.
6. Recent work includes J.E. Bradley, *Religion, Revolution, and English Radicalism: Nonconformity in Eighteenth-century Politics and Society* (Cambridge, 1990); R.J. Morris, *Class, Sect and Party: The Making of the British Middle Class: Leeds, 1820–1850* (Manchester, 1990); and J.A. Phillips, *The Great Reform Bill in the Boroughs: English Electoral Behaviour, 1818–40* (Oxford, 1992).

☐ **7 Source-Oriented Database Systems (pp. 186–217)**

1. Michael Stonebraker, Larry A. Rowe, David Beech, Bruce Lindsay, *et al.*, *The Third Generation Database System Manifesto*, Proceedings of the IFIP, July 1990 (Amsterdam, 1990).
2. Manfred Thaller, 'Data Bases v. Critical Editions', *Historical Social Research*, Vol. 13 No. 3 (1988), pp. 137–8. But also see, *inter alia*, Ian Winchester, 'Priorities for Record Linkage: A Theoretical and Practical Checklist', in Jerome M. Clubb and Erwin K. Scheuch (eds), *Historical Sociological Research* (1980) pp. 429–30; Caroline Bourlet and Jean-Luc Minel, 'A Declarative System for Setting Up a Prosopographical Database', in Peter Denley and Deian Hopkin (eds), *History and Computing* (Manchester, 1987) pp. 186–91.
3. Manfred Thaller, 'Historical Information Science: Is There Such a Thing? New Comments on an Old Idea', in Tito Orlandi (ed.), *Discipline umanistiche e informatica. Il Problema dell'integrazione* (Rome, 1993) p. 52.
4. See, for example, Kevin Schürer and Jim Oeppen, 'Calculating Days of the Week and Some Related Problems with Using Calendars of the Past', *History and Computing*, Vol. 2, No. 2 (1990), pp. 107–18. Some of the problems involved in working with old dating methods are summarised in P. Donche, 'HISTCAL: A Program for Historical Chronology', *History and Computing*, Vol. 2 No. 2 (1990), pp. 97–196.
5. This section is largely based upon a paper by Manfred Thaller entitled 'What is "Source-Oriented Data Processing"? What is a "Historical Information Science"?' All quotations, unless otherwise stated, are from this paper, which has not been published in English. However, a Russian language version is in Leonid I. Borodkin and Wolfgang Levermann (eds), *Istorija i komp'juter: Novye informacionnye technologii v istoricheskich issledovanijach i obrazovanii* (St. Katharinen, 1993) pp. 5–18. Amongst Thaller's most important published works on source-oriented data processing and his concept of the 'Historical Workstation' are: 'Beyond Collecting: The Design and Implementation of CLIO, a DBMS for the Social-Historical Sciences', in Robert F. Allen (ed), *Databases in the Humanities and Social Sciences 2* (Florida, 1985) pp. 328–34; 'A Draft Proposal for a Standard for the Coding of Machine Readable Sources', *Historical Social Research*, Vol. 40 (Oct. 1986), pp. 3–46, reprinted in D. Greenstein (ed), *Modelling Historical Data* (St. Katharinen, 1991) pp. 19–64; 'Methods and Techniques of Historical Computing', in Denley and Hopkin (eds), *History and Computing*, pp. 147–56; 'Data Bases v. Critical Editions', *Historical Social Research*, Vol. 13, No. 3 (1988), pp. 129–39; 'Gibt es eine fachspezifische Datenverarbeitung in den historischen Wissenschaften?', in K.H. Kaufhold and J. Schneider (eds), *Geschichtswissenschaft und elektronische Datenverarbeitung* (Wiesbaden, 1988) pp. 45–83; 'The Need for a Theory of Historical Computing', in Peter Denley, Stefan Fogelvik and Charles Harvey (eds), *History and Computing II* (Manchester, 1989) pp. 2–11; 'Have Very Large Data Bases Methodological Relevance?', in O. Opitz (ed), *Conceptual and Numerical Analysis of Data* (Berlin, 1989); 'Databases and Expert Systems as Complementary Tools for Historical Research', *Tijdschrift voor Geschiedenis*, Vol. 103 (1990), pp. 233–47; 'The Historical Workstation Project', *Historical Social Research*, Vol.

16 No. 4 (1991), pp. 51–61, reprinted in *Computers in the Humanities*, Vol. 25 (1991), pp. 149–62; 'The Need for Standards: Data Modelling and Exchange', in Greenstein (ed), *Modelling Historical Data*, pp. 1–18; *Images and Manuscripts in Historical Computing* (St. Katharinen, 1992); 'Historical Information Science: Is There Such a Thing? New Comments on an Old Idea', in Orlandi (ed), *Discipline unanistiche e informatica*, pp. 51–86; κλειω: *A Database System* (St. Katharinen, 1993).

6. Peter Denley, 'Models, Sources and Users: Historical Database Design in the 1990s', *History and Computing*, Vol. 6 No. 1 (1994), pp. 33–43.

7. For further consideration of techniques for handling currencies and calendar dates, see Thaller, 'A Draft Proposal for the Coding of Machine Readable Sources', in Greenstein (ed), *Modelling Historical Data*, pp. 29–32.

8. Thaller, 'What is "Source-Oriented Data Processing"?'. A more detailed discussion of these issues than is provided here may be found in Denley, 'Models, Sources and Users'.

9. The current version for most applications is version 5, which comprises the command language and non-graphical menu systems, and is machine-independent. As will be discussed below, version 6 is also available; in addition to the features listed above, it also provides a graphical user interface geared to handling images. However, it is restricted to a number of UNIX platforms, though a Windows 95 version is under development. English versions of κλειω are available from the Humanities Computing Centre, Queen Mary & Westfield College, University of London, Mile End Road, London, E1 4NS.

10. Denley, 'Models, Sources and Users', p. 37.

11. This summary is taken from Pöttler, Burkhard, 'Modelling Historical Data: Probate Inventories as a Source for the History of Everyday Life', in Francesca Bocchi and Peter Denley (eds), *Storia & Multimedia* (Bologna, 1994), pp. 494–9.

12. Reference to the development of historical computing in Eastern Europe may be found Leonid I. Borodkin and Wolfgang Levermann (eds), *History and Computing in Eastern Europe* (St. Katharinen, 1993); *idem, Istorija i komp'juter: Novye informacionnye technologii v istoricheskich issledovanijach i obrazovanii* (St. Katharinen, 1993).

13. The manual is Gerhard Jaritz, *Images: A Primer of Computer-Supported Analysis with κλειω IAS* (St. Katharinen, 1993). Also see *idem*, 'The Image as Historical Source, or: Grabbing Contexts', *Historical Social Research*, Vol. 16, No. 4 (1991), pp. 100–5; Jurij Fikfak and Gerhard Jaritz (eds), *Image Processing in History: Towards Open Systems* (St Katharinen, 1993); Manfred Thaller (ed), *Images and Manuscripts in Historical Computing* (St. Katharinen, 1992).

14. Ben Schneiderman, 'Reflections on Authoring, Editing and Managing Hypertext', in E. Barrett (ed), *The Society of Text* (Cambridge, MA, 1989), pp. 115–31.

15. Jakob Nielson, *Hypertext and Hypermedia* (San Diego, CA, 1990), p. 43. Nielson discusses a range of applications suited to hypermedia on pp. 43–82.

16. David Gilbert, 'HyperCard: New Ways of Writing, New Ways of Reading', *History and Computing*, Vol. 3, No. 3 (1991), p. 187.

17. For a full description of the system, and further examples of its use, see David Gilbert and Humphrey Southall, 'Data *Glasnost*: A User-Friendly System for Access to Research Databases across Wide-Area Networks', *History and Computing*, Vol. 3, No. 2 (1991), pp. 119–28. The scope and objectives of the project were described in Humphrey Southall and David Gilbert, 'British Nineteenth-Century Labour Markets Database at Queen Mary & Westfield College', *History and Computing*, Vol. 1, No. 2 (1989), pp. 171–2. Also see Humphrey Southall, 'The Origins of the Depressed Areas: Unemployment, Growth and Regional Economic Structure in Britain before 1914', *Economic History Review*, 2nd series, Vol. XLI, No. 2 (May 1988), pp. 236–58.

18. Researchers from Southampton – including the developers of Microcosm – have considered the impact of multimedia in J. Colson, F. Colson, H.C. Davis and W. Hall, 'Questioning "Authority": The Challenge of Multimedia', in Bocchi and Denley (eds), *Storia & Multimedia*, pp. 597–605.

19. M. Atkinson, F. Bacilhon, D. DeWitt, K. Dittrich, D. Maier and S. Zdonik, 'The Object-Oriented Database System Manifesto', *Proceedings of the First International Conference on Deductive and Object-Oriented Databases* (Kyoto, 1989), pp. 40–57.

20. For an excellent summary of the debate and the issues, see Christopher M. Stone and David Hentchel, 'Database Wars Revisited', *Byte* (Oct. 1990), pp. 223–42.

21. Edward Yourdon, 'Auld Lang Syne: Is it Time for You to Ring out the Old and Ring in the New?', *Byte* (Oct. 1990), p. 258.

22. A brief introduction to object-oriented database management systems (OODBMSs) is supplied by T. Atwood, 'An Introduction to Object-Oriented Database Management Systems', *Hotline on Object-Oriented Technology*, Vol. 1 No. 1 (New York, 1989), pp. 11–12. An excellent introduction to every aspect of OODBMSs, with comprehensive discussion of several applications, is provided by R.G.G. Cattell, *Object Data Management: Object-Oriented and Extended Relational Database Systems* (Reading, MA, 1991). M. Atkinson, *et al.*, 'The Object-Oriented Database System Manifesto', attempts to achieve a consensus on terminology for OODBMSs, and also to define a number of criteria which can be used to judge how object-oriented a DBMS is. Useful collections of essays and conference papers are provided by: A. Cardenas and D. McLeod (eds), *Research Foundations in Object-Oriented and Semantic Database Systems* (Englewood Cliffs, NJ, 1990); S.B. Zdonik and D. Maier (eds), *Readings on Object-Oriented Database Systems* (San Mateo, CA, 1990); K. Dittrick (ed.), *Advances in Object-Oriented Database Systems*, Proceedings of the 2nd International Workshop on Object-Oriented Database Systems, 27–30 September 1988 (Berlin, 1988).

23. Christopher M. Stone and David Hentchel, 'Database Wars Revisited', *Byte* (Oct. 1990), p. 234.

24. Stonebraker *et al.*, *The Third Generation Database System Manifesto*.

25. G. Kappel and M. Schrefl, 'A Behaviour-Integrated Entity-Relationship Approach for the Design of Object-Oriented Databases', *Proceedings of the 7th International Conference on the Entity-Relationship Approach* (Rome, Nov. 1988) pp. 175–92.

26. W.J. Premerlani, M.R. Blaha, J.E. Rumbaugh and T.A. Varwig, 'An Object-Oriented Relational Database', *Communications of the ACM*, Vol. 33 (Nov. 1990), pp. 99–109.

27. L.A. Rowe and M.R. Stonebraker, 'The POSTGRES Data Model', in Zdonik and Maier (eds), *Readings on Object-Oriented Database Systems*, pp. 461–73.

28. On GemStone, see R.G.G. Cattell, *Object Data Management: Object-Oriented and Extended Relational Database Systems* (Reading, MA, 1991), especially pp. 246–8; D. Maier, J. Stein, A. Otis and A. Purdy, 'Development of an Object-Oriented DBMS', *Proceedings of OOPSLA '86 Conference* (New York, 1986), pp. 472–82. On Vbase, see T. Andrews and C. Harris, 'Combining Language and Database Advances in an Object-Oriented Development Environment', *Proceedings of OOPSLA '87 Conference* (New York, 1988), pp. 142–52. On ORION, see Cattell, *Object Data Management*, especially pp. 248–9; J. Banerjee *et al.*, 'Data Modelling Issues for Object-Oriented Applications', *ACM Transactions on Office Information Systems*, Vol. 5 No. 1 (1987), pp. 3–26; W. Kim, *et al.*, 'Integrating an Object-Oriented Programming System with a Database System', *Proceedings of OOPSLA '88, Conference* (New York, 1988) pp. 142–52.

29. For a description of ODDESSY, see J. Diederich and J. Milton, 'Objects, Messages and Rules in Database Design', in W. Kim and H. Lochovsky (eds), *Object-Oriented Concepts, Databases and Applications* (New York, 1989).

30. Gwyn Price and Alec Gray, 'Object Oriented Databases and their Application to Historical Data', *History and Computing*, Vol. 6, No. 1 (1994), pp. 44–51.

31. *Ibid.*, p. 51.

32. J.F. Sowa, *Conceptual Structures: Information Processing in Mind and Machine* (Reading, MA, 1984) p. 280, quoted in Kevin Schürer, 'Artificial Intelligence and the Historian: Prospects and Possibilities', in Richard Ennals and Jean-Claude Gardin (eds), *Interpretation in the Humanities: Perspectives from Artifical Intelligence* (Boston Spa, West Yorkshire, 1990), p. 176.

33. An example of dealing with fuzzy logic is given in Eric Summers, 'ES: A Public Domain Expert System', *Byte* (October 1990), p. 292.

34. Georges Gardarin and Patrick Valduriez, *Relational Databases and Knowledge Bases* (Reading, MA, 1989), Chapter 10, pp. 315–77.

35. Kamran Parsaye, Mark Chignell, Setrag Khoshafian and Harry Wong, *Intelligent Databases* (New York, 1989), p. vi.

36. *Ibid.*, p. 25.

37. Georges Lee, Ruddy Lelouche, Vincent Meissonier, Monique Ornato, Gian Piero Zarri and Lucia Zarri-Baldi, 'Artificial Intelligence, History and Knowledge Representation', *Computers and the Humanities*, Vol. 16 (1982), pp. 25–34.

38. See, in particular, Caroline Bourlet and Jean-Luc Minel, 'A Declarative System for Setting Up a Prosopographical Database', in Denley and Hopkin (eds), *History and Computing*, pp. 186–91; *idem*, 'Constitution d'une base de données prosopographiques à l'aide d'un système expert', in J.-P. Genet (ed), *Standardisation et échange des bases de données historiques* (Paris, 1988) pp. 313–17; *idem*, 'From a Historian's Know-How to a Knowledge-Base: Using a Shell', in Evan Mawdsley *et al.* (eds), *History and Computing III:*

Historians, Computers and Data (Manchester, 1990), pp. 55–9; *idem*, 'An Expert Decision Support System for a Prosopographical Database', in Lawrence J. McCrank (ed), *Databases in the Humanities and Social Sciences 4* (Medford, NJ, 1990), pp. 79–84; C. Bourlet, A. Guillaumont and J.-L. Minel, 'Intelligence Artificielle et Prosopographie', *Le Medieviste et l'Ordinateur*, Vol. 15 (1986), pp. 6–8; C. Bourlet, L. Fossier, A. Guillaumont and J.-L. Minel, 'Construction d'un prototype de système expert dans le domaine historique', *Computers and the Humanities*, Vol. 20, No. 4 (1986), pp. 273–5.

39. Bourlet and Minel, 'A Declarative System for Setting Up a Prosopographical Database', p. 190.
40. Schürer, 'Artifical Intelligence and the Historian', pp. 169–95.
41. *Ibid.*, p. 178.
42. See Joaquin Carvalho, 'Expert Systems and Community Reconstruction Studies', in Denley, Fogelvik and Harvey (eds), *History and Computing II*, pp. 97–102.
43. Schürer, 'Artifical Intelligence and the Historian', p. 187.
44. Theo J. Schulte, 'Artificial Intelligence Techniques for Historians: Expert Systems, Knowledge Representation and High-Level Programming', in Denley, Fogelvik and Harvey (eds), *History and Computing II*, p. 94.
45. *Ibid.*, p. 95. On the prospects for and limitations of artificial intelligence, see Harry Collins, 'Will Machines Ever Think?', *New Scientist*, 20 June 1992, pp. 36–40.
46. Fred R. McFadden and Jeffrey A. Hoffer, *Database Management* (Redwood City, CA, 3rd edn. 1991), p. 126.

□ **8 Coding and Record Linkage (pp. 222–52)**

1. Konrad H. Jarausch, 'Some Reflections on Coding', in M. Thaller (ed), *Datenbanken und Datenverwaltungssysteme als Werkzeuge Historischer Forschung* (St. Katharinen, 1986), pp. 175–8.
2. This example is drawn from Kevin Schürer, 'The Historical Researcher and Codes: Master and Slave or Slave and Master?', in Evan Mawdsley, *et al.* (eds), *History and Computing III: Historians, Computers and Data* (Manchester, 1990), 74–82. This important and challenging article provides an essential introduction to coding issues.
3. *Ibid.*, p. 76.
4. Marija J. Norusis, *SPSS/PC+ for the IBM PC/XT/AT* (Chicago, 1986), pp. B10–B13.
5. Robert J. Morris, 'Occupational Coding: Principles and Examples', *Historical Social Research*, Vol. 15, No. 1 (1990), p. 3.
6. Daniel I. Greenstein, 'Standard, Meta-Standard: A Framework for Coding Occupational Data', *Historical Social Research*, Vol. 16, No. 1 (1991), p. 5.
7. Kevin Schürer, 'Historical Demography, Social Structure and the Computer', in Peter Denley and Deian Hopkin (eds), *History and Computing* (Manchester, 1987), p. 38. Also see Schürer, 'The Historical Researcher and Codes'.
8. See Edward Higgs, *Making Sense of the Census: The Manuscript Returns for England and Wales, 1801–1901* (London, 1989); Higgs, 'Structuring the Past: The Occupational and Household Classification of Nineteenth-Century

Census Data', in Mawdsley *et al.* (eds), *History and Computing III*, pp. 67–73; Higgs, 'Disease, Febrile Poisons and Statistics: The Census as a Medical Survey, 1841–1911', *Social History of Medicine*, Vol. 4 (1991), pp. 465–78; D. Mills and J. Mills, 'Occupation and Social Stratification Revisited: The Census Enumerators' Books of Victorian Britain', *Urban History Yearbook* (1989), pp. 63–77. On coding errors generally, see A.G. Darroch and M.D. Ornstein, 'Error in Historical Data Files: A Research Note on the Automatic Detection of Error and on the Nature and Sources of Errors in Coding', *Historical Methods*, Vol. 12 No. 4 (1979), pp. 157–67.

9. Morris, 'Occupational Coding: Principles and Examples'. Also, by the same author, 'Fuller Values, Questions and Contexts: Occupational Coding and the Historian', in Kevin Schürer and Herman Diederiks (eds), *The Use of Occupations in Historical Analysis* (St. Katherinen, 1993), pp. 5–21.

10. C. Booth, 'Occupations of the People of the United Kingdom, 1801–81', *Journal of the Royal Statistical Society*, Vol. 49 (1886), pp. 314–444; W.A. Armstrong, 'The Use of Information about Occupation', in E.A. Wrigley (ed), *Nineteenth-Century Society: Essays in the Use of Quantitative Methods for the Study of Social Data* (Cambridge, 1972), pp. 191–310; *idem*, 'The Classification of Occupations', in D.E.C. Eversley, Peter Laslett and E.A. Wrigley (eds), *An Introduction to English Historical Demography* (Cambridge, 1966), Appendix D. For other important work on occupational classifications, see R.H. Hall, *Occupations and the Social Structure* (Englewood Cliffs, NJ, 1975); R.M. Hauser, 'Occupational Status in the Nineteenth and Twentieth Centuries', *Historical Methods*, Vol. 14 (1982), pp. 111–26; M.B. Katz, 'Occupational Classification in History', *Journal of Interdisciplinary History*, Vol. 3 (1972), pp. 63–88; P.H. Lindert, 'English Occupations, 1670–1811', *Journal of Economic History*, Vol. 40 (1980), pp. 685–712; J. Patten, 'Urban Occupations in Pre-Industrial England', *Transactions of the Institute of British Geographers*, new series, Vol. 2 (1977), pp. 296–313.

11. For a useful discussion of this point, see also Greenstein, 'Standard, Meta-Standard', pp. 3–22.

12. *Ibid.*, p. 11.

13. Morris, 'Occupational Coding: Principles and Examples', p. 9.

14. On the latter, see Arno Kitts, David Doulton and Elizabeth Reis, *The Reconstitution of Viana do Castelo* (London, 1990), pp. 27–8.

15. *Ibid.*, p. 19.

16. The Pennsylvania Social History Project's coding system, and the program developed to implement it, are described in T. Hershberg *et al.*, 'Record Linkage', *Historical Methods Newsletter*, Vol. IX, Nos. 2–3 (1976), pp. 137–63.

17. J.A. Phillips, *Electoral Behaviour in Unreformed England* (Princeton, NJ, 1982) Appendix 1.

18. J.E. Bradley, *Religion, Revolution and English Radicalism* (Cambridge, 1990) Appendix 1; Edmund Green, 'Social Structure and Political Allegiance in Westminster, 1774–1820' (unpublished PhD thesis, University of London, 1992); *idem*, 'The Taxonomy of Occupations in Late Eighteenth-Century Westminster', in Penelope J. Corfield and Derek Keene (eds), *Work in Towns, 850–1850* (Leicester, 1990), pp. 164–81; *idem*, 'Social Structure and Political Behaviour in Westminster, 1784–1788', in Peter Denley, Stefan

Fogelvik and Charles Harvey (eds), *History and Computing II* (Manchester, 1989) pp. 239–42.

19. For a description of the Henry Soundex code, see Jacques Legaré, Yolande Lavoie and Hubert Charbonneau, 'The Early Canadian Population: Problems in Record Linkage', *Canadian Historical Review*, Vol. 53 No. 4 (1972), pp. 427–42.

20. Gérard Bouchard, Yolande Lavoie and Patrick Brard, 'FONEM: un code de transcription phonétique pour la reconstitution automatique des familles saguenayennes', *Population*, Vol. 6 (1981), pp. 1085–1104.

21. Kevin Schürer, Jim Oeppen and Roger Schofield, 'Theory and Methodology: An Example from Historical Demography', in Denley, Fogelvik and Harvey (eds), *History and Computing II*, p. 136.

22. Daniel Greenstein (ed), *Modelling Historical Data* (St. Katharinen, 1991). Also see Lou Burnard, 'The Text Encoding Initiative: Towards an Extensible Standard for the Encoding of Texts', in S. Ross and E. Higgs (eds), *Electronic Information Resources and Historians: European Perspectives* (St. Katharinen, 1993), pp. 105–18.

23. Manfred Thaller, 'Data Bases v. Critical Editions', *Historical Social Research*, Vol. 13 No. 3 (1988), p. 137.

24. Manfred Thaller, 'A Draft Proposal for a Standard for the Coding of Machine Readable Sources', *Historical Social Research*, Vol. 40 (Oct. 1986), pp. 3–46, reprinted in Greenstein (ed), *Modelling Historical Data*, pp. 19–64.

25. See Manfred Thaller, 'The Historical Workstation Project', *Historical Social Research*, Vol. 16 No. 4 (1991), pp. 56–7; Thaller, 'A Draft Proposal for a Standard Format Exchange Program', in J.-P. Genet (ed), *Standardisation et échange des bases de données historiques* (Paris, 1988), pp. 329–75; Thomas Werner, 'Transforming Machine Readable Sources', *Historical Social Research*, Vol. 16 No. 4 (1991), pp. 62–73. The manual for StanFEP is K. Homann, *StanFEP: Ein Programm zur freien Konvertierung von Daten* (St. Katharinen, 1990). For an introduction in English, see K. Homann, 'StanFEP: Standardisation without Standards', in J. Smets (ed), *Histoire et Informatique* (Montpellier, 1992) pp. 289–99.

26. See Lou Burnard, 'An Introduction to the Text Encoding Initiative', in Greenstein (ed), *Modelling Historical Data*, pp. 81–92.

27. *Ibid.*, p. 84. Encoding principles of the TEI are further discussed in C.M. Sperberg-McQueen, 'Texts in the Electronic Age: Textual Study and Text Encoding, with Examples from Medieval Text', *Literary and Linguistic Computing*, Vol. 6, No. 1 (1991).

28. Lou Burnard and C.M. Sperberg-McQueen (eds), *Guidelines for the Encoding and Interchange of Machine-Readable Texts* (Chicago, IL and Oxford, 1990).

29. Brief summaries of SGML may be found in Lou Burnard, 'What is SGML and How Does it Help?', in Greenstein (ed), *Modelling Historical Data*, pp. 65–80; Michael Hewitt, 'The Battle for Standards', *Personal Computer World* (Feb. 1993), pp. 437–9; R. Lee Humphreys, 'SGML: Marked Improvement', *Personal Computer World* (March 1992), pp. 330–4. For a fuller treatment, see Martin Bryan, *SGML: An Author's Guide to the Standard Generalised Markup Language* (Reading, MA, 1988).

30. Louis Henry and Michel Fleury, *Des registres paroissiaux à l'histoire de la*

population: Manuel de dépouillement et d'éxploitation de l'état civil ancien (Paris, 1956).

31. See, in particular, E. Anthony Wrigley and Roger S. Schofield, 'Nominal Record Linkage by Computer and the Logic of Family Reconstitution', in E. Anthony Wrigley (ed), *Identifying People in the Past* (London, 1973), pp. 64–101; E. Anthony Wrigley, 'Family Reconstitution', in Eversley, Laslett and Wrigley (eds), *Introduction to English Historical Demography*, pp. 96–159; and Kevin Schürer, Jim Oeppen and Roger Schofield, 'Theory and Methodology: An Example from Historical Demography', in Denley, Fogelvik and Harvey (eds), *History and Computing II*, pp. 130–42.

32. Kitts, Doulton and Reis, *The Reconstitution of Viana do Castelo*, especially pp. 21–2 and Bibliography.

33. Ian Winchester, 'What Every Historian Needs to Know about Record Linkage in the Micro-Computer Era', *Historical Methods*, Vol. 25, No. 4 (Fall 1992), pp. 149–65. Also see his earlier papers on linkage strategies: 'On Referring to Ordinary Historical Persons', in Wrigley (ed.), *Identifying People in the Past*, and 'Priorities for Record Linkage: A Theoretical and Practical Checklist', in J. Chubb and E.K. Scheuch (eds), *Historical Social Research* (Frankfurt, 1980), pp. 414–30.

34. K. Schürer and S.J. Anderson (eds), *A Guide to Historical Datafiles Held in Machine-Readable Form* (London, 1992).

35. A useful introduction to methods for undertaking a community study using such data is provided in Alan Macfarlane, S. Harrison and C. Jardine, *Reconstructing Historical Communities* (Cambridge, 1977).

36. See, for example, W.A. Speck and W.A. Gray, 'Computer Analysis of Poll Books: An Initial Report', *Bulletin of the Institute of Historical Research*, Vol. 43 (1970), pp. 105–12; W.A. Speck, W.A. Gray and R. Hopkinson, 'Computer Analysis of Poll Books: A Further Report', *Bulletin of the Institute of Historical Research*, Vol. 48 (1975), pp. 64–90.

37. Frank O'Gorman, *Voters, Patrons and Parties: The Unreformed Electoral System of Hanoverian England, 1734–1832* (Oxford, 1989) Also see *idem*, 'Electoral Behaviour in England, 1700–1872', in Denley, Fogelvik and Harvey (eds), *History and Computing II*, pp. 220–38; *idem*, 'The Unreformed Electorate of Hanoverian England: The Mid-Eighteenth Century to the Reform Act of 1832', *Social History*, Vol. 2, No. 1 (1986), pp. 33–52; J.A. Phillips, *Electoral Behaviour in Unreformed England* (1982); J. Mitchell and J. Cornford, 'The Political Demography of Cambridge, 1832–68', *Albion*, Vol. 9 (1977), pp. 242–72.

38. Daniel I. Greenstein, 'Multi-Sourced and Integrated Databases for the Prosopographer', in Evan Mawdsley *et al.* (eds), *History and Computing III: Historians, Computers and Data* (Manchester, 1990), p. 60.

39. See, for example, R.J. Morris, *Class, Sect and Party: The Making of the British Middle Class: Leeds, 1820–1850* (Manchester, 1990); Charles Harvey and Jon Press, 'The Business Elite of Bristol: A Case Study in Database Design', *History and Computing*, Vol. 3, No. 1 (Spring 1991), pp. 1–11; Stana Nenadic, 'Identifying Social Networks with a Computer-Aided Analysis of Personal Diaries', in Mawdsley *et al.* (eds), *History and Computing III*, pp. 188–94; *idem*, 'The Small Family Firm in Victorian Britain', *Business History*, Vol.

35, No. 4 (Oct. 1993), pp. 86–114; P. Joubert and M. Moss (eds), *The Life and Death of Companies: An Historical Perspective* (New Jersey, 1990).

40. R. Lloyd-Jones and M.J. Lewis, *Manchester and the Age of the Factory: The Business Structure of Cottonopolis in the Industrial Revolution* (London, 1988); *idem*, 'A Database for Historical Reconstruction: Manchester in the Industrial Revolution', in Mawdsley *et al.* (eds), *History and Computing III*, pp. 169–73.

41. Schürer and Anderson (eds), *Guide to Historical Datafiles*, p. 11; R.W. Ambler, R.A. Peese and F.W. Langley, 'SPSS as a Relational Database Management System', *University Computing*, Vol. 12, No. 2 (1990).

42. Schürer and Anderson (eds), *Guide to Historical Datafiles*, pp. 19–20.

43. *Ibid.*, p. 41.

44. This is part of the major project which has been undertaken by researchers at the Memorial University of St John's, Newfoundland. For a description of the project, see Lewis R. Fischer and Eric W. Sager , 'An Approach to the Quantitative Analysis of British Shipping Records', *Business History*, Vol. XXII, No. 2 (1980), pp. 135 *et seq.*

45. François Nault and Bertrand Desjardins, 'Computers and Historical Demography: The Reconstitution of the Early Quebec Population', in Denley, Fogelvik and Harvey (eds), *History and Computing II*, pp. 145–6. Also see Gérard Bouchard, 'The Processing of Ambiguous Links in Computerised Family Reconstitution', *Historical Methods*, Vol. 19 No. 1 (1986), pp. 9–19.

46. Peter Adman, Stephen W. Baskerville and Katharine F. Beedham, 'Computer-Assisted Record Linkage: Or How Best to Optimise Links Without Generating Errors', *History and Computing*, Vol. 4, No. 1 (1992), p. 1.

47. Kitts, Doulton and Reis, *The Reconstitution of Viana do Castelo*, p. 22.

48. Schürer, Oeppen and Schofield, 'Theory and Methodology', p. 138.

49. *Ibid.*, p. 140.

50. This section is drawn from an article by C. Harvey and E. Green, 'Record Linkage Algorithms: Efficiency, Selection and Relative Confidence', *History and Computing*, Vol. 6, No. 3 (1994), pp. 143–52. The authors are grateful to Edmund Green for agreeing to its inclusion here.

51. The contests of 1749, 1788, and 1819 were by-elections in which each voter had one vote only. The other contests were general elections in which both of Westminster's seats were contested and in which electors had two votes at their disposal.

52. Each name standardisation routine used (such as Guth, SOUNDEX, or NYSIIS) makes a further 15 algorithms. Russell Soundex codes have been incorporated into the database since the experiment here reported was conducted, but were not part of that experiment. The Guth algorithm is described in G. Guth, 'Surname Spellings and Computerised Record Linkage', *Historical Methods Newsletter*, Vol. 10 (1976), pp. 10–19. The algorithm of the New York State Intelligence Information System is described in Howard B. Newcombe, *Handbook of Record Linkage: Methods for Health and Statistical Studies, Administration, and Business* (Oxford, 1988), pp. 182–3.

53. No single algorithm linked more records than algorithm 26 (*Stdsur + Shtname + Parish*) which linked 2,868 records, or 34.87 per cent of the voters in 1788. No single algorithm could link records at a higher level of confidence than the 'perfect match' algorithm 1 (*Surname +*

Shtname + Parish + Street + Oclv4) which linked 1,666 records, or 20.25 per cent of the voters in 1788.

54. E.A. Wrigley, 'Introduction', in E.A. Wrigley (ed), *Nineteenth-Century Society: Essays in the Use of Quantitative Methods for the Study of Social Data* (Cambridge, 1972) p. 5.
55. For a consideration of these issues, see Roger S. Schofield, 'Representativeness and Family Reconstitution', *Annales de Démographie Historique* (1972) pp. 121–5.
56. Wrigley, 'Introduction', p. 3.

☐ Case Study H: Researching the Population History of England (pp. 253–6)

1. L.A. Clarkson, 'History Will Never Be The Same Again', *The Times Higher Education Supplement*, 5 February 1982, p. 13, reviewing E.A. Wrigley and R.S. Schofield, *The Population History of England 1541–1871: A Reconstruction* (London, 1981, republished with an Introductory Note Cambridge, 1989), hereafter referred to as *PHE*.
2. The database principally consisted of a matrix of 404 parishes x 280 years x 3 events (baptisms, burials and marriages), in other words 339,360 cells of information.
3. *PHE*, pp. 66–76, Appendix 7. See also D.V. Glass, *Numbering the People: The Eighteenth-Century Population Controversy and the Development of Census and Vital Statistics in Britain* (Farnborough, 1973) and T. Arkell, 'An Examination of the Poll Taxes of the later Seventeenth Century: The Marriage Duty Act and Gregory King', pp. 171–7 and P. Laslett, 'Natural and Political Observations in the Population of Late Seventeenth-Century England: Reflections in the Work of Gregory King and John Gaunt', pp. 18–30, both in K. Schürer and T. Arkell (eds), *Surveying the People: The Interpretation and Use of Document Sources for the Study of Population in the Late Seventeenth Century* (Oxford, 1992).
4. The classic work on parish registers in still J.C. Cox, *The Parish Registers of England* (London, 1910). For a general introduction see R. Finlay, *Parish Registers: An Introduction*, Historical Geography Research Series, Vol. 23 (London, 1981), and for examples of their application see M. Drake (ed), *Population Studies from Parish Registers: A Selection of Readings from Local Population Studies* (Matlock, Derbyshire, 1982). From the point of view of an archival guide and finding aid, see D.J. Steel, *National Index of Parish Registers* (London, several volumes, 1964–).
5. *PHE*, pp. 19–32. But see also P. Razzell, 'The Growth of Population in Eighteenth-Century England: A Critical Reappraisal', *Journal of Economic History*, Vol. 53, No. 4 (1993), pp. 746–8.
6. *PHE*, pp. 49–56.
7. This basic concern is at the root of many of Elton's objections to the applications of quantitative techniques and social science methodology to history. See G.R. Elton, *Return to Essentials: Some Reflections on the Present State of Historical Study* (Cambridge, 1991) and R.W. Fogel, and G.R. Elton *Which Road to the Past? Two Views of History* (New Haven, 1983).

8. R.D. Lee 'Estimating Series of Vital Rates and Age Structures from Baptisms and Burials: A New Technique, with Applications to Pre-Industrial England', *Population Studies*, Vol. 28 (1974), pp. 495–512. The model applied in the *PHE* is described in Jim Oeppen's Appendix 15, and a simple overview of the technique is provided by K. Schürer *et al.*, 'Theory and Methodology: An Example from Historical Demography', in Peter Denley, Stefan Fogelvik and Charles Harvey (eds), *History and Computing II* (Manchester, 1989) pp. 130–42. For critics of the model see R.D. Lee, 'Inverse Projection and Back Projection: A Critical Appraisal and Comparative Results for England, 1539–1871', *Population Studies*, Vol. 39 (1985), pp. 233–48; H.A.W. van Vianen, 'Past Population: A Critique of Back Projection', in B. van Norren and van H.A.W. Vianen (eds), *Profession Demographer: Ten Population Studies in Honour of F.H.A.G. Zwart* (Groningen, 1988); and K.W. Wachter, 'Ergodicity and Inverse Projection', *Population Studies*, Vol. 40 (1986), pp. 275–87. For the most recent commentary on the technique, see J. Oeppen 'Back Projection and Inverse Projection: Members of a Wider Class of Constrained Projection Models', *Population Studies*, Vol. 47 (1993), pp. 245–67 and, by the same author, 'Generalised Inverse Projection', in D.S. Reher and R.S. Schofield (eds), *Old and New Methods in Historical Demography* (Oxford, 1993), pp. 29–39.
9. So-called life tables are a basic tool of both demographers and actuaries and provide, together with a series of other measures, an estimation of the probability of dying (or conversely survivorship) at given ages. For their construction, see A.H. Pollard, F. Yusuf and G.H. Pollard, *Demographic Techniques* (New York, 1990), Chapter 3. Demographers also often use so-called 'model life tables' giving life table statistics for separate 'standard' structural mortality types at differing mortality levels. See A.J. Coale and P. Demeny, *Regional Model Life Tables and Stable Populations* (Princeton, 1966).
10. R.S. Schofield, 'Through a Glass Darkly: *The Population History of England* as an Experiment in History', *Journal of Interdisciplinary History*, Vol. 15 (1985), pp. 571–93, reprinted in R.I. Rotberg and T.K. Rabb (eds), *Population and Economy: Population and History from the Traditional to the Modern World* (Cambridge, 1986), pp. 169–93.
11. T.R. Malthus, *An Essay on the Principle of Population*, and *A Summary View of the Principle of Population* (Penguin edn., Harmondsworth, Middlesex, 1982, first published in 1798 and 1830 respectively). For a full edition of his works, see E.A. Wrigley and D.C. Souden (eds), *The Works of Thomas Robert Malthus* (London, 1986). See also J. Dupâquier, A. Fauve-Chamoux and E. Grebenik (eds), *Malthus Past and Present* (London, 1983).
12. *PHE*, pp. 458–63. See also R.S. Schofield, 'The Impact of Scarcity on Population Change in England, 1541–1871', *Journal of Interdisciplinary History*, Vol. 14 (1983), pp. 265–91.
13. J. Hajnal, 'Two Kinds of Pre-industrial Household Formation System', in R. Wall *et al.* (eds), *Family Forms in Historic Europe* (Cambridge, 1983); and R.M. Smith, 'Fertility, Economy and Household Formation in England over Three Centuries', *Population and Development Review*, Vol. 7, No. 4 (1981), pp. 595–622.

9 Conclusion: Databases and the Future of Historical Computing (pp. 257–60)

1. E.M. Green, 'Social Structure and Political Allegiance in Westminster, 1774–1820' (unpublished PhD thesis, University of London 1992), Chapter 3, p. 169.
2. See 'ESRC Data Archive Establishes History Data Unit', *History and Computing*, Vol. 4, No. 2 (1992), pp. 164–5.
3. For a more in-depth discussion of our view, see Charles Harvey, 'The Nature and Future of Historical Computing', in Evan Mawdsley, *et al.* (eds), *History and Computing III: Historians, Computers and Data* (Manchester, 1990), pp. 204–13.

Glossary

Cross-references are *in italics.*

Access control The task of controlling access to the *database*, usually performed by a *database administrator (DBA)*. Several levels of access may be provided, depending upon the needs of different classes of users.

AI See *artificial intelligence.*

Algorithm A procedure or series of steps which are followed in solving a problem or performing a particular activity.

Alphanumeric characters A character set which draws upon the 26 letters, 10 numerals and punctuation marks, but not special characters like # or @.

ANSI The American National Standards Institute, which defines standards for *(inter alia)* computer hardware and software.

Answer table The temporary *table* which contains the result of a *Query-by-Example* query.

Antecedent Part of the IF clause in a *knowledge base* rule. Provides relation tests; =, <, >, etc.

Application A program used to control processing of data and data output to meet the specific needs of users. Thus one *database* may be accessed by many application programs which perform a variety of tasks.

Artificial intelligence (AI) The use of computers to undertake tasks which would be considered intelligent if performed by humans; systems which imitate human thought processes or decision making.

ASCII American Standard Code for Information Interchange. A code used to represent *alphanumeric characters*, special symbols and certain control functions. Valuable for file transfer because virtually all software can import and export ASCII files. However, conversion to ASCII format does entail loss of some information – emboldening or italicising of text, for example.

Attribute A named characteristic or property of an *entity* or an *object*. An attribute (sometimes called a data item) is the smallest element of data in an information system.

Authorisation rules Controls built into a *DBMS* which restrict access to data and also limit the actions that a user may take when data are accessed.

Backward recovery A procedure which facilitates recovery from a hardware or software crash by undoing (backing out of) incompleted *transactions* (data updates).

Batch processing A method of processing where groups of *transaction* records are processed together; often considered as the opposite of *interactive processing.*

Bitmap An image produced by a *scanner* or painting program which is stored as a set of differently coloured dots (*pixels*).

BLOB Binary Large Object. A large data item (like an image or map) in binary format.

Boolean operator A logical operator – AND, OR and NOT.

Candidate key   One or more *attributes* in a *table* that uniquely identifies an *instance* of an *entity*, and therefore may serve as the *primary key* in that table.

CASE tools   Computer-aided software engineering (CASE) tools are automated tools used to design *databases* and *applications*.

CD-i   CD-i (Compact Disk Interactive) is a format devised by Philips and Sony to run on a specially designed player. Many leading manufacturers produce suitable players, and the format is tightly specified to ensure compatibility from one make to another. A combination of visual and audio data can be stored in various formats. It displays on a standard TV rather than a computer monitor, which may help it to gain general acceptance but limits its use for research projects.

CD-ROM   CD-ROM (Compact Disk – Read Only Memory) is the best defined of the mass storage media. As specified by US and international standards, CD-ROM disks are always single-sided, 12 cm in diameter, and capable of storing 600Mb. As the name suggests, it is a read only format, and most users buy pre-recorded disks rather than create their own. CD-ROM is very effective as a distribution medium for large data sets which do not require frequent modification. A related format is CD-ROM XA. XA stands for Extended Architecture, and it provides a set of extensions to the basic CD-ROM standard. Developed by Microsoft, Sony and Philips, it is intended to provide a computer-based alternative to *CD-i*. Unlike the basic standard, which stores data and audio on different parts of the disk, it allows them to be interlaced, thus permitting faster access for multimedia uses. It includes audio compression techniques. CD-WO (Compact Disk Write Once) allows users to press their own disks using a special gold disk. Unlike magneto-optical drives, where the disks can be rewritten, the CD-WO recording process involves burning the data into the disk's recording layer. It is currently very expensive, but it is likely to become established as an important archiving medium as costs fall. Another format is PhotoCD, developed by Kodak as a standard for storing hgh quality photographic images. It is compatible with both CD-I and CD-ROM XA.

Character   The smallest element in a *file*: a number, letter, or special character.

Class   In an *object-oriented database*, a set of *object instances* which have similar structure and behaviour.

Clipboard   In systems like Windows and the Macintosh operating system, text or graphics may be 'cut' or 'copied' from one document and stored in a part of memory known as the clipboard. From there, it may be 'pasted' into another document – which may have been created by the same program or a different one.

Column   See *field*.

Comma-delimited ASCII   *ASCII* files which have been prepared for importation into a database. Each field is separated by a comma, and each record commences on a new line. Most DBMS allow other characters (e.g. "") to be defined as delimiters instead of commas. This is valuable where text fields containing commas need to be imported.

Common word   See *stopword*.

Composite key   A *primary key* which is composed of two or more *fields* of a *record.* Used where no one field provides a unique identifier for each *record* or row in a *table*.

Conceptual data model The overall model of a *database*, which is independent of a particular *DBMS*.

Conceptual design The process of developing a *database* design that is independent of hardware and software implementation details. The output of conceptual design is an overall information architecture (or *conceptual schema*) for the project.

Conceptual schema An overall *database design* architecture, which is machine- and software-independent.

Concurrency control An essential function in an *multiuser DBMS*, which prevents two or more users trying to change the same data item at once. Also known as file locking. Such locks may be applied at field, record or table levels.

Confidence factor Measure of probability of a rule proving TRUE in an *knowledge base*. Sometimes called a certainty factor.

Consequent Part of the THEN clause in a *knowledge base* rule. It assigns particular conclusions to specified facts if the IF part of the rule proves true.

Context indexing In a *textual information management system (TIMS)*, the concept that the entire contents of the *textbase* should be searchable. In practice, *stopwords* like 'the', 'and', or 'but' are excluded; it is unlikely that anyone would wish to search for them, and because they occur so frequently they would greatly increase the size of the index.

Context-sensitive help On-screen assistance provided by the software which is relevant to the task currently being performed by the user.

Control character A non-printing character that specifies an action to be taken by the printing device, such as carriage return, space, embolden, etc.

Control total A technique for ensuring accuracy when *batch processing* numeric input data. A manually derived total is calculated for the batch, and added to a *header record* which is keyed in before the batch of documents to which it refers. The batch itself is then entered, but is not added to the *database* unless the number of entered records matches the count held in the header record.

Controls Methods for checking the accuracy and completeness of data entry and data processing.

CPU See *central processor unit*.

Critical path In project management, the critical path draws attention to tasks to which a high priority must be given if the project as a whole is to be completed on time.

Data control Refers to the provision made by the *DBMS* for *data recovery*, *data security* and *data integrity*.

Data decomposition The process of extracting different categories of data from a given source.

Data description language (DDL) The language used by a *DBMS* to describe the logical (and sometimes the physical) structure of a *database*.

Data dictionary The repository for all data describing the structure and character of a *database*. Data about data is sometimes called *metadata*.

Data independence The technique of separating data from the *applications* which use it, thus ensuring that any change to the data does not require rewriting the application program. An essential characteristic, and one of the major advantages, of *database management systems.*

Data integrity   The control of data to make sure that it is accurate, fit for purpose, relates correctly to other data and exists where necessary.

Data item   See *attribute.*

Data item list   The starting point in *relational data analysis;* the creation of a list of *data item* names and characteristics.

Data manipulation language (DML)   The *DBMS* language which is used to query and modify the contents of a *database.*

Data model   An abstract representation of the structure and relationships in a *database.*

Data recovery   The range of routines provided by the *DBMS* to cope with hardware, software and disk media errors.

Data redundancy   Occurs when one item of data is stored in more than one location in an information system.

Data security   *DBMS*s provide passwords and other facilities to ensure that the *database* is protected from unauthorised users.

Data set   A collection of logically related data records.

Database   A shared collection of logically related data, designed to meet the information needs of multiple users.

Database administrator (DBA)   The person responsible for documenting the *database,* maintaining security and integrity, controlling access, etc.

Database management system (DBMS)   A software system which is used to create, maintain and permit controlled access to a *database.*

DBMS   See *database management system.*

DDL   See *data description language.*

Deductive database   See *knowledge base.*

Dependencies   In a project, the ways in which tasks depend upon each other. Dependencies may be 'finish to start' (one task must finish before another can start); 'start to start' (where related tasks must start, but not necessarily finish, together); or 'finish to finish' (where related tasks must finish together, regardless of starting time).

Detail record   A single *record* in a batch for data entry. Also see *header record.*

Device driver   A program to control a specific piece of hardware (printers, mice, displays, etc.). It tells the operating system how the hardware is connected and how to use it.

Digital camera   A photosensitive device for capturing digital images, such as Canon's ION camera. Whereas a *scanner* captures flat documents, a digital camera can create images of three-dimensional objects.

Direct access   A means of accessing *files* so that (unlike *sequential access*) each *record*'s location is determined independently of the other records and can be found without reading everything that comes before it.

Distributed database   A *database* that is not stored entirely at a single location, but is spread across a network of computers.

DML   See *data manipulation language.*

Domain   The set of potential values for an *attribute* in a *table.*

DOS   The operating system used by IBM personal computers (PCs) and their clones. Stands for Disk Operating System.

Dynaset In Microsoft Access, the set of records which meets the search criteria of a query.

Electronic edition A *database* which seeks to capture an original source virtually whole.

Entity The object (e.g. person, organisation, transaction) described by the *fields* of a *record*. A key part of the *relational data model*.

Entity description form In *entity-relationship modelling*, a form which is used to record detailed information about the characteristics of the *attributes* of each *table*.

Entity integrity rule In *relational databases*, two integrity rules ensure that linkage between two or more *tables* can be achieved. The entity integrity rule states that once the *primary key* is established, no change may be made that destroys its ability uniquely to identify a *record*. (For instance, no primary key (or any part of the primary key) shall have a *null* value.) This ensures access to all data. The *referential integrity* (q.v.) rule states that the value of a *foreign key* in a table must be null or correspond to a primary key value in the associated table.

Entity-relationship modelling (ERM) A graphical approach to data modelling that uses symbols to represent *entities*, *attributes* and the relationships between entities.

Equi-join A query which involves joining two or more *tables*, where the join condition includes the equals sign.

ERM See *entity-relationship modelling*.

Expanded memory Also referred to as LIM memory, because the standard was agreed by Lotus, Intel and Microsoft. It enables a program to use more memory than *DOS*' 640Kb limit by swapping pages of memory in and out.

Expert shell See *shell*.

Expert system A system that captures the knowledge and experience of human experts in the form of facts and rules, so as to aid others in the process of decison making.

Extended memory On a PC, memory which lies outside the base 640Kb used by *DOS* can be configured as extended memory, and used by Windows programs and other modern software.

External schema Also called an external data model or user view. It describes how each user, or group of users, sees the data in which they are interested. Each user's view of the data is kept as simple as possible, and as the data in which they are interested is normally a subset of the data stored in the *database* such external schemas are also referred to as sub-schemas or user schemas.

FFM See *flat file manager*.

Field Groups of related characters that form a *data item* within a *record*. Also described as a column in a *database table* or as a tuple.

Fieldname The unique name which identifies a *field* in a *table*.

Fifth generation language See *programming language*.

File A collection of logically related *records*. They are usually in a standard format, though some programs such as Idealist allow records to have one of several predefined formats.

File locking   See *concurrency control*.

First generation language   See *programming language*.

First normal form (1NF)   A *table* is in 1NF when for each value of the *primary key* there is no repetition of groups of non-key *data items*.

Flat file   A two-dimensional array of *data items*, which can be visualised as a table with rows representing *records* and columns representing *fields*.

Flat file manager   A software program for the creation, querying and editing of *flat files*.

Foreign key   A non-key *attribute* in one *table* which appears as the *primary key* (or part of the primary key) in another table. Used to enable the two tables to be joined together when querying.

Form   A customised screen layout for data entry, retrieval and updating.

Forms generator   A special program or module which is designed to facilitate the creation of customised screen layouts for data entry, retrieval and updating. It may also include provision for *validation* checks. Sometimes called a screen painter.

Forward recovery   A procedure which facilitates recovery from a hardware or software crash by retrieving the last full backup and then bringing it up to data by rolling forward (redoing) all the changes made since the archive copy was saved. See *transaction, recovery log*.

Fourth generation language   See *programming language*.

Functional dependence   exists between two *data items* in a *database* where the value of one data item depends upon the value of a second.

Gantt chart   A type of bar chart with time as the *x*-axis. Used in project management to indicate how long specific tasks are expected to take to complete.

Gigabyte (Gb)   Approximately 1 billion (2^{30}) bytes; used to measure storage capacity.

Graphical user interface (GUI)   A display which uses graphical rather than character information to communicate between user and computer.

GUI   see *graphical user interface*.

Hard disk, disc   A mass storage device, on which data is magnetically recorded. Data can be accessed randomly, and thus access is faster than with sequential storage devices like magnetic tape.

Header record   The leading *record* in a batch of *detail records*, which contains summary information about the detail records which follow. Used to ensure accuracy when *batch processing* input data. See *transaction count, control total*.

Heuristic problem-solving   involves the use of general strategies or working rules which have been developed through learning and experience. Good or adequate solutions are selected from a wide range of possibilities. An *expert system* uses structured heuristics to codify knowledge into a form that the computer can understand.

Hierarchical database management system   A database management system in which data are represented as a set of *one-to-many relationships*. Each *record* can have many subordinate items (children), but only one parent item directly above it in the hierarchy.

Hierarchical decomposition   A project planning technique for analysing the scope and components of a project.

Historical computing The term used to describe the various ways in which computers are used in historical research.

Historical workstation The concept of a computer which is conceived as a specific response to the historian's needs.

Hit list The result returned by a query; the set of *records* which meet the specified search criteria.

Hollerith code A coding scheme devised by Dr Herman Hollerith for use with the 80-column, 12-row punched card used for data entry.

Hypermedia Software which allows text, still pictures, video and sound to be linked in non-sequential ways; thus allowing the researcher to access information in different sequences according to his/her needs, rather than in a manner prescribed by its original author.

Hypertext Software which allows associative referencing of textual information; in other words, information can be accessed in different sequences according to the needs of the individual researcher, rather than in the manner prescribed by its original author. Systems which accommodate still pictures, video and sound as well as text are often referred to as *hypermedia*.

Indexed sequential file A *file* stored sequentially, with an index to provide direct access to any *record*.

Indexing A method of locating a *record's* physical address by searching a *table* which lists the storage address of record *keys*.

Indirect dependency exists in *tables* which are not fully *normalised*, where some *data items* in a *record* can be identified by a *non-key data item* in that *record*.

Individual transaction processing The entry of individual *records* into a *database*, as opposed to *batch processing*.

Inference engine A processor for manipulating a *knowledge base*.

Inheritance A characteristic of *object-oriented methodology*, where a *subclass* of *objects* acquires the *attributes* and operations of the *class* to which it belongs.

Instance A single occurrence of an *entity*. Thus 'Handel' is an instance of the entity 'composer'.

Integrity See *data integrity*.

Interactive processing Processing method where the user can intervene during program execution, providing input as the program requires (as opposed to *batch processing*).

Internal data model See *internal schema*.

Internal schema The description of the physical storage of data in a database. Also called the internal data model or storage schema.

Item count See *transaction count*.

Key See *primary key*.

Key field See *primary key*.

Knowledge base A stored collection of facts, and rules for deriving facts.

Knowledge base system Allows a computer to make deductions from a stored collection of facts and experience, rather than executing precise *algorithms* that are mathematically guaranteed to solve problems.

Knowledge environment (logical environment) The term used in κλειω to describe the layer of the system which contains the rules and knowledge used to interpret the data.

Laserdisk   See *videodisk.*

Left-hand truncation   See *reverse truncation.*

LIM memory   See *expanded memory.*

List uniqueness   Where each *record* in a *database* is uniquely defined by its *primary key.* An essential prerequisite for data analysis, especially record linkage.

Logical data model   The result of transforming a *conceptual data model* into a model which can be processed by a specific *DBMS.* Most DBMSs currently support the *relational* logical model, though some are based on *network, hierarchical* or *object-oriented* models.

Logical objects   In κλειω, the rules which tell κλειω how to interpret the data.

Lookup table   A separate *table* which contains a list of allowed entries for a particular table and *field.* To ensure accuracy when entering or modifying *records*, data values may only be entered if they already exist in the lookup table.

Macro   Many software programs allow the user to program a single key to carry out complex operations which normally demand a sequence of keystrokes.

Magneto-optical drive   Magneto-optical (MO) drives are the newest form of mass storage technology. They are suitable for projects which need to hold data files on-line which are too large for magnetic disks but do not need to be accessed too rapidly. The recording mechanism fires a laser at the disk, whilst modifying the magnetic charge. Though more complex than *WORM* drives, they permit data to be erased and rewritten. Access time is 2–6 times slower than magnetic hard disks, and prices are higher, which has slowed the adoption of MO drives. However, they are faster and more convenient than magnetic tape. MO disks are usually enclosed in removeable cartridges, and can be transferred between different makes of machine than conform to the ANSI standard.

Main memory   The high-speed storage of a computer, used for programs and data currently in use.

Many-to-many relationship   A relationship in which many instances of one *entity* are associated with many instances of another.

Megabyte (Mb)   Approximately one million (2^{20}) bytes; used to measure storage capacity.

Metadata   Data about data. Thus the *data dictionary* contains metadata because it describes the structure of the *database* of which it is part.

Multimedia   A package of hardware and software which handles digital sound, still images and real-time video (either *window*ed or full-screen) in addition to text.

Multitasking   The ability to have a number of programs loaded and running at the same time.

Multitable database   A *database* which consists of more then one *table* or *file*, ie not a *flat file.*

Multiuser   A computer system which can be used by more than one person at the same time.

Must Fill   In data entry, a feature to ensure that a *field* must be filled in for every record. Also called a mandatory, required or *NOT NULL* field. Used to ensure that essential data is always entered – for example in a *primary* *key*, which must not be null.

Must Match In data entry, a feature to ensure that illegal entries are rejected. Reference is made to a separate *lookup table* which contains a list of allowed entries. Sometimes called a matching values control.

Network A method of connecting computers together so that they can share software, data files and hardware like printers and disk drives.

Network database management system A system based on a *data model* which specifies a set of *records* (known as nodes) and the links (associations) between those records. Supports *many-to-many relationships*.

Nominal record linkage The process of linking historical persons described in one data source with those in another on the basis of their names. The objective is to use an *algorithm* which maximises the number of true links and rejects false links.

Non-equi-join See *theta-join*.

Non-key attribute An *attribute* in a *table* that is not part of the *primary key* of that table.

Non-key data item See *non-key attribute*.

Non-procedural A *programming language* or *query language* which allows the user to specify what is to be done, rather than how to do it. For example, the user does not need to know the physical location of a *data item* in order to retrieve it.

Normalisation The technique of decomposing data into simple *tables* according to a set of rules. Also called *relational data analysis (RDA)*. The process can be summarised by stating that in fully *normalised* tables, each *non-key data item* depends upon the whole *key*, and nothing but the key. Also see *first normal form (1NF)*, *second normal form (2NF)*, *third normal form (3NF)*.

Normalised See *normalisation*.

NOT NULL A field which is not allowed to be left empty when entering data. Typically, a *primary key* field, unique reference number, etc.

Null A value which is not known. Not the same as zero.

Object A packet of data definitions and values, and the procedures (also called *methods*) that act upon that data.

Object instance An individual occurrence of an *object*.

Object-oriented data model A *data model* which is based upon *objects* rather than *entities*.

Object-oriented database A *database* which uses an *object-oriented data model*.

Object-oriented methodology A methodology which uses an *object-oriented data model*.

OCR See *optical character recognition*.

On-line An on-line system is one where data enter the computer directly from the point of origin, and the user can query and update interactively.

One-to-many relationship A relationship in which one instance of one *entity* is associated with many instances of another.

One-to-one relationship A relationship in which one instance of an *entity* is associated with only one instance of another.

Operating system Software which controls and supports a computer system's hardware; loaded first when the computer is switched on.

Optical character recognition (OCR) A data input technique where manuscript, typewritten or printed text is read by a photosensitive device in a *scanner*. The resulting image is then translated into characters by OCR software.

Partial dependency   exists in *tables* which are not fully *normalised*, where some *data items* in a *record* do not depend for their identification on the whole of the *primary key*.

PERT chart   Project Evaluation and Review Technique charts are used in project management to match resources to tasks, ensure that the resource budget is not exceeded, and highlight a *critical path* through the project.

Pixel   A single dot on a screen or display (pixel = picture element).

Pointer   An entry in a *table* which can be used to identify the location of related *records*. For example, in a *textbase*, pointers are used to identify every location of each word.

Primary key   A *field* or group of fields used to provide a unique identifier for each *record* or row in a *table*, and facilitate the linking of related tables.

Programming language   The first generation of programming languages was binary code – a string of ones and zeroes that the computer can manipulate. Also known as machine code, this is now very rarely used by programmers. The second generation consists of low-level assembly languages which convert the programmer's assembly code (typically easily remembered mnemonics) into binary code. The third generation – at a much higher level, and therefore easier to use – are well-known programming languages like BASIC or COBOL. A fourth generation language is a very high-level *query language* or *data manipulation language*. It is *non-procedural* (involves programming what is to be done, rather than how to do it), and enables the user to develop *applications* much quicker than COBOL or any other third generation languages. Fifth generation languages are *artificial intelligence* languages like *PROLOG*.

Project modelling   Takes as input the goals of the project, the task list resulting from *hierarchical decomposition*, and estimates of the resources needed to complete each task. Two sets of constraints are imposed: resource constraints and time constraints. The aims of project modelling are to schedule tasks, match resources to tasks, and effectively limit the duration of the project.

Project reviews   An essential feature of project management, project reviews take place at key points in the project's development, known as milestones. They generally lead to greater or lesser adjustments in the project.

PROLOG (PROgramming in LOGic)   A *programming language* primarily used to develop *expert systems*.

Proximity searching   In a *textual information management system (TIMS)*, enables the user to find all occurrences of a certain search term within a specified distance forwards or backwards from another search term.

QBE   See *Query-by-Example*.

Query-by-Example (QBE)   A method of querying and updating *databases* where search criteria are placed in a blank query form.

Query language   A high-level language which allows a user to create and manipulate a database using English-like statements.

RAM   See *random access memory*.

Random access memory (RAM)   The main memory of a computer, holding programs and data. It can be written to as well as read. It is volatile, only retaining its contents until the computer is switched off.

RDA See *relational data analysis*.

RDBMS See *relational database management system*.

Read only memory (ROM) Memory chips with preprogrammed circuits which cannot be changed by the user.

Record A group of related *fields*, which describe an *entity*. Sometimes referred to as a row in a *table*.

Recovery The process of returning a *database* and *DBMS* to a normal operating condition after a hardware or software crash. Also see *forward recovery*, *backward recovery*, *recovery log*.

Recovery log An automatic record of all modifications to the *database*. In the event of a major failure, this recovery log can be used to reconstruct the database up to the point of failure.

Referential integrity rule In *relational databases*, two integrity rules ensure that linkage between two or more *tables* can be achieved. The *entity integrity* rule (q.v.) states that once the *primary key* is established, no change may be made that destroys its ability uniquely to identify a *record*. (For instance, no primary key (or any part of the primary key) shall have a *null* value.) This ensures access to all data. The referential integrity rule states that the value of a *foreign key* in a table must be null or correspond to a primary key value in the associated table.

Relation See *table*.

Relational data analysis (RDA) The technique of decomposing data into simple *tables* according to a set of rules. Also called *normalisation*. The process can be summarised by stating that in fully *normalised* tables, each *non-key data item* depends upon the whole *key*, and nothing but the key. Also see *first normal form (1NF)*, *second normal form (2NF)*, *third normal form (3NF)*.

Relational data model A *data model* which represents all data as a set of *normalised tables*.

Relational database *Database* constructed using the *relational data model* with a *relational database management system*.

Relational database management system (RDBMS) A software system which is based upon the *relational data model*, and used to create, maintain and permit controlled access to a *relational database*.

Report definition The task of describing the format and layout of printed reports.

Report generator A part or module of a *DBMS* which handles the preparation and printing of customised printouts, providing special commands for inserting headings, summary statistics, etc.

Reverse truncation Reverse truncation (sometimes called left-hand truncation) is used with *wildcards* to retrieve groups of words with different prefixes but the same ending. Thus in ORACLE `'%port'` would retrieve `'Newport'`, `'Bridport'`, etc.

ROM See *read only memory*.

Row See *record*.

Scanner A photosensitive device used for capturing printed text and graphics. Scanning results in a *bitmap*ped image. This is sufficient for importing graphics, but scanned text needs to be processed by *optical character recognition* software to translate it from individual dots into characters.

Schema　A representation of the logical structure of a *database*.

Screen form　See *form*.

Screen painter　See *forms generator*.

Second generation language　See *programming language*.

Second normal form (2NF)　A *table* that is in *first normal form (1NF)* and in which each *non-key* attribute is fully *functionally dependent* upon the *primary key*.

Secondary storage　Bulk storage media (e.g. hard disk, magnetic tape) used to augment the computer's main memory. Usually used for large amounts of data and programs which are not currently needed.

Sequential access　A means of accessing *files* so that (unlike *direct access*) information must be read in the order in which it appears. Each *record*'s location is dependent on the other records and cannot be assessed without reading everything that comes before it.

Sequential file　A *file* in which *records* are arranged in ascending or descending order according to the data in their *key field(s)*.

Shell　A user-friendly front end for building a *knowledge base*.

Source-oriented data processing　An approach to *historical computing* which attempts to model the complete amount of information in an historical source on a computer; it tries to administer such sources for the widest variety of purposes feasible.

Spooling　Sending a print job to the printer queue.

SQL　See *Structured Query Language*.

Stopword　In a *textbase*, words like 'the', 'and', 'but', which are not indexed to save disk space and speeding retrieval times. Also called common words.

Stored query　A query which is saved to disk so that it can be retrieved and rerun whenever necessary. Invaluable where complex querying is needed.

Structured Query Language (SQL)　The standard *query language* for defining and manipulating *relational databases*.

Subclass　A refinement or subset of a generic *superclass*, or parent *class*. An *object* may *inherit* some of its structure and behaviour from its superclass.

Superclass　A generic or parent *class*, which may have one or more *subclasses*.

Synonym ring　In a *textbase*, a group of words which are defined as synonyms. One word is usually defined as the preferred version.

Table　A named collection of *fields* (*attributes*). Data in a table are represented as a *flat file* – a two-dimensional array of *data items*. Throughout this book, the term 'table' is used rather than 'relation' to describe the two-dimensional files that comprise a relational database. Although purists might object that, strictly speaking, the latter term is more correct, its use can lead to confusion between 'relation' and 'relationship'.

Textbase　A *database* consisting largely or wholly of free text as opposed to structured data.

Textual information management system (TIMS)　The software which manages a *textbase*. It provides a variety of features for searching free text, as opposed to structured data.

Theta-join　A query which involves joining two or more *tables*, where the join condition does not use the equals sign. Such joins are also called non-equi-joins and can use any of the following operators: != (not equal), <, >, <=, >=.

Third generation language   See *programming language.*

Third normal form (3NF)   A *table* which is in *second normal form (2NF)*, and in which no *non-key attribute* is *functionally dependent* upon another non-key attribute.

Three schema architecture   A standard way of describing *database* architecture that provides three levels: the conceptual level, the external level, and the internal level. See *conceptual schema, external schema, internal schema.*

TIMS   See *textual information management system.*

Transaction   In a *multitable database*, a single addition or modification to the data may affect several *tables*. A group of inter-related updates is therefore defined as a single transaction. To help maintain *data integrity*, a transaction will either be completed or entirely ignored. If there is a hardware or software failure, the database can automatically be restored by rolling back (undoing) all the transactions being processed at the time of failure to their starting points. Alternatively, if there is a disk media failure, the most recent archive (backup) copy can be reinstalled, and the *DBMS* will then bring it up to date by rolling forward (redoing) all changes made to the database since the archive copy was saved.

Transaction count   A technique for ensuring accuracy when *batch processing* input data. A manually derived count of each transaction or item to be entered is provided along with each batch of transactions. The item count is entered as a data field in a *header record* which is keyed in before the batch of documents to which it refers. The batch itself is then entered, but is not added to the *database* unless the number of entered records matches the count held in the header record.

Transitive dependency   Condition where one *non-key attribute* is *functionally dependent* upon another.

Truncation   Used with *wildcards* to retrieve groups of words with identical prefixes but different endings. For example, it can be used to ensure that plurals and other inflections are selected together. Thus in ORACLE `'Wil%'` retrieves 'Will', 'William', 'Williams', 'William's', etc.

Tuple   Alternative name for one *record* or row in a *relational database.*

Validation   The process of trapping and eliminating errors in data input. May be done at the point of entry, or subsequently through *batch processing.*

Videodisk   Videodisk (sometimes called Laserdisk) differs from other mass storage media in that it holds data in analogue rather than digital form. The disks are 12" in diameter and can carry up to 54,000 individually accessible video frames on each side, with a typical access time of 2.5 seconds. Each frame can be used to store part of a film, animation text, or mixture of these. Access is near-instantaneous, and storage costs are very low. Origination costs are high, however, and the cost of a videodisk system varies considerably, depending upon the needs of the user. Despite continuing advances in digital image compression, the analogue videodisk currently remains an effective way of providing lengthy video sequences for use within computer applications.

View   A subset of a *database* which is available to a particular user.

Virtual field   Used in printing reports, often as a means of calculating sub-totals, and summarising data. A virtual field is a temporary *field*, which only exists during the printing of the report.

Virtual table   A temporary *table* in which data from real (base) tables are combined so that users can work with just one virtual table instead of several base tables. Often used to create a *view* of a *database*.

Wildcard   *DOS* uses ? to mean a single unknown character and * to mean any number of unknown characters (including none). ORACLE uses _ to mean a single unknown character and % to mean any number of unknown characters (including none). Wildcard searching is invaluable when searching for words for which there are alternative spellings.

Window   Windows are an essential feature of any *graphical user interface*. The screen is divided into a number of different areas, each of which may contain a different program. They can be moved around, and stacked one in front of each other. Windows is also the trade name of Microsoft's graphical user interface, which dominates the market for PCs.

WORM drive   WORM (Write Once, Read Many) drives are best used to store data that will not be changed, or where it is desirable to retain all previous version of a file in the interests of security. Data is permanently written to the recording surface by a laser light. Once the disk is full, it is archived and replaced. Depending on the size of disk, WORMs can store between 300Mb and 3Gb per side. Each manufacturer has its proprietary format, which means that disks recorded on one machine can rarely be used on another type. Recent advances in *CD-ROM* and *magneto-optical* technologies mean that WORMs are unlikely to remain a major storage medium in the future.

Bibliography

■ **Contents**

■ **1 Introductory Works on Computer Concepts, Systems and Applications**

Adams, David R. and Wagner, Gerald E., *Computer Information Systems: An Introduction* (Cincinnati, OH, 1986).

Blissmer, R.H., *Introducing Computers: Concepts, Systems and Applications* (New York, 1990).

Capron, H.L., *Computers: Tools for an Information Age* (Redwood City, CA, 1987).

Davis, W.S., *Computing Fundamentals and Concepts* (Reading, MA, 1989).

Greenstein, Daniel I., *A Historian's Guide to Computing* (Oxford, 1994).

Mandell, S.L., *Computers and Information Processing: Concepts and Applications* (St. Paul, MN, 6th edn., 1992).

Slotnick, Daniel L., *et al. Computers and Applications: An Introduction to Data Processing* (Lexington, MA, 1986).

■ **2 General Works on Humanities Computing**

Andrews, Derek and Greenhalgh, Michael, *Computing for Non-Scientific Applications* (Leicester, 1987).

British Library, *Information Technology in Humanities Scholarship* (British Library R&D Report 6097, London, 1993)

Genet, J.-P. and Zampolli, A. (eds), *Computers and the Humanities* (Aldershot, 1992).

Hockey, Susan (ed), *A Guide to Computer Applications in the Humanities* (London, 1980).

Miall, David S. (ed), *Humanities and the Computer: New Directions* (Oxford, 1990).

Rahtz, Sebastian (ed), *A Guide to Computer Applications in the Humanities* (Chichester, Sussex, 1987).

■ 3 Introductory Works on Historical Research

Aydelotte, William O., *Quantification in History* (Reading, MA, 1971).

Colson, Jean, Middleton, Roger and Wardley, Peter, 'Annual Review of Information Technology Developments for Economic and Social Historians, 1991', *Economic History Review*, 2nd series, Vol. XLV, No. 2 (May 1992), pp. 378–412.

Dunn, David, Middleton, Roger and Wardley, Peter, 'Annual Review of Information Technology Developments for Economic and Social Historians', *Economic History Review*, 2nd series, Vol. XLVI, No. 2 (May 1993), pp. 379–409.

Floud, Roderick, *An Introduction to Quantitative Methods for Historians* (London, 1973, 2nd edn. 1979, 3rd edn. 1990), Ch. 9.

Furet, F., 'Quantitative History', *Daedalus* (1971), pp. 151–65.

Hamber, A., Miles, J. and Vaughan, W. (eds), *Computers and Art History* (London, 1989).

Jarausch, K.H and Hardy, K.A., *Quantitative Methods for Historians: A Guide to Research, Data and Statistics* (Chapel Hill, NC, 1991).

Mawdsley, E. and Munck, T., *Computing for Historians: An Introductory Guide* (Manchester, 1993).

Middleton, Roger and Wardley, Peter, 'Information Technology in Economic History: The Computer as Philosopher's Stone or Pandora's Box?', *Economic History Review*, 2nd series, Vol. XLIII, No. 4 (November 1990), pp. 667–96.

Middleton, Roger and Wardley, Peter, 'Review of Information Technology, 1990', *Economic History Review*, 2nd series, Vol. XLIV, No. 2 (May 1991), pp. 343–72.

Middleton, Roger and Wardley, Peter, 'Annual Review of Information Technology Developments for Economic and Social Historians', *Economic History Review*, 2nd series, Vol. XLVIII, No. 2 (May 1994), pp. 374–407.

Thaller, Manfred, 'Historical Information Science: Is There Such a Thing? New Comments on an Old Idea', in Tito Orlandi (ed), *Discipline umanistiche e informatica. Il Problema dell'integrazione* (Rome, 1993), pp. 51–86.

■ 4 History, Development and Future of Historical Computing

Anderson, Sheila, 'The Future of the Present – The ESRC Data Archive as a Resource Centre of the Future', *History and Computing*, Vol. 4, No. 3 (1992), pp. 191–200.

Davis, L.E. and Huttenback, R.A., *Mammon and the Pursuit of Empire* (Cambridge, 1986).

Davis, V., Denley, P., Spaeth, D. and Trainor, R. (eds), *The Teaching of Historical Computing: An International Framework* (St. Katharinen, 1993).

Denley, Peter, 'The Use of Computers in Historical Research', in K. Randell (ed), *The Use of the Computer in the Study and Teaching of History* (London, 1984), pp. 22–30.

Floud, Roderick, Wachter, Kenneth and Gregory, Annabel, *Height, Health and Nutritional Status in the United Kingdom, 1750–1980* (Cambridge, 1990).

Fogel, R.W. and Elton, G.R., *Which Road to the Past? Two Views of History* (New Haven and London, 1983).

Fogel, R.W. and Engerman, S.L., *Time on the Cross: The Economics of American Negro Slavery* (London, 1974), esp. Vol. 2, Evidence and Methods.

Genet, Jean-Philippe, 'L'Ordinateur et le métier d'historien', in *idem* (ed), *L'Ordinateur et le Métier d'Historien* (Bordeaux, 1990), pp. 7–15.

Harvey, Charles, 'The Nature and Future of Historical Computing', in Evan Mawdsley *et al.* (eds), *History and Computing III: Historians, Computers and Data* (Manchester, 1990), pp. 204–13.

Harvey, Charles and Taylor, Peter, 'Computer Modelling and Analysis of the Individual and Aggregate Capital, Stocks, Cash Flows and Performance of British Mining Companies in Spain, 1851–1913', in Peter Denley and Deian Hopkin (eds), *History and Computing* (Manchester, 1987), pp. 115–21.

Herlihy, David, 'Computer-Assisted Analysis of the Statistical Documents of Medieval Society', in James M. Powell (ed), *Medieval Studies: An Introduction* (Syracuse, 1976), pp. 185–211.

Higgs, Edward, 'Machine-Readable Records, Archives and Historical Memory', *History and Computing*, Vol. 4, No. 3 (1992), pp. 183–90.

Lloyd-Jones, Roger and Lewis, M.J., 'A Database for Historical Reconstruction: Manchester in the Industrial Revolution', in Evan Mawdsley *et al.* (eds), *History and Computing III: Historians, Computers and Data* (Manchester, 1990), pp. 169–73.

Morris, Robert J., *Class, Sect and Party: The Making of the British Middle Class. Leeds, 1820–1850* (Manchester, 1990).

Murphy, George G.S., 'Historical Investigation and Automatic Data Processing Equipment', *Computers and the Humanities*, Vol. 3 (1969), pp. 1–13.

Schürer, Kevin, 'Historical Research in the Age of the Computer: An Assessment of the Present Situation', *Historical Social Research*, Vol. 36 (1985), pp. 43–54.

Shorter, Edward, *The Historian and the Computer: A Practical Guide* (New Jersey, 1971).

Silbery, Joel H., 'Clio and Computers: Moving into Phase II, 1970–1972', *Computers and the Humanities*, Vol. 7, No. 2 (1972), pp. 67–79.

Spaeth, Donald, Denley, Peter, Davis, Virginia and Trainor, Richard (eds), *Towards an International Curriculum for History and Computing* (St. Katharinen, 1992).

Speck, W.A., 'History and Computing: Some Reflections on the Achievements of the Past Decade', *History and Computing*, Vol. 6, No. 1 (1994), pp. 28–32.

Sweirenga, Robert, 'Clio and Computers: A Survey of Computerized Research in History', *Computers and the Humanities,* Vol. 5 (1970), pp. 1–22.

Thaller, Manfred, 'Gibt es eine fachspezifische Datenverarbeitung in den historischen Wissenschaften?', in K.H. Kaufhold and J. Schneider (eds), *Geschichtswissenschaft und elektronische Datenverarbeitung* (Wiesbaden, 1988), pp. 45–83.

Thaller, Manfred, 'The Historical Workstation Project', *Historical Social Research,* Vol. 16 No. 4 (1991), pp. 51–61, reprinted in *Computers and the Humanities,* Vol. 25 (1991), pp. 149–62.

Thaller, Manfred, 'Methods and Techniques of Historical Computing', in Peter Denley and Deian Hopkin (eds), *History and Computing* (Manchester, 1987), pp. 147–56.

Thaller, Manfred, 'The Need for a Theory of Historical Computing', in Peter Denley, Stefan Fogelvik and Charles Harvey (eds), *History and Computing II* (Manchester, 1989), pp. 2–11.

Wakelin, Peter, 'Comprehensive Computerisation of a Very Large Documentary Source: The Portbooks Project at Wolverhampton Polytechnic', in Peter Denley and Deian Hopkin (eds), *History and Computing* (Manchester, 1987), pp. 109–14.

Wakelin, Peter, 'Pre-Industrial Trade on the River Severn: A Computer-Aided Study of the Gloucester Port Books, c.1640–c.1770' (unpublished PhD thesis, University of Wolverhampton, 1991).

Zweig, Ronald W., 'Virtual Records and Real History', *Historical Computing,* Vol. 4, No. 3 (1992), pp. 174–82.

■ 5 Databases

Allen, Robert F. (ed), *Databases in the Humanities and Social Sciences 2* (Florida, 1985).

Bowers, David S., *From Data to Database* (London, 2nd edn. 1993).

Bronzite, Michael, *Introduction to ORACLE* (Maidenhead, Berks, 1989).

Courtney, James F. Jr., and Paradice, David B., *Database Systems for Management* (Homewood, IL, 1992).

Date, C.J., *Database: A Primer* (Reading, MA, 1983).

Date, C.J., *A Guide to INGRES* (Reading, MA, 1987).

Date, C.J., *An Introduction to Database Systems* (Reading, MA, 5th edn. 1990), 2 vols.

Goldstein, Robert C., *Database: Technology and Management* (Chichester, Sussex, 1985).

Harris, Wayne, *Databases for Business Users* (London, 1992).

Korth H.F., with Silberschatz, A., *Database System Concepts* (London, 2nd edn. 1991).

Litton, G.M., *Database Management: A Practical Approach* (Dubuque, Iowa, 1987).

McFadden, Fred R. and Hoffer, Jeffrey A., *Database Management* (Redwood City, CA, 3rd edn., 1991).

Oracle Corporation, *ORACLE Overview and Introduction to SQL* (Belmont, CA, 1985).

Oxborrow, Elizabeth, *Databases and Database Systems: Concepts and Issues* (Bromley, Kent, 2nd edn., 1986).

Ricardo, C., *Database Principles, Design and Implementation* (Basingstoke, 1990).

Rolland, F.D., *Relational Database Management with ORACLE* (Reading MA, 2nd edn. 1991).

Stone, Christopher M. and Hentchel, David, 'Database Wars Revisited', *Byte* (Oct. 1990), pp. 223–42.

Stonebraker, Michael (ed), *The INGRES Papers: Anatomy of a Relational Database System* (Reading, MA, 1986).

Stonebraker, Michael, Rowe, Larry A., Beech, David, Lindsay, Bruce, *et al.*, *The Third Generation Database System Manifesto, Proceedings of the IFIP, July 1990* (Amsterdam, 1990).

Tagg, R.M., 'Bibliographic and Commercial Databases – Contrasting Approaches to Data Management with Special Reference to DBMS', *Program*, Vol. 16 No. 4 (Oct. 1982), pp. 191–9.

Thaller, Manfred, κλειω *[kleio]: A Database System* (St. Katharinen, 1993).

Valduriez, Patrick and Gardarin, Georges, *Analysis and Comparison of Relational Database Systems* (Reading, MA, 1989).

■ 6 Textbases

Ashford, J.H., 'Text Storage and Retrieval in the ORACLE Relational Database System', *Program*, Vol. 21 (1987), pp. 108–23.

Ashford, J.H. and Willett, P., *Text Retrieval and Document Databases* (Bromley, Kent, 1988).

Hall, J.L., *Online Bibliographic Databases* (London, 1986).

Harter, S.P. and Peters, A.R., 'Heuristics for Online Information Retrieval: A Typology and Preliminary Listing', *Online Review*, Vol. 9, No. 5 (1985), pp. 407–22.

Mallison, P., 'Development in Free Text Retrieval Systems', *Journal of the Society of Archivists*, Vol. 14, No. 1 (1993), pp. 55–64.

Oracle Corporation UK Ltd, *SQL*TextRetrieval Administrator's Guide* (Chertsey, Surrey, 1990).

Pollit, A.S., *Information Storage and Retrieval Systems: Origin, Development and Applications* (Chichester, Hants, 1989).

Rogers, H.J. and Willett, P., 'Searching for Historical Word Forms in Text Databases using Spelling-Correction Methods: Reverse Error and Phonetic Correction Methods', *Journal of Documentation*, Vol. 47 (1991), pp. 333–53.

Spaeth, D., 'From Relational Database Management System to Textual Database Management System', in J. Oldervoll (ed), *Eden or Babylon? On Future Software for Highly Structured Historical Sources* (St. Katharinen, 1992), pp. 95–106.

Willett, P. (ed.), *Document Retrieval Systems* (London, 1988).

■ 7 Multimedia, Hypermedia and Image Processing

Carvalho, J. and Paiva, J., 'The Use of Hypertext Systems and Artifical Intelligence Techniques in Historical Research', in R. Metz, E. van Cauwenberghe and R. van der Voort (eds), *Historical Information Systems* (Leuven, 1990), pp. 32–47.

Colson, J., Colson, F., Davis, H.C. and Hall, W., 'Questioning "Authority": The Challenge of Multimedia', in Francesca Bocchi and Peter Denley (eds), *Storia & Multimedia* (Bologna, 1994), pp. 597–605.

Conklin, Jeff, 'Hypertext: An Introduction and Survey', *IEEE Computer*, Vol. 17 (1987), pp. 17–41.

Conklin, Jeff, 'Hypertext: An Introduction and Survey', *Computing*, Vol. 20 (Sept. 1987), pp. 17–41.

Davis, H., Hall, W., Heath, I., Hill, G. and Wilkins, R., 'Towards an Integrated Information Environment with Open Hypermedia Systems', *ECHT 92: Proceedings of the Fourth ACM Conference on Hypertext* (Milan, 30 Nov.–4 Dec. 1992), pp. 181–90.

Deegan, M., Timbrell, N. and Warren, L., *Hypermedia in the Humanities* (Oxford, 1992).

Edwards, Deborah M. and Hardman, Lynda, '"Lost in Hyperspace": Cognitive Mapping and Navigation in a Hypertext Environment', in Ray McAleese (ed), *Hypertext: Theory into Practice* (London, 1989), pp. 105–25.

Fikfak, Jurij and Jaritz, Gerhard (eds), *Image Processing in History: Towards Open Systems* (St. Katharinen, 1993).

Foote, K.E., 'Mapping the Past: A Survey of Microcomputer Cartography', *Historical Methods*, Vol. 25, No. 3 (1992), pp. 121–31.

Fountain, A.M., Hall, W., Heath, I. and Davis, H.C., 'MICROCOSM: An Open Model for Hypermedia With Dynamic Linking', in A. Rizk, N. Streitz and J. André (eds), *Hypertext: Concepts, Systems and Applications* (Cambridge), 1990.

Freedberg, David, *The Power of Images* (Chicago and London, 1989).

Gilbert, David, 'HyperCard: New Ways of Writing, New Ways of Reading', *History and Computing*, Vol. 3, No. 3 (1991), pp. 186–94.

Gilbert, David and Southall, Humphrey, 'Data *Glasnost*: A User-Friendly System for Access to Research Databases across Wide-Area Networks', *History and Computing*, Vol. 3, No. 2 (1991), pp. 119–28.

Greenhalgh, Michael, 'Databases for Art Historians: Problems and Possibilities', in Peter Denley and Deian Hopkin (eds), *History and Computing* (Manchester, 1987), pp. 156–67.

Greenhalgh, Michael, 'Graphical Data in Art History and the Humanities: Their Storage and Display', *History and Computing*, Vol. 1, No. 2 (1989), pp. 121–34.

Greenhalgh, Michael, 'An Interactive Text and Image Database for the National Gallery of Australia using Analog and Digital Technologies', in Francesca Bocchi and Peter Denley (eds), *Storia & Multimedia* (Bologna, 1994), pp. 616–28.

Hall, W. and Davis, H., 'Hypermedia Link Services and their Application to Multimedia Information', *Journal of Information Technology* (Special Issue on Multimedia), (1994).

Hardman, L., 'Introduction to Hypertext and Hypermedia', *Historical Social Research/Historische Sozialforschung*, Vol. 15, No. 2 (1990), pp. 94–103.

Jaritz, Gerhard, 'The Image as Historical Source, or: Grabbing Contexts', *Historical Social Research*, Vol. 16, No. 4 (1991), pp. 100–5.

Jaritz, Gerhard, *Images: A Primer of Computer-Supported Analysis with κλειω [kleio] IAS* (St. Katharinen, 1993).

Jaritz, Gerhard, '"New Patterns of Response": Digital Image Processing and the Explanation of Medieval Pictures', in J. Smets (ed), *Histoire et Informatique* (Montpellier, 1992), pp. 261–6.

Li, Z., Davis, H. and Hall, W., 'Hypermedia Links and Information Retrieval', British Computer Society 14th Information Retrieval Colloqium, Lancaster University, 13–14 April 1992.

McAleese, Ray (ed), *Hypertext: Theory into Practice* (London, 1989).

McKnight, Cliff, Richardson, John and Dillon, Andrew, 'The Authoring of HyperText Documents', in Ray McAleese (ed), *Hypertext: Theory into Practice* (London, 1989) pp. 138–47.

Morris, S.J. and Finkelstein, A.C.W., 'An Experimental Hypertext Design Method and Applications in the Field of Art History', *Computers and the History of Art*, Vol. 2, Part 2 (1992), pp. 45–63.

Nielson, Jakob, *Hypertext and Hypermedia* (San Diego, CA, 1990).

Rizk, A., Streitz, N. and André, J., *Hypertext: Concepts, Systems and Applications* (Cambridge, 1990).

Russell, Gill, 'Hypertext', *History and Computing*, Vol. 3 No. 3 (1991), pp. 18–35.

Schneiderman, Ben, 'Reflections on Authoring, Editing and Managing Hypertext', in E. Barrett (ed), *The Society of Text* (Cambridge, MA, 1989), pp. 115–31.

Shneiderman, B. and Kearsley, G., *Hypertext Hands-on!* (Reading, MA, 1989).

Southall, Humphrey, and Gilbert, David, 'British Nineteenth-Century Labour Markets Database at Queen Mary & Westfield College', *History and Computing*, Vol. 1, No. 2 (1989), pp. 171–2.

Spence, Craig, 'Mapping London in the 1690s', in Francesca Bocchi and Peter Denley (eds), *Storia & Multimedia* (Bologna, 1994), pp. 746–56.

Thaller, Manfred (ed), *Images and Manuscripts in Historical Computing* (St. Katharinen, 1992).

Vaughan, W., 'Paintings by Number: Art History and the Digital Image', in A. Hamber, J. Miles and W. Vaughan (eds), *Computers and Art History* (London, 1989), pp. 74–97.

■ 8 Object-Oriented Databases, Knowledge Bases and Expert Systems

Andrews, Timothy and Harris, Craig, 'Combining Language and Database Advances in an Object-Oriented Development Environment', in Stanley B. Zdonik and David Maier (eds), *Readings on Object-Oriented Database Systems* (San Mateo, CA, 1990), pp. 186–96.

Atkinson, M., Bacilhon, F., DeWitt, D., Dittrich, K., Maier, D. and Zdonik, S., 'The Object-Oriented Database System Manifesto', *Proceedings of the First International Conference on Deductive and Object-Oriented Databases* (Kyoto, 1989), pp. 40–57.

Atwood, T., 'An Introduction to Object-Oriented Database Management Systems', *Hotline on Object-Oriented Technology*, Vol. 1, No. 1 (New York, 1989), pp. 11–12.

Banerjee, J., *et al.*, 'Data Modelling Issues for Object-Oriented Applications', *ACM Transactions on Office Information Systems*, Vol. 5, No. 1 (1987), pp. 3–26.

Blaha, M.R., Premerlani, W.J., and Rumbaugh, J.E., 'Relational Database Design using an Object–Oriented Methodology', *Communications of the ACM*, Vol. 31, No. 4 (April 1988), pp. 414–27.

Boden, Margaret A., *Artificial Intelligence and Natural Man* (Cambridge, MA, 2nd edn. 1987).

Bourlet, C., Fossier, L., Guillaumont, A. and Minel, J.-L., 'Construction d'un prototype de système expert dans le domaine historique', *Computers and the Humanities*, Vol. 20, No. 4 (1986), pp. 273–5.

Bourlet, C., Guillaumont, A, and Minel, J.-L., 'Intelligence Artificielle et Prosopographie', *Le Médiéviste et l'Ordinateur*, Vol. 15 (1986), pp. 6–8.

Bourlet, Caroline and Minel, Jean-Luc, 'Constitution d'une base de données prosopographiques à l'aide d'un système expert', in J.-P. Genet (ed), *Standardisation et échange des bases de données historiques* (Paris, 1988) pp. 313–17.

Bourlet, Caroline and Minel, Jean-Luc, 'From a Historian's Know-How to a Knowledge-Base: Using a Shell', in Evan Mawdsley *et al.* (eds), *History and Computing III: Historians, Computers and Data* (Manchester, 1990), pp. 55–9.

Cardenas, A., and McLeod, D. (eds), *Research Foundations in Object-Oriented and Semantic Database Systems* (Englewood Cliffs, NJ, 1990).

Carvahlo, Joaquin, 'Expert Systems and Community Reconstruction Studies', in Peter Denley, Stefan Fogelvik and Charles Harvey (eds), *History and Computing II* (Manchester, 1989) pp. 97–102.

Cattell, R.G.G., *Object Data Management: Object-Oriented and Extended Relational Database Systems* (Reading, MA, 1991).

Collins, Harry, 'Will Machines Ever Think?', *New Scientist*, 20 June 1992, pp. 36–40.

Colson, F. *et al.*, *HiDES: The Historical Document Expert System* (Southampton, 1990).

Diederich, J. and Milton, J., 'Objects, Messages and Rules in Database Design', in W. Kim and H. Lochovsky (eds), *Object-Oriented Concepts, Databases and Applications* (New York, 1989).

Dittrick, K. (ed), *Advances in Object-Oriented Database Systems, Proceedings of the 2nd International Workshop on Object-Oriented Database Systems, Sept. 27–30 1988* (Berlin, 1988).

Ennals, Richard and Gardin, Jean-Claude (eds), *Interpretation in the Humanities: Perspectives from Artificial Intelligence* (Boston Spa, West Yorkshire, 1990).

Fishman, D.H. *et al.*, 'Iris: An Object-Oriented Database Management System', in Stanley B. Zdonik and David Maier (eds), *Readings on Object-Oriented Database Systems* (San Mateo, CA, 1990), pp. 216–26.

Gardarin, Georges and Valduriez, Patrick, *Relational Databases and Knowledge Bases* (Reading, MA, 1989).

Godron, Michael, *Introduction to Expert Systems* (New York, 1986).

Jackson, Peter, *Introduction to Expert Systems* (Reading, MA, 1986).

Khosafian, Setrag and Copeland, George P., 'Object Identity', in Stanley B. Zdonik and David Maier (eds), *Readings on Object-Oriented Database Systems* (San Mateo, CA, 1990), pp. 37–46.

Kim, W. *et al.*, 'Integrating an Object-Oriented Programing System with a Database System', *Proceedings of OOPSLA '88 Conference* (New York, 1988), pp. 142–52.

Lee, G., Lelouche, R., Meissonnier, V., Ornato, M., Zarri, G.P. and Zarri-Baldi, L., 'Artificial Intelligence, History and Knowledge Representation', *Computers and the Humanities*, Vol. 16 (1982), pp. 25–34.

Leung, C.H.C., Page, S. and Mannock, K.L., 'Knowledge-Based Pictorial Database Management', *Computers and the History of Art*, Vol. 1, Part 1 (1990), pp. 19–25.

Loomis, M.E.S., Shah, A.V.S., and Rumbaugh, J.E., 'An Object Modelling Technique for Conceptual Design', in *Proceedings of the European Conference on Object-Oriented Programming (Paris, 15–17 June 1987), Lecture Notes in Computer Science, 276* (New York, 1987), pp. 192–202.

Maier, D., Stein, J., Otis, A. and Purdy, A., 'Development of an Object-Oriented DBMS', *Proceedings of OOPSLA '86 Conference* (New York, 1986), pp. 472–82.

Maier, David and Stein, Jacob, 'Development and Implementation of an Object-Oriented DBMS', in Stanley B. Zdonik and David Maier (eds), *Readings on Object-Oriented Database Systems* (San Mateo, CA, 1990), pp. 166–85.

Moser, J.G., 'Integration of Artificial Intelligence and Simulation in a Comprehensive Decision Support System', *Simulation*, Vol. 47 (Dec. 1986), pp. 22–39.

Parsaye, Kamran, Chignell, Mark, Khoshafian, Setrag and Wong, Harry, *Intelligent Databases* (New York, 1989).

Premerlani, W.J., Blaha, M.R., Rumbaugh, J.E. and Varwig, T.A., 'An Object-Oriented Relational Database', *Communications of the ACM*, Vol. 33 (Nov. 1990), pp. 99–109.

Price, Gwyn and Gray, Alec, 'Object Oriented Databases and their Application to Historical Data', *History and Computing*, Vol. 6, No. 1 (1994), pp. 44–51.

Reynolds, Christopher Finch, 'A Psychological Approach to the Computer Handling of Historical Information', *Historical Social Research*, Vol. 15, No. 1 (1990), pp. 51–8.

Rowe, Lawrence A. and Stonebraker, Michael R., 'The POSTGRES Data Model', in Stanley B. Zdonik and David Maier (eds), *Readings on Object-Oriented Database Systems* (San Mateo, CA, 1990), pp. 461–73.

Rumbaugh, J. *et al.*, *Object-Oriented Modeling and Design* (Englewood Cliffs, NJ, 1991).

Schulte, Theo J., 'Artificial Intelligence Techniques for Historians: Expert Systems, Knowledge Representation and High-Level Programming', in Peter Denley, Stefan Fogelvik and Charles Harvey (eds), *History and Computing II* (Manchester, 1989), pp. 90–6.

Schürer, Kevin, 'Artificial Intelligence and the Historian: Prospects and Possibilities', in R. Ennals and J.-C. Gardin (eds), *Interpretation in the Humanities: Perspectives from Artificial Intelligence* (Boston Spa, West Yorkshire, 1990), pp. 169–95.

Sells, Peter S., *Expert Systems: A Practical Introduction* (London, 1985).

Shah, A. *et al.*, 'DSM: An Object-Relationship Modeling Language', *Proceedings of OOPSLA '89 Conference* (New York, 1989), pp. 191–202.

Snyder, Alan, 'Encapsulation and Inheritance in Object-Oriented Programming Languages', in Stanley B. Zdonik and David Maier (eds), *Readings on Object-Oriented Database Systems* (San Mateo, CA, 1990), pp. 84–91.

Sprague, R.H., and McNurlin, B.C., *Information Systems in Practice* (Englewood Cliffs, NJ, 1986).

Summers, Eric, 'ES: A Public Domain Expert System', *Byte* (Oct. 1990), p. 292.

Thaller, Manfred, 'Databases and Expert Systems as Complementary Tools for Historical Research', *Tijdschrift voor Geschiedenis*, Vol. 103 (1990), pp. 233–47.

Woelk, Darrell, Kim, Won and Luther, Willis, 'An Object-Oriented Approach to Multimedia Databases', in Stanley B. Zdonik and David Maier (eds), *Readings on Object-Oriented Database Systems* (San Mateo, CA, 1990), pp. 592–606.

Yourdon, Edward, 'Auld Lang Syne: Is it Time for You to Ring out the Old and Ring in the New?', *Byte* (Oct. 1990), pp. 257–62.

Zdonik, Stanley B. and Maier, David (eds), *Readings on Object-Oriented Database Systems* (San Mateo, CA, 1990).

■ 9 Database Design Methodologies

Acun, Ramazan, 'Towards the Design and Implementation of an Intelligent Historical Database' (unpublished MSc thesis, University of Birmingham, 1992).

Batini, C., Ceri, S. and Navathe, S.B., *Conceptual Database Design: An Entity Relationship Approach* (Redwood City, CA, 1992).

Burnard, Lou, 'Principles of Database Design' in Sebastian Rahtz (ed), *A Guide to Computer Applications in the Humanities* (Chichester, Sussex, 1987), pp. 54–68.

Checkland, Peter and Scholes, Jim, *Soft Systems Methodology in Action* (Chichester, Sussex, 1990).

Coad, Peter, and Yourdon, Edward, *Object-Oriented Analysis* (Englewood Cliffs, NJ, 1989).

Coad, Peter, with Yourdon, Edward, *Object-Oriented Design* (Englewood Cliffs, NJ, 1991).

Codd, E.F., 'Is Your DBMS Really Relational?', *Computerworld*, 14 Oct. 1985, pp. 1–9.

Codd, E.F., 'Does your DBMS Run by the Rules?', *Computerworld*, 21 Oct. 1985, pp. 49–60.

Codd, E.F., 'A Relational Model of Data for Large Shared Data Banks', *Communications of the ACM*, Vol. 13 No. 6 (June 1970).

Date, C.J., *Relational Database: Selected Writings* (New York, 1986).

Denley, Peter, 'Models, Sources and Users: Historical Database Design in the 1990s', *History and Computing*, Vol. 6, No. 1 (1994), pp. 33–43.

Fischer, Lewis R. and Sager, Eric W., 'An Approach to the Quantitative Analysis of British Shipping Records', *Business History*, Vol. XXII, No. 2 (1980), pp. 135–51.

Greenstein, Daniel, 'Conceptual Models and Model Solutions: A Summary Report of the TEI's Working Group on Historical Studies', in *idem* (ed), *Modelling Historical Data* (St. Katharinen, 1991) pp. 195–204.

Greenstein, Daniel I., 'Historians as Producers or Consumers of Standard-Conformant, Full-Text Datasets? Some Sources of Modern History as a Test Case', in *idem* (ed), *Modelling Historical Data* (St. Katharinen, 1991) pp. 179–94.

Greenstein, Daniel I. (ed), *Modelling Historical Data* (St. Katharinen, 1991).

Greenstein, Daniel I., 'A Source-Oriented Approach to History and Computing: The Relational Database', *Historical Social Research*, Vol. 14, No. 3 (1989), pp. 91–6.

Guttman, Myron P., Fliess, Kenneth H., Holmes, Amy E., Fairchild, Amy L. and Teas, Wendy A., 'Keeping Track of our Treasures: Managing Historical Data with Relational Database Software', *Historical Methods*, Vol. 22, No. 4 (1989), pp. 128–43.

Hartland, Philip and Harvey, Charles, 'Information Engineering and Historical Databases', in Peter Denley, Stefan Fogelvik and Charles Harvey (eds), *History and Computing II* (Manchester, 1989) pp. 44–62.

Harvey, Charles and Press, Jon, 'The Business Elite of Bristol: A Case Study in Database Design', *History and Computing*, Vol. 3, No. 1 (Spring 1991), pp. 1–11.

Harvey, Charles and Press, Jon, 'Relational Data Analysis: Value, Concepts and Methods', *History and Computing*, Vol. 4, No. 2 (1992), pp. 98–109.

Hawryszkiewycz, I.T., *Database Analysis and Design* (London, 2nd edn. 1991).

Howe, D.R., *Data Analysis for Data Base Design* (London, 2nd edn. 1983).

Kappel, G. and Schrefl, M., 'A Behaviour-Integrated Entity-Relationship Approach for the Design of Object-Oriented Databases', *Proceedings of the 7th International Conference on the Entity-Relationship Approach* (Rome, Nov. 1988), pp. 175–92.

Learmouth & Burchett Management Systems Ltd., *Structured Systems Design* (2 vols, London, 1986).

Levermann, Wolfgang, 'Historical Data Bases and the Context Sensitive Handling of Data: Towards the Development of Historical Data Base Management Software', *Historical Social Research*, Vol. 16, No. 4 (1991), pp. 74–88.

Lind, Gunner, 'Data Model and Research Process', in Francesca Bocchi and Peter Denley (eds), *Storia & Multimedia* (Bologna, 1994), pp. 485–90.

Martin, James, *Computer Data-Base Organization* (Englewood Cliffs, NJ, 1977).

Martin, James, *Information Engineering* (2 vols, Carnforth, Lancs, 1986).

Martin, James, *Principles of Database Management* (Englewood Cliffs, NJ, 1976).

Ross, Seamus, 'The Historian and Software Engineering Considerations', *History and Computing*, Vol. 3, No. 3 (1991), pp. 141–50.

Schijvenaars, Toine, 'Data Modelling of Historical Sources in Dutch Historical Research Projects', in Francesca Bocchi and Peter Denley (eds), *Storia & Multimedia* (Bologna, 1994) pp. 501–22.

Senn, J.A., *Analysis and Design of Information Systems* (New York, 1985).

Thaller, Manfred, 'Beyond Collecting: The Design and Implementation of CLIO, a DBMS for the Social-Historical Sciences', in Robert F. Allen (ed), *Databases in the Humanities and Social Sciences 2* (Florida, 1985), pp. 328–34.

Thaller, Manfred, 'Data Bases v. Critical Editions', *Historical Social Research*, Vol. 13, No. 3 (1988), pp. 129–39.

Thaller, Manfred, 'Have Very Large Data Bases Methodological Relevance?', in O. Opitz (ed), *Conceptual and Numerical Analysis of Data* (Berlin, 1989).

Vetter, M., *Strategy for Data Modelling* (Chichester, 1987).

Weatherill, Lorna and Hemingway, Vivienne, *Using and Designing Databases for Academic Work: Practical Guide* (Newcastle, 1994).

Woollard, Matthew and Denley, Peter, *Source-Oriented Data Processing for Historians: A Tutorial for* κλειω *[kleio]* (St. Katharinen, 1993).

■ 10 Programming and Querying

Breure, Leen, 'How to live with XBASE; The Socrates Approach', in Francesca Bocchi and Peter Denley (eds), *Storia & Multimedia* (Bologna, 1994), pp. 477–85.

Breure, Leen, *The Socrates SLX Programming Environment* (Utrecht, 1992).

Burnard, Lou, 'Relational Theory, SQL and Historical Practice', in Peter Denley, Stefan Fogelvik and Charles Harvey (eds), *History and Computing II* (Manchester, 1989), pp. 63–71.

Date, C.J., *A Guide to the SQL Standard* (Reading, MA, 1987).

Donche, P., 'HISTCAL: A Program for Historical Chronology', *History and Computing*, Vol. 2, No. 2 (1990), pp. 97–106.

Emerson, S.L,, Darnovsky, M. and Bowman, J.S., *The Practical SQL Handbook: Using Structured Query Language* (Reading, MA, 1989).

Harvey, Charles and Press, Jon, 'Structured Query Language and Historical Computing', *History and Computing*, Vol. 5, No. 3 (1993), pp. 154–168.

Hedderson, John, *SPSS-X Made Simple* (Belmont, CA, 1987).

Lusardi, F., *The Database Expert's Guide to SQL* (New York, 1987).

Newcomer, L.R., *SELECT . . SQL: The Relational Database Language* (London, 1992).

Norusis, Marija J., *The SPSS Guide to Data Analysis for SPSS-X* (Chicago, 1987).

Zloof, M.M., 'Query-by-Example: A Data Base Language', *IBM Systems Journal*, Vol. 16, No. 4 (1977), pp. 324–43.

■ 11 Data Coding

Armstrong, W.A., 'The Classification of Occupations', in D.E.C. Eversley, Peter Laslett and E. Anthony Wrigley (eds), *An Introduction to English Historical Demography* (London, 1966), Appendix D.

Armstrong, W.A., 'The Use of Information about Occupation', in E.A. Wrigley (ed), *Nineteenth-Century Society: Essays in the Use of Quantitative Methods for the Study of Social Data* (Cambridge, 1972), pp. 191–310.

Blumin, Stuart, 'The Classification of Occupations in Past Time: Problems of Fission and Fusion', in Evan Mawdsley *et al.* (eds), *History and Computing III: Historians, Computers and Data* (Manchester, 1990), pp. 83–9.

Booth, C., 'Occupations of the People of the United Kingdom, 1801–81', *Journal of the Royal Statistical Society*, Vol. 49 (1886), pp. 314–444.

Bouchard, Gérard, 'The Saguenay Population Register and the Processing of Occupational Data: An Overview of the Methodology', *Historical Social Research*, Vol. 32 (1984), pp. 37–58.

Bouchard, Gérard, Lavoie, Yolande and Brard, Patrick, 'FONEM: un code de transcription phonétique pour la reconstitution automatique des familles saguenayennes', *Population*, Vol. 6 (1981), pp. 1085–1104.

Corfield, P.J., 'Class by Name and Number in Eighteenth-Century Britain', *History*, Vol. 72 (1987), pp. 38–61.

Corfield, P.J., 'Computerising Urban Occupations', in Peter Denley and Deian Hopkin (eds), *History and Computing* (Manchester, 1987), pp. 68–71.

Darroch, A.G. and Ornstein, M.D., 'Error in Historical Data Files: A Research Note on the Automatic Detection of Error and on the Nature and Sources of Errors in Coding', *Historical Methods*, Vol. 12 No. 4 (1979), pp. 157–67.

Diederiks, H.A. and Tjalsma, H.D., 'The Classification and Coding of Occupations of the Past: Some Experiences and Thoughts' in K. Schürer and H. Diederiks (eds), *The Use of Occupations in Historical Analysis* (St. Katharinen, 1993), pp. 29–40.

Gevers, Michael, Long, Gillian and McCulloch, Michael, 'The DEEDS Database of Medieval Charters: Design and Coding for the RDBMS Oracle 5', *History and Computing*, Vol. 2, No. 1 (1990), pp. 1–11.

Glasco, Laurence and Baker, Reginald, 'CONVRT: A Computer System for the Conversion of Free-Field Data to Fixed-Field Format', *Historical Methods Newsletter*, Vol. 7, No. 3 (1974), pp. 12–58.

Goldthorpe, J. and Hope, K., *The Social Grading of Occupations; A New Approach and Scale* (Oxford, 1974).

Green, Edmund M., 'The Taxonomy of Occupations in Late Eighteenth-Century Westminster', in Penelope J. Corfield and Derek Keene (eds), *Work in Towns, 850–1850* (Leicester, 1990), pp. 164–81.

Greenstein, Daniel I., 'Encoding Standards for Computer-Aided Historical Research: The Problems Reassessed', in *idem* (ed), *Modelling Historical Data* (St. Katharinen, 1991), pp. 93–110.

Greenstein, Daniel I., 'Standard, MetaStandard: A Framework for Coding Occupational Data', *Historical Social Research*, Vol. 16, No. 1 (1991), pp. 3–22.

Hall, R.H., *Occupations and the Social Structure* (Englewood Cliffs, NJ, 1975).

Hauser, R.M., 'Occupational Status in the Nineteenth and Twentieth Centuries', *Historical Methods*, Vol. 14 (1982), pp. 111–26.

Hausmann, F., Härtel, R., Kropac, I. and Becker, P. (eds), *Data Networks for the Historical Disciplines? Problems in Standardisation and Exchange of Machine-Readable Data* (Graz, 1987).

Higgs, Edward, 'Structuring the Past: The Occupational and Household Classification of Nineteenth-Century Census Data', in Evan Mawdsley *et al.* (eds), *History and Computing III: Historians, Computers and Data* (Manchester, 1990), pp. 67–73.

Hubbard, W. and Jarausch, K., 'Occupations and Social Structure in Modern Central Europe: Some Reflections on Coding Professions', *Quantum Information*, Vol. 11 (July 1979), pp. 10–19.

Jarausch, K.H., 'Some Reflections on Coding', in M. Thaller (ed), *Datenbanken und Datenverwaltungssysteme als Werkzeuge Historischer Forschung* (St. Katharinen, 1986), pp. 175–8.

Katz, M.B., 'Occupational Classification in History', *Journal of Interdisciplinary History*, Vol. 3, No. 1 (1972), pp. 63–88.

Lindert, P.H., 'English Occupations, 1670–1811', *Journal of Economic History*, Vol. 40 (1980), pp. 685–712.

Mills, D. and Mills, J., 'Occupation and Social Stratification Revisited: The Census Enumerators' Books of Victorian Britain', *Urban History Yearbook* (1989), pp. 63–77.

Morris, Robert J., 'Fuller Values, Questions and Contexts: Occupational Coding and the Historian', in Kevin Schürer and Herman Diederiks (eds), *The Use of Occupations in Historical Analysis* (St. Katherinen, 1993), pp. 5–21.

Morris, Robert J., 'Occupational Coding: Principles and Examples', *Historical Social Research*, Vol. 15, No. 1 (1990), pp. 3–29.

Patten, J., 'Urban Occupations in Pre-Industrial England', *Transactions of the Institute of British Geographers*, new series, Vol. 2 (1977), pp. 296–313.

Schofield, Roger S. and Davies, Ros, 'Towards a Flexible Data Input and Record Management System', *Historical Methods Newsletter*, Vol. 7, No. 3 (1974), pp. 115–24.

Schürer, Kevin, 'The Historical Researcher and Codes: Master and Slave or Slave and Master?', in Evan Mawdsley *et al.* (eds), *History and Computing III: Historians, Computers and Data* (Manchester, 1990), pp. 74–82.

Schürer, Kevin, 'Understanding and Coding the Occupations of the Past: The Experience of Analyzing the Census of 1891–1921' in K. Schürer and H. Diederiks (eds), *The Use of Occupations in Historical Analysis* (St. Katharinen, 1993), pp. 101–62.

Schürer, Kevin and Diederiks, Herman (eds), *The Use of Occupations in Historical Analysis* (St. Katherinen, 1993).

Schürer, Kevin and Oeppen, Jim, 'Calculating Days of the Week and Some Related Problems with Using Calendars of the Past', *History and Computing*, Vol. 2, No. 2 (1990), pp. 107–18.

Thaller, Manfred, 'A Draft Proposal for a Standard for the Coding of Machine Readable Sources', *Historical Social Research*, Vol. 40 (Oct. 1986), pp. 3–46, reprinted in D. Greenstein (ed), *Modelling Historical Data* (St. Katharinen, 1991), pp. 19–64.

Thaller, Manfred, 'The Need for Standards: Data Modelling and Exchange', in Daniel Greenstein (ed), *Modelling Historical Data* (St. Katharinen, 1991), pp. 1–18.

Wardley, Peter and Woollard, Matthew, 'Retrieving the Past: A Reclamation and Reconstruction of the Social Survey of Bristol, 1937', *History and Computing*, Vol. 6, No. 2 (1994), pp. 85–105.

Werner, Thomas, 'Transforming Machine Readable Sources', *Historical Social Research*, Vol. 16, No. 4 (1991), pp. 62–73.

■ 12 Record Linkage, Demography and Family Reconstitution

Acheson, E.D., *Medical Record Linkage* (Oxford, 1967).

Acheson, E.D. (ed), *Record Linkage in Medicine* (Edinburgh and London, 1968).

Adman, Peter, Baskerville, Stephen W. and Beedham, Katharine F., 'Computer-Assisted Record Linkage: Or How Best to Optimise Links Without Generating Errors', *History and Computing*, Vol. 4, No. 1 (1992), pp. 21–5.

Åkerman, Sune, 'An Evaluation of the Family Reconstitution Technique', *Scandinavian Economic History Review*, Vol. 25 (1977), pp. 160–70.

Baldwin, J.A., Acheson, E.D. and Graham, W.J. (eds), *Textbook of Medical Record Linkage* (Oxford, 1987).

Bean, Lee. L., May, Dean L. and Skolnick, Mark, 'The Mormon Historical Demography Project', *Historical Methods*, Vol. 11, No. 1 (1978), pp. 45–53.

Beauchamp, P., Charbonneau, H., Desjardins, B. and Légaré, J., 'La reconstitution automatique des familles: un fait acquis. La mésure des phénomenes demographiques. Hommages à L. Henry', *Population*, Vol. 32 (1977), pp. 375–99.

Bouchard, Gérard, 'Computerised Family Reconstitution and the Measure of Literacy: Presentation of a New Index', *History and Computing*, Vol. 5, No. 1 (1993), pp. 12–24.

Bouchard, Gérard, 'Current Issues and New Prospects for Computerised Record Linkage in the Province of Quebec', *Historical Methods*, Vol. 25, No. 2 (1992), pp. 67–73.

Bouchard, Gérard, 'The Processing of Ambiguous Links in Computerised Family Reconstitution', *Historical Methods*, Vol. 19, No. 1 (1986), pp. 91–9.

Bouchard, Gérard and Brard, Patrick, 'Le programme de reconstruction automatique des familles saguenayennes: données de base et résultats provisionnes', *Histoire Sociale* (Ottawa), Vol. 12 (1979), pp. 170–85.

Bouchard, Gérard and Lavoie, Yolande, 'Le project d'histoire social de la population du Saguenay: l'appariel méthodologique', *Revue d'Histoire de l'Amérique Française*, Vol. 32, No. 1 (1978), pp. 41–56.

Bouchard, Gérard and Pouyez, Christian, 'Name Variations and Computerised Record Linkage', *Historical Methods*, Vol. 13, No. 2 (1980), pp. 119–25.

Cambridge Group for the Study of Population and Social Structure, 'Automatic Record Linkage for Family Reconstitution', *Local Population Studies*, Vol. 40 (1988), pp. 10–16.

Copas, J.B. and Hilton, F.J., 'Record Linkage: Statistical Models for Matching Computer Records', *Journal of the Royal Statistical Society*, Vol. 153, Part 2 (1990), pp. 1–26.

Danell, Christina, 'The Demographic Data Base at Umeå University', in A. Brandström and J. Sundin (eds), *Tradition and Transition: Studies in Microdemography and Social Change* (Umeå, Sweden, 1981).

Davies, H.R., 'Automated Record Linkage of Census Enumerators' Books and Registration Data: Obstacles, Challenges and Solutions', *History and Computing*, Vol. 4 No. 1 (1992), pp. 16–26.

De Bron, David and Olsen, Mark, 'The Guth Algorithm and the Nominal Record Linkage of Multi-Ethnic Populations', *Historical Methods*, Vol. 19 (1986), pp. 20–4.

Desjardins, Bertrand and Nault, François, 'Recent Advances in Computerised Population Registers', *Historical Methods*, Vol. 21 (1988), pp. 29–33.

Doulton, David, and Kitts, Arno, 'The Storing and Processing of Historical Data', in Peter Denley, Stefan Fogelvik and Charles Harvey (eds), *History and Computing II* (Manchester, 1989), pp. 81–9.

Eversley, D.E.C., Laslett, Peter and Wrigley, E. Anthony (eds), *An Introduction to English Historical Demography* (London, 1966).

Felligi, I.P. and Sunter, A.B., 'A Theory for Record Linkage', *Journal of the American Statistical Association*, Vol. 64 (1969), pp. 1183–1210.

Genealogical Society of Utah, *How to Transcribe the British Census* (Salt Lake City, UT, 1988).

Guth, Gloria J.A., 'Surname Spellings and Computerized Record Linkage', *Historical Methods Newsletter*, Vol. 10 (1976), pp. 10–19.

Henry, Louis and Fleury, Michel, *Des registres paroissiaux à l'histoire de la population: Manuel de dépouillement et d'éxploitation de l'état civil ancien* (Paris, 1956).

Hershberg, T. *et al.*, 'Record Linkage', *Historical Methods Newsletter*, Vol. IX (1975/76), pp. 137–63.

Higgs, Edward, 'Disease, Febrile Poisons and Statistics: The Census as a Medical Survey, 1841–1911', *Social History of Medicine*, Vol. 4 (1991), pp. 465–78.

Higgs, Edward, *Making Sense of the Census: The Manuscript Returns for England and Wales, 1801–1901* (London, 1989).

Kennedy, J.M., 'File Structures for the Automatic Manipulation of Linked Records', in E.D. Acheson (ed), *Record Linkage in Medicine* (Edinburgh and London, 1968).

King, Steve, 'Record Linkage in a Protoindustrial Community', *History and Computing*, Vol. 4, No. 1 (1992), pp. 27–33.

Kitts, Arno, Doulton, David, Diamond, Ian and Reis, Elizabeth, 'Using the Data Base Management System SIR to Link Political Data from Viana do Castelo, Minho, Portugal, 1827–95', in Peter Denley and Deian Hopkin (eds), *History and Computing* (Manchester, 1987), pp. 177–85.

Kitts, Arno, Doulton, David and Reis, Elizabeth, *The Reconstitution of Viana do Castelo* (London, 1990).

Lamm, Doron, 'British Soldiers of the First World War: Creation of a Representative Sample', *Historical Social Research*, Vol. 13, No. 4 (1988), pp. 55–98.

Legaré, Jacques, Lavoie, Yolande, and Charbonneau, Hubert, 'The Early Canadian Population: Problems in Record Linkage', *Canadian Historical Review*, Vol. 53, No. 4 (1972), pp. 427–42.

Lipp, Carola, 'Symbolic Dimensions of Serial Sources: Hermeneutical Problems of Reconstructing Political Biographies Based on Computerized Record Linkage', *Historical Social Research*, Vol. 15, No. 1 (1990), pp. 30–40.

Macfarlane, Alan, Harrison, S. and Jardine, C., *Reconstructing Historical Communities* (Cambridge, 1977).

Morris, Robert J., 'Does Nineteenth-Century Nominal Record Linkage have Lessons for the Machine Readable Century?' *Journal of the Society of Archivists*, Vol. 7 (1985), pp. 503–12.

Nault, François and Desjardins, Bertrand, 'Computers and Historical Demography: The Reconstitution of the Early Quebec Population', in Peter Denley, Stefan Fogelvik and Charles Harvey (eds), *History and Computing II* (Manchester, 1989), pp. 14–38.

Newcombe, Howard B., *Handbook of Record Linkage: Methods for Health and Statistical Studies, Administration, and Business* (Oxford, 1988).

Newcombe, Howard B., 'Record Linking: The Design of Efficient Systems for Linking Records into Individual and Family Histories', *American Journal for Human Genetics*, Vol. 19 (1967), pp. 335–59.

Newcombe, Howard B. and Kennedy, James M., 'Record Linkage: Making Maximum Use of the Discriminating Power of Identifying Information', *Communications of the Association for Computing Machinery*, Vol. 5 (1962), pp. 563–7.

Nygaard, Lars, 'Name Standardisation in Record Linking: An Improved Algorithmic Strategy', *History and Computing*, Vol. 4, No. 2 (1992), pp. 63–74.

Oeppen, Jim, 'Aggregative Back Projection' in Anthony E. Wrigley and Roger

S. Schofield, *The Population History of England, 1541–1871: A Reconstruction* (London, 1981, revised edn. 1989), Appendix 15.

Oldervoll, Jan, 'The Machine-Readable Description of Highly Structured Historical Documents: Censuses and Parish Registers', in Daniel Greenstein (ed), *Modelling Historical Data* (St. Katharinen, 1991), pp. 169–78.

Phillips, W., 'Record Linkage for a Chronic Disease Register', in E.D. Acheson (ed), *Record Linkage in Medicine* (Edinburgh and London, 1968), pp. 120–53.

Pouyez, Christian, Roy, Raymond and Martin, François, 'The Linkage of Census Name Data: Problems and Procedures', *Journal of Interdisciplinary History*, Vol. 14, No. 1 (1983), pp. 129–52.

Rhodri Davies, H., 'Automated Record Linkage of Census Enumerators' Books and Registration Data: Obstacles, Challenges, Solutions', *History and Computing*, Vol. 4, No. 1 (1992), pp. 16–26.

Schofield, Roger S., 'Automatic Family Reconstitution: The Cambridge Experience', *Historical Methods*, Vol. 25 (1992), pp. 75–9.

Schofield, Roger S., 'Representativeness and Family Reconstitution', *Annales de Démographie Historique* (1972), pp. 12–15.

Schofield, Roger S., 'The Standardisation of Names and the Automatic Linking of Historical Records', *Annales de démographie historique* (1972), pp. 359–64.

Schofield, Roger S. and Wrigley, E.A., 'English Population History from Family Reconstruction: Summary Results, 1600–1799', *Population Studies*, Vol. 37 (1983), pp. 157–84.

Schürer, Kevin, 'Census Enumerators' Returns and the Computer', *Local Historian*, Vol. 16 (1985), pp. 335–42.

Schürer, Kevin, 'Historical Demography, Social Structure and the Computer', in Peter Denley and Deian Hopkin (eds), *History and Computing* (Manchester, 1987), pp. 33–44.

Schürer, Kevin, 'Standards or Model Solutions? The Case of Census-Type Documents', in Daniel Greenstein (ed), *Modelling Historical Data* (St. Katharinen, 1991), pp. 205–23.

Schürer, Kevin, Oeppen, Jim and Schofield, Roger, 'Theory and Methodology: An Example from Historical Demography', in Peter Denley, Stefan Fogelvik and Charles Harvey (eds), *History and Computing II* (Manchester, 1989), pp. 130–42.

Skolnick, Mark H., 'The Resolution of Ambiguities in Record Linkages', in Anthony E. Wrigley (ed), *Identifying People in the Past* (London, 1973).

Stephenson, C., 'The Methodology of Historical Census Record Linkage: A User's Guide to the Soundex', *Journal of Family History*, Vol. 12, No. 4 (1980), pp. 151–3.

Sunter, A.B., 'A Statistical Approach to Record Linkage', in E.D. Acheson (ed), *Record Linkage in Medicine* (Edinburgh and London, 1968).

Tepping, Benjamin J., 'A Model for Optimal Linkage of Records', *Journal of the America Statistical Association*, Vol. 63 (1968), pp. 1321–32.

Vetter, John E., Gonzalez, Jesus R. and Gutmann, Myron P., 'Computer-Assisted Record Linkage Using a Relational Database System', *History and Computing*, Vol. 4, No. 1 (1992), pp. 34–51.

Winchester, Ian, 'A Brief Survey of the Algorithmic, Mathematical and Philosophical Literature Relevant to Historical Record Linkage', in Anthony E. Wrigley (ed), *Identifying People in the Past* (London, 1973).

Winchester, Ian, 'The Linkage of Historical Records by Man and Computer: Techniques and Problems', *Journal of Interdisciplinary History*, Vol. 1 (1970), pp. 107–24.

Winchester, Ian, 'On Referring to Ordinary Historical Persons', in Anthony E. Wrigley (ed), *Identifying People in the Past* (London, 1973).

Winchester, Ian, 'Priorities for Record Linkage: A Theoretical and Practical Checklist', in J. Chubb and E.K. Scheuch (eds), *Historical Social Research* (Frankfurt, 1980), pp. 414–30.

Winchester, Ian, 'What Every Historian Needs to Know about Record Linkage in the Micro-Computer Era', *Historical Methods*, Vol. 25, No. 4 (Fall 1992), pp. 149–65.

Wrigley, E. Anthony, 'Family Reconstitution', in D.E.C. Eversley, Peter Laslett and E. Anthony Wrigley (eds), *An Introduction to English Historical Demography* (London, 1966).

Wrigley, E. Anthony (ed), *Identifying People in the Past* (London, 1973).

Wrigley, E. Anthony (ed), *Nineteenth-Century Society: Essays in the Use of Quantitative Methods for the Study of Social Data* (Cambridge, 1972).

Wrigley, E. Anthony and Schofield, Roger S., 'English Population History from Family Reconstitution: Summary Results, 1600–1799', *Population Studies*, Vol. 37 (1983).

Wrigley, E. Anthony and Schofield, Roger S., 'Nominal Record Linkage by Computer and the Logic of Family Reconstitution', in E. Anthony Wrigley (ed), *Identifying People in the Past* (London, 1973).

Wrigley, E. Anthony and Schofield, Roger S., *The Population History of England, 1541–1871: A Reconstruction* (London, 1981, revised edn. 1989).

■ 13 Psephology

Adman, Peter, Baskerville, Stephen W. and Beedham, Katharine F., 'Manuscript Poll Books and English County Elections in the First Age of Party: A Reconsideration of their Provenance and Purpose', *Archives*, Vol. 19, No. 86 (1991), pp. 384–403.

Baskerville, Stephen W., '"Preferred Linkage" and the Analysis of Voter Behaviour in Eighteenth-Century England', *History and Computing*, Vol. 1, No. 2 (1989), pp. 112–20.

Bradley, J.E., *Religion, Revolution and English Radicalism* (Cambridge, 1990), Appendix 1.

Drake, M. (ed), *Introduction to Historical Psephology* (Milton Keynes, 1982).

Green, Edmund M., 'Social Structure and Political Allegiance in Westminster, 1774–1820' (unpublished PhD thesis, University of London, 1992).

Green, Edmund M., 'Social Structure and Political Behaviour in Westminster, 1784–1788', in Peter Denley, Stefan Fogelvik and Charles Harvey (eds), *History and Computing II* (Manchester, 1989), pp. 239–42.

Mitchell, J. and Cornford, J., 'The Political Demography of Cambridge, 1832–68', *Albion*, Vol. 9 (1977), pp. 242–72.

O'Gorman, Frank, 'Electoral Behaviour in England, 1700–1872', in Peter Denley, Stefan Fogelvik and Charles Harvey (eds), *History and Computing II* (Manchester, 1989), pp. 220–38.

O'Gorman, Frank, 'The Unreformed Electorate of Hanoverian England: The Mid-Eighteenth Century to the Reform Act of 1832', *Social History*, Vol. 2, No. 1 (1986), pp. 33–52.

O'Gorman, Frank, *Voters, Patrons and Parties: The Unreformed Electoral System of Hanoverian England, 1734–1832* (Oxford, 1989).

Phillips, John A., 'Achieving a Critical Mass while Avoiding an Explosion', *Journal of Interdisciplinary History*, Vol. 9, No. 3 (1978), pp. 493–508.

Phillips, John A. (ed), *Computing Parliamentary History* (special book issue of *Parliamentary History*, Edinburgh, 1994).

Phillips, John A., *Electoral Behaviour in Unreformed England* (Princeton, NJ, 1982).

Phillips, John A. and Wetherell, Charles, 'Probability and Political Behaviour: A Case Study of the Municipal Corporations Act of 1835', *History and Computing*, Vol. 5, No. 3 (1993), pp. 135–153.

Speck, W.A. and Gray, W.A., 'The Computer Analysis of Poll Books: An Initial Report', *Bulletin of the Institute of Historical Research*, Vol. 43 (1970), pp. 105–12.

Speck, W.A., Gray, W.A. and Hopkinson, R., 'Computer Analysis of Poll Books: A Further Report', *Bulletin of the Institute of Historical Research*, Vol. 48 (1975), pp. 64–90.

■ 14 Prosopography

Barman. J., Barman, R. and Kirshaw, W.T., 'Prosopography by Computer: The Development of a Data Base', *Historical Methods Newsletter*, Vol. 10 (1977), pp. 102–8.

Best, H., 'Reconstructing Political Biographies of the Past: Configurations, Sequences, Timing, and the Impact of Historical Change', in H. Millet (ed), *Informatique et Prosopographie* (Paris, 1985), pp. 247–60.

Bourlet, Caroline and Minel, Jean-Luc, 'A Declarative System for Setting Up a Prosopographical Database', in Peter Denley and Deian Hopkin (eds), *History and Computing* (Manchester, 1987), pp. 186–91.

Bourlet, Caroline and Minel, Jean-Luc, 'An Expert Decision Support System for a Prosopographical Database', in Lawrence J. McCrank (ed), *Databases in the Humanities and Social Sciences 4* (Medford, NJ, 1990), pp. 79–84.

Bulst, N., 'Prosopography and the Computer: Problems and Possibilities', in P. Denley, S. Fogelvik and C. Harvey (eds), *History and Computing II* (Manchester, 1989), pp. 12–18.

Bulst, N. and Genet J.-P. (eds), *Medieval Lives and the Historian: Studies in Medieval Prosopography* (Kalamazoo, MI, 1986).

Denley, Peter, 'Prosopography and Computer', in V. Davis, P. Denley, D. Spaeth and R. Trainor (eds), *The Teaching of Historical Computing: An International Framework* (St. Katharinen, 1993), pp. 69–71.

Denley, Peter, 'Source-Oriented Prosopography: κλειω [kleio] and the Creation of a Data Bank of Italian Renaissance University Teachers and Students', in Francesca Bocchi and Peter Denley (eds), *Storia & Multimedia* (Bologna, 1994), pp. 150–60.

Greenstein, Daniel I., 'Multisourced and Integrated Databases for the Prosopographer', in Evan Mawdsley *et al.* (eds), *History and Computing III: Historians, Computers and Data* (Manchester, 1990), pp. 60–6.

Kropač, Ingo H., 'Who's Who in the Southeast of Germany: The Design of the Prosopographical Data Base at Graz University', in Peter Denley, Stefan Fogelvik and Charles Harvey (eds), *History and Computing II* (Manchester, 1989), pp. 27–39.

Mathisen, R.W., 'Medieval Prosopography and Computers: Theoretical and Methodological Considerations', *Medieval Prosopography*, Vol. 9, No. 2 (1988), pp. 73–128.

Millet, H. (ed), *Informatique et Prosopographie* (Paris, 1985).

Morgan, Nicholas, and Moss, Michael, 'Urban Wealthholding and the Computer', in Peter Denley, Stefan Fogelvik and Charles Harvey (eds), *History and Computing II* (Manchester, 1989), pp. 181–92.

Morgan, Nicholas, and Moss, Michael, '"Wealthy and Titled Persons" – The Accumulation of Riches in Victorian Britain: The Case of Peter Denny', *Business History*, Vol. 31, No. 2 (1989), pp. 28–42.

Müller, Walter, 'The Analysis of Life Histories: Illustrations of the Use of Life History Plots', *Historical Social Research* (1980), pp. 164–91.

Nenadic, Stana, 'Identifying Social Networks with a Computer-Aided Analysis of Personal Diaries', in Evan Mawdsley *et al.* (eds), *History and Computing III: Historians, Computers and Data* (Manchester, 1990), pp. 188–94.

Pöttler, Burkhard, 'Modelling Historical Data: Probate Inventories as a Source for the History of Everyday Life', in Francesca Bocchi and Peter Denley (eds), *Storia & Multimedia* (Bologna, 1994), pp. 494–9.

Sandström, Goran and Sundin, Jan, 'Computer Analysis of Life Histories from Swedish Church Records: A Case Study from the Demographic Data Base at Umeå University', *Historical Social Research* (1980), pp. 192–202.

■ 15 Literary and Linguistic Computing

Fielding, N. and Lee, R. (eds), *Wordworking: Using Computers in Qualitative Research* (London, forthcoming).

Grishman, R., *Computational Linguistics: An Introduction* (Cambridge, 1989).

Kenny, Anthony, *The Computation of Style* (Oxford, 1982).

Leiter-Köhrer, Ursula, 'Linguistic Knowledge as a Background Component of an Application Oriented Workstation', *Historical Social Research*, Vol. 16 No. 4 (1991), pp. 89–99.

Rudall, B.H. and Corns, T.N., *Computers and Literature* (Cambridge, MA, 1987).

Smith, P.D., *An Introduction to Text Processing* (Cambridge, MA, 1990).

■ 16 Text Markup

Botzem, Susanne and Kropač, Ingo H., 'Integrated Computer Supported Editing: Approaches and Strategies' *Historical Social Research*, Vol. 16, No. 4 (1991), pp. 106–15.

British Standards Institute, *Guide to Establishment and Development of Monolingual Thesauri (BS 5723)* (London, 1987).

Bryan, Martin, *SGML: An Author's Guide to the Standard Generalised Markup Language* (Reading, MA, 1988).

Burnard, L.D., 'An Introduction to the Text Encoding Initiative', in Daniel Greenstein (ed), *Modelling Historical Data* (St. Katharinen, 1991), pp. 81–92.

Burnard, Lou, 'The Text Encoding Initiative: Towards an Extensible Standard for the Encoding of Texts', in S. Ross and E. Higgs (eds), *Electronic Information Resources and Historians: European Perspectives* (St. Katharinen, 1993), pp. 105–18.

Burnard, Lou, 'Tools and Techniques for Computer-Assisted Text Processing', in C.S. Butler (ed), *Computers and Written Texts* (Oxford, 1992), pp. 1–28.

Burnard, Lou, 'What is SGML and How Does it Help?', in Daniel Greenstein (ed), *Modelling Historical Data* (St. Katharinen, 1991), pp. 65–80.

Burnard, Lou and Sperberg-McQueen, C.M. (eds), *Guidelines for the Encoding and Interchange of Machine-Readable Texts* (Chicago, IL and Oxford, 1990).

Concepcion, Vicente P. and D'Amato, Donald P., 'A String-Matching Algorithm for Assessing the Results of an OCR Process', in Francesca Bocchi and Peter Denley (eds), *Storia & Multimedia* (Bologna, 1994), pp. 694–701.

Coombs, J.H., Renear, A.H. and DeRose, S.J., 'Markup Systems and the Future of Scholarly Text Processing', *Communications of the ACM*, Vol. 30, No. 11 (1987), pp. 933–47.

Ginter, Donald E., Grogono, Peter and Bode, Frederick A., 'A Review of Optimal Input Methods: Fixed Field, Free Field, and the Edited Text', *Historical Methods Newsletter*, Vol. 10 (1977), pp. 166–76.

Homann, K., *StanFEP: Ein Programm zur freien Konvertierung von Daten* (St. Katharinen, 1990).

Homann, K., 'StanFEP: Standardisation without Standards', in J. Smets (ed), *Histoire et Informatique* (Montpellier, 1992), pp. 289–99.

Humphreys, R. Lee, 'SGML: Marked Improvement', *Personal Computer World* (March 1992), pp. 330–4.

Sperberg-McQueen, C.M., 'Texts in the Electronic Age: Textual Study and Text Encoding, with Examples from Medieval Text', *Literary and Linguistic Computing*, Vol. 6, No. 1 (1991).

Thaller, Manfred, 'A Draft Proposal for a Standard Format Exchange Program', in J.-P. Genet (ed), *Standardisation et échange des bases de données historiques* (Paris, 1988), pp. 329–75.

■ 17 Project Management

Ashworth C. and Goodland, M., *SSADM: A Practical Approach* (Maidenhead, Berkshire, 1990).

Avison, D.E. and Fitzgerald, G., *Information Systems Development: Methodologies, Techniques and Tools* (Oxford, 1988).

Bergen, S.A., *Project Management: An Introduction to Issues in Industrial Research and Development* (Oxford, 1986).

Breure, Leen, 'The Management of Historical Computer Projects', in V. Davis, P. Denley, D. Spaeth and R. Trainor (eds), *The Teaching of Historical Computing: An International Framework* (St. Katharinen, 1993), pp. 48–54.

Hoare, H.R., *Project Management using Network Analysis* (Maidenhead, Berkshire, 1973).

Howard, K. and Sharp, J.A., *The Management of a Student Research Project* (Aldershot, 1989).

Lock, Dennis, *Project Management* (London, 1989).

Meredith, Jack R. and Mantel, Samuel J., Jr., *Project Management: A Managerial Approach* (Chichester, Sussex, 2nd edn. 1989).

van Horik, René, 'Optical Character Recognition and Historical Documents: Some Programs Reviewed', *History and Computing*, Vol. 4, No. 3 (1992), pp. 211–20.

van Horik, René, and Doorn, P.K., 'Scanning and Optical Character Recognition of Historical Sources', in Hans J. Marker and Kirsten Pagh (eds), *Yesterday: Proceedings from the 6th International Conference of the Association for History and Computing, Odense 1991* (Odense, 1994), pp. 344–55.

Woollard, Matthew, 'Project Management and the 1881 Census' (unpublished MA dissertation, University of London, 1991).

Yeates, Don, *Project Management for Information Systems* (London, 1991).

■ 18 Collected Essays and Conference Papers

Best, H., Mochmann, E. and Thaller, M. (eds), Computers in the Humanities and the Social Sciences: *Achievements of the 1980s, Prospects for the 1990s* (Munich, 1991).

Bocchi, Francesca and Denley, Peter (eds), *Storia & Multimedia* (Bologna, 1994).

Borodkin, Leonid I. and Levermann, Wolfgang (eds), *Istorija i komp'juter: Novye informacionnye technologii v istoricheskich issledovanijach i obrazovanii* (St. Katharinen, 1993).

Borodkin, Leonid I. and Levermann, Wolfgang (eds), *History and Computing in Eastern Europe* (St. Katharinen, 1993).

Denley, Peter and Hopkin, Deian (eds), *History and Computing* (Manchester, 1987).

Denley, Peter, Fogelvik, Stefan and Harvey, Charles (eds), *History and Computing II* (Manchester, 1989).

Genet, Jean-Philippe (ed), *Standardisation et échange des bases de données historiques* (Paris, 1988).

Gilmour-Bryson, Anne (ed), *Computer Applications to Medieval Studies* (Kalamazoo, 1984).

Jarausch, Konrad H. and Schröder, Wilhelm H. (eds), *Quantitative History of Society and Economy: Some International Studies* (St. Katherinen, 1987).

Marker, Hans J. and Pagh, Kirsten (eds), *Yesterday: Proceedings from the 6th International Conference of the Association for History and Computing, Odense 1991* (Odense, 1994).

Mawdsley, Evan, Morgan, Nicholas, Richmond, Lesley and Trainor, Richard (eds), *History and Computing III: Historians, Computers and Data* (Manchester, 1990).

McCrank, Lawrence J. (ed), *Databases in the Humanities and Social Sciences 4* (Medford, NJ, 1990).

Moberg, Thomas F. (ed), *Databases in the Humanities and Social Sciences 3* (Florida, 1987).

Raben, J. and Marks, G. (eds), *Databases in the Humanities and Social Sciences* (Amsterdam & New York, 1980).

Smets, J. (ed), *Histoire et Informatique* (Montpellier, 1992).

■ **19 Journals**

Computers and the Humanities.
Histoire et Mesure.
Historical Methods, formerly *Historical Methods Newsletter.*
Historical Social Research/Historische Sozialforschung.
History and Computing, formerly *Computing and History Today.*
History Microcomputer Review.
Literary and Linguistic Computing.

■ **20 Bibliographies**

Birch, Debra, Denley, Peter and Ruusalepp, Raivo, *A Historical Computing Bibliography* (London, v2.0 1995), available on disk or hard copy.

Hall, J.L., *Online Bibliographic Databases: A Directory and Sourcebook* (London, 4th edn. 1986, or subsequent editions).

Kimberley, R., *Text Retrieval: A Directory of Software* (Aldershot, 1987).

Laboratoire d'Etudes et de Recherches sur l'Information et la Documentation, *History and Computing: An International Bibliography* (St. Katharinen, 1994).

Lancashire, Ian and McCarty, Willard, *The Humanities Computing Yearbook, 1988* (Oxford, 1989).

Ross, Seamus and Higgs, Edward (eds), *Electronic Information Resources and Historians: European Perspectives* (St. Katharinen, 1993).

Schürer, Kevin and Anderson, Sheila J. (eds), *A Guide to Historical Datafiles Held in Machine-Readable Form* (London, 1992).

Index